C0-APQ-257

Reptiles y anfibios

Joanne Mattern

Traducción al español: Leticia Molinero

The Rosen Publishing Group's
Editorial Buenas Letras™
New York

Published in 2002 for The Rosen Publishing Group, Inc.
29 East 21st Street, New York, NY 10010

First Library Edition in Spanish 2002
First Library Edition in English 2002

Book Design: Haley Wilson

Photo Credits: Cover, p. 1 © E.R. Degginger/Joe McDonald/Animals Animals; p. 4 © Stan Osolinski/FPG International/T. Jackson/Animals Animals; p. 6 © Telegraph Colour Library/FPG International/George Bernard/Animals Animals; p. 9 © Trevor Barrett/E. R. Degginger/Paul Freed/Ken G. Preston-Mafham/ Animals Animals; p. 10 © Bill Beatty/E. R. Degginger/John Netherton/ Animals Animals; p. 12 © Michael Habicht/Animals Animals; pp. 14–15 © Larry West/FPG International; p. 17 © Gail Shumway/FPG International/ Joe McDonald/Zig Leszczynski/Animals Animals; p. 18 © Marian Bacon/ Animals Animals; p. 20 © Jerry Driendl/FPG International.

Library of Congress Cataloging-in-Publication Data

Mattern, Joanne, 1963-
   Reptiles and amphibians / Joanne Mattern; traducción al español Leticia Molinero.
      p. cm. — (The Rosen Publishing Group's reading room collection)
Summary: Describes the basic attributes of reptiles and amphibians and provides examples of various species.
      ISBN: 0-8239-8317-X (pbk)
      ISBN: 0-8239-6515-5 (hc)
      6-pack ISBN 0-8239-6578-3
  1. Reptiles—Juvenile literature. 2. Amphibians—Juvenile literature.
[1. Reptiles. 2. Amphibians. 3. Spanish Language Materials] I. Title. II. Series.
  QL644.2 .M316 2002
  567.9--dc21

                                        2001006833
Manufactured in the United States of America

Contenido

¿Qué son los reptiles?

Los reptiles son animales especiales. Los reptiles tienen una **columna vertebral** como los seres humanos, pero tienen **sangre fría**. Esto significa que sus cuerpos están tan calientes o tan fríos como el aire que los rodea. La mayoría de los reptiles no paren crías vivas. En vez, ponen huevos.

Algunos reptiles, como los caimanes, son grandes. Otros, como los lagartos, son pequeños. Algunos viven cerca del agua. Otros viven en el desierto donde hace calor y el clima es seco.

Los reptiles tienen piel seca y con escamas. Hay unas 6,500 clases de reptiles diferentes.

¿Qué son los anfibios?

Los anfibios se parecen a los reptiles de muchas maneras: tienen columna vertebral, ponen huevos y son de sangre fría.

Pero hay algo que hace que los reptiles y los anfibios sean diferentes: los anfibios viven en el agua cuando son jóvenes. Cuando crecen, viven en la tierra. Un anfibio bebé y un anfibio adulto tienen aspectos muy diferentes. El cuerpo del anfibio cambia para **adaptarse** a su nueva casa. El cuerpo del reptil no cambia. Sigue agrandándose al crecer.

◀ Las ranas y los sapos son anfibios. Los bebés de rana y sapo se ven muy diferentes de las ranas y los sapos adultos.

7

Ponen huevos

La mayoría de los reptiles y los anfibios hacen bebés poniendo huevos. El reptil pone sus huevos sobre la tierra y están protegidos por una cáscara o cascarón. El anfibio pone sus huevos diminutos en el agua o sobre el suelo mojado. Los huevos no tienen cáscara, y están unidos por una especie de gelatina que los ayuda a pegarse a las plantas en el agua.

Algunas clases de **salamandras**, serpientes y lagartos no ponen huevos. Paren crías vivas.

La mayoría de las madres reptiles y anfibias no cuidan a sus hijos. Las crías se las arreglan por su cuenta desde el momento en que nacen.

Ranas

Tortuga

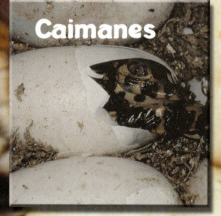

Caimanes

Serpientes

9

Primera fase

Tercera fase

Segunda fase

10

Cambian de cuerpo

Cuando nacen los anfibios, sus cuerpos están preparados para vivir en el agua. No tienen ni patas ni brazos. Tienen colas que les ayudan a nadar. También tienen **agallas**, que les permiten respirar agua en vez de aire.

Al crecer, los anfibios cambian por completo. Sus agallas desaparecen y se forman los pulmones que les permiten respirar aire. A los anfibios les crecen patas. Su corazón, estómago y boca también cambian para ayudarles a vivir sobre la tierra.

¡Las ranas son anfibios y han existido desde hace unos 190 millones de años!

11

¡Algunas ranas son tan pequeñas que pueden pararse en la yema de tu dedo!

12

Ranas y sapos

Las ranas y los sapos son anfibios. Hay unas 3,800 clases diferentes de ranas y sapos.

A las ranitas y los sapitos recién nacidos se les llama **renacuajos**. Los renacuajos tienen agallas y colas. Comen plantas, huevos de rana ¡y hasta otros renacuajos!

Al poco tiempo de nacer su cuerpo comienza a cambiar. Le crecen patas y pulmones. Ahora el renacuajo es una rana o un sapo y puede saltar sobre la tierra. Su cola desaparece. En vez de comer plantas, come animales más pequeños y atrapa insectos con su lengua larga y pegajosa.

Salamandras

Las salamandras son los únicos anfibios que tienen colas largas cuando crecen. Usan sus colas para mantener el equilibrio al caminar. Sus colas también les ayudan a nadar.

La mayoría de las salamandras están activas de noche. Es cuando andan de un lado a otro y cazan para comer. Las salamandras necesitan mantener sus cuerpos fríos y mojados. Para lograrlo, pasan mucho tiempo debajo de rocas y hojas.

La mayoría de las salamandras son pequeñas, pero una salamandra gigante japonesa como la de la fotografía, ¡puede crecer hasta más de 5 pies de largo!

Serpientes

Las serpientes son reptiles. Hay muchas clases diferentes de serpientes. Algunas serpientes son venenosas. Matan a sus **presas** mordiéndolas con sus afilados **colmillos**. Sus colmillos contienen una sustancia que se llama **ponzoña**. Otras serpientes matan a sus presas apretándolas con sus cuerpos.

Las serpientes tragan sus alimentos enteros. Después de una gran comida, una serpiente no vuelve a comer durante varios días o semanas. ¡Algunas serpientes grandes no vuelven a comer durante más de un año!

Serpiente de cascabel

Coral ratonera

Pitón

¡Hay unas 2,500 clases diferentes de serpientes!

Serpiente rey

Boa Constrictor

17

Algunos camaleones se pelean para
ver quién cambia de color más rápido.

18

Lagartos

Un lagarto es una clase de reptil. La mayoría de los lagartos tienen cuatro patas y una larga cola. Al igual que los demás reptiles, los lagartos tienen sangre fría. Si un lagarto se enfría demasiado, sale al sol para calentarse. Si un lagarto se calienta demasiado, descansa a la sombra para enfriarse.

Muchos lagartos, como los camaleones, pueden cambiar el color de la piel para confundirse con el medio ambiente y protegerse de sus enemigos. Algunos lagartos tienen colas especiales. Si un enemigo rompe la cola del lagarto, el lagarto puede escaparse y después le crece una cola nueva.

La tortuga con caparazón tipo laúd
puede crecer hasta 8 pies de largo.
¡Puede pesar una tonelada!

Tortugas

Las tortugas son reptiles. Las tortugas que viven sobre la tierra tienen caparazones duros para protegerse de sus enemigos. Si una tortuga está en peligro, esconde su cabeza y sus patas adentro del caparazón.

Las tortugas de mar tienen caparazones blandos. También tienen **aletas**. Las aletas funcionan bien para nadar, pero no para caminar sobre la tierra. A diferencia de las tortugas de tierra, las tortugas de mar no pueden esconder sus cabezas o aletas adentro de sus caparazones.

Las tortugas no tienen dientes. Usan sus narices afiladas para destrozar sus alimentos.

Caimanes y cocodrilos

Los caimanes y cocodrilos son reptiles. Pasan una parte de sus vidas en el agua y otra parte sobre tierra. Estos animales son buenos nadadores y pueden recorrer distancias cortas rápidamente. Usan sus poderosas quijadas y filosos dientes para atrapar sus presas. Comen cualquier animal que puedan atrapar, tal como pescados, aves, mapaches, serpientes ¡y hasta ganado!

Los caimanes y cocodrilos son animales peligrosos, pero muchos reptiles, y muchos anfibios, son muy dóciles. ¡La mayoría te tiene más miedo a ti que lo que tú tienes de ellos!

Glosario

adaptarse
Cambiar para responder a nuevas condiciones.

agallas (las)
Parte del cuerpo de algunos animales que se usa para respirar debajo del agua.

aletas (las)
Parte del cuerpo ancha y plana que tienen algunos animales para ayudarse a nadar.

colmillo (el)
Diente largo y puntiagudo.

columna vertebral (la)
El hueso principal en el medio de la espalda de muchos animales, incluidos los seres humanos. La columna vertebral está constituida de muchos huesos pequeños.

de sangre fría
Cuando el cuerpo tiene la misma temperatura que el aire que lo rodea.

ponzoña (la)
El veneno que producen algunas serpientes y otros animales.

presa (la)
Un animal que es cazado por otro animal que lo quiere comer.

renacuajo (el)
Una rana o sapo recién nacido.

salamandra (la)
Un anfibio que se parece mucho a un lagarto.

Índice

Labor Markets and Firm Benefit Policies in Japan and the United States

**A National Bureau
of Economic Research
Conference Report**

Labor Markets and Firm Benefit Policies in Japan and the United States

Edited by **Seiritsu Ogura, Toshiaki Tachibanaki, and David A. Wise**

The University of Chicago Press

Chicago and London

SEIRITSU OGURA is professor of economics at Hasei University in Tokyo. TOSHIAKI TACHIBANAKI is professor of economics at the Kyoto Institute of Economic Research, Kyoto University. DAVID A. WISE is the John F. Stambaugh Professor of Political Economy at the John F. Kennedy School of Government, Harvard University, and the director for Health and Retirement Programs at the National Bureau of Economic Research.

The University of Chicago Press, Chicago 60637
The University of Chicago Press, Ltd., London
© 2003 by the National Bureau of Economic Research
All rights reserved. Published 2003
Printed in the United States of America
12 11 10 09 08 07 06 05 04 03   1 2 3 4 5
ISBN: 0-226-62094-8 (cloth)

Library of Congress Cataloging-in-Publication Data

Labor markets and firm benefit policies in Japan and the United States /
    edited by Seiritsu Ogura, Toshiaki Tachibanaki, and David A. Wise.
        p. cm. — (A National Bureau of Economic Research conference report)
        This volume consists of papers presented at the Japan Center for Economic Research-National Bureau of Economic Research Joint Conference on Labor Markets and Firm Benefits Policies held in Hawaii, US in January 2002.
    Includes bibliographical references (p.) and index.
    ISBN 0-226-62094-8 (cloth : alk. paper)
    1. Labor market—Japan—Congresses.   2. Labor market—United States—Congresses.   3. Employee fringe benefits—Japan—Congresses.   4. Employee fringe benefits—United States—Congresses.   I. Ogura, Seiritsu.   II. Tachibanaki, Toshiaki, 1943–   III. Wise, David A.   IV. Series.

HD5827 .A6L3 2003
331.12′0952—dc21

                                                    2003041000

⊗ The paper used in this publication meets the minimum requirements of the American National Standard for Information Sciences—Permanence of Paper for Printed Library Materials, ANSI Z39.48-1992.

Since this volume is a record of conference proceedings, it has been exempted from the rules governing critical review of manuscripts by the Board of Directors of the National Bureau (resolution adopted 8 June 1948, as revised 21 November 1949 and 20 April 1968).

Contents

Acknowledgments

This volume consists of papers presented at the Japan Center for Economic Research–National Bureau of Economic Research Joint Conference on Labor Markets and Firm Benefits Policies held in Hawaii in January 2000. Financial support from the U.S. Department of Health and Human Services, National Institute on Aging (grants P01-AG05842 and P20-AG12810); the Japan Foundation Center for Global Partnership; Japan's National Institute for Research Advancement; and the Toyota Foundation is gratefully acknowledged. The conference also received support from Toyota Motor Corporation, IBM Japan, Nippon Telegraph and Telephone Corporation, and Japan Tobacco, Inc. Additional funding sources are noted in individual papers.

The editors wish to thank Leemore Dafny and Bengte Evenson for their help in editing the papers, and Richard Woodbury for his help in putting together the introduction to the volume.

Any opinions expressed in this volume are those of the respective authors and do not necessarily reflect the views of the National Bureau of Economic Research, the Japan Center for Economic Research, or the sponsoring organizations.

Introduction

David A. Wise

This is the fourth in a series of Japan Center for Economic Research–National Bureau of Economic Research volumes dealing with population aging, economic systems, and economic behavior in the United States and Japan. The first three volumes—*Aging in the United States and Japan: Economic Trends* (1994), *The Economic Effects of Aging in the United States and Japan* (1997), and *Aging Issues in the United States and Japan* (2001)—focus on the challenges of an older population in these two countries, and on the aging-related influences of each country's economic and social institutions, public policies, and employment traditions.

Following up on this earlier work, this volume focuses more intensively on the employment policies in each country, including both general employment practices and more specific fringe benefit systems. Population aging, an older workforce, and the associated explosion in costs in both employer-provided and publicly supported retirement benefit programs affect every aspect of employment policy. The papers in this volume take an important step in relating these economic and demographic changes to employment practices and labor market trends in Japan and the United States, as well as to economic vitality and productivity more generally. The volume also highlights some common characteristics and important differences in employment policies and traditions between the two countries.

For example, Japan is widely recognized for offering long-term employment security with one firm, broad participation of employees at all levels in business decision making, and, in at least some industries, significant

This introduction was completed with the collaboration of Richard Woodbury.

David A. Wise is the John F. Stambaugh Professor of Political Economy at the John F. Kennedy School of Government, Harvard University, and the director for health and retirement programs at the National Bureau of Economic Research.

information sharing across business components. This volume devotes a chapter to each of these employment traditions in Japan and to examining how these employment traditions are evolving over time in relation to Japan's changing economic and demographic circumstances. The findings from these studies suggest a very gradual erosion of participatory employment practices in Japan and a higher degree of employment level flexibility in Japanese firms than conventionally assumed. And at least some of this evolution in traditional employment practices in Japan results from the economic slowdown of the 1990s and the aging of the workforce in Japan. These employment practices, as well as the interactive dynamics of youth and senior labor market opportunities, are explored in chapters two through five.

The increasing cost of employer-provided fringe benefits and the economic incentives associated with fringe benefit systems represent another important employment-related issue in Japan and the United States, and this issue is addressed in chapters six through thirteen. Trends, economic incentives, and potential innovations in a number of specific benefit programs are considered.

Four of the studies focus on health care and employer-provided health benefit programs. Chapter six looks at the potential for stronger demand-side incentives to contain health care costs, focusing on an innovative "medical savings account" approach to employee health benefit provision in the United States. Chapter nine focuses on the disproportionately large amount spent on prescription medications in Japan relative to the United States and how the current health benefit system in Japan may have encouraged distortions in pharmaceutical spending by as much as 50 percent. Chapter ten looks at the potential for investments in preventive health care both to decrease the long-term cost of acute health care services (by decreasing hospitalizations, for example) and to reduce work absenteeism. Chapter seven looks at how private health insurance supplements to publicly supported health care programs affect the overall use (and cost) of health care services, based on a worldwide view of health policy. Each of these studies has implications for the design of health benefit policies and for the cost of employer-provided health benefits as the population ages in Japan and the United States.

The economic characteristics and incentives of other fringe benefit programs are also explored in the volume. For instance, chapter eight shows how the structure of firm pension plans in the United States has a large effect on workers' retirement decisions, as does the amount of money saved in both employer-sponsored retirement accounts and nonretirement accounts. This has important economic implications, not just for the individuals choosing retirement, but also for the larger economic vitality of a country with increasing numbers of retirees. Chapter eleven explores similar issues of welfare and retiree benefits in Japan, and the role of the employer in supporting such benefits. Finally, chapters twelve and thirteen deal with the economics of providing benefits to part-time workers, the economics of vacation benefits, and how unionization affects worker time off. The volume as a whole compiles these analyses of employee benefit programs to highlight the trends, economic incentives, and cross-national differences between Japan and the United States.

The volume begins (in chapter one) with a big-picture perspective of economic growth and decline in Japan and the United States over the past several decades and the factors that may have contributed to each country's successful economic results in different periods of recent history. It lays a broad foundation for the more focused discussion of individual employment practices and firm benefit policies that follow. Together, the studies in the volume provide a diversity of new information about employment practices and firm benefit policies in these two economies.

The remainder of this introduction previews the individual studies in the volume, drawing heavily on the authors' descriptions of their own papers.

Employment Practices

In "Changing the Guard: The Rise of the United States to Peak Capitalist Economy," Richard B. Freeman assesses the spectacular performance of the U.S. economy during the 1990s and relates it to the economic performance of Japan in the 1970s and 1980s. What is it, he asks, that makes different economies successful at different times?

"There are some similarities in the institutions, policies, and economic developments that made the United States the 1990s' peak economy and those that made Japan the 1980s' peak economy," says Freeman. The most notable similarity is the importance of variable pay in the two economies. Bonuses became a common form of variable pay in Japan in the 1980s, with the amount of bonuses rising in booms and falling in recessions. A similar move to variable pay in the United States occurred in the 1990s. According to Freeman, "variable pay should increase employment and reduce fluctuations in employment, and it thus may have contributed to the peak performance of both economies in the two periods."

But Freeman suggests that the differences between the United States and Japan are more striking than the similarities. For example, workers change jobs frequently in their early career years in the United States, whereas workers in Japan typically stay with one firm throughout their careers. Substantially more immigration and entry of women in the labor force has occurred in the United States than Japan. Japan has a more equalized distribution of income, whereas earnings in the United States are more unequal. The United States encourages new business development and has lenient bankruptcy laws, whereas Japan targets government support toward helping companies maintain their employment. Perhaps most important, Japan saves and invests and runs trade surpluses, whereas the United

States carries substantial private domestic debt and a massive trade deficit. "In short," says Freeman, "the overall picture is that these are economies with very different institutions, policies, and roads to full employment."

So what is it that has made both economies successful at different times in recent history? Freeman offers two hypotheses. "The diverse capitalism hypothesis interprets the evidence as reflecting a multipeaked landscape with different institutions producing more or less economic success in different periods. In a multipeaked world, there is no real peak economy and thus it is no surprise that one economy does better in one period and another in another period. The adaptionist hypothesis makes the stronger claim that Japanese institutions and policies fit the 1980s environment whereas U.S. institutions and policies fit the 1990s environment." Although Freeman offers some perspective on both hypotheses, he looks toward the future to better assess their relative merits, and he predicts the likely occurrence of another "changing of the guard" ahead.

Following this broad overview of employment traditions and economic performance in Japan and the United States, the remainder of the volume focuses in a more targeted way on particular employment practices or firm benefit programs. The next group of studies considers four aspects of employment in Japan: the participation of employees in all levels in business decision making; information sharing across business divisions; the interactions between an older population and an aging labor force, on the one hand, and youth employment, on the other; and the ability of firms in Japan to make labor cost and employment adjustments despite the long-term career stability of Japanese employees.

Takao Kato considers "The Recent Transformation of Participatory Employment Practices in Japan." The broad participation of employees in business decision making in Japan was at one time modeled around the world as an innovative approach to business management. Kato looks at how the 1990s slowdown in the Japanese economy has affected participatory employment practices in Japan. He finds some evidence of a decline and some adjustments in how participatory practices are being applied in firms, but he concludes overall that participatory employment practices appear to be surviving in general in the economic slowdown in the 1990s.

From a historical perspective, Kato points out how the relatively higher job security and strong group cohesiveness of Japanese workers in large manufacturing firms in the postwar period created an environment favorable to successful employee participation. This was enhanced by relatively more rapid and stable growth in the Japanese economy of the postwar period. As a result of this favorable environment, particularly in manufacturing, it is perhaps not surprising that participatory practices spread widely in Japan. Indeed, these practices became the hallmark of "Japanese management," which has been inspiring (or necessitating in some instances) many corporations elsewhere in the world to experiment with employee involvement and labor-management cooperation in recent years. In short, the postwar Japanese economy (especially in manufacturing) clearly represents one of the most important examples of experimentation with participatory employment practices.

The economic slowdown in the 1990s and a rapidly aging workforce have allegedly been eroding the aforementioned participation-friendly environments. Kato suggests that a closer look at the recent Japanese experience with participatory employment practices will help us better understand two key questions regarding participation: (a) what are the conditions under which participatory employment practices are best introduced and best sustained, and (b) in what way participatory employment practices will need to evolve when external environments change. To address these questions, Kato has analyzed both quantitative data from national surveys and qualitative data from his own field research on evolving employment practices in the 1990s.

Among the results, Kato finds evidence of complementarities in participatory employment practices that have served to protect participatory practices over time. Terminating a single practice (such as financial participation in business performance, or information sharing, for example) may not only eliminate its own positive effect on worker productivity but also reduce the positive effects of other practices at the same firm. In the extreme case, the termination of a single practice may jeopardize the whole system of employee participation and labor-management cooperation. These complementarities appear to have deterred management from any major steps back from participatory practices.

This is particularly true in large unionized firms. Such Japanese firms appear to be responding to the economic slowdown in the 1990s and the recent financial crisis in particular by fine-tuning the existing practices, not by dismantling them. Even in these firms, however, there are early signs of change, such as a decreasing number of full-time union officials, and overloaded work demands that prevent union officials from resisting management initiatives. In small to medium-sized firms with no union, Kato finds much more evidence of management's trying to weaken employee participation. Thus, with potentially decreasing union representation at large firms, and a growing number of small and medium-sized firms without unions and with less participatory environments, the participatory traditions of employment in Japan may well have started a very gradual decline.

Information sharing within firms is one of the participatory employment practices that has been applied in Japan. In "Determinants of the Shadow Value of Simultaneous Information Sharing in the Japanese Machine-Tool Manufacturing Industry," Hiroyuki Chuma analyzes the role of information sharing in enhancing productivity in the machine-tool industry. The machine-tool industry in Japan became the world output leader in 1982 and has maintained this leadership ever since. Chuma makes the case that information-sharing practices in this industry contributed importantly to its success.

There have been a number of technological advances in Japan that relate to the machine-tool industry, and there have been spillover effects from other manufacturing industries that related in important ways to the market for machine tools. Among the most widely recognized technological and cross-industry developments are the growth of the Japanese auto industry, the leap forward in mechatronics manufacturing, the growth of precision-parts manufacturing, and the basic development of foundry engineering technology. What Chuma emphasizes is the complementary role of "human-related" factors. He gives special attention to the existence of simultaneous and formal information-sharing systems between production workers and design and development engineers.

Chuma's analysis is based on both field research and survey results. The field research reveals that the machine-tool industry employs a simultaneous and rather egalitarian information-sharing system linking production workers and design and development engineers. The computerized numerical control (CNC) machines used in this industry are so complex, according to Chuma, that without close collaboration among the various professionals, mechanical designers could not effectively design the details of the production machines while at the same time keeping lead times short. Information sharing is a critical aspect of the production process.

The importance of information sharing is identified generally in the field interviews, and it is statistically confirmed using the survey data. Indeed, Chuma says, the statistical analysis predicts that simultaneous information-sharing systems are more likely to be implemented by machine-tool manufacturers that retain highly skilled assemblymen and machinists, produce (CNC) lathes or machining centers (MCs), and have more than 100 full-time workers. The implication is that information sharing has increased importance to productivity as the complexity of the manufacturing process increases.

In many countries, there is a concern that aging populations may change the employment opportunities of youth. For example, some analysts speculate that increased retirement at older ages will create new opportunities for workers at younger ages. Who will do the work, it is sometimes asked in the United States, when the baby boomers retire? Although there are clearly interactions between the labor market for young and older workers, any potential excess demand for young workers does not appear to have occurred in Japan, at least not yet. In fact, just the reverse has been happening. In "Who Really Lost Jobs in Japan? Youth Employment in an Aging Japanese Society," Yuji Genda analyzes the recent *decline* in youth employment in Japan. Genda concludes in his study that declining youth employment is primarily due to a drop in demand for products (and workers) in Japan, but that the delay in retirement of older workers is an important contributing factor in aggravating youth unemployment.

In analyzing recent trends in employment in Japan, Genda also points to the side effects of government policy. Following extensive corporate restructuring in Japan, the Japanese government, media, labor unions, and even employers have made a big deal out of the job losses of older, and especially white-collar, workers. Consequently, in 1999, in response to this perceived crisis, the Japanese Ministry of Labor introduced emergency measures to create employment opportunities for older people. By stimulating opportunities for older workers, however, the government may have at the same time caused a reduction in the employment opportunities of youth.

Genda also makes the case that the change in government policy may have been an overreaction. Indeed, Genda questions whether the employment situation for middle-aged and older white-collar workers was, in fact, deteriorating as much as Japanese newspapers claimed. According to Genda, only 70,000 out of 3 million unemployed persons (about 2 percent) were aged 45–54 and had a university education in 1999. This contrasts with the very large proportion of newly unemployed young people, and especially those without a college degree. The relative unemployment of middle-aged and older college graduates has not increased to the degree claimed, Genda says.

Genda's research illustrates the important interactions between youth and senior labor markets—how policies designed to affect employment opportunities for one group can have secondary effects on the other. Genda concludes that a decline in overall labor demand in Japan largely resulted in reduced employment opportunities for youth, whereas the employment of middle-aged and older workers was safeguarded. Indeed, a large part of the contraction in the labor demand for younger workers has been due to job displacement by the delayed retirement of a graying workforce, especially within large firms in Japan.

The tradition of long-term job security in Japan implies some potential impediments to downsizing at Japanese firms, or at least raises the question of how companies in Japan respond to a decline in demand for their products. Yoshifumi Nakata and Ryoji Takehiro consider this issue in "Total Labor Costs and the Employment Adjustment Behavior of Large Japanese Firms." The study looks at how firms absorb demand fluctuation in Japan, focusing on the role of adjusted work hours, the inflow of new workers, the retirement of older workers, and layoffs. Nakata and Takehiro present evidence that substantial employment variation can (and does) take place in Japan—even without layoffs—through adjusted work hours, restricted inflow of new workers, and stimulated retirement of older workers. Thus employment and labor cost adjustments at Japanese firms are much more responsive to demand fluctuations than conventionally assumed.

The study analyzes employment adjustments using a twenty-five-year firm-level panel data set for thirty-three large Japanese firms in three industries: automobile manufacturing, department stores, and supermarkets. The data set includes consistent employment data on regular full-time workers. Nakata and Takehiro apply the data set to an empirical employment adjustment model, and the calibrated model is found to explain very well the employment adjustment behavior of leading Japanese firms. The model is applied separately to the data from each industry, as well as for all three industries combined.

In both the industry-specific and industry-consolidated results, Nakata and Takehiro find negative relationships between the adjustment parameter and the output and price elasticities of employment. They interpret this negative relationship as evidence that firms compensate for slow *long-run* labor market adjustments by making faster *short-run* employment adjustments. The supplementary analysis of work hour adjustments at eleven of the firms in the database reinforces this interpretation. Indeed, the inclusion of work hours improves the overall fit of the employment adjustment model for most firms.

Nakata and Takehiro conclude that leading Japanese firms do make significant employment adjustments even in an environment of long-term job security: "Firms adjust employment levels and work hours in response to fluctuations in output and the relative price of labor."

Fringe Benefits and Labor Markets

Three papers address aspects of fringe benefits in the United States: the potential for medical saving accounts to support employer-provided health insurance, the economic implications of supplementing public health insurance with private insurance, and the relationship between employer-provided pension benefits and employee retirement decisions.

Only a few years ago most private health insurance plans in the United States paid for care on a fee-for-service basis, with any limits on expenditures provided through typically small copayments and deductibles. The rising cost of medical care encouraged a progression to managed care plans, and now the majority of plan participants are enrolled in plans that to some extent limit cost through supply-side restrictions. But health care costs are rising rapidly again, even in managed care environments. In "Individual Expenditures and Medical Saving Accounts: Can They Work?" Matthew J. Eichner, Mark B. McClellan, and I consider an innovative approach to health insurance that reintroduces demand-side cost containment characteristics and improves the efficiency of individual spending decisions for health care.

The plan we consider is the Medical Saving Account (MSA). Most

Americans have very little financial asset savings. This has limited the practical feasibility of high-deductible "catastrophic" health insurance, as traditionally structured, despite the efficiency benefits of such policies. Medical saving accounts would address this limitation. By providing a savings account that could be used to pay for substantial medical costs, without causing major short-term disruptions in family budgets, the MSA is intended to make insurance plans with high deductibles and copayments practical for a larger number of Americans. The typical plan would allow tax-free contributions to an MSA. Then, at retirement, the MSA balance could be used for general financial support, much like an individual retirement account (IRA) or 401(k) savings plan. An MSA thus combines the desirable features of catastrophic coverage for reducing medical expenditures with a mechanism that creates a reserve for paying individual expenses.

In the paper in this volume, we analyze an important potential impediment to the practical application of MSA plans. Specifically, MSA plans might not be practical if the same individuals have high medical expenditures year after year. In this study, we explore the likely variation in MSA balances that would occur over a working career, based on actual patterns of individual health care spending over time.

The key results are in the form of simulations, based on model estimates. Under the illustrative plan we have simulated, most employees would approach retirement with a substantial proportion of MSA contributions remaining in the account. Only a small fraction would approach retirement with very small balances. Based on our illustrative plan, if investments of MSA assets were in equities, fewer than 10 percent of participants would retire with a balance in their MSA plan of less than they had contributed— even after paying for health care expenses throughout their working careers. Over half of participants would accumulate MSA balances greater than 300 percent of their contributions. If investments were in bonds, balances would be much lower. In this case about 10 percent of workers would retain less than 50 percent of contributions. Thus, we conclude that persistence of medical expenditures seems not to present an overriding obstacle to the adaptation of MSA plans.

All countries insure a significant part of the population through public insurance. However, not all services are covered publicly, or the services covered may not be of the highest quality. A central question for countries designing medical care systems is whether to allow people to supplement the public insurance policy, and if so under what restrictions. An important aspect of this question is how the supplementary coverage changes medical care decisions, including decisions made about care that is already covered under the public benefits. For example, the supplementary coverage could increase or decrease the cost of the public program, depending on how the public and private programs interact with one another. David M. Cutler considers these issues in "Supplementing Public Insurance Coverage with Private Coverage: Implications for Medical Care Systems."

To better understand the issue, Cutler categorizes three types of supplemental health insurance coverage. The first, and most straightforward, form of supplemental insurance is for services that are not covered under the public insurance system. The second type of supplemental insurance is for the cost sharing required in public insurance systems. Some public health insurance systems require high beneficiary copayments. If it is allowed, recipients of public insurance may purchase secondary insurance, which pays for this cost sharing. The third type of insurance is for services that are covered under the public plan but for which private provision might be preferred to public provision. Because of the tight budget constraints on service availability, some countries have waiting lines for access to specialty services. Some people purchase private insurance to see doctors outside of the public system, in effect jumping the public queue.

Each category of supplemental health insurance has different economic implications. Most countries do allow supplemental insurance for services not covered under the public program—Cutler's first category. Under these types of policies, people may use more or less of the publicly provided health care services, depending on whether the covered and uncovered services in the public program are complements or substitutes. Public spending may rise or fall as a result. Further, the availability of private insurance might reduce poverty among people, saving money on health and other support services.

Insurance for the cost-sharing component of the public system—Cutler's second category—is more complex. On the one hand, allowing people to purchase such insurance increases welfare by reducing exposure to financial risk. On the other hand, such insurance creates moral hazard, leading people to use more medical care than they would without the insurance. This increases the cost of the public system. Because these public costs are not passed back to individuals purchasing private insurance, these policies are in effect subsidized by the public sector, making the insurance too generous. Whether supplemental policies to reduce the cost sharing are welfare improving or welfare decreasing depends on whether the gains from risk reduction are greater or smaller than the losses from increased moral hazard.

Supplemental insurance for queue jumping—the third category—is perhaps the most controversial form of insurance. Some countries, such as Canada, prohibit physicians from accepting payment for services that are covered under the private sector. The government is concerned that if such payments are possible, the rich will get more services and the poor will get less. But this concern ignores supply effects of the supplementary coverage. If increased demand by those with supplemental insurance leads to increased supply of resources, the total resources available for the poor may increase as well.

In addition to the discussion of economic incentives, Cutler's paper includes some empirical findings about the Medicare program in the United States, where supplemental insurance is extremely common. About 85 percent of Medicare recipients have some supplemental insurance. In the United States, queue jumping is not important (because supply is essentially unlimited), but the insurance for cost sharing and uncovered services (particularly prescription drugs) is very important. Cutler estimates that people with supplemental insurance coverage paying for Medicare cost sharing spend about 50 percent more on health care than people without supplemental insurance coverage—a sizable moral hazard effect of the supplementary coverage. Cutler does not find significant effects of covering prescription drugs on Medicare spending. In total, therefore, Cutler concludes that allowing supplemental insurance leads to substantial cost increases for the public sector.

Employer-provided pension benefits are an important source of retirement support in the United States. However, the typical defined benefit pension plans offered by employers in the United States also induce earlier retirement than would occur without the plans. In "Option Value Estimation with Health and Retirement Study Data," Andrew Samwick and I begin to explore how pension plan provisions, and other individual attributes, affect retirement decisions, using data from the Health and Retirement Study.

In most defined benefit pension plans, there is an extremely uneven accrual of pension benefits over a working career. Vesting rules, ages of eligibility for benefits, service credit rules, early retirement provisions, and the adjustment formulas used to determine pension benefits for retirement at different ages—all affect the pattern of pension accrual. This leads to large jumps in benefit entitlement for working an additional year at some ages, small increases at other ages, and very often a loss in benefits for working beyond certain ages.

To most accurately estimate the effect of pension provisions on retirement, it is therefore critical to consider the specific provisions of the plans and how they relate to the pension accrual patterns for an individual employee, based on that individual employee's wage and career service history. The Health and Retirement Study (HRS) is perhaps the first database in the United States that combines information on employment history, detailed and accurate earnings histories, and the detailed provisions of the employer-sponsored pension plan. The HRS also includes a diversity of other information about individuals that would be likely to influence retirement, such as health and functional ability, and the accumulation of assets in both retirement and nonretirement savings accounts. It therefore provides new opportunities to examine retirement in a very comprehensive way.

This paper does three things. The first is to describe the critical content of the HRS and confirm that these new data are important components of comprehensive analysis of retirement. The second is to make preliminary calculations of pension incentives and to estimate their effect on the probability of retirement, incorporating at the same time the effects of other nonpension characteristics on retirement. The third goal, by way of the first two, is to provide guidance that we hope will help analysts in other countries who may wish to conduct such analysis and indeed may wish to develop HRS-like surveys.

We show that when the financial incentives of pension plans are calculated over a sufficiently long time period, higher financial incentives to delay retirement predict lower retirement rates. However, pensions have a much larger effect on the decision to leave one particular firm than they do on the decision to leave the labor force entirely, as the pension benefits from one employer are still paid, even if a person continues working for another employer. So a sizable number of workers "retire" from one firm, with a pension from that firm, and then continue working with another firm. Thus the incentive effects of firm pension programs are somewhat different from the incentive effects of Social Security, which does not differentiate regarding whether an individual is working for one firm or another.

In addition to the effects of pensions on retirement, we also find that wealth influences retirement, whether wealth is measured by the present value of traditional pension benefits, by the accumulation of assets in retirement accounts, or by wealth in nonretirement assets. Finally, as expected, there is a strong effect of health status on retirement, particularly for the roughly 10 percent of the HRS sample reporting fair or poor health.

The U.S. papers are followed by five papers that address aspects of benefits programs in Japan: the cost of prescription drugs in health care benefit programs, the potential for preventive health care to better contain health benefit costs, the role of firms in providing welfare benefits, the economics of providing benefits to part-time workers, and the economics of vacation benefits and worker absenteeism.

Relative to other countries, a comparatively large portion of health care spending in Japan is for pharmaceutical expenses. For example, in terms of the per-patient costs of drugs, Japan spends more than three times as much as the United States. The importance of drugs in Japan seems to be most heavily concentrated among elderly patients for their outpatient care. Seiritsu Ogura and Takehiko Hagino consider the disproportionately high spending on pharmaceuticals in Japan in their paper, "Why Do the Japanese Spend So Much on Drugs?"

Among the reasons for high spending on drugs, Ogura and Hagino point to enormous distortions in the price regulation of drugs that have been generated over the last five decades. Although there is significant regulatory intervention in all aspects of the health care system in Japan, there are some distinct characteristics about the regulations on drug prices.

First, regulated drug prices vary by brand names, even if the drugs are chemically identical. In general, when the Japanese government purchases any other good or service, it has to observe a set of stringent procurement procedures that are designed to assure the lowest possible prices. With drugs, however, physicians are allowed to prescribe more expensive brand-name drugs even when cheaper alternatives are available. Second, the government sets the reimbursement (or retail) price for drugs based on wholesale prices almost eighteen months earlier, and they are fixed for the following two years. This lag time can create significant gaps between the reimbursed price and the price that would otherwise prevail in an unregulated market. Third, drug markets have been very tightly regulated and, at the same time, protected by high barriers to entry for new suppliers. The regulations concerning the introduction of new drugs, in effect, prohibit the entry into the drug market of new suppliers, and they make it easy for existing suppliers to establish noncompetitive prices.

In addition to the descriptive discussion of economic incentives in the drug industry in Japan, Ogura and Hagino present empirical evidence on the effects of these price distortions on resource allocation in the health care sector. The empirical work uses a new and comprehensive microdata set not previously available for statistical analysis in Japan. The authors estimate distortionary effects of between 20 percent and 50 percent of drug costs. They then show that the government's attempts to directly control drug prices have been ineffective, because drug companies have simply offset the price control efforts by offering alternative drug choices—what Ogura and Hagino call "drug switching" effects. And the economic incentives for drug switching are already strong, because of the built-in profit margins for "new" drugs that are given generous prices by the regulator.

The study as a whole suggests that the disproportionately high spending on pharmaceuticals in Japan is to a significant extent a result of the economic incentives in the pharmaceutical market and the use of higher priced pharmaceutical products, when identical or similar products could be prescribed at lower prices.

Preventive health care—such as routine checkups—is often mentioned as a means to reduce total health care expenditures, by identifying and addressing health care issues as they arise and before they become serious (and expensive) problems. By improving health, routine checkups may also reduce worker absenteeism and, as a consequence, increase worker productivity. On a more individual level, moreover, most would agree that routine checkups are just a good idea. But according to the 1995 *National Survey of Life,* administered by the Japanese government, only about half of

Japan's population undergoes health checkups. In "The Demand for Health Checkups Under Uncertainty," Tadashi Yamada and Tetsuji Yamada look at the characteristics of individuals that lead them to seek more or fewer routine checkups.

The study is based on a sample of about 630,000 observations from people in the twenty to sixty-four age group in the National Survey of Life, focusing in particular on those between ages thirty and sixty. Yamada and Yamada find a significant gender differential in the demand for health checkups even after controlling for other socioeconomic and demographic characteristics. This differential tends to disappear as age increases. Age is also a major determinant of health checkups. The type of health insurance coverage and the size of one's employer also affect the likelihood of a health checkup. Finally, Yamada and Yamada identify a strong negative correlation between the health checkup rate and the probability of becoming ill, as well as the duration of hospitalization.

In the short run, the authors find, health checkups increase medical expenditures. These expenditures are offset, however, by reductions in the incidence and duration of hospitalization. In other words, an individual who has had a health checkup has a much lower risk of being hospitalized than one who has not. Furthermore, if this individual is hospitalized, he or she is likely to have a shorter hospital stay. Thus, in the long run, checkups will reduce not only monetary expenditures, but also psychological burdens associated with illness and hospitalization. In conclusion, the author says: "This paper finds that health checkups constitute a highly cost-effective means of illness prevention within the context of the current comprehensive system of national health care. We must increase the relatively low health checkup rate of 56 percent in the twenty- to sixty-four-year-old population, if only because good health is, by itself, of great value."

In "The Role of Firms in Welfare Provision," Toshiaki Tachibanaki discusses the ways firms support welfare benefit programs in Japan, and how this role might evolve in the future. Firms in Japan support welfare provision in various ways. First, firms help finance public social security benefits by contributing to social insurance programs such as public pensions, unemployment compensation, and medical care. Second, firms organize together and manage their own system of welfare provision for their employees. Typical examples of this are enterprise pensions (or occupational pensions) and health insurance benefits. Third, large firms in particular often provide their employees with direct benefits, such as housing services and other nonstatutory welfare benefits.

The distinction between direct and indirect methods of welfare provision is particularly important, the author says. An indirect method implies that firms contribute to both employees and citizens who are anonymous from the firm's point of view. An example is a social insurance system, in which firms contribute to a pool of resources that supports the overall citizenry of the country, rather than the employees of any one firm. A direct method implies that firms contribute directly and exclusively to their own employees. Thus, firms can identify the actual beneficiaries of the welfare provision because they support only their own employees. Typical examples are enterprise pensions, health insurance systems, and housing services. An interesting question is whether such direct and indirect methods have different effects on workers' behavior, welfare system management, or firms' economic performance.

In addition to elaborating on these various forms of benefit provision, and their economic characteristics for the firm, the author also looks at the potential future evolution of the firm's role. For instance, he considers the possibility of a transformation of nonstatutory fringe benefits to wage payments, a reduction in the statutory social security contributions of firms, and the introduction of a progressive expenditure tax to compensate for such a reduction.

In many countries, benefit provision for part-time workers is an important labor market concern. Part-time work has expanded rapidly in Japan in the 1980s and 1990s. According to the Employment Status Survey, the number of female part-time workers increased from 3.9 million in 1982 to 8.5 million in 1997. In light of this expansion, labor market policies affecting part-time workers have generated increased interest. In "Fringe Benefit Provision for Female Part-Time Workers in Japan," Yukiko Abe considers this issue.

Although Japan has universal public pension and health insurance coverage, the benefits are provided through a somewhat more complicated interaction of employee benefit programs (mandated by the government), eligibility for spousal benefits, and regional plans for self-employed and nonworking individuals. As a result of these multiple programs, how one receives benefits and who pays for those benefits are closely related to an individual's employment status. The demographic group most often in the "gray" area in this respect in Japan is women who work part-time. Some may be covered as employees, some may be covered as spouses of full-time employees, and some may be covered as nonworking individuals—all depending on the nature of their employment and the characteristics of the various benefit programs. In this paper, Abe focuses on women who work part-time and provides new empirical evidence on their fringe benefit coverage.

Social insurance programs in Japan (in this case, public pension, health insurance, and employment insurance) do not require all part-time workers to enroll. Participation is only necessary for workers with sufficiently high working hours or earnings. It has been pointed out that many married women working part-time do not participate in employer-provided plans but are still covered by the spousal provisions in their husbands' benefit programs. In these situations, neither income taxes nor social security taxes are collected out of the wife's earnings, but she still receives benefits. This raises questions of both efficiency and equity, says Abe.

In this study, using microdata on part-time workers, Abe examines the enrollment patterns of female part-time workers in employment insurance (EI) programs, public pensions (EP), and employer-provided health insurance plans. The conditions for participating in EP and employer-provided health insurance are the same (for those younger than sixty-five): Part-time workers who work thirty or more hours are required to enroll in public pension and employer-provided health insurance. The coverage for EI is wider: Workers who work more than twenty hours per week or earn 0.9 million yen or more have to participate.

Abe hypothesizes that the financial incentives in the current system will induce less direct benefit participation among married women and older workers, because these demographic groups are more likely to receive benefits already through alternative programs. She finds that, conditional on satisfying the hours and earnings conditions mandating participation in employees' pensions and health insurance, married and older female workers are no less likely to participate than others. However, married and older female workers who do *not* meet the mandatory participation conditions are significantly less likely to participate, just as the financial incentives would suggest. Abe also notes an overall increase in participation in social insurance programs by female part-time workers between 1990 and 1995.

Vacation time is another important fringe benefit in most industrialized countries. In "Unions, the Costs of Job Loss, and Vacation," Fumio Ohtake explores the relationship between unionization, on the one hand, and the cost of vacations and other worker absenteeism (what Ohtake refers to as "bad" vacation time) on the other. In the terminology of the study, good vacations are paid holidays, sick leaves, or other legally contracted vacations. Bad vacations consist of worker absenteeism, shirking, and other absences without authorized leave. Although the loss in worker productivity is somewhat larger for bad vacations, the distinction between fully authorized time off and other worker absenteeism is apparently weak in Japan.

Ohtake makes the case that unionization is an important factor in worker decisions about how much time off to take. He argues, specifically, that workers represented by a union will feel greater job security and will therefore take more time off than workers not represented by a union. Because unions reduce the threat of job loss (by making it more difficult for employers to dismiss workers), vacation time is less responsive to such threats in unionized firms than in nonunionized firms. Ohtake tests this hypothesis using data from the 1985 and 1993 *General Survey on Working Hours and Conditions in Japan,* and the findings support his supposition.

Ohtake relates these findings to mainstream economic models of efficiency wages, the mechanisms for worker discipline, and the ways employment practices are applied differently to unionized and nonunionized firms in Japan. According to Ohtake, since Japanese case law severely restricts unionized firms from dismissing workers, the simple worker discipline model based on dismissal does not apply in Japan. Instead, unionized firms motivate workers using more costly monitoring and merit pay systems than nonunionized firms. In nonunionized Japanese firms, however, efficiency wages and the threat of dismissal may have much larger applicability. Thus, it may be more appropriate to characterize the Japanese labor market as a three-sector market, with a unionized sector of full-time workers, a nonunionized sector of full-time workers, and a part-time workforce—each governed by different employment practices.

Changing the Guard
The Rise of the United States to
Peak Capitalist Economy

Richard B. Freeman

1.1 Introduction

At the turn of the twenty-first century, many analysts view the United States as the peak capitalist economy—the economy whose institutions other countries should emulate. With an unemployment rate below 4 percent in 1999-2000—lower than in Japan or Germany or other European Union countries—a huge federal budget surplus, declines in crime, a booming stock market, rapid productivity growth, and the integration of welfare mothers into work, the United States seemingly found the magic formula for economic success in the new millennium.

A decade or so earlier, analysts saw the United States in a very different light. In the 1970s and 1980s most viewed Japan as the peak capitalist economy, whose institutions other countries should emulate. American business leaders feared Japanese competitors to the extent that they made the fourteenth-century samurai warrior Miyamoto Musashi's *A Book of Five Rings* (1982) a best-seller on the business charts. Financial experts saw Japanese banks as the 800-pound gorillas on financial markets and wondered if lead bank-financing and monitoring firms worked better than stock market monitoring of performance. Labor economists argued that job rotation, permanent employment, consensual decision making, and other Japanese institutions contributed to labor market success. Few doubted that Ezra Vogel was right when he described *Japan as Number One* (1979).

Richard B. Freeman is the Herbert Ascherman Chair in Economics at Harvard University and is co-director of the Labor and Work Life Forum at Harvard Law School. He is director of the Labor Studies Program at the National Bureau of Economic Research, co-director of the Centre for Economic Performance at the London School of Economics, and visiting professor at the London School of Economics.

The "changing of the guard" from Japan to the United States as peak capitalist economy raises important questions about the relation between economic institutions and outcomes. Is there in fact a single capitalist model that deserves the title of peak economy? Does the performance of the U.S. and Japanese economies support the notion that in the 1990s the United States had the right stuff, whereas in the 1980s Japan had the best economic institutions? What features of the U.S. system enabled it to outperform other capitalist countries in the 1990s? How do these features compare to those that enabled Japan to outperform other capitalist countries in the 1990s?

This paper examines these questions. Section 1.2 develops criteria to judge whether any economy merits peak economy status in a particular period. Section 1.3 assesses how well the United States fits this position in the 1990s and compares the U.S. record with that of Japan in its peak economy period of the 1980s. Section 1.4 assesses the features of the U.S. capitalist model that contributed to its economic success in the 1990s and 2000. The final section contrasts these features with the features of the Japanese model that contributed to its success in the 1970s and 1980s. The similarities and differences between the institutions of these two peak economies highlight the difficulty of linking with any surety institutions, policies, and economic outcomes in a changing world.

1.2   Single-Peaked versus Diversified Capitalism

Behind the claim or belief that the United States or Japan or any other country has developed *the* ideal form of capitalism is the notion that economic outcomes are related to institutions and policies according to a single-peaked social maximand. When institutions or policies produce a single peak in the space of social outcomes, one set of arrangements is indeed the global optimum. This is shown in the first landscape in figure 1.1. The horizontal axis measures institutions along some dimension such as centralization of wage setting or the role of unions or the state in economic decision making, whereas the vertical axis represents some aggregate social output. In the first landscape the set of institutions N (for nirvana) produces the highest output, and every move in the direction of N raises well-being. It behooves all economies to adopt the nirvana institutions as quickly as they can.

But there is nothing in economic logic that rules out different institution-outcome landscapes. One alternative is a landscape with multiple peaks separated by valleys. Some of the multiple peaks may have similar heights, so that different institutional arrangements produce the same well-being, but most peaks are local optima, separated from higher optima by valleys that make it costly to change. The peak economy might have better outcomes than others, but it may not be worthwhile for countries with slightly lower outcomes to invest in change by going down from their peak.

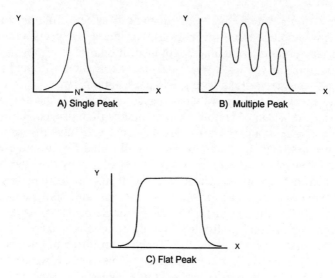

Fig. 1.1   Economic institutions: Outcome landscapes

It is also possible, however, that different institutions produce similar levels of output with little cost to changing them. This produces the flat peak in figure 1.1. This is a Coasian world side payments guarantee that whatever the initial property arrangements, the economy reaches an efficient outcome. This diagram predicts similar gross domestic product (GDP) per capita (other social maximands) within a wide range of institutional settings. Each country can do it its own way without suffering any economic penalty.

Belief in a single-peaked outcome function is deeply ingrained in economics. Models of optimizing behavior assume convex functions so that first derivatives yield the maximizing conditions and second derivatives or matrices thereof have the appropriate sign for the second order conditions. Even if individuals choose blindly, persons who pick points around the peak do better and eventually increase their share of markets. Marxian analysis also takes a single-peaked view of capitalism, predicting the growth of monopolies and proletariat in all countries.

There is a case for diversified capitalism as well, however. Since the end of World War II, living standards in advanced capitalist economies with differing institutions have converged. The coefficient of variation of GDP per capita, measured in purchasing power parity terms, declined over time among major Organization for Economic Cooperation and Development (OECD) countries as Japan and European Union (EU) countries closed much of the income gap with the United States. Comparative advantage argues for diversity. If Japan can operate a consensual stake-holder model of the firm better than the United States and the United States is more adept at a high-mobility or decentralized wage-setting model, Japan will do better with its system than to mimic the U.S. system, and the converse is true as well. Game theory teaches us that interactive decision making creates many potential outcomes, with institutional rules or norms determining equilibrium (Kreps 1990). This is more consistent with multiple or flat peaks—diversity—than with single-peak optima.

Finally, there is a third possibility: that some economic institutions are better adapted to some economic environments than others. Perhaps indicative planning and corporatist arrangements were peak institutions in an era of mass factory production but are ill suited for an information-based economy, whereas high mobility and flexibility work better in that environment than in others. The notion that institutions are better suited for some environments than for others is a more subtle and demanding interpretation of economic history than the single-peak "X works best" claim or the "many roads to Rome" diversified capitalism claim. It requires that we understand how institutions function in different environments and how they learn to adapt to changing circumstances. If we are to draw policy lessons from current successes, this view requires that the current environment maintain itself for some period of time. The evidence is consistent with an adaptionist interpretation, in part because it affords us an additional degree of freedom with which to interpret events.

1.2.1   Criteria for Peak Status

What factors might help us determine which landscape best describes the economics world, and whether the United States or some other economy represents the economic peak in any given time period?

Table 1.1 lists six factors that differentiate peak landscapes from other landscapes and that can thus guide any assessment of whether any economy has achieved peak status.

The first criterion for a single-peak landscape is that the peak economy does better than other economies in sustainable aggregate economic performance. The natural measure of aggregate performance is long-term sustainable GDP per capita or GDP per hour worked. If there was general agreement how to weigh the impact of outcomes like inflation, balance of payments, unemployment, fiscal deficits, and so forth on long-term

Table 1.1   **Criteria for a Single-Peak Economy**

Static Criteria of N* as Optimum	Dynamic Criteria of N*
1. N* dominates on several key aggregate outcomes	4. Large and small movements toward N raise well-being
2. N* has higher well-being in much of distribution	5. N* dominates over extended period
3. Near neighbors are also high	6. Institutions converge (or outcomes diverge)

output, we could form a single weighted average of those outcomes, per so-called misery indexes of various forms. But whereas some economists weigh inflation heavily, others weigh unemployment heavily in judging how well an economy does in the aggregate. In some periods, there is wide-spread consensus that a negative balance of payments is a critical constraint on long-term growth. In other periods, as in the United States in the late 1990s, many ignore trade imbalances. In any case, the peak economy must do better on some dimensions of aggregate performance.

The second criterion is distributional. The peak economy should produce higher incomes throughout much of the income distribution than competing economies. If one economy produces higher outcomes at *all* points in the income distribution, who would not declare it the peak economy? Beyond that, however, there is no universally accepted ordering of distributions. Rawls values how the poorest fare; your local billionaire may value how the richest fare; and political economy considerations make the middle of the distribution important. My criterion is again vague, simply that the peak economy has higher incomes throughout much of the distribution. This is a way of saying that distributional factors must enter any assessment.

The third criterion relates to the convexity of the landscape space. As figure 1.1 shows, N^* lies at the top of a mountain, so neighbors with characteristics close to those of N^* should also have good social outcomes, and the more features of the single-peak economy they have, the higher their social outcome should be. This is the standard calculus requirement for a local maximum.

The next three criteria relate to changes over time.

Since there is only one peak in the figure 1.1 landscape, any change in the direction of the peak—large-scale as well as small-scale—ought to improve well-being. In practice, an economy that chooses radical reform in the direction of the peak economy ought to see economic improvements. By contrast, economies that, for whatever reason, move away from peak institutions should suffer economic losses. This is the requirement for a global maximum.

Criterion five requires that the economy with peak institutions dominate other economies for some period—probably at least a decade or so. Given that candidates for the peak, such as the United States, are likely to have high income per capita and that other economies can take advantage of catch-up, I do not require that the peak economy grow more rapidly than other economies, only that it maintain an edge on outcomes over an extended period.

The sixth criterion requires that the peak economy be an attractor in institution-outcome space. Other economies seeking to improve their performance should imitate the features of the peak economy. That U.S. firms tried to copy Japanese modes of production in the 1970s-1990s indicates that businesses, at least, saw Japan as the peak economy. The fact that European and Japanese policymakers tried to alter the way they regulated markets in the 1990s in the direction of the United States indicates that they now see the United States in that light.

In short, economic institutions merit peak status if they fulfill the standard calculus conditions for a global optimum for extended periods of time and are an attractor to other economies.

1.3   Comparing the Peak Economies

How well did the candidate for peak economy in the 1990s through 2000, the United States, fare by these criteria? How did the 1980s candidate for peak economy, Japan, fare by these criteria in the earlier period?

Table 1.2 examines the performance of the United States, Japan, and the leading EU economy, Germany, in the late 1990s, when the United States moved into peak status in the eyes of many observers; in the early 1990s, when U.S. economic performance was more uncertain; and in the 1980s, when few analysts saw the United States as a candidate for peak economy. The exhibit records data on employment, unemployment, growth of GDP, productivity, and earnings growth.

The strongest case for the United States as peak economy is its success in increasing employment—what I have labeled the magnitude of work. Throughout the 1990s the United States had higher ratios of employment to population than Japan or Germany and the rest of the EU. If we look back to 1970, the Bureau of Labor Statistics files show that the United States had a higher employment-population rate than Germany and a markedly lower rate than Japan. Since then the U.S. rate rose by 6.9 points, while the German rate fell by 4.4 points and the Japanese rate fell by the same 4.4 points. Unemployment rates tell a similar story for the United States and EU in the 1990s but show that even in the late 1990s, the United States had higher unemployment than Japan. Not until 1998-99 did U.S. unemployment rates fall below Japanese rates. Along with employment, hours worked also rose in the United States compared to Japan and the EU. Using the magnitude of work as indicator of economic success, the United States has a strong case for peak economy in the 1990s.

The economic growth figures in table 1.2 make a weaker case for the United States. In the late 1990s the United States outperforms both Japan and Germany in growth of GDP per capita and GDP per worker, but in the earlier 1990s, it falls behind both countries. Both in Japan and Germany, however, productivity measured by GDP per employee or per hour worked grew more rapidly than in the United States, so that by the mid-1990s output per hour worked in Japan and major EU countries was roughly on a par with output per hour worked in the United States (Freeman 1996; van Ark and McGuckin 1999; McKinsey Global Institute 1997).

Table 1.2 **Comparisons of the United States, Japan, and Germany, 1980s and 1990s**

Magnitude of Work (averages over years)

	1995–1999		1990–1994		1980–1989	
	Employment to population rate	Unemployment Rate	Employment to population rate	Unemployment Rate	Employment to population rate	Unemployment Rate
United States	63.7	4.9	62.0	6.6	60.1	7.3
Japan	60.5	3.8	61.6	2.4	60.8	2.5
Germany	52.2	9.1	53.7	6.7	51.5	6.0

Growth of Aggregate Economy

	1995–1998		1990–1995		1980–1990	
	GDP per Capita	GDP per Employment	GDP per Capita	GDP per Employment	GDP per Capita	GDP per Employment
United States	3.2	2.4	1.4	1.5	2.2	1.4
Japan	1.2	1.1	2.0	1.6	4.1	2.7
Germany	1.3	2.3	1.9	2.8	2.0	1.7

Growth of Productivity and Real Hourly Compensation in Manufacturing

	1995–1998		1990–1995		1980–1990	
	Manufacturing Output per Hour	Real Hourly Compensation	Manufacturing Output per Hour	Real Hourly Compensation	Manufacturing Output per Hour	Real Hourly Compensation
United States	2.7	1.3	3.2	0.1	3.1	0.1
Japan	2.4	1.1	2.7	2.4	4.1	2.3
Germany	3.3	1.4	2.3	2.4	2.5	2.6

Sources: U.S. Bureau of Labor Statistics (2000a, tables 2 and 5; 2000b, tables 1 and 4 [these figures use EKS purchasing power parity]; 2000c, tables 1 and 13).

Finally, the manufacturing productivity data in table 1.2 show the United States doing well over the entire 1990s—better than Japan and slightly better over than period than Germany. The hourly real compensation data, however, show that even in the late 1990s, the United States had lower growth of pay than Germany, although faster growth than Japan. It is the fact that the United States combined substantial productivity growth and employment growth, rather than its productivity record per se, that makes it a candidate peak economy in the 1990s. The late-1990s boom in the United States continued longer than expected (and is going strong at this writing) because productivity growth associated with high-tech industries and the "new economy" keep inflation low despite the low unemployment.

1.3.1 The Problem of Distribution

The flaw in the U.S. candidacy for peak economy is on the distributional criterion. As table 1.3 shows, although the United States is first in per capita income, it is thirteenth in per capita income for workers in the lower decile of earnings. Not until the thirtieth to fortieth decile does the United States surpass most other advanced countries in per capita income. In addition, the fact that Americans work so much more than citizens of other countries implies that the U.S. advantage in living standards is less than what is indicated by GDP per capita. Greater hours worked per adult

Table 1.3   **Per Capita Income by Position in the Income Distribution, Relative to U.S. Per Capita Income, 1996**

	Per Capita	Lower Decile	Upper Decile
United States	100	36	208
Switzerland	91	52	168
Norway	88	49	139
Japan	84	39	161
Denmark	81	44	126
Belgium	79	46	129
Canada	77	36	141
Austria	77	43	144
Germany	76	41	131
The Netherlands	75	43	130
France	74	41	143
Australia	73	33	141
Italy	72	40	127
Sweden	69	39	110
Finland	68	39	107
United Kingdom	67	29	138
New Zealand	63	34	119

Sources: Income per capita, U.S. Bureau of the Census (1998, table 1355). Income Distribution estimates based on percentile figures relative to median for household income, Gottschalk and Smeeding (1997), usually 1991–1992 figures.

means less leisure, so that any welfare function that values leisure brings EU countries closer to the United States in overall economic well-being. With hours per worker and per adult rising in the United States relative to other countries, moreover, the U.S. advantage in living standards eroded even in the 1990s.

However, the boom of the late 1990s did improve U.S. performance in the distribution of economic benefits. With a national unemployment rate around 4 percent and unemployment around 2 to 3 percent in many areas of the country, the real wages of low-skilled workers rose; young blacks whom employers had previously shunned have found jobs; welfare reforms that seemed conservative madness moved many single mothers from dependence into the workforce. Although these changes have not reversed the 1970s and 1980s fall in real earnings for low-skilled workers, they raise the possibility that the extended economic boom may ameliorate the U.S. failure to meet the distributional criterion for peak economy status (Freeman 2000b).

All told, however, although U.S. performance has been superior for an extended period on full employment and has been good on one other outcome, productivity during a period of rising employment, it still falls short of peak status on distributional grounds.

1.3.2   Other Criteria

According to the peak-economy view of the economic landscape, neighbors to the peak should also do well, and economies that adopt peak-economy institutions should improve their outcomes. The view of the United States as peak economy fails these criteria.

Close neighbors refers to neighbors in institution space, not in geography, but the United States' closest geographic neighbor, Canada, is also its closest institutional neighbor. The 1990s were an economic disaster for Canada. In 1990, Canada stood third in the GDP per capita league tables, below Switzerland and the United States, and sufficiently above most EU countries to support the notion that North American institutions generated higher average living standards than those in other advanced countries. In 1997, following a decade of economic decline and stagnation, Canada was in seventh position in the league tables. One interpretation of the disparate performances of the United States and Canada is that the small differences between the two countries matter a lot, and that Canada has just not gone far enough toward the U.S. model. Alternatively, some argue that Canada suffered from egregious macroeconomic policy. A broader interpretation, however, is that countries with similar institutions can do differently in any given time period, a conclusion that rejects the single-peak view of the world.

In the EU, the United Kingdom is generally viewed as the economy most similar to the United States, and the reforms enacted by the Thatcher, Major, and Blair governments have brought the United Kingdom even closer to the American model. Has this improved the position of the United Kingdom in the league per capita income tables? No. In 1980, the United Kingdom was sixteenth in the league tables; in 1997, it was eighteenth (U.S. Bureau of the Census 1999, table 1363). Perhaps the United Kingdom was not radical enough. Mrs. Thatcher's reforms never touched the National Health Service, did not reduce the ratio of tax revenues to GDP to U.S. levels, and left monetary policy in the hands of the government rather than the Bank of England. Perhaps without the reforms the United Kingdom would have fallen further in the league tables. But again, perhaps the correct interpretation is that the institutions-outcome space does not fit the single-peak model.

Outside Europe, the economy that has undertaken the most radical reforms is New Zealand. New Zealand deregulated much of its labor market, freed its central bank from political control, and introduced a variety of free trade measures. It out-Thatchered Mrs. T. With what result? In 1997, New Zealand ranked last in per capita income among advanced OECD countries, with an income per capita 14 percent below that of its natural partner, Australia. In 1980, New Zealand was also last among the countries, with an income per capita 19 percent below that of Australia. Extenuating circumstances may explain the failure of radical reform: New Zealand had such serious problems prior to its reforms that absent the reforms it might have fallen even further. New Zealand may have screwed up its monetary policy so badly that its labor and product market reforms had no chance to bring about recovery. Perhaps—but once more a simpler explanation is that the single-peak landscape vision of capitalism is wrong.

What about the sixth criterion—the predicted movement of economies toward the peak institutional form? Because there are many factors that differentiate the U.S. model from others, it is difficult to determine whether economies are becoming Americanized. In one readily measurable dimension, the extent of unionization and collective bargaining coverage, they are not becoming more like the United States. Table 1.4 shows that union density and collective bargaining coverage rates diverged across OECD countries between 1980 and 1997. If the countries that moved further from the United States on this dimension did especially poorly in GDP per capita, we might reconcile this pattern with a single-peaked world (they screwed up), but the data do not show such a pattern. Sweden fell in per capita income, but so too did New Zealand. On the other hand, many EU countries and Japan moved their regulatory policies toward the American model, so that on many areas beyond collective bargaining, the United States does seem to be an attractor to other countries.

1.3.3   Japan as Number One in the 1980s

How good was the case for Japan as number one in the 1980s?

The table 1.2 evidence for the 1980s suggests that the case for Japan as

Table 1.4   **The Increasing Diversity of Labor Institutions, 1980–1994**

	Density		Coverage	
	1980	1997	1980	1994–1997
Declining density and coverage				
United Kingdom	50	30	70	44
United States	22	16	26	18
Japan	31	21	28	18
New Zealand	56	30	67	31
Australia	48	35	88	80
Declining density and stable/rising coverage				
Austria	52	39	98	98
France	22	10	85	95
Germany	36	29	91	92
Italy	50	37	85	82
The Netherlands	35	24	76	81
Portugal	52	30	70	71
Stable density/coverage				
Belgium	53	53	90	90
Canada	36	38	37	36
Denmark	79	76	69	69
Norway	55	55	75	74
Switzerland	31	23	53	50
Rising density and stable/rising coverage				
Finland	69	88	95	95
Spain	8	17	76	78
Sweden	78	86	86	89
#5 relative to #15	1.6	2.3	1.3	1.8

Sources: OECD (1997, table 3.3), with updates from Blanchflower (2000).

peak economy in that decade was much stronger than the 1990s case for the United States. Japan outperformed other economies on all of the relevant criteria, whereas table 1.3 shows that the distribution of income in Japan approaches the distribution of income in EU countries.

In the 1980s, Japan had higher employment rates and lower unemployment than the United States and EU countries.

Its rate of productivity growth closed much of the gap with the United States and brought Japan from nineteenth in GDP per capita tables to sixth.

Its rate of real wage growth closed much of the gap with the United States as well.

Japan ran huge trade surpluses and expanded its multinational production overseas. Perhaps most indicative of Japanese success was its remarkable record in the automobile sector, where Japanese firms and transplants had higher productivity than U.S. or EU automobile companies. Most observers traced the superior Japanese performance to team production, job rotation, and related human resource or personnel policies.

The other area in which Japan did well was high-tech production. In 1980, Japan produced 53 percent as much as the United States did in high tech; in 1990, it produced 81 percent as much as the United States. More than anything, it was the Japanese success in automobiles and high-tech manufacturing that made Japan seem the country best poised to progress rapidly in succeeding years.

Few if any analysts saw that Japan had underlying problems that were going to cause it great economic problems in the 1990s.

1.4   What Explains U.S. Employment Success in the 1990s?

Economies have many institutional features and policies, and different observers select different features of peak economies to highlight in their analysis and recommendations. Given that we have relatively few observations of economies with particular institutional settings, and that seemingly similar economies, like those of the United States and Canada, have performed differently in a given period, the problem of identifying what really matters for any peak performance is a difficult one. In the aggregate, there are more candidate arrangements that could contribute to peak status than empirical observations. This identification problem is particularly severe if one believes that performance depends on a configuration of institutions. If you thought that U.S. peak performance depended on four factors—flexible labor market, weak unions, deregulated product markets, and, say, tax and bankruptcy laws favorable to venture capital—you would have to analyze 2^4 or sixteen cases to show that in fact all four were necessary.[1] Although the lack of experimental or pseudoexperimental data severely limits what we can see, it is still possible to rule out some factors as contributing to the stellar employment performance of the United States and to direct attention to factors that are associated with the relevant performances.

1.4.1   Misunderstandings

There is considerable misunderstanding about the institutions and policies that contributed to the United States stellar 1990s performance in employment.

Many have claimed that U.S. job growth has consisted largely of low-level, fast-food-type jobs, of which McDonald's is the archetype. This is erroneous.

Looking at the industrial composition of U.S. jobs growth from the 1980s through the 1990s, there is some support for this argument. Ameri-

---

1. Measure each of the four institutions as a 0-1 variable, reflecting presence or absence. With four institutions, this gives 2^4 cases, ranging from situations with only two of the features to three of the features, and so on.

can job creation has been concentrated in the broadly defined service sector, particularly retail trade, which pays less than, say, manufacturing. But in the 1990s, when the United States attained full employment, the retail trade share of employment has fallen. In 1990, 17.9 percent of nonagricultural employment was in retail trade; in 1999, 17.7 percent of employment was in retail trade. Employment grew rapidly in many high-paying and skilled service industries as well as low-paying and less skilled industries. Average hourly earnings for production workers in services was 48 percent higher than in retail trade in March 2000 and 1.5 percent above the national average (U.S. Bureau of Labor Statistics 2000d).

Looking at the occupational composition of U.S. job growth, we see that the McJobs story has never been true. In 1999, 30 percent of the U.S. workforce was in managerial and professional specialties compared to 23 percent in 1983. Although the growth of employment was bifurcated, with fast growth at both the top and bottom of the skill and wage distributions, on net U.S. employment was more skilled in 2000 than in 1990 or 1980.

The notion that U.S. job growth has come at the cost of falling real wages and productivity has greater empirical support over the long run, but it does not the fit the pattern of change in employment among groups in the United States or the 1990s expansion, when the United States became a candidate for peak economy. From the 1970s through the mid-1990s, the real wages of American production workers fell while the real wages of workers in most OECD countries rose, suggesting that declining wages account for U.S. job growth relative to other countries.

Examined closely, however, the trade-off claim loses its appeal. The wages of low-skilled men fell absolutely and relative to the wages of more skilled men, but so too did the employment and hours worked of the low-skilled. Women, whose wages rose relative to men, increased employment. The 1980s reductions in the real minimum wage did not improve employment of low-skilled youth, and the 1990s increases in the minimum did not reduce it. Comparisons of employment growth in Canada, France, and the United States (Card, Lemieux, and Kramarz, 1996) or between Germany and the United States (Freeman and Schettkat 2000) also show no clear relation across countries in the growth of employment among groups and in the pattern of wage changes.

Most important, the move to full employment in the 1990s was associated with rising real wages for the low-skilled. In the late 1990s, as unemployment dropped to 4 percent or so, diverse groups of low-wage workers enjoyed significant increases in real wages. For example, the usual weekly earnings of men aged sixteen to twenty-four deflated by the consumer price index rose by nearly 8 percent from 1994 to 1999, after having fallen steadily since 1980. In retail trade, the real earnings of production workers rose by 7.0 percent; in services, they rose by 6.8 percent, whereas in low-paying occupations, median weekly earnings of full-time workers rose between 1996 and 1999 by 7.2 percent among information clerks, by 5.2 percent among food preparation and service workers, and by 3.3 percent among handlers, cleaners, and laborers (Freeman 2000b). To be sure, the earnings of the low-paid and disadvantaged did not rise to their levels of the 1970s or reduce the overall level of earnings inequality. What the boom did was to raise both employment and earnings of low-skilled workers, showing that falling real pay is not the magic bullet for increased employment.

The link between productivity growth and job growth is more complicated. Productivity grew less rapidly in the United States than in other advanced OECD countries in the 1980s through the mid-1990s, suggesting that the United States paid for its employment expansion through slower productivity advance. But output per hour rose rapidly in the United States during the late-1990s period of expanding employment, reducing inflationary pressures and thus helping maintain the boom. Indeed, it is the combination of low unemployment, a high employment-population ratio, and rising productivity that makes the U.S. performance so good.

The notion that U.S. job growth benefits from an unregulated labor market is also a misreading of American economic institutions. The United States has a considerable corpus of labor laws covering everything from hours worked to occupational health and safety to protection of minorities and women. In the 1990s, Congress enacted new laws enhancing individual employee rights—the Americans with Disabilities Act of 1990, the Civil Rights Act of 1991, and the Family and Medical Leave Act of 1993. Most states adopted rules on wrongful dismissals that allow employees to sue for wrongful dismissal in court. Congress twice increased the minimum wage and rejected businesses efforts to modify the Fair Labor Standards Act that requires time and a half overtime and to ease "company union" restrictions on employee involvement committees.

Because the federal government has few regulators to monitor these laws, the main mode of enforcement has been through courts or by workers' bringing complaints to agencies. Most large firms in the United States face some court suit about employment practices every year. Firms have found the burden of employment law sufficiently large to lead many to seek private dispute resolution alternatives.

The notion that U.S. employment growth consists of virtual or short-term temporary jobs is also erroneous. In the mid-1990s, *Fortune* Magazine heralded the "end of the job." The United States was, the story ran, moving from permanent jobs to temporary work, in which firms put together teams for short periods to accomplish specific tasks, much as Hollywood producers produce a movie. Employment in temporary help agencies has, in fact, risen greatly, and there is a growing internet-based industry of "e-working," which means that employers contact employees over the web to undertake specific tasks. However, this is not the world of work. Job tenure—the number of years a worker is with an employer—has held steady or risen modestly because women have more permanent attachments to work than in the past. Tenure has fallen for less skilled men, due to the decline in their job market opportunities, not a movement toward on-line or virtual work.

What, then, underlies growth of employment in the United States?

1.4.2   Contributors to Employment Success

There are five important features to the growth of employment in the United States: institutions and policies that favor inclusion of new groups of workers into the job market, namely women and both unskilled and skilled immigrants; modes of compensation that share the benefits and risks of new undertakings among workers and investors; a linkage between higher education and business that moves science and technology rapidly; and ease of forming new businesses and declaring bankruptcy that encourages entrepreneurship.

New Workers: Growth of Jobs for Women

Perhaps the most important fact about U.S. employment growth is that growth has been most pronounced among women. Had the ratio of employment to population of U.S. women increased from 1973 to 1997 by the same percentage points as did the employment-population ratio of EU women, the aggregate U.S. employment to population rate would have been virtually constant at 65 percent. The biggest increase in female employment was among married women with young children. In 1996 the proportion of married women with children less than six who were working was 63.6 percent—which exceeds the proportion of all European women, including those without children, working. This occurred without national day care facilities or with the hiring of a majority of women by the state, as in some Nordic countries, or with labor laws that give parents paid leave or other benefits to ease the burden of child care. In addition, the position of women in the occupational hierarchy improved. In 1983, women were less likely to be in the high-wage executive and professional occupations than men (22 percent of women versus 25 percent of men). In 1997, they were more likely to be in those occupations (28 percent for women versus 25 percent form men; U.S. Bureau of the Census 1999, table 672).

New Workers: Influx of Immigrants

The 1990s were a period of substantial immigration to the United States. Of the 7.3 million additional persons who obtained jobs from 1990 to 1997, nearly half (3.5 million or 48 percent) were immigrants who entered the country from 1990 to 1997 (comparable to the early 1900s). The immigrants have a bifurcated distribution of skills. Some, largely from Mexico and Latin America, tend to have levels of education far below those of Americans, and they fill unskilled jobs at relatively low U.S. wages, but at wages far above what they could make in their native country. Others, largely from Asia, Europe, and Canada, are highly skilled and contribute to the U.S. higher education and high-tech sectors. Industry has pushed for special visas for some of these immigrants to alleviate alleged skill shortages. As immigrants have become increasingly important in science and engineering, the best and brightest young Americans have moved into business careers. Although we do not know the extent, if any, to which the influx of immigrants spurred U.S. economic success in the 1990s, the influx has been a major part of the employment growth story.

New Businesses: Venture Capital and Bankruptcies

In the United States it is relatively easy to form new ventures (even if they are not dotcoms), and it is relatively easy to go bankrupt and suffer no major stigma: If you are energetic and have a good idea, you can start up again. In the 1990s there were over 150,000 new business starts per year, and about half as many business failures (U.S. Bureau of the Census 1999, table 885). Between 1990 and 1998, the number of business bankruptcy cases averaged over 50,000 a year, while the number of personal bankruptcies more than doubled to over 1.3 million. But perhaps the most important statistic is that venture capital commitments increased from 4 billion dollars in 1993 to 47 billion dollars in 1997. There was a veritable gold rush mentality in exploiting the new Internet and related information technology (IT) and biotechnological advances.

New Modes of Pay: Shared Capitalist Compensation

During the 1980s and 1990s, the United States greatly increased the extent to which workers were paid through some form of financial sharing of company rewards, so that by the mid-1990s about one-half of the U.S. work force received compensation related to company performance (Dube and Freeman 2000). Table 1.5 shows that approximately 25 percent of the private-sector work force had a stake in their firm through some form of ownership—8 percent had employee stock ownership plans, another 8 percent had an all-employee stock option plan, about 10 percent had a substantial proportion of their retirement funds invested in company stocks, and another 8 percent or so buy shares at a discount from the firm. A quarter of the work force was covered by profit or gain sharing. In 1998, 55 million workers were covered by a defined contribution private pension plan, giving them a stake in the performance of the economy outside their own firm. In principle, by making pay more variable, these modes of compensation should reduce the variability of employment. Perhaps more important, the shared modes of pay have been accompanied by increased

Table 1.5   **Estimates of the Percentage of Employees with Pay Related to Company/Group Performance**

Basis	Percentage
Worker Representation and Participation Survey	54
Diverse surveys of programs	45
Stock ownership programs	≈25
Profit-gain-sharing	≈25
Defined contribution pensions invested heavily in company stock	≈11

Source: Dube and Freeman (2000).

Notes: If workers were covered by only one form of variable pay, our estimate would be the sum of the estimates for the bold categories in the table: 61 percent, of which 50 percentage points consists of ownership and incentive pay. But there is considerable overlap in coverage. On the basis of overlaps in the *Worker Representation and Participation Survey,* I estimate that the proportion of workers with any form of performance pay and ownership exceeds the sum of the proportions covered by each form separately by 33 percent = (41.9 + 29.6)/53.8. Thus, I reduce the 50 percent to 38 percent. I do not have data on the overlap with the estimated 11 percent of workers with 401k or other plans with sizable amounts of company shares, but I anticipate that this will be modest, giving the 45 percent in the text.

worker decision making through employee involvement programs and teams, which should improve productivity.

The Higher Education-Industry Link

Higher education is more closely linked to industry in the United States than in most countries, and this has helped the United States apply advanced technology to the economy, with consequences for employment and earnings. As business opportunities have blossomed, top American students have chosen business careers in place of academic work. The United States has also positioned itself to allocate resources to other important areas of scientific and technological progress. Biotechnology, including genetically modified food, which many in the EU deplore, and nanotechnology have the potential to be the technological breakthroughs of the twenty-first century, with impacts on employment, productivity, and wages. The federal government has allocated half a billion dollars to research and development in this area (National Science and Technology Council 2000).

1.5   Conclusion: U.S. versus Japanese Peak Economy Institutions

There are some similarities in the institutions, policies, and economic developments that made the United States the 1990s' peak economy and those that made Japan the 1980s' peak economy. The most notable similarity is in the importance of variable pay. In the 1980s, Japan used bonuses as a form of variable pay, with the amount of bonuses rising in booms and falling in recessions (Freeman and Weitzman 1987). As pointed out above, the United States also moved heavily into variable pay in the 1990s. In principle, variable pay should increase employment and reduce fluctuations in employment, and it thus may have contributed to the peak performance of both economies in the two periods. Both countries have also had declines in their rate of unionization (see table 1.4), and both countries have substantially invested in high-tech industries.

But the differences between the United States and Japan are more striking. Employment in the United States is flexible, with workers changing jobs frequently in their early career years. By contrast, Japanese workers often find permanent employment with the firm they join immediately after school. The U.S. employment growth has been women and immigrant dominated. Japan has not made great use of its female work force and has never encouraged immigration even with very low unemployment. U.S. earnings inequality is high, whereas Japan looks more like an EU country than the United States in terms of earnings inequality (table 1.3). The United States encourages new businesses and has lenient bankruptcy laws and freedom of dismissal for economic reasons. By contrast, the Japanese government has often helped companies maintain employment with subsidies. At the macro level, the differences are even more remarkable. Japan saves and invests and runs trade surpluses. By contrast, U.S. expansion in the late 1990s was spurred by an increase in private domestic debt and a massive trade deficit.

In short, the overall picture is that these are economies with very different institutions, policies, and roads to full employment. What, then, explains Japan's peak economy performance in the 1980s and the United States peak performance in the 1990s? How should we understand the "changing of the guard"?

Two hypotheses fit this experience. The diverse capitalism hypothesis interprets the evidence as reflecting a multipeaked landscape with different institutions producing more or less economic success in different periods. In a multipeaked world, there is no real peak economy and thus it is no surprise that one economy does better in one period and another in another period. The adaptionist hypothesis makes the stronger claim that Japanese institutions and policies fit the 1980s environment whereas U.S. institutions and policies fit the 1990s environment. Developments in the early 2000s will support one explanation or the other. If the U.S. job boom proves sustainable, the case that the United States has peak institutions and policies for the information economy will be enhanced, lending support to the adaptionist claim. If the U.S. economy has a "hard landing," we will be comparing the 2000s fall of the United States as the economic wonder to the 1990s fall of Japan as numero uno in the economic world, strengthening the case for the diverse capitalism hypothesis. Given the penchant that analysts have for picking a peak economy, there will undoubtedly be another changing of the guard.

References

van Ark, Bart, and Robert H. McGuckin. 1999. International comparisons of labor productivity and per capita income. *Monthly Labor Review* 122 (7): 33-41.
Blanchflower, David. 2000. Globalization and the labor market. Report to Trade Deficit Review Commission. http://www.ustdrc.gov.<http://www.ustdrc.gov/>.
Card, David, Thomas Lemieux, and Francis Kramarz. 1999. Changes in the relative structure of wages and employment: A comparison of the United States, Canada, and France. *Canadian Journal of Economics* 32 (4): 843-77.
Dube, Arindrajit, and Richard B. Freeman. 2001. Shared compensation systems and decision-making in the U.S. job market. In *Incomes and productivity in North America: Papers from the 2000 seminar,* 159-214. Washington, D.C.: Secretariat of the Commission for Labor Cooperation.
Freeman, Richard B., ed. 1996. *Working under different rules.* New York. Russell Sage Foundation.
———. 2000a. Single peaked vs. diversified capitalism: The relation between economic institutions and outcomes. In *Advances in macroeconomic theory,* ed. Jacques Dreze, 139-70. London: Palgrave.
———. 2000b. The U.S. "underclass" in a booming economy. *World Economics* 1 (2): 89-100.
Freeman, Richard B., and Ronald Schettkat. 2001. Skill compression, wage differentials, and employment: Germany vs. the U.S. *Oxford economic papers,* 582-603. Oxford: Oxford University Press.
Freeman, Richard, and Martin L. Weitzman. 1987. Bonuses and employment in Japan. *Journal of the Japanese and International Economics* 1:168-94.
Gottschalk, Peter, and Tim Smeeding. 1997. Empirical evidence on income inequality in industrialized countries. Luxembourg Income Study Working Paper no. 154. Luxembourg, Belgium: Luxembourg Income Study.
Kreps, David. 1990. *Game theory and economic modelling.* New York: Oxford University Press.
McKinsey Global Institute. 1997. *Removing barriers to growth and employment in France and Germany.* Frankfurt, Germany: McKinsey Global Institute.
Miyamoto, Musashi. 1982. *A book of five rings* (Gorin no sho), trans. Victor Harris. Woodstock, N.Y.: Overlook Press.
National Nanotechnology Initiative. 2002. http://www.nano.gov. (accessed 20 December 2002).
Organization for Economic Cooperation and Development (OECD). 1997. *OECD employment outlook.* Paris: OECD.
U.S. Bureau of the Census. 1998. *Statistical abstract of the United States: 1998.* Washington, D.C.: U.S. Bureau of the Census.
———. 1999. *Statistical abstract of the United States: 1998.* Washington, D.C.: U.S. Bureau of the Census.
U.S. Bureau of Labor Statistics. 2000a. Comparative civilian labor force statistics, ten countries, 1959-1999. ftp://ftp.bls.gov/pub/special.requests/ForeignLabor/flslforc.txt. (accessed 25 April 2000).

————. 2000b. Comparative real gross domestic product per capita and per employed person, fourteen countries, 1960-1998. http://www.bls.gov/fls/flsgolp.pdf. (accessed 30 March 2000).

————. 2000c. Foreign labor statistics. http://www.bls.gov. (accessed April).

————. 2000d. *Monthly Labor Review* (May).

Vogel, Ezra F. 1979. *Japan as number one: Lessons for America.* Cambridge: Harvard University Press.

The Recent Transformation of Participatory Employment Practices in Japan

Takao Kato

2.1 Introduction

This paper presents findings from our most recent research on the transformation of participatory employment practices of Japanese firms in the 1990s, during which the Japanese economy slowed down considerably. The Japanese experience of employee participation and labor-management cooperation appears to be of particular public policy interest for many countries considering participatory employment practices as a way to improve their productivity performance and thus competitiveness.

As Levine and Tyson (1990) suggest, relatively higher job security and strong group cohesiveness (supported by the compression of wage and status differentials) of workers in large manufacturing firms in the postwar Japanese economy point to an industrial relations system favorable to successful employee participation. Moreover, relatively more rapid and stable growth, lower unemployment, and stable financial corporate grouping (banks and institutional shareholders as stable, long-term suppliers of capital) point to an external environment favorable to successful employee participation.

Takao Kato is professor of economics and Presidential Scholar at Colgate University and a research associate of the Center on Japanese Economy and Business at Columbia Business School and at the Tokyo Center for Economic Research.

I owe my greatest debt of gratitude to the National Bureau of Economic Research (NBER), National Institute for Research Advancement, Japan Center for Economic Research (JCER), Japan Institute of Labour, Rengo-Soken, and Japan Productivity Center for Socio-Economic Development (JPC-SED); and to Richard Freeman, David Wise, Toshiaki Tachibanaki, Seiritsu Ogura, Motohiro Morishima, Professor Koike and Professor Fujimura of Hosei University, Mr. Nakashima and Mr. Koike of Rengo-Soken, Mr. Fukutani of JPC-SED, and the managers, foremen, and union officials of Japanese companies who granted me the opportunities to interview them. I benefited greatly from comments made by Richard Freeman, Professor Chuma of Hitotsubashi University, and other conference participants.

Probably as a result of these favorable environments in the postwar Japanese economy, particularly in manufacturing, participatory employment practices spread widely and were established firmly (e.g., see Kato and Morishima 2002). Indeed, these practices became the hallmark of "Japanese management," which in recent years has been inspiring (or in some instances necessitating) U.S. corporate experimentation with employee involvement and labor-management cooperation (Levine 1995).

The economic slowdown in the 1990s and a rapidly aging workforce have allegedly been eroding the aforementioned participation-friendly environments. A closer look at the recent Japanese experience with participatory employment practices will help us better understand two key questions regarding participation: (a) What are the conditions under which participatory employment practices are best introduced and best sustained? and (b) in what way will participatory employment practices need to evolve when external environments change? To address these questions, we have been gathering and analyzing both quantitative data from national surveys and qualitative data from our own field research on evolving employment practices in the 1990s. This paper reports the first findings from our analysis of these data on the responses of Japanese firms in their use of participatory employment practices to the economic slowdown in the 1990s.

The paper is organized as follows. In the next section, we provide an overview of the scope, nature, and effects of participatory employment practices in postwar Japan (including quantitative evidence on evolving practices in the 1990s). Section 2.3 presents findings from our field research on the responses of Japanese firms in their use of participatory employment practices to the economic slowdown in the 1990s, and section 2.4 concludes.

2.2 The Scope, Nature, and Effects of Participatory Employment Practices in Japan

We first provide an overview of participatory employment practices in Japan, followed by a brief review of the evidence of their effects on firm performance. For a couple of participatory employment practices (joint labor management committees and employee stock ownership plans), our overview also includes quantitative evidence on evolving practices in the 1990s.

2.2.1 Joint Labor-Management Committees: Employee Participation and Involvement at the Top

One of the core mechanisms for labor-management relations within a large Japanese firm is joint labor-management committees (JLMCs). Established at the top (corporate or establishment) level and involving both management and union representatives, JLMCs serve as a mechanism for employee participation and involvement at the top level on a large variety of issues ranging from basic business policies to working conditions.

When there is a union, labor-side representatives are almost always union representatives, while even in the absence of unions, the majority of labor-side JLMC members are elected by employee vote (about 70 percent; Koike 1978). Thus, labor-side JLMC members usually legitimately represent the interests of the firm's workforce.

According to Shimada (1992), JLMCs were one of the many labor-management institutions proposed at the beginning of 1950s by the Japan Productivity Center. After a decade of tumultuous labor-management relations between 1945 and 1955, Japanese unions and management, with the endorsement from the central government, began to implement a number of well-known human resource management techniques, including JLMCs and semiannual bonus payments to all employees. According to Kato and Morishima (2002), in 1960 about 38 percent of all firms, including both manufacturing and nonmanufacturing firms (close to 50 percent for manufacturing), had standing JLMCs. During the next decade, use of the institution spread rapidly. Thus, by 1970 the figure had risen to close to 60 percent (70 percent for manufacturing). For the next two decades the use of this institution increased steadily and, as of 1992, fully 80 percent of all firms (nearly 90 percent for manufacturing) reported to have standing JLMCs.

Many observers attribute the peaceful firm-level labor relations observed in Japanese firms to the establishment of JLMCs (Shimada 1992; Inagami 1988). Within JLMCs, which meet almost once a month, a number of issues are discussed, ranging from basic business policies to social and athletic activities sponsored by the firm (see Kato and Morishima 2002).

Finally, we have been collecting and analyzing quantitative data from recent national surveys on the transformation of JLMCs in the 1990s. We present the first findings from our analysis of such data. The *Survey of Labor-Management Communications* conducted in 1995 by the Ministry of Labor provides the most recent aggregate data on JLMCs. The same survey was conducted also in 1988 by the ministry. Using various cross tabulations published from the 1995 survey as well as those from the 1988 survey, we produced figure 2.1 and tables 2.1 and 2.2.

First, figure 2.1 shows how the proportion of establishments with JLMCs has changed from 1988 to 1995. For all establishments (labeled "total" in the figure), the proportion of those with JLMCs has not fallen significantly over this time period, remaining a little below 60 percent.[1] In

1. This figure is substantially lower than what Kato and Morishima (2002) report. The sample universe of the survey conducted by Kato and Morishima was the Toyo Keizai Kaisha Shiki Ho, which provides a list of all firms listed on Japan's three major stock exchanges (Tokyo, Osaka, and Nagoya). The *Ministry of Labor Survey* is, however, an establishment-

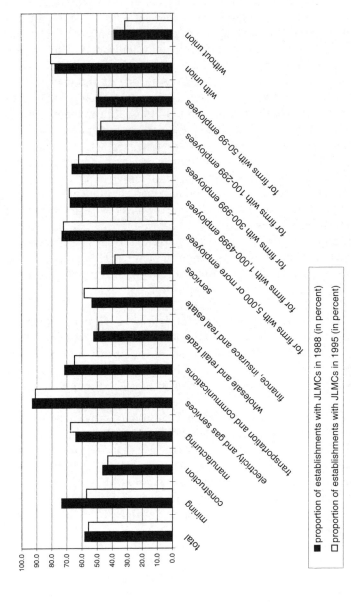

Fig. 2.1 Proportion of establishments with JLMCs in 1998 and 1995

■ proportion of establishments with JLMCs in 1988 (in percent)
□ proportion of establishments with JLMCs in 1995 (in percent)

Table 2.1   Average Number of JLMC Meetings per Year and Average Number of
                   Special Subcommittees in 1988 and 1995 for Establishments with
                   Varying Characteristics

	Average Number of Meetings per Year		Average Number of Special Subcommittees	
	1988	1995	1988	1995
Total	14.2	9.1	3.3	2.8
Mining	5.9	6.6	3.4	2.7
Construction	8.3	7.8	2.8	2.5
Manufacturing	12.5	9.3	3.8	2.7
Electricity and gas services	25.0	18.7	2.8	3.1
Transportation and communications	25.0	11.4	2.4	2.8
Wholesale and retail trade	9.9	8.1	3.7	3.3
Finance, insurance, and real estate	10.8	6.4	3.0	2.5
Services	7.4	8.1	3.4	2.4
For firms with 5,000+ employees	21.3	12.4	3.2	3.2
For firms with 1,000–4,999 employees	10.6	8.7	3.8	3.7
For firms with 300–999 employees	10.3	10.1	3.5	3.0
For firms with 100–299 employees	8.7	7.6	2.2	2.5
For firms with 50–99 employees	7.1	7.9	2.2	1.8
With union	15.4	9.8	3.3	3.1
Without union	7.7	7.2	2.7	1.8

Sources: Japan Ministry of Labor (1988, 1995).

other words, overall, the economic slowdown in the 1990s in general and
the recent banking crisis in particular have not caused any significant dismantling of JLMCs.[2]

Conceivably, the adverse shock might have hit certain sectors of the
economy particularly hard, and for those hard-hit sectors the dismantling
of JLMCs might have begun. To see if this is indeed the case, we repeated
the same analysis for establishments in different industries, establishments
of firms of differing size, and establishments of firms with and without
unions. As shown in the figure, the proportion of establishments with
JLMCs has declined noticeably for mining, services, transportation, and
communications, and for nonunion sectors (although it is still premature

---

level survey and the sample universe in all establishments with more than thirty workers. It
follows that the *Ministry of Labor Survey* includes many establishments of small private firms
that are not included in the sample universe of the survey conducted by Kato and Morishima.
This probably accounts for the discrepancy. Fortunately, the *Ministry of Labor Survey* also reports the proportion of establishments with JLMCs for establishments of unionized firms that
are probably closest to the sample universe of Kato and Morishima. Reassuringly, the figures
for those establishments were very close to those Kato and Morishima report.

2. We recognize that 1995 may be a little too early to detect the full impact of the economic
slowdown in the 1990s. As shown in the next section, however, qualitative evidence from our
field research of summer 1999 tends to confirm this finding from the quantitative data.

Table 2.2   Changes in Varying Attributes of JLMCs from 1988 to 1995

Attribute of Establishments with JLMCs	With Union (%)		Without Union (%)	
	1988	1995	1988	1995
Discusses corporate restructuring	65.4	60.3	48.0	55.9
Discusses hiring and staffing	54.0	51.8	44.7	52.1
Discusses transfer of employees	65.0	66.5	45.1	53.8
Discusses layoff	67.3	71.8	51.2	59.0
Discusses mandatory retirement	71.4	75.8	67.0	60.9
Discusses severance pay or pension	67.9	74.2	61.4	56.8
Establishments with JLMCs that discuss each issue				
Asks employee representatives for prior consent on corporate restructuring	6.1	6.6	6.8	7.0
Asks employee representatives for prior consent on hiring and staffing	7.0	5.7	8.4	5.5
Asks employee representatives for prior consent on transfer of employees	15.4	16.0	19.4	4.0
Asks employee representatives for prior consent on layoff	26.2	34.6	22.8	12.2
Asks employee representatives for prior consent on mandatory retirement	31.8	37.2	31.2	12.1
Asks employee representatives for prior consent on severance pay or pension	33.3	38.6	17.2	9.7
Unionized establishment, union representatives participate as employee representatives	88.1	91.4		
Nonunionized establishment, employee representatives elected by employees			75.2	78.1

Sources: See table 2.1.

Note: Establishments with JLMCs, with or without unions.

to consider this an early sign of the crumbling of JLMCs for these sectors).

The absence of evidence for the formal dissolution of JLMCs is probably not too surprising since, if they decided to end JLMCs, Japanese firms would likely make them dormant by changing their attributes (e.g., reducing the frequency of meetings drastically and trivializing the content of information shared) rather than formally dissolving them. To this end, we created tables 2.1 and 2.2, which demonstrate whether various attributes of JLMCs have changed from 1988 to 1995—and if so, in what way.

Table 2.1 shows the average number of JLMC meetings per year and the average number of special subcommittees in 1988 and 1995. For all establishments, the frequency of JLMC meetings fell substantially from fourteen times a year to nine times a year over the time period. It appears that when news is consistently bad, JLMCs meet much less frequently. The figure also points to considerable differences among sectors. Thus, JLMCs in transportation and communications held JLMC meetings twenty-five times a year in 1988 but only eleven times a year in 1995. The frequency of JLMC meetings in finance, insurance, and real estate has also decreased sharply, from eleven times a year in 1988 to only six times a year in 1995. JLMCs in larger and unionized firms experienced a sharper drop in the frequency of meetings from 1988 to 1995.

Case histories of Japanese JLMCs suggest that JLMCs tend to function well with a number of special subcommittees, such as a special subcommittee on productivity and a special subcommittee on safety and health (Japan Productivity Center 1990). As table 2.1 shows, the average number of special subcommittees for all establishments has declined somewhat from 3.3 in 1988 to 2.8 in 1995. Some differences among sectors are also present. Manufacturing, services, and nonunion sectors experienced larger decline.

A possible way to weaken information-sharing is to undermine the democratic process of selecting employee representatives. In unionized establishments, the democratic selection of employee representatives is typically ensured by union representatives participating in JLMCs as employee representatives. In nonunion establishments, it is normally ensured through election by employees. The last two rows of table 2.2 show the proportion of unionized establishments with JLMCs in which union representatives participate in JLMCs as employee representatives in 1988 and 1995, and the proportion of nonunion establishments with JLMCs in which employee representatives are elected by employees in 1988 and 1995. We failed to find any sign of erosion of the democratic selection of employee representatives over this time period.

The nature of employee participation and involvement changes considerably, depending on (a) the content of information shared (e.g., more or less sharing of information on business and strategic plans, such as sales and production plans and the introduction of new technology and equipment, as compared to information on labor issues such as layoffs, working hours, wages, and bonuses, fringe benefits, and cultural activities or sports), and (b) the nature of "consultation" (for instance, whether labor representatives are "informed only" or "asked for prior consent"). The *Survey of Labor-Management Communication* selects sixteen issues (plus two more issues in 1995), such as basic business strategies, corporate restructuring, layoffs, and mandatory retirement, and asks each establishment with JLMCs whether it discusses each of these issues during its JLMC meetings. When the establishment responds positively, it is then asked whether management asks employee representatives for prior consent.

We selected six issues that are of particular relevance to the economic slowdown in the 1990s, especially the recent economic crisis, and created the rest of table 2.2. The table shows the proportion of unionized establishments with JLMCs that discussed each of these six issues (corporate restructuring, hiring and staffing, transfer of employees, layoffs, mandatory retirement, and severance pay and pension) in 1988 and 1995. It also shows the same figures for nonunionized establishments. In addition, the table shows the proportion of union and nonunion establishments with JLMCs discussing each of these six issues that asked employee representatives for prior consent in 1988 and 1995.

For both unionized and nonunionized establishments, JLMCs are more likely to discuss transfer of employees and layoffs in 1995 than in 1988. For unionized establishments, JLMCs are more likely to discuss mandatory retirement and severance pay or pension in 1995 than in 1988, while they are less likely to discuss corporate restructuring and hiring and staffing in 1995 than in 1988. The opposite pattern is observed for nonunionized establishments. Overall, it is unclear whether JLMCs are more or less likely to discuss issues of topical relevance in 1995 as compared to 1988.

Nevertheless, when one takes a close look at the nature of consultation on each of these six issues, a noteworthy difference between unionized and nonunionized establishments is revealed. As shown in table 2.2, JLMCs of unionized establishments discussing transfer of employees, layoffs, mandatory retirement, and severance pay or pension are more likely to ask employee representatives for prior consent in 1995 as compared to 1988. In stark contrast, JLMCs of nonunionized establishments discussing transfer of employees, layoffs, mandatory retirement, and severance pay or pension are much less likely to ask employee representatives for prior consent in 1995 as compared to 1988. This contrast in the changing nature of consultation over this time period between unionized and nonunionized establishments may suggest that unions effectively prevent JLMCs from becoming dormant by keeping the strong consultative role of JLMCs, whereas for small to medium-sized firms with no union, such role may be weakening. As such, unions and JLMCs may be complements rather than substitutes. At the same time, it suggests that the overall importance of participation in the Japanese economy may be diminishing with the rising proportion of the nonunion sector in the economy.[3]

2.2.2   Shop-Floor Committees and Small-Group Activities: Employee Participation and Involvement at the Grassroots Level

Aside from JLMCs and formal trade unions, many Japanese corporations have shop-floor committees (SFCs) in which supervisors and employees on the shop floor discuss issues such as shop-floor operations and shop-floor environments. Although the potentially important role of SFCs

---

3. According to the *Basic Survey on Labor Unions* (Japan Ministry of Labor), the estimated unionization rate (the number of union members divided by the number of employees) has been falling in the last three decades, from 35 percent in 1970 to 22 percent in 1999.

in the Japanese industrial relations system has been suggested (e.g., see Koike 1978), the nature and scope of these SFCs have not been studied extensively, largely due to the absence of reliable data. A recent survey conducted by Kato and Morishima (2002) reveals that the average SFC meets about nine times a year (slightly less frequently than JLMCs), and that information shared during the SFC meetings tends to go beyond standard shop-floor issues—such as safety and health, fringe benefits, training and development, and grievances—and includes business and strategic plans. As such, SFCs are aimed at employee participation and involvement at the grassroots level.

Kato and Morishima (2002) also reveal the diffusion of SFCs among Japanese firms in the postwar era. In 1960, a little over 10 percent of all firms including both manufacturing and nonmanufacturing firms (15 percent for manufacturing) each had a standing SFC. Since then, the institution spread steadily; in 1992 more than 40 percent of all firms reported having standing SFCs (45 percent for manufacturing firms).

Small-group activities (SGAs) are those such as quality control (QC) circles and "zero defects" in which small groups at the workplace level voluntarily set plans and goals concerning operations and work together to accomplishing these plans and goals. The widespread use of SGAs such as QC circles by Japanese firms is, by now, quite well known (e.g., see Cole 1989). In 1950 almost no firms (only 3 percent) used SGAs. In 1960 only 6 percent of publicly traded firms had SGAs. The rapid diffusion of the institution began in 1960s. By the beginning of 1970s, about one in four publicly traded firms were practicing an SGA, and the figure reached 44 percent in 1980. Since then the institution has grown steadily; in 1993, 70 percent of publicly traded firms reported practicing SGAs (Kato 1995).

Small-group activities are clearly more popular among larger firms (80 percent of firms with 5,000 or more employees practice SGAs as opposed to 43 percent of firms with 299 or fewer). Moreover, SGAs are more widespread in the unionized sector (Kato 1995).

2.2.3   Employee Stock Ownership Plans:
        Financial Participation via Stock

Japanese employee stock ownership plans (ESOPs) are perhaps best understood by comparison of their main features with the better-known U.S. ESOPs. Unlike U.S. ESOPs, Japanese corporations establishing ESOPs (called *mochikabukai*) do not receive any tax incentive to do so. To induce individual employees to participate in the ESOPs, companies offer subsidies (typically the firm matches each employee's contribution by giving 5 to 10 percent of the contribution as well as bearing the administrative costs). Whereas ESOPs elsewhere frequently are structured so as to encourage strong participation by top management, in Japan executives (as well as part-time and temporary employees) are normally ineligible for membership. As is the norm elsewhere, individual participants' shares (and dividends) in the ESOP are held in trust. Unusually, however, each participant has a right to withdraw his or her shares, and share withdrawals are privately owned. Withdrawals are permitted only in 1,000 shares, round lots. While members may freely exit completely from the ESOP, reentry is restricted. Exiting employees will receive their shares in 1,000 shares, round lots, and must sell the remaining shares to the trust at the prevailing market price. Upon retirement, model rules adopted by most ESOPs require retiring workers to exit completely from the ESOP. Finally, the general director (*rijicho*) represents stockholders in the ESOP. The general director is chosen by other participants, on a one-participant, one-vote basis. At the general meeting of shareholders, the general director votes the stock held by the plan, deciding independently rather than by tabulating votes of employee participants. The general director must be a participant in the ESOP and thus is not an executive (Jones and Kato 1993, 1995).

The survey conducted by Kato and Morishima (2002) shows that the ESOPs are a relatively new and the most rapidly spread innovation among various Japanese human resource management practices. Thus, in 1960 the proportion of firms that had ESOPs was only 4 percent. The proportion grew rapidly during the next decade, reaching 26 percent by 1970. In 1967, a special government committee on foreign capital advocated employee ownership as a way to help prevent foreign takeovers of domestic firms. The government, using informal channels, encouraged firms to set up new ESOP trusts to accommodate employee investments in their stock. While the fear of foreign takeovers diminished in the 1970s, the idea of employee ownership took root. Perhaps partly due to this government initiative of 1967, the 1970s were characterized by an astonishing rate of spread of the institution, and more than two-thirds of firms came to have ESOPs by 1980. The diffusion continued even after 1980, and in 1992 it became almost a universal phenomenon (96 percent of firms reported to have ESOPs in that year, and there is no significant difference between manufacturing and nonmanufacturing firms).

The survey also shows that in 1993, almost 50 percent of the labor force in firms with ESOPs participated in ESOPs. Furthermore, concerning employee stakes, Jones and Kato (1995) report that in 1988 ESOPs owned stock worth 4.1 trillion yen (about 32 billion dollars); this amounts to 1.7 million yen (about 14,000 dollars) per participant.

However, according to Jones and Kato (1995), these plans do not own large percentages of company stock. For listed companies the average proportion of stock owned by ESOPs has varied between 0.66 percent and 1.42 percent from 1973 to 1988. In 1988 the average was lower than 1 percent and holdings over 5 percent were rare.

Finally, we have been collecting and analyzing quantitative data from recent national surveys on the transformation of ESOPs in the 1990s. The

National Conference Board of Securities Exchanges has been conducting annually the *Survey of Stock Distribution* to which *all* firms listed on Japan's stock exchange markets respond. The National Conference Board has recently released summary tables from their 1997 survey. Using these most recently published summary tables as well as earlier tables, we created figure 2.2.[4]

In the 1980s, the share prices of most large corporations in Japan rose steadily. It is not too surprising under such steady growth of corporate profitability that ESOPs gained increasing popularity in Japan. Thus, as shown in figure 2.2, both the proportion of firms with ESOPs and the ESOP participation rate (the proportion of the labor force employed by firms with ESOPs and participating in those ESOPs) grew steadily in the 1980s. Moreover, the real market value of outstanding shares owned by ESOPs more than quadrupled and the real market value of outstanding shares owned by ESOPs per participant (the real value of the average stake) more than doubled in the 1980s. The National Conference Board also published the average price of shares owned by ESOPs (the market value of outstanding shares owned by ESOPs divided by the total number of shares owned by ESOPs). The real value of this average price tripled in the 1980s.

The steady growth of share prices ended rather abruptly at the end of the 1980s. For instance, the average firm listed on the Tokyo Stock Exchange lost more than half its value in the early 1990s (Kang and Stulz 1997). Reflecting this rapid asset price deflation in the early 1990s, the real market value of outstanding shares owned by ESOPs, the real value of the average stake, and the real value of the average price of shares owned by ESOPs fell sharply in the early 1990s. As shown in figure 2.2, recovery from this sharp drop has been anemic.

A natural question concerning the responses of ESOPs to this seemingly powerful adverse shock is whether this shock has been discouraging employees from participating in ESOPs. Figure 2.2 shows a surprisingly calm response of the labor force in firms with ESOPs. The ESOP participation rate has not fallen in any significant way in the 1990s although its steady increase in the 1980s did stop in the 1990s: The ESOP participation rate rose in the 1980s by 9 percentage points, from 40 to 49 percent, and has remained at the 49 percent level in the 1990s. It is unclear, however, whether the stagnation of the participation rate in the 1990s was caused by the adverse financial shocks. At any rate, there has been no sign of a frenzied exit of participants from ESOPs in response to the adverse financial shock in the 1990s.

---

4. Although the survey began in 1973, data on the market value of outstanding shares owned by ESOPs became available only in 1979. Thus, our complete data on the evolution of ESOPs begin in 1979.

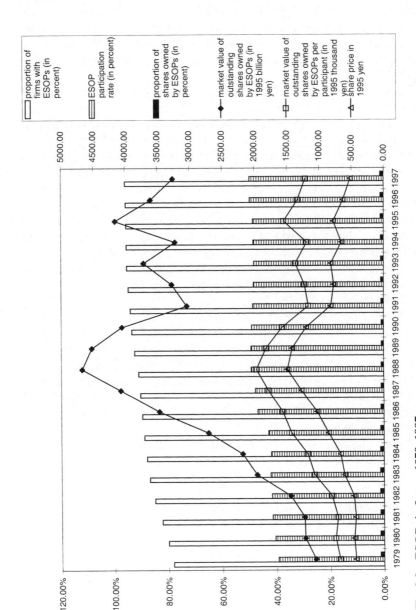

Fig. 2.2 ESOPs in Japan: 1979–1997

Consistent with this relatively calm employees response, very few employers have terminated their ESOPs in response to the adverse financial shock. Thus, as shown in figure 2.2, the proportion of firms with ESOPs has not fallen in the 1990s and ESOPs have continued to be a nearly universal phenomenon among publicly traded firms in Japan (95 percent of all publicly traded firms have ESOPs).

Overall, it appears that neither employees nor employers have panicked in the face of the adverse financial shock in the 1990s. In addition to the summary table for all publicly traded firms, the National Conference Board publishes the summary table for two-digit industries. Conceivably, the adverse shock might have hit certain industries particularly hard, and for those hard-hit industries, many ESOPs might have been terminated and the ESOP participation rate might have fallen significantly. To see if this is the case, we repeated the same analysis for each of 28 two-digit industries. We failed to find any noteworthy example of such industries.

2.2.4   Profit-Sharing Plans: Financial Participation via Bonus

A profit-sharing plan (PSP) is a pay system in which the total amount of bonuses is linked to a measure of firm performance, such as profit. The Japanese bonus payment system has attracted considerable attention and controversy (e.g., Freeman and Weitzman 1987; Nakamura and Nakamura 1989; Hashimoto 1990; Hart and Kawasaki 1995). In light of the ongoing debate between those who stress the profit-sharing aspect of the Japanese bonus system (e.g., Freeman and Weitzman 1987) and those who downplay it (e.g., Ohashi 1989; Brunello 1991), we consider only the least controversial (with respect to the profit-sharing aspect) types of the bonus payment system—that is the bonus payment system with a formal contract stipulating the presence of the PSP.

According to Kato and Morishima (2002), one in four publicly traded firms had a PSP in 1993 (with no appreciable difference between manufacturing and nonmanufacturing firms). The proportion of publicly traded firms with PSPs was only 5 percent in 1960 and grew steadily to 14 percent by 1980. Significant growth occurred during the 1980s, however, with the proportion of publicly traded firms with PSPs reaching more than 20 percent by 1990.

Profit-sharing plans are found to be more prevalent in smaller firms. For instance, the proportion of publicly traded firms with 5,000 or more employees and having any PSP was only 11 percent. The large majority (70 percent) of firms with PSPs reported separate profit-sharing plans for officers and nonofficers. However, Japanese PSPs do not normally distinguish between union and nonunion members (only one-third of firms with PSPs reported separate PSPs for union and nonunion members). Profit-sharing plans are mostly company-wide, with only 12 percent of firms with PSPs reporting separate plans for different divisions and occupations. Moreover, nearly all Japanese PSPs (98 percent) are cash plans, which is in sharp contrast to the United States where deferred plans are more popular (see Kruse 1993, 16–17). Because they are almost always cash plans, Japanese PSPs have no tax advantage (Kato and Morishima 2002).

Kato and Morishima (2002) also report that the majority (55 percent) of Japanese PSPs lack set formulas (or are fully discretionary) for how the contribution should be tied to profits, which is also in contrast to PSPs in the United States, where only 22 percent are fully discretionary (Kruse 1993, 75).

2.2.5   Evidence on Their Effects

In spite of the importance of the postwar Japanese experience with participatory employment practices, there has been little systematic investigation of the economic effects of participatory employment practices in Japan.[5] For the economic effects of financial participation, the Japanese bonus payment system has attracted considerable attention and controversy, in particular the claim that it is a form of PSP. Earlier studies focused on the effects on employment of the Japanese bonus payment system (e.g., see Freeman and Weitzman 1987 and Brunello 1991). More recent studies turned to the issue of the productivity effects of the Japanese bonus payment system. Jones and Kato (1995) use firm-level panel data to find that there is a modest productivity gain from the bonus system. Ohkusa and Ohtake (1997) find that firms with statistically significant positive correlation between their wages and per capita profits are 9 percent more productive than firms with no such correlation. For ESOPs, Jones and Kato (1995) use firm-level panel data to find that the introduction of an ESOP will lead to a 4 to 5 percent increase in productivity and that this productivity payoff does not appear immediately.

For the economic effects of information sharing at the top level, Mor-

---

5. For U.S. corporations, however, we are presently witnessing an impressive growth of evidence. See, for example, Ichniowski, Shaw, and Prennushi (1997), Black and Lynch (2001), Freeman and Kleiner (1998), Helper (1998), Bartel (2000), Freeman and Kleiner (2000), and articles featured in a special issue of *Industrial Relations* (July 1996, vol. 35). Many of these recent studies in the United States use plant-level (branch-level) panel data within a narrowly defined industry. The benefits of using such data are probably less dramatic for Japan than for the United States since Japanese firms generally are substantially smaller (e.g., see Kato and Rockel's 1992 comparative study of the 1,000 most valuable corporations between the two nations), and their management appears to be less decentralized than that of U.S. firms. Based on our interviews with managers in human resources at the corporate level and top managers in marketing/sales and accounting/finance at the business-unit level of Japanese and U.S. corporations, the power of human resource departments at the corporate level relative to top management at the business-unit level appears to be much stronger in Japan than in the United States. In addition, as Jones and Kato (1995) and Kato and Morishima (2002) show, there are substantial lags (up to seven years) in the productivity effects of participatory employment practices in Japan. Plant-level data seldom provide long longitudinal data and thus may not be as useful in the context of the postwar Japanese experience as in the context of the current U.S. experimentation.

ishima (1991a, b) use firm-level microdata to find the statistically significant positive correlations between the extent of information sharing through JLMCs and productivity, and the statistically significant correlations between stronger JLMCs and shorter and smoother wage negotiation. More recently, Tsuru and Morishima (1999) use two unique data sets, one from a survey of firms and the other from a survey of employees, and find evidence for positive correlations between the presence of JLMCs and the strength of "employee voice."

Finally, Kato and Morishima (2002) find evidence of the importance of introducing groups of participatory employment practices in the following three areas: (a) employee participation and involvement at the top level; (b) employee participation and involvement at the grassroots level; and (c) financial participation. Specifically, moving from the traditional system of no participatory employment practices to a highly participatory system with participatory employment practices in all three areas led to a significant 8 to 9 percent increase in productivity. The full productivity effect, however, is felt only after a fairly long developmental phase (seven years). At the same time, they find no evidence for significant productivity gains from changing the industrial relations system from the traditional system to any intermediate systems that lack participatory employment practices in at least one of the three key areas.

In sum, there is evidence for the positive effects of participatory employment practices in Japan in the postwar period, supporting the idea that such practices help align the interest of the firm with the interest of its employees and encourage specific human capital accumulation of employees.[6] In addition, recent findings from Kato and Morishima (2002) suggest that the goal alignment process needs to be supported by both direct methods (financial participation) and indirect ones (information sharing). Furthermore, information sharing needs to take place not only at the top level but at the grassroots level, as well. In other words, the goal-alignment process occurs most strongly when the interests of the two parties are aligned through financial participation and when this interest alignment is facilitated by mechanisms at both the top and the grassroots levels, which curtails parties' opportunistic behavior.

Kato and Morishima's (2002) findings also point to the importance of a long-term perspective in evaluating the success of participatory employment practices. First, it does take time for the goal alignment process to take root. It is highly unlikely that instituting a participatory employment practice will instantly create significant interest alignment of groups of employees with the firm.[7] Furthermore, there is substantial learning by doing

6. See Kato and Morishima (2002) for further discussion on the goal-alignment and human-capital effects of these practices, as well as their complementarity effects.
7. For similar arguments, see Pil and MacDuffie (1996) and Ichniowski and Shaw (1995).

in the evolution of participatory employment practices, which "mature" over time—and only mature participatory employment practices tend to yield significant productivity gains.

2.3 Evolving Practices in the 1990s: Evidence from Field Research

In the summer of 1999, we conducted field research at a number of Japanese firms. We had written them the previous winter, asking them to locate and assemble some specific data on participatory employment practices of their firms and detailing what kind of questions we intended to ask when we visited them that summer.[8] An obvious advantage of field research is that such research allows for more detailed and richer analysis; but there is also an added advantage. The quantitative data from national surveys are usually not available for the latter half of the 1990s. For example, in the previous section, the lack of available data on JLMCs after 1995 forced us to compare 1988 to 1995. Conceivably, the impact of the economic slowdown in general and financial crisis in particular on JLMCs may be felt only after 1995. Our field research from summer 1999 provides the most recent picture of employment practices. Below we present a number of key findings from the field research.[9]

2.3.1 The Quantity and Quality of Information Shared During JLMC Meetings

In general, our field research provides very little evidence for reduction in the quantity and quality of information shared through JLMCs in the 1990s.

Firm A is a large manufacturing firm with sales of more than 3 trillion yen (nearly half of which is export sales) and employment of close to 40,000 workers in 1998. It is listed in the first section of the Tokyo Stock Exchange. In the 1990s the firm's performance worsened substantially and became much more volatile. It cut 30 percent of its labor force throughout the 1990s, from about 57,000 to about 40,000. The corporation consists of eleven establishments.

On 10 June 1999 we visited the headquarters of firm A. We met with the personnel manager, our primary interviewee, in the personnel department. The interview lasted about four hours. The manager's young subordinate

---

8. We asked Professor Koike of Hosei University, Mr. Nakashima and Mr. Koike of Rengo-Soken (RENGO Research Institute for Advancement of Living Standards), and Mr. Fuku-tani of JPC-SED to introduce us to more than a dozen large Japanese firms, including both manufacturing and nonmanufacturing. We wrote all of these firms to which they introduced to us. In our letters, we asked them to collect specific data on their participatory employment practices, and explained what sort of questions we planned to ask when we visited them. All of the firms we wrote agreed to cooperate with us fully. In addition, Professor Fujimura of Hosei University introduced us to a medium-sized firm (referred to as firm C later in the text).

9. See Kato (2000) for a more detailed report of the field research.

was also present during the interview and provided some additional information. We had written them several months prior to our visit, asking them to locate and assemble some specific data and detailing what kinds of questions we intended to ask. They took our request very seriously and spent much time and effort to prepare confidential data for us.

On the next day, we visited establishment P of this firm and spent over half an hour observing a number of shop floors of this establishment. We then interviewed a foreman who is in charge of a section (called *kakari*). He reports to department chief (*kacho*) and has six unit chiefs (*kocho*) reporting to him. Each unit consists of about ten to fifteen workers. The foreman had spent over thirty years in this department and was about to be promoted to *kacho*. The interview lasted a little over an hour, focusing on SFCs and SGAs.

On 16 June 1999 we visited firm A's union headquarters and interviewed our primary interviewee (the vice president of the union) for about two hours. We were also given an opportunity to interview his young staff members (full-time union officials) for a little over an hour. Our primary interviewee was the union's number-two person and attended all JLMCs at the headquarters level. Our secondary interviewees worked very closely with him and engaged in the day-to-day activities of JLMCs. Several months prior to our visit, we had also written them a letter similar to the one we had sent to our personnel interviewees, asking them to locate and assemble some specific data and detailing what kind of questions we intended to ask. They, too, took our request very seriously and spent a lot of time and effort preparing confidential data for us.

At firm A, JLMCs existed at least in 1955. Initially, JLMCs were functioning as mechanisms for management to explain their decisions ex post to union representatives. However, due in part to the presence of charismatic and aggressive union leader, JLMCs by 1985 had changed their role from information sharing to joint decision making. For example, during JLMC meetings, union representatives tried to veto management's decision to open a new plant overseas. Following the resignation of the union leader in 1985, the joint-decision-making aspect of JLMCs was significantly reduced in 1986, and the current form of JLMC was established.

JLMCs at the headquarters level of firm A consist of five types of meetings: (a) management council meetings; (b) committee meetings; (c) restructuring meetings; (d) production meetings; and (e) individual item meetings. At management council meetings, six to seven top managers (chief executive officer [CEO], vice-CEOs, and the director of personnel) meet with six to seven top full-time union officials regularly. Each meeting lasts half a day. Business strategies and plans and the current status of corporate performance are discussed. The management council meetings are normally held twice a year. They are scheduled right before spring wage offensive and fall collective bargaining so that they can help facilitate each collective bargaining. There was no major change in the basic framework of JLMCs in the 1990s.

The union begins its preparation for management council meetings a month prior to each meeting. A full-time union official visits various shop floors and talks to union representatives of establishments to find out what union members are concerned about and what they want to know from management. This is very time and effort consuming. Based on this field research, the official writes up a list of questions. It is imperative to have careful field research to gather information from shop floors. For example, careful field research at the shop-floor level revealed that in spite of management's overall decision to reduce a number of products it sells, the reduction was not really happening—although on paper it looked as if it were happening.

A list of questions is then given to management seven to ten days prior to the meeting, and management prepares responses to those questions. At the management council meeting, management presents an answer to each question and the union asks further questions about the answer. After the meeting, both management and union prepare separate proceedings and exchange each other's proceedings before dissemination. Some information shared during meetings is designated as confidential and is excluded from the proceedings. Union proceedings are distributed to all union members and management proceedings are distributed to all managers.

JLMCs at the headquarters level of firm A have a number of subcommittees, including the subcommittee on production, the subcommittee on employee benefits and welfare, the subcommittee on sales, and the subcommittee on development. Subcommittee meetings on production are held regularly twice a year and are attended by six to seven managers from the production department, domestic sales department, export sales department, and personnel department, and six to seven top full-time union officials. Biannual production and staffing plans are discussed. In addition to production subcommittee meetings, occasionally other subcommittee meetings (such as those of the subcommittee on employee benefits and welfare, the subcommittee on sales, and subcommittee on development) are also held.

Restructuring meetings are held on an ad hoc basis. Decentralization, outsourcing, and plant closures are discussed. Production meetings are also held on an ad hoc basis.[10] Unlike committee meetings on production that discuss the overall framework of employment adjust-

10. Our primary union interviewee and personnel interviewee provided slightly conflicting views on production meetings. According to our personnel interviewee, they are held regularly on a monthly basis. According to the data provided by our union interviewee, as shown in figure 2.3, there were fourteen production meetings in 1998. As far as 1998 is concerned, they were indeed held monthly (actually, slightly more often than monthly). However, in the previous years, it was clear that they met less often than monthly.

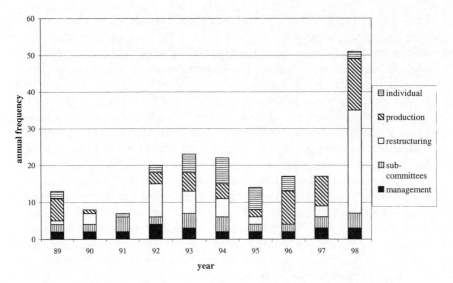

Fig. 2.3   Changes in the frequency of JLMC meetings at the headquarters level over time: Firm A

ments, production meetings deal with actual employment changes in response to changes in output demand. Individual item meetings are held also on an ad hoc basis to discuss items other than what is covered in other meetings.

There is no evidence for reduction in the quantity of information shared through JLMCs in the 1990s. First, there has been no apparent decline in the frequency of meetings in the 1990s. As shown in figure 2.3, the total number of JLMC meetings at the headquarters level reached twenty per year in 1992 and kept exceeding twenty until 1995. The number fell a little for the next three years. This is somewhat consistent with our national survey finding of a declining meeting frequency from 1988 to 1995, as presented in the previous section. However, in 1998, it reached an all-time high level of fifty-one meetings a year. Most of the increase came from restructuring meetings and production meetings. Management council meetings and subcommittee meetings on production stayed pretty much the same over this period.

To be consistent with this increased frequency of meetings, our union interviewee felt that the amount of information shared during JLMC meetings increased in the 1990s. Our personnel manager interviewee noticed that unions have been increasingly concerned about basic business-strategy questions that only the CEO or chief financial officer (CFO) could answer. Consequently, the information shared during JLMC meetings has become more concerned with business strategies than with more directly labor-related issues (such as employee welfare and benefits) and can be said to be more "confidential." Our personnel interviewee added that discussion on restructuring (such as decentralization, outsourcing, plant closures, or selling off segments of the business) naturally had increased in the last few years. This is reflected in an increase in the number of restructuring meetings in the last few years.

Our union interviewee believed that the quality of information shared had also risen in the 1990s. In the 1970s and 1980s, news was almost always good. Wages and bonuses were rising faster than those of the firm's major competitors. There was very little concern about firm performance, wages, bonuses, and employment security among employees. The quality of information shared during JLMC meetings was not of prime concern. In the 1990s, however, firm performance worsened, annual raises of wages and bonuses stagnated, and employees became more concerned about their employment security. The quality of information shared began to be of major concern. Our primary union interviewee said, "When the rank and files are asked to accept zero increase in bonus, for example, they do demand a detailed and convincing justification."

Our primary union interviewee believed that some of the information he received from top management could be considered "insider information" and that top management asked him not to release it to other union members. To maintain a good relationship with top management, he did keep such information in strict confidence. Our secondary union interviewees echo this by saying that most information was shared with them before it was made public knowledge and that it would be possible to use some of the information shared during JLMC meetings to make money in the stock market (i.e., some of the information shared during JLMC meetings could be insider-trading material). They quickly added that they did not engage in such activities.

Firm B is a large manufacturer with sales of a few trillion yen (about one-quarter of which is export sales) and employment of close to 20,000 workers in 1998. It is also listed in the first section of the Tokyo Stock Exchange. The firm has over ten establishments. Similar to that of firm A, the firm performance of firm B continued to worsen in the 1990s, and it cut almost 50 percent of its labor force during that time. On 26 May 1999 we visited the headquarters of the firm. We met with our primary interviewee in personnel (the general manager of labor relations in the personnel and labor relations division) first. The interview lasted about three hours, including lunch. After lunch, we met with our secondary interviewee in personnel (the manager of labor relations) for an hour and half. As in the case of firm A, we had written these individuals several months earlier, asking them to locate and assemble some specific data and detailing what kind of questions we intended to ask. They took our request seriously and spent much time and effort to prepare a variety of in-house data for us.

After our visit to firm headquarters, we went to the union headquarters of firm B and met with our union interviewee (the general secretary, number two in the organization). The interview lasted over one hour. Several months earlier we had written him a letter similar to the one we had sent our personnel interviewees, asking them to locate and assemble some specific data and detailing what kind of questions we intended to ask. They also took our request very seriously and prepared in-house data for us.

JLMCs existed at least in 1970 in firm B. JLMCs at the headquarters level consist of two types of meetings: (a) management council meetings and (b) labor-management committee meetings. Management council consists of a group of top management (CEO, vice-CEOs, and other directors) and a group of ten full-time union officials at the headquarters. There are two biannual council meetings and four quarterly council meetings a year at the headquarters level. The chief executive officer and vice-CEOs attend the biannual meetings, which convene right at the biannual accounting-report time, but do not attend the quarterly meetings. Union representatives from each establishment also attend these biannual council meetings. Each meeting normally begins at 11 A.M. and ends at 5 P.M. with an informal luncheon. Management explains its production plans, introduction of new equipment, temporary and permanent closing of plants and equipment, and major organizational changes. The union asks for their justifications.

The labor-management committee consists of the director of personnel, his or her subordinates, and a group of ten full-time union officials at the headquarters level. The committee meets on an ad hoc basis. Depending on the issue, full-time union representatives of relevant establishments may attend these committee meetings. Management explains staffing changes resulting from new production plans, such as worksharing, layoffs, substantial transfers of employees, welfare benefits, fringe benefits, and health and safety. The union negotiates with management on these issues.

Management council meetings and labor-management committee meetings are complementary. For example, a plant closure plan is proposed to the management council meeting and the union asks for its justification there. Labor-management committee meetings work out an agreement on the size of and conditions for labor transfers as a result of the plant closure. There has not been any major change in the basic framework of JLMCs.

Like in the case of firm A, our primary personnel interviewee at firm B strongly objected to the popular notion of a weakening of JLMCs in recent years, by arguing that both the quantity and quality of information shared during JLMC meetings increased in the 1990s. "When things are going well, it may not be crucial to have a good labor-management relationship. However, when the firm is faced with serious competition, it is imperative to have a good labor-management relationship and make decisions, based on good discussion between labor and management."

To be consistent with his remarks, there has been no indication of a de-

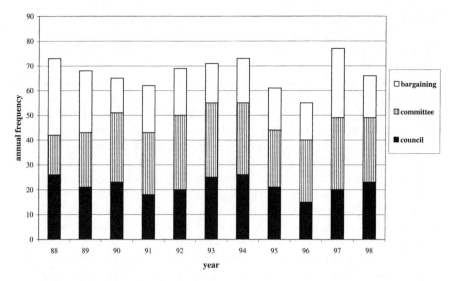

Fig. 2.4   Changes in the frequency of JLMC meetings and collective bargaining over time: Firm B

cline in the frequency of JLMC meetings. As shown in figure 2.4, we see no downward trend in the total number of JLMC meetings per year in the 1990s. Please note that the numbers for management council meetings and labor-management committee meetings include headquarters-level meetings as well as establishment-level meetings, and therefore that they tend to be quite high.

We were fortunate to be able to study the proceedings of their most recent biannual management council meeting and those from ten years ago. These proceedings are distributed to union representatives from each establishment. Those from ten years ago were very detailed and were close to a word-for-word transcription of the actual meetings. In stark contrast, more recent proceedings were less detailed and were closer to executive summaries. According to our union interviewee, compared to ten years ago the firm is facing a much more competitive environment and union members are much more concerned about firm performance and their employment and earnings. To reflect these changes, the union's needs for deeper information about firm performance and business strategies and plans have risen substantially. As a result, the union has been asking more and deeper questions during JLMC meetings, and therefore has been acquiring deeper and more detailed information about firm performance and business strategies and plans. The word-for-word proceedings of such meetings might lead to leaking of some confidential information. Also, he suggested that the union is looking for more than superficial answers to their questions from management and that management tends to be more forthcoming when they know that their words are not going to be published in the proceedings. In parallel to this increased quality and quantity of information shared during JLMCs, the union offers alternative plans more often than before.

In addition to firm A and firm B, we also conducted field research at six other large manufacturing firms, two large retail chain stores, and one large city bank, all of which tell essentially the same story. However, we learned a somewhat different tale from firm C, a medium-sized manufacturing firm with sales of 150 billion yen and employment of over 2,000 workers in 1997. Unlike firm A, firm B, and other large firms that we visited, firm C is not publicly traded. On 23 June 1999, we visited the headquarters of that firm and interviewed the president of the firm's union. He has been the president over twenty years. The interview lasted about two hours. After that, we met with our interviewee in personnel (manager of the personnel department) for about an hour. Again, we had written these individuals a few weeks prior to our visit, asking them to locate and assemble some specific data and detailing what kind of questions we intended to ask. They took our request seriously and prepared confidential data for us.

Performance of firm C clearly worsened in the 1990s. Inflation-adjusted real sales peaked in 1990 and then continued to fall until 1994, when real sales were at almost half their 1990 level. Since then, recovery of real sales has been sluggish at best. Real net profit (after tax), return on assets and return on equity continued to decline in the early 1990s and experienced negative profit two years in a row (until this time, the firm had never experienced negative profit since its founding in 1945). Since then, recovery of profitability has still been rather weak. The firm began downsizing its workforce in 1993, and by 1997 the firm's employment became almost 80 percent of its 1992 level.

The firm has JLMCs only at the headquarters level. JLMCs began in 1970. However, until 1978, JLMCs held informal meetings three or four times a year in which labor and management exchanged ideas with no specific agenda. JLMCs were formalized in 1978, with specific agenda set for each meeting. In the 1990s, they started to hold meetings regularly once a month. In addition, upon request of either management or the union, JLMC meetings can be held on an ad hoc basis. In fact, to discuss the present issue of permanent transfers of workers to related firms, one of those ad hoc JLMC meetings was scheduled in the afternoon of our visit to the firm. Each meeting lasts four hours. In addition, subcommittees are occasionally formed to discuss specific issues. For example, currently they have one subcommittee on the issue of extending the mandatory retirement age from sixty to sixty-two.

Unlike in the case of large, publicly traded firms, top management of this firm proposed to reduce the frequency of JLMC meetings and shorten the length of each meeting from four to two hours. Top management argued that this proposed change was necessary for more efficient and timely management. Our union interviewee was skeptical about this proposal. He feared that this might make JLMCs more superficial. Based on his twenty-year experience with JLMCs, only with ample time for discussion is important information revealed during JLMC meetings.

Regular participants in the JLMC from the management side include vice-CEOs, other executives, and the director of personnel (six to seven executives in total). The CEO used to attend all JLMC meetings before 1990. However, at the union's suggestion, since 1990 the CEO has attended only a couple of meetings a year when wage negotiation is complete. Depending on the agenda items, top managers of the relevant establishments also attend. Regular participants from the union side include union officials at the headquarters level and union representatives from each of the five establishments (ten to twelve officials in total).

Unlike in the case of large, publicly traded firms, most of the time the union does not tell management in advance what kinds of questions it will ask. However, when either management or the union has a particularly important issue, the issue will be discussed prior to JLMC meetings between the director of personnel and top union officials at the headquarters level. By the time an actual proposal is submitted to the JLMC, it has already been revised to incorporate union input.

During each monthly JLMC meeting, management presents and explains monthly data on orders, sales, production, and sales profit for each establishment. Occasionally, management does share some very confidential information, such as development of new products and the opening and closure of plants, with the union during JLMC meetings. Management asks the union to keep such information in confidence. Since JLMC meetings were formalized in 1978, there has not been any incidence of confidential information leaking outside the firm. Our union interviewee felt that he had developed a good, trusting relationship with management and that management did not hide confidential information from him.

To conclude the section on the quantity and quality of information shared during JLMC meetings, we address an issue raised by critics of participatory management—in particular, of JLMCs—that participatory management is too time consuming and that it cannot adjust effectively to a rapidly changing competitive environment. Critics also argue that it consumes too much management, union, and general-employee effort that could be used for more productive activities.

Both management and the unions of our large, publicly traded firms argued that JLMCs rarely delay important management decisions, and stressed the benefits of having a labor force that is thoroughly educated about and supportive of management's plans, which results from having good JLMCs. When management decisions are actually implemented, there are no surprises, no misunderstandings, and no confusion among employees, which makes the process of implementation smooth and prompt. Our personnel interviewee of firm A, however, recognized that the firm did experience a major delay in its decision to open a plant overseas due to its union's strong objection in 1985, and that the current system was built on the premise that the same problem should not happen again. He further added that restructuring meetings and individual item meetings could be held immediately at either management's or labor's request. The increased use of these meetings (as opposed to more regular meetings, such as management council meetings) can be viewed as a mechanism to achieve timely management within the existing framework of JLMCs.

In contrast, top management of our medium-sized, privately held firm, firm C, appears to subscribe somewhat to the beliefs held by critics of participatory employment practices, by proposing to reduce the frequency of JLMC meetings and shorten the length of each meeting from four to two hours.

2.3.2   The Nature of Employee Participation at JLMCs

The basic nature of employee participation at JLMCs can be summarized as "consultation on business strategies and plans, yet joint determination on their implementation." Specifically, labor representatives ask for and receive detailed justifications for business strategies and plans yet do not try to change the overall framework of the plans. However, on the implementation of these plans, labor representatives decide jointly with management when the plans have significant effects on employees.

For example, at firm A, during management council meetings and subcommittee meetings on production, management explains and the union asks questions. The union receives detailed explanations from management on business strategies and plans (including investment, opening and closing of plants, sales and production plans, introduction of new products) during management council meetings and committee meetings on production. The union then asks questions, in particular asking for justifications for these plans, but does not try to change the overall framework of the plans. Our primary union interviewee of firm A stated plainly, "We do not have any right to change these plans. We do not have any intention to decide on basic business strategies jointly with management." As a result, it is rare for union representatives to offer alternative plans to management insofar as basic business strategies are concerned. Nonetheless, union representatives sometimes offer ideas about what kinds of products may sell. Our personnel interviewee recalled that union representatives suggested that some redundant factory workers could support the sales department by handing out sales ad fliers.

However, when they discuss the consequences for employees of these business strategies and plans during restructuring meetings, production meetings, and individual item meetings, they decide jointly with management. For example, plant closures and outsourcing were proposed several years ago from top management to union representatives during their management council meetings. Although the union did ask many detailed questions about why these steps were necessary, they did not try to change the decision to close the plant and outsource. Instead, they successfully negotiated with top management during restructuring meetings to delay the plant closure for several months and to get favorable conditions for those employees who were transferred as a result of the plant's closure and outsourcing. For example, when employees are transferred to subsidiaries, they usually face poorer working conditions, such as lower wages and longer working hours. The union negotiated diligently during JLMC meetings to set up a policy of minimizing changes in working conditions as a result of transfers to subsidiaries.

In the 1990s, however, in response to worsening firm performance, discussion on basic business strategies and plans between management and labor became more extensive and intensive. Unions tend to ask more and harder questions on basic firm performance and business strategies, such as why a certain product is not selling or why the firm has so much debt. This reflected an increased interest and concern in the overall firm performance and hence employment security among employees. Nonetheless, there have not been any major changes in the overall nature of employee participation at JLMCs, that is, consultation on business strategies and plans yet joint determination on their implementation.

To repeat, in all cases neither management nor the union viewed the JLMC as a joint decision-making mechanism through which management and labor decide jointly on basic business strategies. However, both recognized that decisions made by management rarely turn out to seem "unreasonable" in the eyes of the employees. First, management and union representatives, in particular the top three union officials, tend to engage in extensive informal prenegotiation prior to formal JLMC meetings. As a result, management proposals submitted to JLMCs have already been revised to incorporate input from the union. Second, when management works out its business strategies, it is fully aware of what will be viewed as "unreasonable" by employees and thus tends to avoid proposing unreasonable plans for fear of destroying its good working relationship with the union, or wasting time and effort by lengthy and costly negotiations.

For example, at firm B, during management council meetings, management explains its production plans, introduction of new equipment, temporary and permanent closing of plants and equipment, and major organizational changes. The union asks for management's justifications. Labor-management committee meetings deal with more direct labor issues such as staffing, worksharing, transfers, layoffs, and benefits. Naturally, the union is often asked for its views on various issues and sometimes offers alternative plans. According to collective agreement, unlike collective bargaining (which deals only with wages and changes in collective agreement), management may implement its plans even if no agreement is reached with labor. However, our primary personnel interviewee of firm B reported that management rarely has to resort to this clause in order to implement its plans. He offered two reasons. First, according to our primary personnel interviewee, the union is very well informed about the competitive environment of the firm, and its overall understanding of current market conditions is close to that of management. Second, management and top union officials engage in extensive informal communication prior to JLMC meetings, and actual plans proposed by management in various formal meetings often have already been modified to incorporate union input. If the union objects strongly to management's plans, then management—rather than resorting to its right to implement without an agreement—is likely to withdraw its plans. Our union interviewee of firm B confirmed this point.

2.3.3   Employee Interest in JLMCs

Interest in JLMCs among employees rose in the 1990s. For example, at firm A, participation in union meetings increased in general. In particular, white-collar union members at the headquarters were traditionally somewhat apathetic to the newsletters unions use to disseminate the information shared at JLMCs. In the last few years, however, they have started to read these newsletters more often and more carefully. Our primary personnel interviewee of firm B felt that the union is taking JLMCs more seriously, and that the union's need for getting good information at JLMCs and for understanding and explaining that information well to its members are increasing in the face of increased competition. This point was confirmed by our primary union interviewee. Employees are more sensitive to firm performance and competitive environment. The rising employee interest in JLMCs was observed for firm C, a medium-sized, privately owned firm. Our union interviewee believed that general employee interest in JLMCs rose in the 1990s. Lately he had received more feedback (personal letters to him concerning the proceedings of JLMC meetings that are distributed to all union members). He even received requests from plant-level managers to send the proceedings to them. More important, our union interviewee felt an increasing desire among the employees for the union to help management make good decisions through JLMCs.

2.3.4   The Importance of SFCs

In general, the management philosophy of large Japanese firms in recent years has been leaning toward more-decentralized decision making. In other words, the power and authority of headquarters has been weakening while the power and authority of business units has been rising. In parallel to this trend, the importance of SFCs, or information sharing at the grassroots level, appears to be rising.

For example, at firm A, there are more than 400 shop floors (each shop floor consists of about 50 to 100 employees). The firm used to have no formal standing shop floor committees, although upon request from the union each shop floor did hold committee meetings occasionally. In spring 1996, the union felt a need for better communication at the shop-floor level and requested the firm to establish more formal, standing SFCs and to hold regular meetings. Management and the union jointly decided to establish more formal SFCs and to hold regular meetings (with a target of three to four times a year for white-collar shop floors and once a month for blue-collar shop floors). Since then, the union has been gathering monthly data on the incidence of meetings at each shop floor. As shown in table 2.3, for the last two years, the average SFCs met four times a year. The incidence of meetings, however, has been far from uniform. Our union interviewee remarked that there are negative correlations between the number of SFC meetings and the number of shop-floor complaints made to upper-level union organizations.

At firm A, SFCs have two functions: (a) resolving shop-floor-level work condition issues (such as air conditioning, smoking vs. nonsmoking environments, bathrooms, paid vacations, and cafeteria menus), and (b) giving explanations of shop-floor production plans and related staffing issues by a manager in charge of the shop floor. The link between JLMCs and SFCs is strong. First, what is not resolved at SFCs goes up to JLMCs (at the establishment level). (For example, labor representatives requested the introduction of air conditioners to its shop floor during SFC meetings. However, a manager in charge of the shop floor did not have the budget to pay for them. The issue was discussed at the next JLMC meetings at the establishment level, and top management of the establishment decided to purchase several spot air conditioners for the shop floor.) Second, SFCs discuss shop-floor production plans, which are derived from establishment production plans that are discussed during JLMC meetings at the establishment level.

The meetings are held outside regular working hours and usually last one to two hours. More time is usually spent on the first function of resolving shop-floor work condition issues than on the second function of discussing shop-floor plans.

Both our union and personnel interviewees recognized the benefit of SFCs and their increasing importance in the future. Employees are generally interested in SFCs. However, if SFCs fail to produce concrete results, such as satisfactory resolution of employee requests for air conditioning, employees tend to lose interest in SFCs quickly.

Our personnel interviewee considered the benefit of SFCs quite substantial. Complaints that are resolved at SFC meetings are not really earth-shattering, but when they are resolved employees can actually see, feel, and touch the results and their morale is enhanced.

Table 2.3 Number of SFC Meetings per Month at Each Establishment, September 1996–August 1998: Firm A

	Establishment Number											
	1	2	3	4	5	6	7	8	9	10	11	Total
September 1996	3	16	3	18	9	4	20	12	1	4	12	102
October 1996	3	16	3	18	9	4	20	12	1	4	12	102
November 1996	45	11	1	16	11	7	21	4	2	3	7	128
December 1996	1	19	3	15	7	4	27	9	4	4	11	104
January 1997	12	14	0	13	8	5	15	12	12	5	3	99
February 1997	9	19	0	13	7	4	13	13	6	8	12	104
March 1997	1	10	2	7	11	1	16	7	4	8	2	69
April 1997	12	7	0	9	8	7	13	12	4	6	11	89
May 1997	4	14	1	9	8	3	14	10	4	12	10	89
June 1997	1	7	1	6	8	3	13	7	2	8	6	62
July 1997	5	9	0	2	4	0	10	8	0	3	8	49
August 1997	14	1	4	0	0	2	6	6	0	0	0	33
Total	110	143	18	126	90	44	188	112	40	65	94	1,030
Number of shop floors, September 1996–August 1997	42	42	3	27	17	16	31	19	12	19	35	263
Annual average number of meetings, September 1996–August 1997	2.62	3.40	6.00	4.67	5.29	2.75	6.06	5.89	3.33	3.42	2.69	3.92
September 1997	11	20	4	10	3	3	12	8	0	15	35	121
October 1997	21	14	2	14	5	6	14	11	4	10	26	127
November 1997	5	17	1	11	4	2	13	9	6	12	19	99
December 1997	0	28	1	10	5	6	19	9	4	9	9	100
January 1998	79	29	1	9	9	6	14	6	8	14	21	196
February 1998	1	24	1	11	9	2	11	7	5	13	22	106
March 1998	0	18	1	6	7	1	11	6	2	10	69	131

(*continued*)

Table 2.3   (continued)

	Establishment Number											Total
	1	2	3	4	5	6	7	8	9	10	11	
April 1998	0	22	0	7	4	3	10	3	2	7	28	86
May 1998	0	17	2	3	4	1	13	9	2	6	37	94
June 1998	0	18	0	4	4	1	11	6	6	5	31	86
July 1998	2	20	0	1	4	4	10	3	6	8	36	94
August 1998	4	11	0	6	4	6	10	4	0	7	29	81
Total	123	238	13	92	62	41	148	81	45	116	362	1,321
Number of shop floors, September 1997–August 1998	41	55	4	25	17	16	32	18	12	19	69	308
Annual average number of meetings, September 1997–August 1998	3.00	4.33	3.25	3.68	3.65	2.56	4.63	4.50	3.75	6.11	5.25	4.29

Source: Internal documents of firm A (see text).

Grievance procedures deal with personal complaints that cannot be expressed in public. For example, those who feel their bosses give them unfairly low subjective performance evaluations never voice their complaints at SFC meetings but submit their complaints to grievance committees.

Our personnel interviewee stressed the importance of the manager's ability to communicate for successful SFCs, and pointed out that some SFCs do not function well due to the manager's lack of ability to listen to labor representatives. When managers lack the ability to listen, SFCs become an extension of regular supervisor-supervisee relationships and labor representatives do not feel at ease expressing their views—hence the SFCs stagnate.

Establishment P of firm A holds its SFC meetings at the section level (about 500 employees). Section Q regularly holds an off-hours meeting on a monthly basis. These usually last one hour. In addition, upon request of the section's union representative, additional meetings can be held. During the previous year, section Q held two meetings a month on average. Our foreman interviewee added that it had been an unusually busy year in terms of SFCs.

The section chief and all foremen attend the SFC meetings. The union representatives for the section also attend. Once a month, the union representatives for the section hold a meeting of union representatives for *kakari* to prepare for their SFC meeting for that month. Three days prior to the meeting, a written list of suggested discussion topics are given to the section chief. Work environment issues, such as shower rooms, water leaks, smoking, bathrooms, cafeterias, and air conditioning, are of central concern for their SFC meetings. There is no discussion of production plans at the section level. This is somewhat different from what our personnel and union interviewees explained. The operation of SFCs appears to be left to each shop floor, and there seems to be quite a variation in the actual operation of SFCs among various shop floors. There was no major change in SFCs at this section in the 1990s.

2.3.5 Enduring SGAs

We did not find any evidence for a major decline in the quantity and quality of SGAs. For example, at firm A, the firm currently has 2,090 QC circles, amounting to 10.6 employees per circle. In 1965, the first QC circles were registered in establishment P. Since then, QC circles have been established at each new plant upon its opening. The union is neither negative nor positive about these SGAs. Part-timers are not included, and the firm maintains the voluntary nature of QC circles. Thus, activities are held after hours and there is no compensation for those hours. Not all employees volunteer to participate (e.g., older employees approaching retirement tend not to participate). Our personnel interviewee spent two and a half years as a plant-level personnel manager and did not recall any sign of stagnation of QC circle activities over time. One reason for the overall lack of stagnation of SGAs is that employees are generally very proud of the success of their groups. When a group wins the annual QC circle contest, its members usually have a major celebration and are extremely proud. The sense of pride seems to have carried them through over the last three decades. Our personnel interviewee was somewhat concerned about the future of SGAs, since it is uncertain whether new generations of Japanese workers will continue to participate in them wholeheartedly largely for the sense of group pride.

Most recently, however, plants have not been very busy and QC activities have been somewhat stagnant. Our personnel interviewee argued that when plants are not busy, possible sources of productivity and product quality improvements tend to be disguised. The SGAs for white-collar occupations have not been as active and successful as those for blue-collar occupations.

Neither our personnel interviewee nor our union interviewee was aware of any relationship between SGAs and SFCs, except that both take place at the shop-floor level. As a result of aging of the labor force, which was accelerated by limited hiring in the last few years (the average age of employees at this firm rose from thirty-seven to forty in the last decade), the transmittal of the skills and ethos of SGAs to the next generation is increasingly becoming a major concern.

We were very fortunate to be able to spend half a day in establishment P of firm A, observing the actual operations of shop floors and QC circles and interviewing a veteran foreman. The smallest organizational unit of establishment P is called a *han*. Each *han* consists of fifteen to twenty employees, and the *kocho* is in charge of each *han*. In addition to the *kocho*, each *han* normally has one to two *shidoin* and four leaders. Each leader is in charge of one of the four main objectives: (a) safety, (b) high quality, (c) cost reduction, and (d) punctual delivery. Each leader will carry out various activities to achieve the assigned goal. These activities may take the form of SGAs. At any rate, these activities are not voluntary, are fully directed by the *kocho*, and are part of work, and hence are done during regular hours. On the other hand, a QC circle *is* voluntary; and depending on the project, it will change its QC captain, who is not necessarily a leader (people with one year of tenure can and will become QC circle captains). Projects are also chosen by circle members with some indirect guidance from the *kocho*. Each QC circle carries out six to twelve projects a year.

On average, each QC circle meets four to six times a month and each meeting lasts one to one and a half hours. Sometimes, for other activities (such as safety, cost reduction, and punctual delivery), each employee spends two to three hours a month after regular hours. All these after-hours activities are considered voluntary and are thus without pay. In addition, for a couple of hours a month, on average, employees are also engaged in machine-maintenance *kaizen* activities after hours. For these activities, they are paid at an overtime premium rate. Each employee's performance in all these activities, including voluntary QC circles, is evaluated by the *kocho*.

Our foreman interviewee believed that QC circle activities are more active and more voluntary then ten years earlier. For example, in the 1980s, the firm used to provide some modest compensation for QC activities. However, in the 1990s, the firm abolished this QC circle compensation and made it clear that QC activities were voluntary. Both the quantity and quality of QC activities increased substantially in the 1990s. To meet increasing needs for more technically sophisticated projects and quick turnaround time, the firm introduced a special full-time *kaizen* group (a handful of veteran workers) who could perform some experiments for various ideas suggested by QC circles. Our interviewee attributed this rise in the quantity and quality of QC activities to the increased competition and sense of crisis among employees: "Our means for living have been threatened by the increased competition and if we do not produce a better and cheaper product, we will lose out." In other words, employee interest in SGAs has clearly increased. Our foreman interviewee strongly believed that ideas for improvement have not been exhausted.

Firm B has a long history of SGAs, dating back to 1962. The firm outlines the purposes for its SGAs as follows:

- To organize voluntary group activities by employees in equal positions and on the basis of each employee's voluntary participation.
- To select themes at each job site and to attain goals.
- To realize each employee's self-fulfillment in his job through improvement of ability and demonstration of creativity.
- To build respect for fellow employees and to create an energetic job site with a happy atmosphere.
- To contribute to the development of the company's businesses, thereby contributing to society.

According to the statistics provided by the firm, there is no evidence for stagnation of SGAs in the 1990s. The total number of SGA groups declined from close to 4,000 in 1992 to close to 2,500 in 1997 as the firm has downsized its labor force. However, since the number of SGA groups did not fall as fast as the total number of employees, the number of groups per employee (dividing the total number of SGA groups by the total number of employees) increased during this time period.

The total number of projects completed during each year also diminished, from 22,000 in 1992 to 16,000 in 1997. Nonetheless, the number of projects completed per group actually rose from 5.86 to 6.40 because the total number of SGA groups fell faster than the total number of projects completed. The proportion of blue-collar workers participating in SGAs remained stable, at around 95 percent. In short, in the 1990s, there was no sign either of a declining employee participation rate in SGAs or of a diminishing number of projects completed by each group. We failed to obtain any systematic data on the quality of the projects over time at firm B.

2.3.6   Employee Commitment to ESOPs

There is some evidence for weakening commitment of employees to ESOPs. For example, firm A has a standard ESOP with 5 percent subsidy from the firm. The ESOP participation rate (proportion of the labor force participating in an ESOP) remained around 30 percent in the 1980s. The firm embarked on a major ESOP promotion campaign during 1987, and as a result the ESOP participation rate jumped to 70–80 percent. Since then it has been falling steadily, and it is currently a little below 50 percent. The share price of the firm is currently one-third of what it was in 1989. Many employees who joined the ESOP during the firm's ESOP promotion campaign in 1987 are experiencing substantial capital loss. For 1998, the firm experienced over 1,000 employees exiting from the ESOP for reasons other than separation from the firm, and only 204 people joined the ESOP.

The initial objective of the ESOP at firm A was threefold: (a) enhancing the sense of participation and motivating employees, (b) providing a source of retirement income, and (c) acquiring a stable shareholder group. With substantial capital loss in the 1990s and highly volatile share prices in recent years, our personnel interviewee felt that the ESOP's ability to achieve its objectives diminished in the 1990s. The average contribution of participants is 5,000 to 10,000 yen from monthly pay and 20,000 to 30,000 yen from bonus.

Firm B has a similar situation. It introduced its ESOP in September 1988, which is unusually late compared to its competitors who introduced their ESOPs in the 1970s. During the first year of its ESOP, over 4,000 employees signed up for it. However, only 800 employees joined during the next two years. To boost the ESOP membership, the firm introduced a standard 5 percent subsidy in 1993. Close to 1,500 employees joined during that year. However, since then, on average, fewer than 100 employees joined each year. Currently, only about 10 percent of the labor force in the firm participates in its ESOP and 0.2 percent of the total number of outstanding shares are owned by its ESOP. The share price of the firm is one-quarter of what it was in 1989. Many employees who joined the ESOP during the firm's ESOP introduction year are experiencing substantial capital loss. Our primary personnel interviewee attributed the firm's low ESOP participation rate to a combination of rapidly falling share prices and falling income of employees.

To shed further light on the nature of the recent transformation of ESOPs, we were able to obtain unusually rich data on the subject from firm D, a large manufacturing firm with sales of a few trillion yen (about one-third of which was export sales) and employment of close to 40,000 workers in 1998. The firm is listed in the first section of the Tokyo Stock Exchange. Unlike the first three firms, firm D's sales and employment did not fall dramatically in the 1990s although its share price did fall as drastically as those of the other firms over the same time period.

Firm D introduced its ESOP in 1971. Like in the case of firm A, the initial objective of the ESOP was threefold: (a) enhancing the sense of participation and motivating employees, (b) providing a source of retirement income, and (c) acquiring a stable shareholder group. By the end of 1980, the ESOP participation rate reached one in four employees and the average monthly contribution reached 13,000 in 1995 yen. Since 1990, the participation rate has fallen to almost one in five employees. The average monthly contribution also decreased in the early 1990s to less than 12,000 yen, and the subsequent recovery has not been strong.

The falling ESOP participation rate is accounted for by a decrease in new participants and an increase in exiting participants. The number of new participants has fallen from nearly 1,000 a year in 1990 to a little over 200 a year in 1998. On the other hand, the number of exiting participants doubled from 400 in 1990 to 800 in 1998. It follows that in 1998, there was a net loss of 600 participants. Unfortunately, the data do not allow us to find out how many of these exiting participants were exiting from the trust while remaining in the firm and thus were "voluntarily leaving the ESOP trust." However, according to our primary interviewee in personnel, nearly all exiting participants were also leaving the firm.

However, ESOP participants, although remaining in the trust, fine-tuned their commitments to the trust by changing their monthly contributions. During 1990, as shown in figure 2.5, more than 1,000 continuing par-

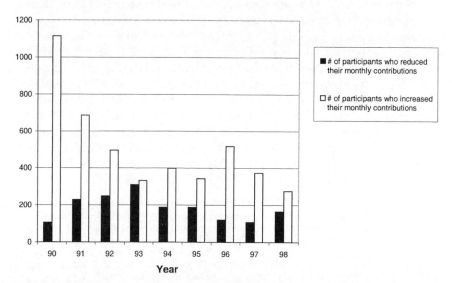

Fig. 2.5   ESOP participants who reduced and increased contributions: Firm D

ticipants increased their monthly contributions, whereas only 100 reduced their monthly contributions. In the early 1990s, fewer and fewer of these continuing participants were increasing their monthly contributions and more and more were reducing them. By 1993, the number of those reducing their monthly contributions became nearly identical to the number increasing them. Since then, the number of those increasing their contributions has stopped falling, whereas the number reducing their contributions has declined somewhat. As a result, during 1998 there were still more continuing participants who increased their contributions than those who reduced them. However, the difference between the two (about 100) was much smaller than it used to be in early 1990s (e.g., more than 900 in 1990). In short, although most ESOP participants remain in the trust unless they separate from the firm, fewer participants increase their contributions to the trust and more reduce their contributions. The overall commitment of ESOP participants to the trust appears to be falling somewhat as a result of worsening stock performance of the firm.

2.3.7   Complementarity of Employment Practices[11]

We asked both our union and personnel manager interviewees the following question: Suppose it is necessary to streamline and downsize a set of participatory employment practices consisting of JLMCs (at the headquarters level and at the establishment level), SFCs, SGAs, ESOPs, and PSPs. Would it be possible to eliminate one of those employment practices? If so, which one? The general response to this question was, "It would not be possible to take out any of the following three: JLMCs at the headquarters level, JLMCs at the establishment level, and SFCs since they actually work hand in hand." However, when pressed to choose one of those three to eliminate, our union interviewee of firm A mentioned that he would choose SFCs because in the past industrial relations did work fine without them. Our personnel interviewee's response turned out to be almost identical. However, he added that SFCs are not really costly (they are held outside regular working hours) and that their positive morale effects would be rather substantial. In other words, according to him, SFCs are probably the most cost effective participatory practice. In addition, he anticipated that in the future, as decentralization of the firm progresses, the importance of JLMCs at the headquarters level will naturally diminish and the importance of establishment-level JLMCs and SFCs will increase.

Our field research also revealed two kinds of complementary relations

---

11. For complementarity of various employment practices, see, for instance, Fitzroy and Kraft (1987); Weitzman and Kruse (1990); Levine and Tyson (1990); Jones and Pliskin (1991); Ben-Ner and Jones (1995); Kandel and Lazear (1992); Kruse (1993); Holmstrom and Milgrom (1994); Baker, Gibbons, and Murphy (1994); Milgrom and Roberts (1995); Ichniowski, Shaw, and Prennushi (1997); Black and Lynch (2001); Helper (1998); Kato and Morishima (2002); Eriksson (2003); and articles featured in a special issue of *Industrial Relations* (July 1996, vol. 35).

between collective bargaining and JLMCs: (a) complementarity in scope and (b) complementarity in time. According to the complementarity-in-scope model, collective bargaining deals with wages, bonuses, working hours, and agreement revision whereas JLMCs deal with all other items. Thus, depending on an item to be discussed, either JLMCs or collective bargaining will be used. According to the complementarity-in-time model, all items will be discussed first at JLMCs and collective bargaining will be used only when JLMCs cannot resolve differences between management and labor. The majority of our firms subscribe to the complementarity-in-scope model. No firm suggested that they are substitutes.

2.3.8   Gap between Full-Time Union Officials and the Rank and File

For JLMCs to work well, management needs to prove credibly that it trusts union representatives by providing them with confidential information. Based on our observations of top union officials, it seems to be almost impossible to continue to deceive them by providing them with superficial information while claiming it to be "confidential." It appears to be the case that top management does provide top union officials with truly confidential information. By the very nature of confidentiality, top management cannot allow such information to go beyond top union officials since it will be prohibitively costly to monitor the information flow of all employees. Thus, management asks top union officials to keep such information among themselves. A problem with this solution is that it produces a gap between top union officials and the rank-and-file employees. When the latter find out about important business decisions such as alliance with another firm from newspapers and television instead of hearing about it from their own management, they will naturally be upset that management would release such important information to the media before releasing it to its own employees. When that happens, the employees will ask their union officials whether they knew. When the union officials deny it, sooner or later the rank and file start to consider their own union officials as incompetent or, even worse, as working for management and not for the employees. Eventually, a good, cooperative relationship between labor and management will turn into a complicated, not always cooperative, three-way relationship among the rank and file, union officials, and top management. We are not suggesting this is actually happening in our sample firms; we are simply pointing out a possible cause for the breakdown of the system of participatory employment practices.

2.3.9   Overloaded Labor Representatives and Limited
Supply of Full-Time Union Officials

Many firms have been downsizing. For example, firm A reduced its labor force by more than 30 percent in the 1990s. To keep pace with this downsizing, the number of full-time union officials in firm A has also fallen in the 1990s. However, as shown in figure 2.3, the activities of JLMCs have not diminished accordingly. Rather they have recently intensified. This is making full-time union officials exceedingly busy while there is no sufficient monetary compensation for this increased work load. For example, our secondary union interviewees at firm A complained that the amount of work they were asked to do had recently increased substantially, and they appeared to be looking forward to returning to some management positions within the firm after their current union posts end.

If this trend of overloading of labor representatives continues in the future, the system of participatory employment practices may break down. First, labor representatives may not be as well prepared for JLMC meetings as before since they are simply too busy. Second, the increased work load with no monetary compensation for it makes union posts somewhat less attractive to young, capable employees (who are increasingly becoming scarce due to the aging of the labor force in general). In addition, substantially diminished employment opportunities outside the firm may make full-time union officials more dependent on the firm for their future employment after they have finished their union posts. Furthermore, as a result of downsizing, managers may become more reluctant to send their best people from their organizations to union posts. All these things may make labor representatives for JLMCs less effective and less committed to the interest of the rank and file. Without well-prepared, firmly committed, and effective labor representatives, JLMCs will become a mere formality. A real danger to the survival of participatory employment practices might come not from management but from union. If participatory employment practices disappear from Japanese firms in the future, it might be due not to management initiatives but to the lack of capable and committed labor representatives.

2.4   Conclusions

In this paper we have shown that participatory employment practices appear to be generally surviving the economic slowdown of the 1990s, whereas subtle yet potentially important changes in their attributes are taking place.

Kato and Morishima (2002) provide econometric evidence for the complementarity of these participatory employment practices. Terminating a single practice may not only eliminate its own positive effect but reduce the positive effects of other practices. In the extreme case, the termination of a single practice may cause the whole system of employee participation and labor-management cooperation to halt. For example, it was found that the goal alignment process needed to be supported by both direct methods (financial participation) and indirect ones (employee participation and involvement). Removing financial participation will cause employee participation and involvement to be ineffective and vice versa. Furthermore, we found it is necessary for participation to take place not only at the top level but at the grassroots level. Discontinuing participation at the grassroots level will cause participation at the top level to be ineffective, and vice versa.

Moreover, research points to the importance of taking a long-term perspective in evaluating the success of participatory employment practices. Coupled with the importance of the long-term perspective, the complementarity of participatory employment practices will probably make individual practices in Japan more enduring than the popular rhetoric of "the end of Japanese employment practices" suggests. Our findings on the responses of Japanese firms in their use of participatory employment practices to the economic slowdown in the 1990s do point to the enduring nature of such practices for large, unionized firms. Such Japanese firms appear to be responding to the 1990s slowdown and to the recent financial crisis in particular by fine-tuning the existing practices, not by dismantling them. For small to medium-sized firms with no unions, we find some evidence of management's trying to weaken the role of employee participation. Combined with the rising proportion of the nonunion sector in the Japanese economy, the overall importance of participation in the Japanese economy may be falling.

There are a few early signs of trouble even for large, unionized firms that might eventually result in the breakdown of the system if left untreated. First, the number of full-time union officials has been falling as a result of continued downsizing of firms' labor forces. The amount of time and effort that union officials need to put into participatory employment practices have not been falling. This often results in an uncompensated increase in work load for union officials. If this trend continues, labor representatives for JLMCs will become less prepared and less committed to the interest of the rank and file, and thus less effective. Second, at least in our medium-sized firm case, top management is finding its participatory management system detrimental to timely and efficient management, and has begun to streamline the system. Overloaded union officials may offer less resistance to such management initiatives. Third, the current system tends to produce a gap in the quantity and quality of information acquired from management between top union officials and their general membership. It is conceivable that such a gap may eventually result in the breakdown of the system. These are still preliminary observations. Clearly, more work is necessary to find more definitive answers to these important questions.

References

Baker, George, Robert Gibbons, and Kevin J. Murphy. 1994. Subjective performance measures in optimal incentive contracts. *Quarterly Journal of Economics* 108 (November): 1125–56.

Bartel, Ann P. 2000. Human resource management and performance in the service sector: The case of bank branches. NBER Working Paper no. 7467. Cambridge, Mass.: National Bureau of Economic Research, January.

Ben-Ner, Avner, and Derek C. Jones. 1995. Employee participation, ownership, and productivity: A theoretical framework. *Industrial Relations* 34 (October): 532–54.

Black, Sandra E., and Lisa M. Lynch. 2001. How to compete: The impact of workplace practices and information technology on productivity. *Review of Economics and Statistics* 8 (3): 434–45.

Brunello, Giorgio. 1991. Bonuses, wages, and performances in Japan: Evidence from micro data. *Ricerche Economiche* 45 (April–September): 377–96.

Cole, Robert E. 1989. *Strategies for learning: Small-group activities in American, Japanese, and Swedish industry.* Berkeley, Calif.: University of California Press.

Eriksson, Tor. 2003. The effects of new work practices: Evidence from employer-employee data. In *Advances in the economic analysis of participatory and labor-managed firms.* Vol. 7, *The determinants of the incidence and the effects of participatory organizations,* ed. Takao Kato and Jeffrey Pliskin. Amsterdam: Elsevier. Forthcoming.

Fitzroy, Felix R., and Kornelius Kraft. 1987. Cooperation, productivity, and profit sharing. *Quarterly Journal of Economics* 102 (February): 23–35.

Freeman, Richard B., and Morris M. Kleiner. 1998. The last American shoe manufacturers: Changing the method of pay to survive foreign competition. NBER Working Paper no. 6750. Cambridge, Mass.: National Bureau of Economic Research, October.

———. 2000. Who benefits most from employee involvement: Firms or workers? *American Economic Review* 90 (May): 219–23.

Freeman, Richard B., and Martin L. Weitzman. 1987. Bonuses and employment in Japan. *Journal of the Japanese and International Economies* 1 (June): 168–94.

Hart, Robert A., and Seiichi Kawasaki. 1995. The Japanese bonus system and human capital. *Journal of the Japanese and International Economies* 9 (September): 225–44.

Hashimoto, Masanori. 1990. *The Japanese labor market in a comparative perspective with the United States.* Kalamazoo, Mich.: Upjohn Institute for Employment Research.

Helper, Susan. 1998. Complementarity and cost reduction: Evidence from the auto supply industry. NBER Working Paper no. 6033 (rev.). Cambridge, Mass.: National Bureau of Economic Research, May.

Holmstrom, Bengt, and Paul Milgrom. 1994. The firm as an incentive system. *American Economic Review* 84 (September): 972–91.

Ichniowski, Casey, and Kathryn Shaw. 1995. Old dogs and new tricks: Determinants of the adoption of productivity-enhancing work practices. *Brookings Papers on Economic Activity, Microeconomics*: 1–55.

Ichniowski, Casey, Kathryn Shaw, and Giovanna Prennushi. 1997. The effects of human resource management practices on productivity: A study of steel finishing lines. *American Economic Review* 87 (July): 291–313.

Inagami, Takeshi. 1988. *Industrial relations series. Vol. 14: Japanese workplace industrial relations.* Tokyo: Japan Institute of Labour.

Japan Ministry of Labor. 1988. *Survey of labor-management communications.* Tokyo: Japan Ministry of Finance, Printing Bureau.

———. 1995. *Survey of labor-management communications.* Tokyo: Japan Ministry of Finance, Printing Bureau.

Japan Productivity Center. 1990. *To improve joint labor management committees* (Roshikyogisei no jujitsu o motomete). Tokyo: Japan Productivity Center.

Jones, Derek C., and Takao Kato. 1993. On the scope, nature, and effects of employee stock ownership plans in Japan. *Industrial and Labor Relations Review* 46
(January): 352–67.

———. 1995. The productivity effects of employee stock ownership plans and
bonuses: Evidence from Japanese panel data. *American Economic Review* 85
(June): 391–414.

Jones, Derek C., and Jeffrey Pliskin. 1991. The effects of worker participation, employee ownership, and profit sharing on economic performance: A partial review. In *Ownership and participation: International handbook of participation in
organizations.* Vol. 2, ed. Raymond Russell and Veljko Rus, 43–63. Oxford: Oxford University Press.

Kandel, Eugene, and Edward Lazear. 1992. Peer pressure and partnerships. *Journal of Political Economy* 100 (August): 801–17.

Kang, Jun-Koo, and Rene M. Stulz. 1997. Is bank-centered corporate governance
worth it? A cross-sectional analysis of the performance of Japanese firms during
the asset price deflation. NBER Working Paper no. 6238. Cambridge, Mass.: National Bureau of Economic Research, October.

Kato, Takao. 1995. Cooperate to compete, Employee participation and productivity: Evidence from a new survey of Japanese firms. Public Policy Brief no. 19. An-
nandale-on-Hudson, N.Y.: The Jerome Levy Economics Institute, Bard College.

———. 2000. The recent transformation of participatory employment practices.
NBER Working Paper no. 7965. Cambridge, Mass.: National Bureau of Economic Research, October.

Kato, Takao, and Motohiro Morishima. 2002. The productivity effects of participatory employment practices: Evidence from new Japanese panel data. *Industrial Relations* 41 (October): 487–520.

Kato, Takao, and Mark Rockel. 1992. The importance of company breeding in the
U.S. and Japanese managerial labor markets: A statistical comparison. *Japan and
the World Economy* 4 (June): 39–45.

Koike, Kazuo. 1978. *Worker participation* (Rodosha no keiei sanka). Tokyo: Nihon
Hyoron Sha.

Kruse, Douglas L. 1993. *Profit sharing: Does it make a difference?* Kalamazoo,
Mich.: W. E. Upjohn Institute for Employment Research.

Levine, David I. 1995. *Reinventing the workplace.* Washington, D.C.: Brookings Institution.

Levine, David I., and Laura D'Andrea Tyson. 1990. Participation, productivity,
and the firm's environment. In *Paying for productivity,* ed. Alan S. Blinder, 183–
236. Washington, D.C.: Brookings Institution.

Milgrom, Paul, and John Roberts. 1995. Complementarities and fit: Strategy, structure, and organizational change in manufacturing. *Journal of Accounting and
Economics* 19 (April): 179–208.

Morishima, Motohiro. 1991a. Information sharing and collective bargaining in
Japan: Effects on wage negotiations. *Industrial and Labor Relations Review* 44
(April): 469–85.

———. 1991b. Information sharing and firm performance in Japan: Do joint consultation committees help? *Industrial Relations* 30 (Winter): 37–61.

Nakamura, Masao, and Alice Nakamura. 1989. Risk behavior and the determinants of bonus versus regular pay in Japan. *Journal of the Japanese and International Economies* 3 (September): 270–91.

Ohashi, Isao. 1989. On the determinants of bonuses and basic wages in large Japanese firms. *Journal of the Japanese and International Economies* 3 (December):
451–79.

Ohkusa, Yasushi, and Fumio Ohtake. 1997. The productivity effects of information sharing, profit-sharing and ESOPs. *Journal of the Japanese and International Economies* 11 (September): 385–402.

Pil, Frits K., and John Paul MacDuffie. 1996. The adoption of high-involvement work practices. *Industrial Relations* 35 (July): 423–55.

Shimada, Haruo. 1992. Japan's industrial culture and labor-management relations. In *The political economy of Japan. Vol. 3: Cultural and social dynamics,* ed. Shumpei Kumon and Henry Rosovsky, 267–91. Stanford, Calif.: Stanford University Press.

Tsuru, Tsuyoshi, and Motohiro Morishima. 1999. Nonunion employee representation in Japan. *Journal of Labor Research* 20 (Winter): 93–110.

Weitzman, Martin L., and Douglas L. Kruse. 1990. Profit sharing and productivity. In *Paying for productivity,* ed. Alan S. Blinder, 95–140. Washington, D.C.: Brookings Institution.

3

Determinants of the Shadow Value of Simultaneous Information Sharing in the Japanese Machine-Tool Manufacturing Industry

Hiroyuki Chuma

3.1 Introduction

As discussed in more detail in the previous chapter, Japan is widely known for its use of participatory employment practices, involving employees in a substantive way in many firm decision-making processes. Information sharing is one such participatory employment practice. Information sharing and collaboration across business components have proved to be important and valuable employment practices in Japanese firms, enabling workers with different core responsibilities to interact more effectively. The value of such information sharing is particularly apparent in the interaction between those who design production processes and those who execute them. This paper is a case study of the value of information sharing to the machine-tool industry, and how information sharing has contributed to the success of the machine-tool industry in recent decades.

Until the mid-1970s, Japanese machine-tool manufacturers lagged far behind their U.S. and German counterparts. The advent of computerized numerical control (CNC) complex lathes or machining centers (MCs)[1] drastically changed this situation (Finegold 1994; Finegold et al. 1994; Fleischer 1997; or Kobayashi and Ohdaka 1995). Indeed, since 1982, Japanese machine-tool manufacturers have led the industry, producing the world's largest (U.S. dollar) amount of machine tools.[2] The following external and technological factors are normally credited with spurring the

Hiroyuki Chuma is professor of economics at the Institute of Innovation Research, Hitotsubashi University.

1. Most of these are flexible, general-purpose machines.
2. In 1975, Japan occupied the fourth position, just after the former Soviet Union. The United States occupied the first position and the former West Germany the second.

rapid development of the Japanese machine-tool industry since the late 1970s:[3] (a) the extensive expansion of the Japanese automobile industry, represented by Toyota, Nissan, and Honda, which in 1981 surpassed all other countries in unit sales; (b) the "leap-forward" development of Japanese mechatronics manufacturers, represented by Fanuc, Mitsubishi Electric, and Yaskawa Electric, who provided superior numerical control devices and software; (c) the rapid development of precision-parts manufacturers, such as NSK, NTN, or THK, who could supply bearings, ball screws, and linear guideways; and (d) the basic development of foundry engineering technology, represented by automatic control technology for annealing, which effectively removes casting stresses.

Needless to say, each of these factors has played a very important role in the rise of the machine-tool industry. Chuma (1998) shows, however, that there is a very important human-related factor: (e) the existence of a formal simultaneous information-sharing system in which, even in the early stages of fundamental machine design, development and design (D&D) engineers can exchange opinions with production shop managers. Mechanical designers have multitudinous details to bear in mind when designing complex, modern CNC machine tools. Except in very rare cases, keeping track of everything is almost impossible, even for first-rate designers. Introducing a simultaneous information-sharing system linking highly skilled machinists and D&D engineers at early stages of product development will reduce lead time.[4]

The ever-increasing importance of information-sharing systems has generated an increase in the premium paid to broadly skilled production workers (ones with so-called "integrated skills"; Koike 1999). As machines have become more and more complex both mechanically and electrically, problem-solving skills have become more important for shortening lead time in machine development. Here, "problem-solving skills" broadly refers to the ability to anticipate and prevent problems with machines. These skills require logical thinking and abundant experience with machine problems. Without this broad skill base, production workers and engineers could not properly communicate and would therefore be unable to anticipate and improvise solutions to the diversity of problems that invariably arise in newly developed complex machines.[5]

3. The strong role of the government, especially that played by the Ministry of International Trade and Industry (MITI) could be added to these four factors. However, there are contrasting views on this subject. Thus, we do not consider it. For more on this factor, see Friedman (1988), Holland (1992), Kobayashi and Ohdaka (1995), or Miwa (1998).

4. A similar point, based on a few case studies of new machine development processes used by German, Italian, Japanese, and U.S. machine-tool manufacturers, can be found in several papers in Jurgens (1999). However, the argument has never been statistically validated. Moreover, the cases profiled are not rich enough to introduce a specific machine development process, as is done in this paper.

5. In this sense, contrary to Braverman's (1978) naive conjecture, the advent of CNC complex lathes, or MCs, through the mechatronics revolution is apt to induce upskilling rather than deskilling of machine-tool manufacturers.

The main purpose of this paper is to empirically test these conjectures using information from basic field research as well as a statistical analysis of an original survey.

The structure of this paper is as follows. In the next section, an outline of the research method is introduced. In section 3.3, I briefly summarize the external and technological factors that have favored Japanese machine-tool manufacturers since 1970. Sections 3.4 and 3.5 are the main sections of the paper. Section 3.4 introduces the gist of the simultaneous information-sharing system for developing new machines, based on field research. Section 3.5 considers economic rationales for such a system and statistically confirms my conjectures using an original survey. The final section summarizes the results.

3.2   The Research Method

I investigated twelve representative Japanese machine-tool manufacturers from September 1996 to March 2000. Seven of these firms are large-scale manufacturers, with more than 1,000 full-time employees. The other five have less than 500 full-time employees.[6] These firms can be classified into four groups. The first group produces high- or medium-class machines that are mass-produced abroad as well as in Japan. The second group mass-produces high- or medium-class machines that are only domestically produced and are largely exported to the United States or Europe. The third group mass-produces low-cost machines that are only domestically produced and are largely exported to developing countries such as Asian newly industrialized economies. The final group consists of mother-machine-type MCs with extraordinary tolerances that are only domestically produced. Thus, these firms are nicely varied for my research purposes.[7] In selecting these firms, I was advised by an industry specialist who is actively involved in the top-rated machine-tool industry journal in Japan, *Seisan-zai Marketing Shi* (*Capital Goods Marketing Journal*), which is analogous to *American Machinists* in the United States.[8]

In addition to the field research, I also conducted a survey of about 600 machine-tool and related firms in March 1998. These firms constitute the population of firms in the machine-tool industry as identified by the *Almanac of Office Automation,* a publication issued annually by *Seisan-zai Marketing Shi.* This almanac includes nearly all of the machine-tool manufacturers in Japan. I asked a supervisor (such as a foreman) in the as-

---

6. Although the results are not explicitly introduced here, I also visited an NC manufacturer, an LM guideway manufacturer, and three German machine-tool manufacturers.

7. I visited each shop floor or R&D section at least twice, and each interview lasted approximately two hours excluding time for factory tours. The details of this research are in Chuma (1998).

8. I was introduced to this expert by a researcher from the Association of the Japanese Machine Tool Industry.

sembly or machining shop of each company to fill out the questionnaire. The response rate was approximately 20 percent.

3.3   External and Technological Factors

In this section, I briefly introduce external and technological factors that have aided the development of the Japanese machine-tool industry since 1970. The human factors emphasized in this paper must be analyzed in the context of these other factors. As illustrated in the statistical analysis that follows, it is the combination of all of these factors that has induced the development (albeit a discontinuous one) of this industry.

One crucial factor has been the rapid development of the Japanese auto industry, represented by Toyota, Nissan, and Honda. About 60 percent of domestic machine tools are demanded by auto and auto parts manufacturers. Moreover, if auto-related molding and electric equipment manufacturers are included, the corresponding percentage is much higher. The link between the machine-tool and auto industries is reflected by the fact that Japanese auto makers produced the world's largest output in their industry in 1981, and Japanese machine-tool manufacturers accomplished the same feat in 1982. Japanese machine-tool manufacturers are also considered expert at making CNC composite lathes, or MCs, whose prices range from $100,000 to $500,000.

Another primary factor has been the development of the Japanese mechatronics industry, represented by Fanuc, Mitsubishi Electric, and Yaskawa Electric. The numerical control (NC) technology owned by these companies has long been considered very sophisticated in world markets, particularly since the early 1980s (for details, see Finegold 1994 or Kobayashi and Ohdaka 1995). Normally, machine-tool manufacturers collaborate with NC manufacturers in order to enhance the motion controllability of their machines. This is one reason Japanese machine-tool manufacturers continue to enjoy a substantial advantage in the advanced controllability of high-speed and high-precision machines. Of course, mechatronics manufacturers must be compensated for their contributions. Indeed, my field research suggests that 30 to 40 percent of total machine-tool costs are spent in order to utilize this high NC technology (including both software and hardware), regardless of whether the technology was developed by the machine-tool manufacturers themselves.[9]

A third important factor has been the development of the Japanese bearing, ball screw, and guideway manufacturing industries, represented by NSK, NTN, and THK. As is the case for NC technology, these high-

---

9. Such heavy reliance on the mechatronics industry has been interpreted by many Japanese machine-tool manufacturers as an industry crisis, and the demand for open NC interfaces has greatly increased.

precision parts are typically specific to individual machine-tool manufacturers. Therefore, a long-term relationship between these parts suppliers and machine-tool manufacturers is again desirable.[10] In other words, having easy access to high-precision parts manufacturers is quite beneficial to machine-tool manufacturers. One of the most influential of the high-precision parts is the linear motion guideway (LM guide), which was invented by THK about twenty-five years ago. Before the LM guide, slide guideways that required highly advanced hand-scraping skills[11] in order to guarantee a micron level of precision were quite common. The LM guide, however, significantly reduced the need for hand scraping without sacrificing the controllability of machines.[12] This is reflected in the fact that most of the machine-tool manufacturers I visited claimed that their payments to parts manufacturers constitute 10 to 20 percent of their total costs.

The fourth factor has been the rapid development of foundry engineering as represented by the automatic control technology for annealing to promptly remove casting stresses. In fact, this technology was invented about twenty years ago. In my field research, many engineers emphasized the fact that high-quality iron castings became cheaper due to the spread of annealing furnaces equipped with advanced automatic process control technology. The modern casting process uses open-arc or annealing furnaces. It requires precision in all aspects of the production process, including time, temperature, and ingredients, and so it must be automatically controlled in order to produce high-quality products. Many Japanese machinery manufacturers have invented very precise controlling technologies. Before these innovations, manufacturers placed iron castings around their factories for (natural) aging. In fact, one reason German and Swiss machine-tool manufacturers of the pre-innovation era were very proud of the stability of their high-precision machines was that they used high-quality iron castings that had undergone long-term aging. Nowadays, similar aging effects can easily be achieved by three to six hours of stress relief annealing inside a furnace of 500 to 550 degrees centigrade (Monma 1997). Many of the research and development (R&D) engineers I interviewed mentioned that the availability of high-quality iron castings is no longer a bottleneck in the production of high-quality machines.

3.4   Simultaneous Information Sharing during the Development Process

In this section we examine the types of simultaneous information sharing that take place in the Japanese machine-tool industry. We use manufacturer

---

10. Several representative machine-tool manufacturers produce their own ball screws.

11. Hand-scraping skills are among the most difficult craft-type skills, even though the motion is seemingly repetitive and physically demanding.

12. It is sometimes claimed that slide guideways are still much better than LM guides for maintaining micron or submicron levels of machine precision for heavy-duty jobs (Bates 1999).

B, a leading Japanese machine-tool manufacturer, as an example of how new machine ideas are developed and what kind of information sharing takes place when a firm produces experimental machines in anticipation of commercial production. Similar machine development processes have been introduced in most of the twelve machine-tool manufacturers I investigated.

Before continuing, however, we need to distinguish among three types of drawings: prototype drawings, conceptual drawings, and component drawings. Prototype drawings outline the basic ideas for a potential new machine.[13] Conceptual drawings break the prototype drawings down into elaborately detailed sections. Conceptual drawings are sometimes called "drawings for assembly." After the conceptual drawings are complete, it is possible to make component drawings, which indicate the exact form and size of each part.[14] The recent development of computer-aided design (CAD) makes it possible to use the conceptual figures to calculate such things as the strength of the machine, the frequency of vibrations, and the thermal transformations that occur when the machine is heated up.

3.4.1   Examples of Leading Newly Developed Machines

We use the MC FF63S (not the real name) as an example of a leading machine at manufacturer B. This machine is characterized by a highly respected trade journal as a horizontal machining center "developed based on both the high-speed and high-precision technology that applies to high-level heat-control systems." More concretely, it can rapidly and precisely process medium- or large-sized output; its work-feeding speed reaches 30 meters per minute when special square-angled slide guideways are used. The development designer at manufacturer B, whom I interviewed, said that the main objective of this machine was to reduce total costs by 30 percent over the previous prototype, and that it actually reduces the processing time by 35 percent for certain auto parts manufacturers. This MC has sold well, especially in the United States.

3.4.2   The Process of Machine Development

Manufacturer B uses a rolling five-year development plan that lists each type of machine and its expected year of completion. This plan is closely

---

13. In these drawings, users' needs, competitors' machine specifications, and relevant concepts for strategically important components are clarified. Details are given on the forms and structures of ball screws and guideways, as well as the main spindle, which make it possible to attain the targeted cutting speed and precision. Designers try to simulate the main objectives in these drawings.

14. In the case of main spindle units, the corresponding conceptual drawings consist of a three-dimensional figure and two-dimensional drawings that indicate the placement of bearings, springs, spacers, and so on. In these drawings, exact sizes, intervals between bearings, torque for screwing, and the like are given. The drawing for each main spindle, bearing, spacer, and so forth is called a component figure. Therefore, whether a drawing is a component or conceptual drawing depends to some extent on the mechanism of each machine.

aligned with the fundamental management plan. It clearly stipulates market conditions based on sales information, user feedback, related literature, newspapers, and other sources. A plan with a concrete timetable is created for each type of machine, such as grinding machines, machining centers, and made-to-order machines. The machines are principally planned by members of the machine-tool planning sections in the machine-tool and mechatronics divisions. Most of these planners were originally in the development and design division. In addition, participants from other departments, such as sales, production planning, machining and assembling, purchasing, quality control, and R&D give input. The FF63S was developed mainly in response to users' feedback.

3.4.3   Information Sharing in the Design Review 1

The development of the machining center FF63S was initiated in December 1994, when the machine was added to the five-year development plan. It was completed in 1995. Usually, a project manager is selected as soon as it is decided that a machine is to be developed. The manager immediately starts to make a commodity design plan, which verifies such strategic details as sales points, main specification comparisons with similar machines made by competitors, sales and profit plans, and users' current and future demands. In the case of FF63S, the project team studied sales information from the previous prototype machine, FF60B. They considered examples of inquiries about FF60B, an analysis of the main reasons why these specific inquiries did or did not lead to actual orders, and feedback from users after the sale. Section or department heads of the aforementioned departments typically join in making the commodity design plan.

After the commodity design plan has been successfully completed, the project manager[15] and his or her subordinates create a product design plan, which usually takes about two months. This plan includes the machine's main development objective, mechanical specifications, costs, expected development time, selling points, expected difficulties, quality target, design quality, method of product maintenance, and so on. In addition, it stipulates previously developed parts that are to be used. For example, a plan might include a comment such as "some parts of the main spindle of the previous machine can be used as they are." Moreover, in going from the commodity design plan to the product design plan, it is quite common to reevaluate the relevance of the users' development requests, which had been submitted early in the commodity design phase. Again, planning participants from various departments, especially department heads, provide input for revisions of the product design plan. For example, representatives from the machinists' division theorize on how they may or may not be able

---

15. I interviewed the project manager of FF63S himself.

to overcome the difficulties specified in the product design plan, and representatives from purchasing comment on the expected costs.

At manufacturer B, the meeting to discuss the product design plan proposed by the project manager is called the DR1 (design review 1). The basic ideas for the drawings (including the prototype drawings) are all decided upon in the DR1, and they are rarely modified thereafter. During the DR1 for the FF63S, the project chief was asked to clarify the precision and efficiency of the machine if used on the special projects of the specific users for whom the FF63S was being produced.

3.4.4   Information Sharing in the Design Review 2

If the product design plan passes the DR1, conceptual drawings are made based on the commodity design plan. The relevance of these drawings is discussed in the design review 2 (DR2). At this stage, even the exterior face of the machine is sketched in detail. In other words, the conceptual drawings are quite complicated and precise. The section managers of the sales, production planning, machining and assembling, purchasing, quality control department, and R&D departments participate in the DR2. For example, representatives from the assembly shop may comment on the feasibility of the tolerances indicated in the drawings.

In order to estimate the total costs of the new machine, the conceptual drawings specify the man-hours needed to build the machine and the corresponding total and unit labor costs. In addition, materials costs, energy costs, and the costs of using the company's facilities are specified. Then, representatives from the machining and assembly shops voice their opinions on the accuracy of the proposed man-hours, and sometimes change the estimates. Of course, it is desirable for assembly workers and machinists to secure sufficient time in which to complete their assigned tasks. Indeed, the man-hours determined in the DR2 become the standard against which actual man-hours are measured in the commercial production phase. However, since management insists on optimal cost-efficiency, the man-hours needed for assembly or machining must be as small as possible. It is in the DR2 that such adjustments are made. I should note that, for most projects, there is a general consensus among the planning participants regarding required man-hours for assembly or machining, based on past job experience or working records. Lastly, when tolerances required by the conceptual drawings exceed the level attainable using existing hardware, representatives from the machining shops are likely to request permission to purchase new hardware.

3.4.5   Information Sharing in the Design Review 3

After the conceptual design is accepted in the DR2, work on various component drawings begins immediately. Only drawings of important parts (e.g., the main spindle) that have been drastically changed from the previous prototype are reviewed in the design review 3 (DR3). The designers in charge decide whether or not a drawing needs to be reviewed. I should note here that reviewers from all departments utilize the same set of drawings during all the design reviews, regardless of affiliation. In other words, representative reviewers from sales, services, and production shops all review every DR3 drawing. Their opinions are also applied to the DR1 and DR2 drawings. For example, in the DR3, representatives from the assembly shop may claim that the assembly tasks depicted in a certain drawing are quite difficult and must be changed. Or representatives from the machining shop may claim that the shape of the machine as depicted in the drawings requires too many man-hours and so ought to be changed. In this way, professionals from various departments exchange opinions about the feasibility and reliability of the proposed machine.

3.4.6   Information Sharing during Experimental Production

After the DR3, experimental production begins. This used to be done by assembly workers and machinists on the shop floor. Recently, however, firms have begun to form special teams on a trial basis that specialize in experimental production. Standard working manuals are also written in this phase. To create these manuals, factory engineers conduct time studies using stopwatches or by interviewing the workers in charge in order to determine the standard working time for each task. However, the factory engineers do not unilaterally determine standard working time. Rather, it is determined by a combination of discussion and this evidence. Work improvement proposals are also written at this stage. In the case of the FF63S, about a year passed between the proposal of the commodity design plan and the completion of the first experimental machine. Five months passed between the beginning of experimental production and the completion of test cutting.

Normally, only one or two experimental machines are produced. After that, about ten commercial machines are produced for specific users. These twelve machines are used in part to uncover and eliminate bugs. For example, if cut chips tend to block efficient cutting, the chip-handling system is redesigned. If some part of the machine is not strong enough, the design flaw will be corrected. In the case of the FF63S, a new technology was used that automatically controls the thermal expansion expected to occur around the main spindle. However, this control system did not work reliably in the experimental production stage, and several technological breakthroughs were needed to fix it.

It is not uncommon for mechanical designers to try to immediately correct machine defects in the assembly shops. They are apt to stay in the shops during the whole of experimental production. Project leaders or chief design managers sometimes instruct their subordinates to work alongside the assembly workers while they are assembling the machine.

The objective is to avoid delays caused by insufficiently detailed drawings, because the ambiguity can be clarified immediately. The project manager of the FF63S explained,

> Without experience, it is very difficult to understand the gist of machine-tool mechanics. It can be quite dangerous to design machines without knowing how each machine is processed and assembled in the shop. To effectively design new machines and machine parts, mechanical designers have to have an understanding of the skill level of the assemblymen and machinists as well as the production capacity and finishing ability of company-owned facilities.

3.5   The Necessity for Simultaneous Information Sharing

3.5.1   Intuition Acquired from Field Research

The simultaneous information-sharing system linking mechanical designers and production workers has been broadly utilized and institutionalized by all of the machine-tool manufacturers we investigated. However, many have begun to criticize it, saying that the Japanese practice of regarding the common consensus as first best is outdated. However, the head of the technology department of manufacturer B pointed out the following very interesting fact:

> It is an established fact that we think highly of simultaneous information sharing among our various departments and divisions. This practice has been well established for about ten years—since the so-called TQC began to be widely practiced. Certainly, people shared a sense of family even before then, and consensus was important in various aspects of our production process. The current, rather egalitarian information-sharing system, however, was established in the 1980s, at which point certain types of sectionalism were almost wiped out and collaboration started to play a more important role. Twenty or thirty years ago, the technology department unilaterally presided over the production department. In a sense, engineers in the technology department encouraged production workers to do a good job in a paternalistic way. Also, they had the arrogance to say that the production workers had only to faithfully follow their instructions in order to produce good machines. However, such a unilateral relationship could not produce good products. As a result, the current design review system was introduced, based on the idea that, because only assembly and machining shops produce actual products, machine drawings must respect the shops' ways of doing things and take into account the various shops' constraints.

Total quality control (TQC) practices were well established by the 1960s in the Japanese automobile and household appliance industries (Udagawa et al. 1995). They have been utilized well into the 1980s, at least for manufacturer B (see the foregoing quotation). If this were true for all other machine-tool manufacturers, we could claim, contrary to the generally accepted notion, that the simultaneous information-sharing system linking production workers and engineers was established only recently. In other words, the system is not indigenous to Japan, but came into existence as the efficient production system of the period of rapid globalization in the 1980s. Indeed, our survey revealed the following: About 62 percent of machine-tool manufacturers[16] with close information sharing between mechanical designers and production workers answered that their system was initiated after 1980. This number increases to 74 percent when we include manufacturers who reported initiating their systems after 1970.

Why was the current egalitarian system of information sharing introduced fairly recently? The following comments from the mechanical designers of one of the largest machine-tool manufacturers in the industry help to answer this question:

> When traditional non-NC lathes or milling machines used to be produced, mechanical designers were very overconfident relative to the current standard. This was because they could theorize much of how these non-NC machines were built. However, their ability to do this gradually diminished as the machines became multifunctional, as in the case of machining centers or complex lathes, and equipped with CNC. This was reinforced by the advent of high-speed and high-precision machines equipped with ATC (auto tool changer) and APC (auto pallet changer). In the case of such complex machines, designers must take many factors into account beforehand in order to design a good machine. However, except in very rare cases, this is almost impossible. This is when the present simultaneous and egalitarian information-sharing system among our departments and divisions started to play an important role. Compared with the skills of machinists, the skills of first-rate assemblymen are primarily based on experience with a large number of fundamental laws. These skills are quite durable, even in the face of rapid technological development. As a result, assembly shops have become increasingly powerful.

Many engineers in the machine-tool manufacturing firms I investigated support the above statements. It is very interesting to note that, in contrast to automobile or household appliance manufacturers, none of the investigated machine-tool manufacturers have production or factory engineering sections (for assembly shops). These sections normally standardize assembling processes, manage production processes, or serve as an interface between production workers and R&D engineers or designers. Their absence underscores the necessity for close and simultaneous information sharing during the development process.[17]

---

16. Only 7 percent say they have no such close information-sharing system.
17. Only one of the machine-tool manufacturers I visited had such a section. However, upon further investigation, this section was found not to play the same role as an ordinary production engineering section.

Lastly, some people maintain that information sharing between production workers and engineers was practiced even in the prewar period. The following examples support this claim. According to Tokyo Gas Electric (now Hitachi Fine Machinery),

> The first stage of production management is design. In 1933, when we were still in a depression, the company employed 2 to 3 university graduates as designers of milling machines in a particular series. We had established a system in which the designers were responsible for all defects in the machines, so that it was quite troublesome when machines could not be produced as designed. All members of the production team thought hard about any problems that arose, and tried to improve the machines. It was not rare for young designers to take special on-the-job lessons in machining or assembly from skilled workers. Such an environment created excellent designers. (Miyazaki 1997)

According to Seiko,

> Around the last half of the 1920s, university graduates in the engineering section responsible for design who had insufficient knowledge of manufacturing technology were grouped together with assembly workers who had strong project-specific skills but were weak in theoretical understanding. They developed new products together. In this process, new products were revised again and again by both designers and skilled workers. They were put into commercial production only when no more defects could be found by any of the group's members. The close relationship between designers and skilled workers at that time reminds us of the current-style production process. (Odaka 1993, 151)

To be sure, it can be surmised from these statements that a form of mutual understanding between engineers and production workers played an important role in manufacturing even in the prewar period. However, Yamashita (1999) also introduces evidence collected from interviews with several former Tokyo Gas Electric engineers that suggests that even informal communication between production workers and engineers was quite rare in the prewar Tokyo Gas Electric, in direct contradiction to the above example. Thus, it is doubtful that the current type of simultaneous information system existed in the prewar period.[18]

3.5.2 Statistical Analysis

As indicated in the previous section, the advent of CNC complex lathes or MCs increased the need for simultaneous information sharing between production workers and design and development engineers. To show this statistically, we estimate a probit equation (1) allowing for heteroskedas-

---

18. Prewar evidence of informal and rather sporadic information sharing in Nihon Denki (the current NEC), Shibaura Seisaku-sho (the current Toshiba), and Mitsubishi Electric (a part of the former Mitsubishi Heavy Industry) is introduced in Sasaki (1998).

ticity. In this equation, the dependent dummy variable d_sinfo1 takes on a value of one if the firm answered "yes" to the following question: "Does your company (or factory) have a formal design review system in which, even in the early states of machine development, both R&D (or D&D) engineers and production workers simultaneously and directly exchange opinions?"

In the sample of 108 respondents, 67 percent answered "yes." In addition to this dependent variable (d_sinfo1), we also use two other dependent variables: d_sinfo2 and d_sinfo3. The dummy variable d_sinfo2 takes on a value of one if d_sinfo = 1 and the firm introduced this information-sharing system in 1980 or later. The dummy variable d_sinfo3 takes on a value of one if d_sinfo1 = 1 and the system was introduced in 1970 or later. These additional variables are utilized because the field research suggests that information-sharing systems were mainly introduced after 1980. Indeed, 41 percent of firms are in the d_sinfo2 = 1 sample and 50 percent are in the d_sinfo3 = 1 sample, so a large number of manufacturers introduced the system after 1980. Description of the independent variables (X_i) used are provided in the appendix.

$$(1) \quad \text{d\_sinfo1} = 1 \text{ if } \left(\alpha_0 + \sum_{i=1}^{i=n} \alpha_i X_i + \varepsilon \geq 0 \right); = 0 \text{ otherwise for } j = 1, 2, 3$$

where α_i = coefficients, X_i = independent variables ($i = 1, 2, \ldots n$), $\varepsilon \in \phi \, (0, 1)$ (the standard normal distribution).

The estimation results are shown in tables 3.1 through 3.3. Generally speaking, the most favorable results employ the dependent variable d_sinfo2, the next most favorable use d_sinfo3, and the least favorable use d_sinfo1. This indicates that the need for simultaneous information sharing between production workers and design and development engineers has increased, especially since 1980. This is also the period during which Japanese machine-tool manufacturers have consistently maintained the world's largest machine-tool production.

According to table 3.1, d_sinfo1 is positively correlated with the explanatory variables d_integ, d_ptime and d_TQC, all of whose coefficients are significant at the 1 percent level. The dummy variable d_integ takes on a value of one if the manufacturer answered "Yes" to the question: "In training your regular assemblymen, do you basically make them gain broad skills and know-how for both main- and parts-assembling processes?" The dummy variable d_ptime indicates that the sampled manufacturer employs nonregular employees such as part-timers. The dummy variable d_TQC that takes on a value of one if the firm has introduced TQC activities. The negatively correlated variables, significant at the same level, are OVERSEAS and d_pswar. The dummy variable OVERSEAS indicates that the firm has directly produced machines overseas using a production process that is quite different from that used for domestic production. The

Table 3.1   The Effects of Firm Characteristics on the Probability of Adoption of a Simultaneous Information-Sharing Design Review System (d_sinfo1)

d_sinfo1	Coefficient	Standard Error	z	$P > \|z\|$	95% Confidence Interval (1)	(2)	dP/dx
_cons*	−1.42	0.81	−1.75	0.08	−3.01	0.17	—
method	0.47	0.35	1.33	0.19	−0.22	1.16	0.1
d_integ*	**1.14**	**0.42**	**2.73**	**0.01**	**0.32**	**1.95**	**0.4**
d_early	**0.72**	**0.32**	**2.20**	**0.03**	**0.08**	**1.35**	**0.2**
d_mfunc*	1.41	0.83	1.70	0.09	−0.22	3.04	0.3
d_mfunc2	0.15	0.76	0.20	0.84	−1.34	1.63	0.0
d_scrape	**1.11**	**0.56**	**1.98**	**0.05**	**0.01**	**2.21**	**0.3**
d_tshoot	**1.10**	**0.47**	**2.35**	**0.02**	**0.18**	**2.01**	**0.4**
skillrat	−0.14	0.23	−0.61	0.54	−0.58	0.30	(0.0)
d_ptime*	**0.94**	**0.36**	**2.62**	**0.01**	**0.24**	**1.65**	**0.3**
d_TQC*	**0.87**	**0.32**	**2.73**	**0.01**	**0.25**	**1.49**	**0.3**
d_experi	0.41	0.40	1.03	0.30	−0.37	1.18	0.1
overseas*	**−1.69**	**0.47**	**−3.61**	**0.00**	**−2.61**	**−0.78**	**(0.6)**
d_pubedu	0.18	0.39	0.45	0.65	−0.59	0.95	0.1
d_intwar	−0.77	0.56	−1.37	0.17	−1.87	0.33	(0.3)
d_pstwar*	**−1.44**	**0.52**	**−2.76**	**0.01**	**−2.47**	**−0.42**	**(0.4)**
d_lathe	0.07	0.43	0.16	0.87	−0.78	0.91	0.0
d_MC	−0.09	0.42	−0.20	0.84	−0.92	0.75	(0.0)
d_Drill	−0.94	0.75	−1.25	0.21	−2.41	0.53	(0.3)
d_Boring	0.15	0.83	0.18	0.86	−1.49	1.78	0.0
d_GeaGrd*	0.69	0.36	1.92	0.06	−0.02	1.40	0.2
d_IND	−0.04	0.38	−0.10	0.92	−0.78	0.71	(0.0)
d_Misc	−0.33	0.32	−1.03	0.30	−0.96	0.30	(0.1)
d_spoint	−0.55	0.37	−1.50	0.13	−1.27	0.17	(0.2)
d_spoint2	−0.07	0.30	−0.25	0.81	−0.66	0.51	(0.0)
scale100	0.54	0.39	1.39	0.16	−0.22	1.30	0.2
N	108						
Pseudo-R^2	0.32						
Log-likelihood	46.59415						

Notes: Probit estimates of equation (1) with robust standard errors. Obs. $P(\text{d\_sinfo1} = 1) = 0.67$; pred. $P(\text{d\_sinfo1} = 1) = 0.75$ (at x-bar). Boldface indicates that the variables are statistically significant.
***$P \le .01$.
**$P \le .05$.
*$P \le .10$.

variable d_pswar is a dummy variable that takes on a value of one if the manufacturer was founded after World War II (WWII).

The result that d_integ positively and significantly increases the probability of introducing a simultaneous information-sharing system is expected a priori because, other things being equal, it suggests that assembly workers are broadly skilled. The positive and significant impact of d_TQC

Table 3.2   The Effects of Firm Characteristics on the Probability of Adoption of a Simultaneous Information-Sharing Design Review System since 1980 (d_sinfo2)

d_sinfo2	Coefficient	Standard Error	z	$P > \|z\|$	95% Confidence Interval (1)	(2)	dP/dx
_cons***	–3.25	1.01	–3.23	0.00	–5.23	–1.28	—
method***	1.42	0.51	2.81	0.01	0.43	2.41	0.5
d_integ*	0.94	0.49	1.90	0.06	–0.03	1.90	0.3
d_early**	0.87	0.42	2.08	0.04	0.05	1.69	0.3
d_mfunc***	2.36	0.86	2.75	0.01	0.67	4.04	0.7
d_mfunc2	0.58	0.82	0.71	0.48	–1.03	2.19	0.2
d_scrape***	1.94	0.64	3.03	0.00	0.68	3.19	0.6
d_tshoot***	1.97	0.59	3.31	0.00	0.80	3.13	0.6
skillrat	–0.15	0.27	–0.55	0.59	–0.67	0.38	(0.1)
d_ptime***	1.97	0.46	4.24	0.00	1.06	2.87	0.7
d_TQC***	1.07	0.41	2.62	0.01	0.27	1.87	0.4
d_experi***	1.40	0.51	2.77	0.01	0.41	2.39	0.4
overseas***	–2.65	0.72	–3.70	0.00	–4.06	–1.25	(0.5)
d_pubedu***	1.92	0.50	3.82	0.00	0.94	2.91	0.6
d_intwar***	–4.24	0.83	–5.10	0.00	–5.87	–2.61	(0.7)
d_pstwar***	–2.69	0.78	–3.46	0.00	–4.21	–1.16	(0.8)
d_lathe***	1.52	0.53	2.86	0.00	0.48	2.56	0.6
d_MC*	1.22	0.70	1.74	0.08	–0.16	2.61	0.5
d_Drill**	–2.08	0.85	–2.45	0.02	–3.76	–0.41	(0.5)
d_Boring	–1.22	0.79	–1.54	0.13	–2.77	0.34	(0.3)
d_GeaGrd	0.48	0.49	0.98	0.33	–0.47	1.43	0.2
d_IND	0.46	0.49	0.95	0.34	–0.49	1.42	0.2
d_Misc***	–2.00	0.45	–4.43	0.00	–2.88	–1.11	(0.6)
d_spoint***	–1.35	0.45	–3.02	0.00	–2.22	–0.47	(0.4)
d_spoint2	–0.46	0.38	–1.21	0.23	–1.20	0.28	(0.2)
scale100***	1.50	0.52	2.91	0.00	0.49	2.52	0.5
N	108						
Pseudo-R^2	0.56						
Log-likelihood	32.03						

Notes: Probit estimates of equation (1) with robust standard errors. Obs. P(d_sinfo1 = 1) = 0.41; pred. P(d_sinfo1 = 1) = 0.37 (at x-bar). Boldface indicates that the variables are statistically significant.
***$P \leq .01$.
**$P \leq .05$.
*$P \leq .10$.

is also consistent with my conjectures. As for the OVERSEAS dummy, my field research suggests that most machine-tool manufacturers involved in overseas production (12 percent of the sample) mass-produce machine-tools based on expected demand. Compared with user-specific machines, mass-produced machines are less demanding of assembling and machining skills. Thus, OVERSEAS has a negative and significant impact. In addi-

Table 3.3   **The Effects of Firm Characteristics on the Probability of Adoption of a Simultaneous Information-Sharing Design Review System since 1970 (d_sinfo3)**

d_sinfo3	Coefficient	Standard Error	z	$P > \lvert z \rvert$	95% Confidence Interval (1)	(2)	dP/dx
_cons*	−1.43	0.85	−1.68	0.09	−3.09	0.24	—
method	0.47	0.37	1.26	0.21	−0.26	1.20	0.2
d_integ***	**1.28**	**0.48**	**2.68**	**0.01**	**0.35**	**2.22**	**0.5**
d_early**	**0.84**	**0.37**	**2.28**	**0.02**	**0.12**	**1.56**	**0.3**
d_mfunc	0.48	0.60	0.81	0.42	−0.68	1.65	0.2
d_mfunc2	0.09	0.75	0.12	0.90	−1.37	1.56	0.0
d_scrape***	**1.10**	**0.57**	**1.93**	**0.05**	**−0.02**	**2.22**	**0.4**
d_tshoot	0.29	0.50	0.58	0.56	−0.68	1.26	0.1
skillrat	−0.14	0.22	−0.63	0.53	−0.58	0.30	(0.1)
d_ptime***	**1.58**	**0.40**	**3.94**	**0.00**	**0.80**	**2.37**	**0.6**
d_TQC**	**0.74**	**0.36**	**2.08**	**0.04**	**0.04**	**1.44**	**0.3**
d_experi*	0.69	0.38	1.80	0.07	−0.06	1.44	0.3
overseas***	**−1.84**	**0.49**	**−3.75**	**0.00**	**−2.81**	**−0.88**	(0.6)
d_pubedu***	**1.29**	**0.46**	**2.78**	**0.01**	**0.38**	**2.19**	**0.4**
d_intwar***	**−3.07**	**0.73**	**−4.20**	**0.00**	**−4.51**	**−1.64**	(0.8)
d_pstwar***	**−2.07**	**0.65**	**−3.20**	**0.00**	**−3.34**	**−0.80**	(0.7)
d_lathe**	**1.06**	**0.47**	**2.25**	**0.02**	**0.14**	**1.98**	**0.4**
d_MC**	**1.11**	**0.50**	**2.24**	**0.03**	**0.14**	**2.09**	**0.4**
d_Drill	−1.17	0.79	−1.47	0.14	−2.72	0.39	(0.4)
d_Boring**	**−1.45**	**0.74**	**−1.96**	**0.05**	**−2.91**	**0.00**	(0.5)
d_GeaGrd	0.10	0.37	0.26	0.79	−0.62	0.81	0.0
d_IND	0.47	0.37	1.25	0.21	−0.27	1.20	0.2
d_Misc***	**−1.05**	**0.35**	**−3.03**	**0.00**	**−1.73**	**−0.37**	(0.4)
d_spoint	−0.64	0.42	−1.51	0.13	−1.47	0.19	(0.3)
d_spoint2	−0.35	0.33	−1.04	0.30	−1.00	0.31	(0.1)
scale100***	**1.35**	**0.44**	**3.06**	**0.00**	**0.48**	**2.22**	**0.5**
N	108						
Pseudo-R^2	0.46						
Log-likelihood	−40.16						

Notes: Probit estimates of equation (1) with robust standard errors. Obs. P(d_sinfo1 = 1) = 0.50; pred. P(d_sinfo1 = 1) = 0.56 (at x-bar). Boldface indicates that the variables are statistically significant.
***$P \leq .01$.
**$P \leq .05$.
*$P \leq .10$.

tion, firms founded after WWII are more apt to specialize in mass-produced machines than are the more established firms. This is why d_pswar has as significant and negative an impact as OVERSEAS. I do now know why d_ptime has a significant, positive impact. However, my field research yields no definitive evidence that mass-producers use more nonregular workers. Accordingly, it is possible for d_ptime to a priori have either a positive or negative impact.

There are additional variables in table 3.1 that are significant at the 5 percent level. These are d_early, d_scrape, and d_tshoot. The dummy variable d_early takes on a value of one if the firm answered "yes" to the following question: "In order to foster your prospective leaders, are you concerned about putting talented assemblymen in charge of a wider range of work beginning in the early stages of their careers, so that they can gain integrated skills?" The dummy variable d_scrape implies that the most advanced job for assemblyworkers in the firm is hand scraping, which is required to attain the static or dynamic precision called for by the drawings. The dummy variable d_tshoot indicates that the most advanced job for assemblyworkers in the firm is that of troubleshooting in the shops (diagnosing and correcting both new and previously encountered bugs). All three of these variables indicate that the assemblyworkers in the firm are highly skilled. They significantly enhance the need for simultaneous information sharing between production workers and design and development engineers.

We note here that there are two or three other variables that are significant at the 10 percent level. Their significance, however, is highly dependent on the total sample size, so it is dangerous to draw conclusions based on these data alone. The highly significant coefficients are also significant in tables 3.2 and 3.3, whereas the less significant coefficients are not always robust to changes in the dependent variable.

As previously mentioned, the field research suggests that the need for simultaneous information sharing between production workers and design and development engineers has increased since the late 1970s. The fact that the number of significant (at the 1 percent or 5 percent level) variables jumps appreciably in tables 3.2 and 3.3 supports this suggestion.[19] It is especially apparent in table 3.2 for the dependent variable d_sinfo2, which takes on a value of 1 if d_sinfo1 = 1 and the system was introduced in 1980 or later. Additional variables with positive and significant coefficients in tables 3.2 and 3.3 are d_method, d_mfunc, d_experi, d_pubedu, d_lathe, d_MC, and scale100. The variables d_intwar, d_Drill, d_Misc, and d_spoint all have negative and significant coefficients.

The dummy variable d_method takes on a value of 1 if the total assembly method of high-speed/high-accuracy machines differs significantly from that of other machines. The dummy variable d_mfunc indicates that the firm tries to make its machinists multifunctional, since being responsible for many machines at once might allow them to troubleshoot more effectively. The variable d_experi indicates that, compared to machining skills, assembling skills in a firm are apt to withstand rapid technological innovation.[20] The dummy variable d_pubedu indicates that the firm requires

---

19. The significance of d_integ drops a little, but it is still significant at the 6 percent level.

20. Actually, about 80 percent of the manufacturers interviewed for my survey reported that assembling skills are more likely to be internalized in a specific person than machining skills. Moreover, compared with machining skills, assembling skills are more dependent on many experienced laws.

public trade skill licenses for promotion. If the firm produces (CNC) lathes, the dummy variable d_lathe takes on a value of 1. If the firm produces machining centers, drilling machines, or miscellaneous machines, the dummy variables d_MC, d_Drill, and d_Misc respectively take on a value of 1. The dummy variable scale100 indicates that the firm has more than 100 full-time employees. The dummy variable d_intwar indicates that the firm was founded during the interwar period. Finally, the dummy variable d_spoint indicates that the firm's sales point is "low price."

The variable d_method is a proxy for whether the firm has highly skilled assemblyworkers; if the firm produces high-speed and high-precision machines, such workers are necessary. Thus, the positive and significant coefficient on d_method is consistent with a priori expectations. The variable d_mfunc implies that the machinists have broad skills. Hence, its significant and positive impact is also acceptable. The same interpretation is applicable to the coefficient on the variable d_experi because assembling skills rely heavily on rules of thumb. Insights from the field research are helpful in interpreting the significant positive impact of the variable d_pubedu. Machine-tool manufacturers that recommend acquiring public trade skill licenses also make the licenses mandatory for promotion in order to cope with fierce competition among production workers and to maintain the objectivity of promotion criteria. Hence, the significant positive result is comprehensible to some extent. The positive, significant impact of d_lathe or d_MC is also quite understandable because most of these lathes and MCs are the complex CNC machine types, through which Japanese machine-tool manufacturers attained their current leading position in the world market in the early 1980s.[21] The variable d_Drill indicates that the firm is still producing traditional drilling machines, so the significant negative impact can be given the opposite interpretation of d_lathe and d_MC. Only innovative manufacturers that maintained a certain firm scale could effectively survive the cutthroat competition among rival producers of high-speed and high-precision complex machines. Therefore, the positive and significant coefficient on scale100 is reasonable. Lastly, the negative and significant coefficient on d_spoint is quite natural, given that d_spoint represents a "low price" sales point.

Finally, the last columns in tables 3.1 through 3.3 show each variable's impact on the probability that simultaneous information sharing is introduced. Except for the constant (cons) and the skillrat variable, all the independent variables are dummies, so the impact is actually equivalent to the elasticity. In table 3.1, only d_integ and d_tshoot have a large, positive elasticity. Still, the impact of these variables is at most 0.4. In table 3.2, however, the number of variables with a large positive impact is much higher. Furthermore, the magnitudes are far greater than in table 3.1. Indeed, the following variables have an elasticity greater than 0.5: d_method,

---

21. Note that both d_lathe and d_MC are significant and positive even in table 2.3.

d_mfunc, d_scrape, d_tshoot, d_ptime, d_pubedu, d_lathe, d_MC, and scale100. These results suggest that simultaneous information-sharing systems are more likely to be introduced by machine-tool manufacturers that retain highly skilled assemblyworkers and machinists, produce (CNC) lathes or MCs, or have more than 100 full-time workers.

3.6 Summary and Conclusion

The Japanese machine-tool industry attained the position of world output leader in 1982 and has maintained this status ever since. This paper analyzes the factors that enabled this success. In this analysis, I assert the importance of human-related factors in addition to such popular technological factors as the extensive development of Japanese automakers, the "leap-forward" development of Japanese mechatronics manufacturers, the rapid development of precision-parts manufacturers, and the basic development of foundry engineering technology. I pay special attention to the existence of simultaneous and formal information-sharing systems between production workers and design and development engineers.

My analysis utilizes both field research and survey results. The field research reveals that the machine-tool industry employs a simultaneous and rather egalitarian information-sharing system linking production workers and design and development engineers. It is typically asserted that this kind of system is indigenous to Japan. However, the field research indicates that these systems have largely been implemented since 1980. I also investigate why the system was introduced so recently. One promising reason is that current CNC machines are so complex that, without close collaboration among the various professionals, mechanical designers could not effectively design machines to the last detail and keep lead times short. This last conjecture is statistically confirmed by the survey data. Indeed, the statistical analysis predicts that simultaneous information-sharing systems are more likely to be implemented by machine-tool manufacturers that retain highly skilled assemblyworkers and machinists, produce (CNC) lathes or MCs, and have more than 100 full-time workers.

Appendix
Legend

d_sinfo1   A dummy variable that takes on a value of one if the firm answered "yes" to the following question: "Does your company (or factory) have a formal design review system in which, even in early stages of machine development, both R&D (or D&D) engineers and production workers simultaneously and directly exchange opinions?"

d_sinfo2   A dummy variable that takes on a value of one if d_sinfo1 = 1 and the firm introduced this information-sharing system in 1980 or later

d_sinfo3   A dummy variable that takes on a value of one if d_sinfo1 = 1 and the system was introduced in 1970 or later

method   A dummy variable that takes on a value of one if the total assembly method of high-speed/high-accuracy machines differs significantly from that of other machines

d_integ   A dummy variable that takes on a value of one if the maker answered "yes" to the question: "In training your regular assemblymen, do you basically make them gain broad skills and know-how for both main- and parts-assembling processes?"

d_early   A dummy variable that takes on a value of one if the firm answered "yes" to the following question: "In order to foster your prospective leaders, are you concerned about putting talented assemblymen in charge of a wider range of work beginning in the early stages of their careers, so that they can gain integrated skills?"

d_mfunc   A dummy variable that takes on a value of one if the firm tries to make its machinists multifunctional because this might allow the machinists to understand the interaction between the machine tools and the parts they process

d_mfunc2   A dummy variable that takes on a value of one if the firm tries to make its machinists multifunctional because this might allow the machinists to troubleshoot more effectively

d_scrape   A dummy variable that takes on a value of one if the most advanced job for assemblyworkers in the firm is hand scraping

d_tshoot   A dummy variable that takes on a variable of one if the most advanced job for assemblyworkers in the firm is troubleshooting in the shops

skillrat   The percentage of (full-time) assemblyworkers that could fully manage all of the advanced jobs indicated in the question

d_ptime   A dummy variable that takes on a value of one if the manufacturer employs nonregular employees such as part-timers

d_TQC   A dummy variable that takes on a value of one if the firm conducts TQC activities and expects these to lead to a simultaneous information-sharing system

d_experi   A dummy variable that takes on a value of one if, compared to machining skills, assembling skills are apt to withstand rapid technological innovation

overseas	A dummy variable that takes on a value of one if the sampled firm has directly produced machines overseas using a production process that is quite different from that used for domestic production
d_intwar	A dummy variable that takes on a value of one if the firm was founded during the interwar period
d_pswar	A dummy variable that takes on a value of one if the maker was founded after WWII
d_pubedu	A dummy variable that takes on a value of one if the firm requires public trade skill licenses for promotion
d_lathe	A dummy variable that takes on a value of one if the firm produces (CNC) lathes
d_MC	A dummy variable that takes on a value of one if the firm produces MCs
d_Drill	A dummy variable that takes on a value of one if the firm produces drilling machines
d_Boring	A dummy variable that takes on a value of one if the firm produces boring machines
d_GeaGrd	A dummy variable that takes on a value of one if the firm produces gear-cutting machines or grinders
d_IND	A dummy variable that takes on a value of one if the firm produces industry machines
d_Misc	A dummy variable that takes on a value of one if the firm produces miscellaneous machines
d_spoint	A dummy variable that takes on a value of one if the firm's sales point is "low price"
d_spoint2	A dummy variable that takes on a value of one if the firm's sales point is "high-speed and high-precision machines"
scale100	A dummy variable that takes on a value of one if the firm has more than 100 full-time employees

References

Bates, C. 1999. Applications show the way. *American Machinists* (January): 50–56.

Braverman, H. 1978. *Labor and monopoly capital: The degradation of work in the twentieth century.* New York: Monthly Review Press.

Chuma, H. 1998. Genba-shugi ka no Jinzai-keisei to Joho Kyoyu: Kosakukikai maker 9 sha no Jireikara (Skill formation and information sharing under "shop sovereignty": Examples from 9 machine-tool makers). *Keizai-Kenkyu* 49 (3): 218–30.

Finegold, D., ed. 1994. *The decline of the U.S. machine-tool industry and prospects for its sustainable recovery.* Vol. 1. Santa Monica, Calif.: RAND.

Finegold, D., K. W. Brendley, R. Lempert, D. Henry, P. Cannon, B. Boultinghouse, and M. Nelson. 1994a. *The decline of the U.S. machine-tool industry and prospects for its sustainable recovery.* Vol. 2: *Appendices.* Santa Monica, Calif.: RAND.

Fleischer, M. 1997. *The inefficiency trap: Strategy failure in the German machine tool industry.* Berlin: Edition Sigma.

Friedman, D. 1988. *The misunderstood miracle: Industrial development and political change in Japan.* Ithaca, N.Y.: Cornell University Press.

Holland, M. 1992. *When the machine stopped.* Cambridge: Harvard Business School Press.

Jurgens, U., ed. 1999. *New product development and production networks.* New York: Springer.

Kobayashi, M., and Y. Ohdaka. 1995. Kosaku-kikai Sangyo (History of the machine tool industry). In *Sengo Nihon Sangyo-shi* (Postwar history of Japanese industry), ed. Sangyo Gakkai. Tokyo: Toyokeizai Shinpo-sha, 382–412.

Koike, K. 1999. *Ishigoto no Keizaigaku, Toyokeizai-Shinpo-sha* (Economics of working). Tokyo: Toyokeizai-Shinpo-sha.

Miwa, Y. 1998. *Seifu no Noryoku* (Capability of government). Tokyo: Yuhikaku.

Miyazaki, M. 1997. Hanaoka Hiroshi-Shi-Showa no Kosakukikai Retsuden (Sono 6) (Mr. Seishu Hanaoka: Great people involved in the machine-tool industry in the Showa period), *Kikai Gijyutsu,* 35 (11): 77–82.

Monma, K. 1997. *Daigaku-Kiso: Kikai-Zairyo* (Fundamental book: Materials for machines). Tokyo: Jikkyo Shuppan-sha.

Odaka, K. 1993. *Kigyonai Kyoiku no Jidai* (World of skilled workers and world of factories). Tokyo: Libroport.

Sasaki, S. 1998. *Kagaku-teki Kanriho no Nihon-teki Tenkai* (Development of Japanese-style scientific management). Tokyo: Yuhikaku.

Udagawa, M., H. Sata, K. Nakamura, and I. Nonaka. 1995. *Nihonkigyo no Hinshitsu Kanri: Keiei-shi Kenkyu* (Quality management in Japanese firms: History of management). Tokyo: Yuhikaku.

Yamashita, M. 1999. *Kohsakukikai-sangyo no Shokuba-shi 1889–1945* (Workshop history in the machine-tool industry 1989–1945). Tokyo: Waseda University Press.

4

Who Really Lost Jobs in Japan?
Youth Employment in an Aging Japanese Society

Yuji Genda

4.1 Introduction

This paper looks at how the rapid aging of Japanese society has changed employment opportunities for youth. In the second half of the 1990s, the job insecurities of middle-aged and older workers have received much attention. The Japanese government, media, labor unions, and even employers often admit that corporate restructuring measures have resulted in massive job loss among older, especially white-collar, workers. In 1999, in response to this perceived crisis, the Ministry of Labor introduced emergency measures to create employment opportunities for older people.

However, we should question whether the employment situation for middle-aged and older white-collar workers is, in fact, deteriorating as much as is often claimed by the major Japanese newspapers. Only 70,000 unemployed persons were aged forty-five to fifty-four and had a university education in 1999 (Statistics Bureau 1999). This figure was a little more than 2 percent of the approximately three million unemployed persons. A large proportion of the increasing number of unemployed is accounted for by young people, especially those without a college degree. The relative unemployment of middle-aged and older college graduates has not increased to the degree claimed.

In contrast, the job insecurities of young people have been virtually ignored. The media has been relatively unconcerned about the labor market

Yuji Genda is associate professor of the Institute of Social Science at University of Tokyo.
The author benefited a great deal from useful comments at the National Bureau of Economic Research and Japan Center for Economic Research meetings, especially from comments by Richard Freeman and Takao Kato. He is also grateful for helpful comments from Hiroyuki Chuma, David Cutler, Yutaka Kosai, Yoshi Nakata, Seiritsu Ogura, Fumio Ohtake, and Toshiaki Tachibanaki. He takes responsibility for any errors.

problems of Japanese youth. In fact, the youth unemployment rate has remained low in Japan relative to that in other developed countries. And Japan's increasing rate of job turnover among youth, even during the recessions of the 1990s, mostly tends to be explained away by citing evidence of changing work attitudes among Japanese youth.

This paper explains changes in job opportunities in Japan in the late 1990s, especially for youth. It is one of only a few economic studies that focus on labor demand by age. It concludes that a decline in overall labor demand largely resulted in reduced employment opportunities for youth, while the employment of middle-aged and older workers was relatively safeguarded. A large part of the contraction in the labor demand for younger workers has been due to job displacement by a graying workforce, especially within large firms.

4.2   Youth Unemployment and Parasite Singles

Figure 4.1 shows unemployment rates by age category. The unemployment rate for each age category rose rapidly in the 1990s. In particular, the monthly unemployment rate for fifteen- to twenty-four-year-old males increased significantly, surpassing 10 percent in 1999 for the first time since 1953. The difference in the unemployment rate between younger and older age groups has expanded over time. From 1999 to 2001, the Japanese unemployment rate has exceeded that of the United States. Figure 4.2 presents monthly unemployment rates by age category and gender for the

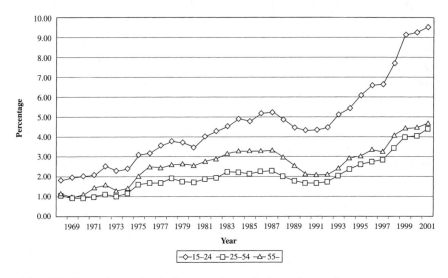

Fig. 4.1   Unemployment rates by age category in Japan (percent)
Source: Statistics Bureau (1968–2001)

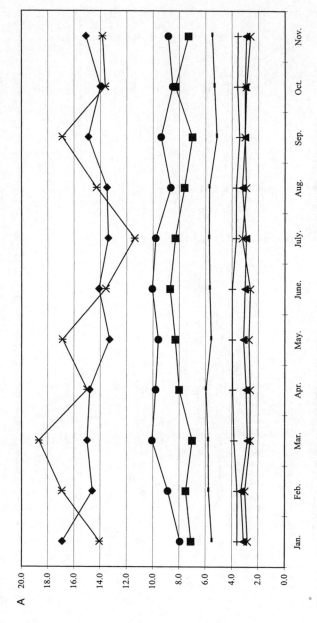

Fig. 4.2   Monthly unemployment rates in Japan and the United States in 1999: *A,* **Men;** *B,* **Women**

Sources: Japan: Statistics Bureau (1999); United States: U.S. Department of Labor, Bureau of Labor Statistics (1999).

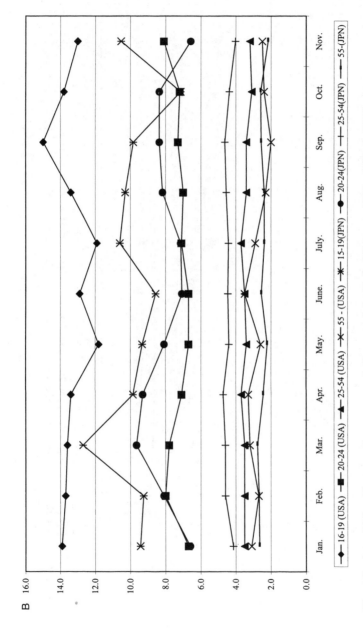

Fig. 4.2   (cont.) Monthly unemployment rates in Japan and the United States in 1999: *A,* **Men;** *B,* **Women**

Sources: Japan: Statistics Bureau (1999); United States: U.S. Department of Labor, Bureau of Labor Statistics (1999).

United States and Japan. The unemployment rates of twenty- to twenty-four-year-olds were consistently higher in Japan than in the United States for both males and females. In addition, the teenage male unemployment rate was also higher in Japan for several months. The long-term unemployment ratio (defined as the number of people who have looked for jobs for more than one year over the total number of unemployed) is shown in figure 4.3. The long-term unemployment ratio is higher for older workers and has gradually increased over time in every age category. Even younger workers aged fifteen to thirty-four experienced a jump in this ratio from less than 10 percent in the mid–1980s to over 20 percent in 2001.

Nevertheless, few economists or policymakers have analyzed youth employment because they believe that it is mostly voluntary.[1] There have been few economic studies of youth unemployment in Japan, even though it has been widely studied in western countries (Blanchflower and Freeman 2000).[2] Table 4.1 shows reasons why unemployed persons left their previous jobs, as reported in the *Job Seeking Situation Survey* of 1998 (Statistics Bureau 1998). About 28 percent of unemployed fifteen- to twenty-four-year-olds left because their expectations of working conditions prior to entering the workforce had not been met. This contrasts starkly with middle-aged and older workers, who mainly lost their jobs through bankruptcy, dismissal, or mandatory retirement.

What is behind the increase in resignations among young people? One argument, which focuses on the upbringing and outlook of the current generation, suggests that values and attitudes toward work have changed. It claims that young people now lack a traditional work ethic, such as persistence in keeping working. It also asserts that, since couples are having fewer children, young people are able to reside with and financially depend upon their parents longer.

These youths, known as "parasite singles" in Japan, have drawn public attention to the link between rising unemployment and increased job switching by the younger generation. In a book entitled *Days of the Parasite Single,* Yamada (1999), a Japanese sociologist, defines "parasite singles" as "unmarried persons who live with their parents even after graduation, and depend on their parents for basic living necessities" (11). Using national census data, he calculates that there are no fewer than 10 million unmarried persons aged twenty to thirty-four still living with their parents. And this number is most probably increasing. These parasite singles prefer the higher standard of living they achieve by continuing to live in their parents' homes. They are unwilling to lower their living standards by marrying or living independently from their parents. Accordingly, this increase

---

1. For example, a principal author of the *White Paper on Labor* by the Ministry of Labor expresses the opinion that the most serious concern of labor market policy is the unemployment of middle-aged and older persons (Muraki et al. 1999, 76).
2. One exception is Tachibanaki (1984).

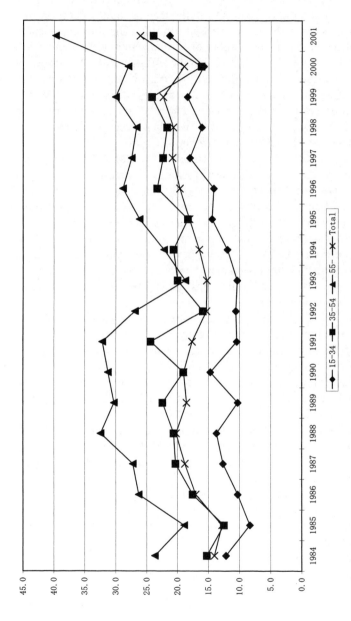

Fig. 4.3   The long-term unemployment ratio (percent)

Source: Statistics Bureau (1984–2001).

Notes: Figures are examined in February of each year. The long-term unemployed are defined as those unemployed for more than one year.

Table 4.1   **Reasons Cited by Unemployed Workers for Previous Job Separation**

		Age		
	Total	15–24	25–54	55+
Total	100.0	100.0	100.0	100.0
Bankruptcy of firm, closing of establishment, or self-employment	10.9	5.1	13.0	10.9
Dismissal or personal retrenchment	17.9	5.1	20.0	23.9
Mandatory retirement or expiration of employment contract	11.4	0.0	4.0	34.8
Business prospects were poor	7.6	12.8	7.0	0.0
Working conditions such as earnings, working hours, and days off deteriorated	6.0	7.7	6.0	4.3
Working conditions were different from what had been expected before starting work	10.9	28.2	9.0	0.0
Pursuing jobs or something more favorable even without dissatisfaction at previous jobs	9.8	15.4	11.0	0.0
Own convenience or family reasons (marriage, maternity leave, housekeeping, taking care of sick family members, failing health, etc.)	13.6	12.8	17.0	8.7
Other	11.4	12.8	13.0	8.7
Unknown	1.1	0.0	0.0	2.2

Source: Statistics Bureau (1998).

in the number of parasite singles is correlated with rapid increases in the numbers of late marriages and couples with fewer children.

The emergence of parasite singles has cast a shadow over the labor market for young people in Japan. Since parasite singles are free of financial responsibilities, they do not look for jobs with high wages, treating work as a hobby. Because they have this attitude, they immediately give up jobs that they find uncongenial. The resulting unemployment of young people is "luxury unemployment;" it does not involve real financial necessity. To them, work is a discretionary pastime or a means of earning pocket money.

4.3   Long-Term Employment, Seniority Wages, and Displaced Youth

These changes in labor supply may partly explain the long-term rise in youth unemployment. However, there is no precise empirical economic research confirming this. Another plausible explanation is that a decline in labor demand has played a central role in reducing the number of jobs available to youths.

The belief that changing attitudes toward work and a decline in the work ethic are the main causes of youth employment turnover can be challenged on factual grounds. Figure 4.4 presents the mean number of years spent working at a given firm for full-time employees. Males over the age of fifty

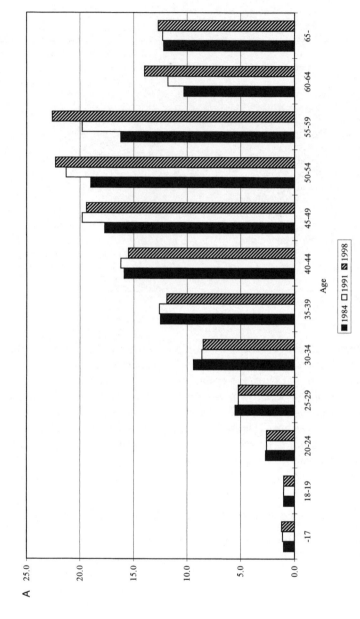

A

Fig. 4.4 Mean number of years worked at a given firm for full-time employees: *A*, **Men;** *B*, **Women**
Source: Ministry of Labor (1984, 1991, 1998).

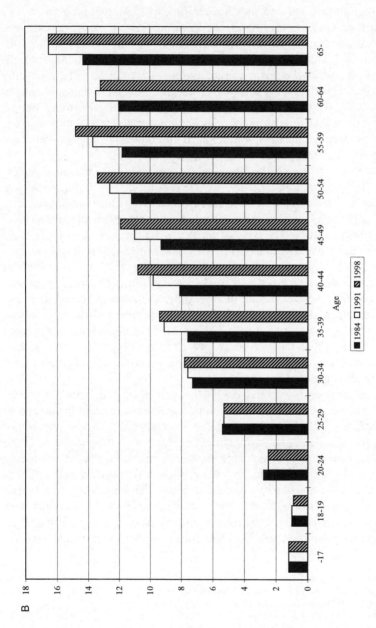

Fig. 4.4   (cont.)

and females aged thirty to fifty-nine tend to work more years at a given firm now than in the past, and they have stronger long-term employment ties than before. On the other hand, the mean number of working years at a given firm has been relatively stable for twenty- to thirty-four-year-old full-time workers in the 1990s, for both males and females. I also find from alternative data that the turnover rate among all young workers, especially young female workers, has gradually increased since the 1980s. These facts conclusively show that, although a small proportion of young people found jobs as full-time workers, many more were forced to choose part-time jobs. Meanwhile, most middle-aged and older full-time workers kept their positions throughout the 1980s and 1990s.[3]

With the bursting of the so-called bubble economy, business performance declined in most Japanese firms. In addition, the graying workforce (i.e., the increasing numbers of middle-aged and older employees) has raised labor costs, particularly for firms most likely to maintain seniority-based compensation. The ratio of workers aged forty-five and older to all full-time male employees at firms with 1,000 or more employees soared from 22 percent in 1979 to 36 percent in 1998. The creation of an intrafirm structure clustered around older workers is the result of both demographic and economic changes. Broad demographic shifts have resulted in an aging population and a shrinking birth rate. Members of the baby boom generation—those born between 1947 and 1949 in Japan and employed en masse during the economic boom years of the 1960s and early 1970s— were over fifty by the late 1990s. Finally, the oil crisis curbed employment of succeeding generations.

Higher labor costs lead to a decline in optimal labor demand. However, since separation costs of firing existing employees are high, firms tend to concentrate on adjusting employment through reducing the number of young recruits. The other employment adjustment option that firms have available during times of poor business performance is that of enhancing labor mobility between firms, by means including transfers and reallocation. Until the mid-1990s, sufficient labor demand from small- and medium-sized firms enabled large firms with excess labor to adjust employment levels downward by transferring workers to smaller firms. However, the recession of the late 1990s, unlike previous recessions, has sub-

---

3. I can also observe the time series of turnover rates for new graduates by education level. The turnover rate is defined as the proportion of workers who changed jobs within three years of graduation. This statistic can be computed from the *Survey on Employment Insurance* conducted by the Ministry of Labor (1997). The turnover rate tended to rise during the 1990s. Almost 70 percent of junior high school graduates and half of high school graduates gave up their first job within three years. The turnover rate among college graduates has increased since 1992, and almost one-third of 1995 graduates have changed their first job. The concept of lifetime employment, working for a particular company from graduation until retirement, no longer has any meaning for many young people. On the other hand, the average number of years spent working at the same firm has continued to increase among employees aged fifty to fifty-nine. Long-term employment of older workers is still observable in Japan (Chuma 1997).

stantially reduced labor demand from even small- and medium-sized firms. Consequently, large firms have had no choice but to cut new employment of young people in order to reduce employment.

Declining employment opportunities for the young may be conceptualized in terms of a job displacement effect created by middle-aged and older workers displacing younger workers. In order to examine the job displacement effect more precisely, I focus on employment adjustment from the labor demand side. However, the unemployment rate may also be influenced by adjustments in labor supply. Therefore, in the next section I use a gross job creation and destruction framework to analyze changes in formal job opportunities.

Of course, a scarcity of full-time job openings for young people does not necessarily lead to an immediate fall in employment. If price is flexible enough to adjust downward in response to the change in demand, a certain level of supply is assured. The labor market for Japan's young people is, however, far from ideal. Under excess labor demand an upward wage adjustment is observed, such as a rise in the initial salary for newly hired employees. But when supply greatly exceeds demand, the downward adjustment of wages is limited (Ishikawa 2001, chap. 6). As a result, employment adjustment must occur in isolation from wage adjustment in firms' responses to excess labor supply.

The seniority-based wage system of Japanese firms is well known (Hashimoto and Raisian 1985). During the 1980s and early 1990s, the influence of years worked in a firm on earnings has gradually weakened, especially among older male college graduates in large firms. Their supply rapidly expanded due to population aging and growth in college enrollment. This led to a shortage of managerial positions and a decrease in the importance of seniority for wages and promotions (Genda 1998). Nevertheless, this decrease has been very slow, and the seniority-based wage schedule was maintained, at least in principle, during the 1990s. Figure 4.5 shows the relationship between the log of scheduled real monthly wages and average years worked in a firm for full-time males by education status.[4] For both high school and college graduates, the wage-tenure profile flattened in the 1980s due to a rise in youth wages, and hardly changed in the 1990s. As long as wage adjustment is slow there will be a quantity adjustment of employment, or a job displacement effect.

4.4 Gross Job Flows by Age of Employees

I examine gross job flows by age of employee in order to capture changes in labor demand across different age groups. Gross job flows are defined in the job creation and destruction literature as net changes in employment

---

4. Monthly scheduled wages in each year are deflated by a consumer price index equal to 100 in 1995.

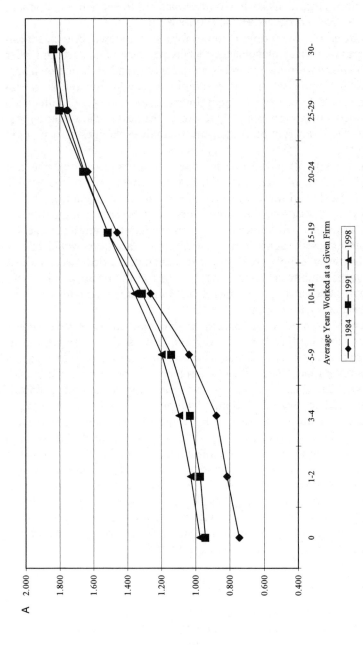

Fig. 4.5 Wage-tenure profile for full-time male workers: *A*, **College graduates;** *B*, **High school graduates**

Source: Ministry of Labor (1984, 1991, 1998).

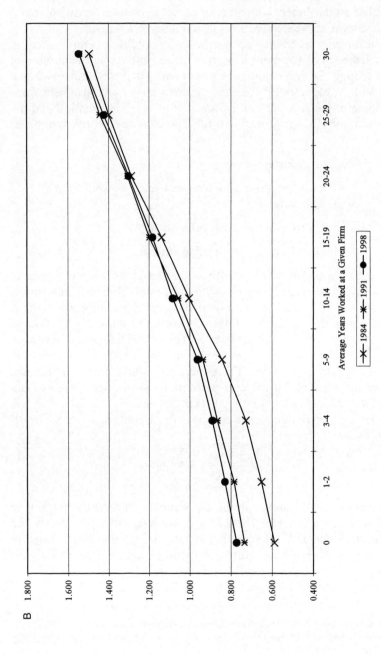

B

Average Years Worked at a Given Firm

—✕— 1984   —✱— 1991   —●— 1998

Fig. 4.5 (cont.)

opportunities at the establishment level (Davis, Haltiwanger, and Schuh 1996).[5] The establishment is an office or plant (*jigyosho* in Japanese) that is a physical location where business or production takes place.

Job turnover is based on a comparison of the stocks of employment in an establishment at two points in time. Let n_{ij0} and n_{ij1} be the number of regular employees who belong to age category j at establishment i in period 0 and 1, respectively.[6] Then job growth at the establishment for a given age group can be defined as $\Delta n_{ij} = n_{ij1} - n_{ij0}$. The creation and destruction of jobs for age group j at establishment i can be broken down as follows:

(1) Δn_{ij} = hires − separations

+ net workers flows across establishments within firms (*haichi-tenkan*)

+ net worker flows across firms (*shukko*)

+ inflows from $n_{ij-1,0}$ − outflows into $n_{ij+1,1}$

It is worth noting that job growth as defined in equation (1) includes movements between age categories within the establishment. Take, for example, a job filled by a twenty-nine-year-old employee. Suppose that in the following year this worker continues to work and there is no inflow of workers aged twenty-five to twenty-nine. Then one job for employees aged twenty-five to twenty-nine is destroyed, but one job for employees aged thirty to thirty-four is created. Therefore, even if there are no inflows and outflows at the establishment level, job destruction for age category j can occur if the proportion of older workers is growing.

The net job growth rate for age group j in the overall economy can be defined as follows:

(2)
$$\frac{\Delta n_j}{n_j} = \frac{\sum_i m_{i1} \cdot n_{ij1} - \sum_i m_{i0} \cdot n_{ij0}}{\sum_i m_{i0} \cdot n_{ij0}}$$

In equation (2), m_{i0} and m_{i1} represent sample establishment weights in period 0 and 1, respectively.[7] These weights are determined by industry and size of establishment. A difference between m_{i0} and m_{i1} suggests a change in the number of establishments through openings and closings between the periods.

Net job growth can be broken into

---

5. Job turnover measures the creation or disappearance of positions. Labor turnover, on the other hand, measures the movement of workers into and out of jobs (hires and separations, respectively; Davis and Haltiwanger 1999).

6. Establishments that open or close within a period are not sampled.

7. In the analysis of Davis, Haltiwanger, and Schuh the sample weights do not change during the ongoing panel's life (1996, 209).

(3) $$\Delta n_j = \sum_i m_{i0}(n_{ij1} - n_{ij0}) + \sum_i (m_{i1} - m_{i0}) \cdot n_{ij1}.$$

The first term on the right-hand side (RHS) of equation (3) represents the estimated net employment changes at establishments sampled in both periods. The second term on the RHS of equation (3) represents the estimated changes in employment due to changes in the number of establishments with n_{ij1} employees.

The net employment changes at establishments that are continuously sampled can be further broken down:

(4) $$\sum_i m_{i0}(n_{ij1} - n_{ij0}) = \sum_{n_{ij1} > n_{ij0}} m_{i0}(n_{ij1} - n_{ij0}) + \sum_{n_{ij1} < n_{ij0}} m_{i0}(n_{ij1} - n_{ij0})$$

The first term on the RHS of equation (4) represents estimated gross job gains at establishments that are expanding employment in age category j. The second term represents estimated gross job losses at establishments that are reducing employment.

Similarly, employment changes due to changes in the number of establishments can also be further decomposed:

(5) $$\sum_i (m_{i1} - m_{i0}) \cdot n_{ij1} = \sum_{m_{i1} > m_{i0}} (m_{i1} - m_{i0}) \cdot n_{ij1} + \sum_{m_{i1} < m_{i0}} (m_{i1} - m_{i0}) \cdot n_{ij1}$$

The first term on the RHS of equation (5) represents estimated gross job gains due to an increase in the number of establishments. The second term represents estimated gross job losses due to a decrease in the number of establishments.

I examine the reasons behind changes in employment opportunities by employee age category using the above equations. I calculate an establishment's annual change in net employment using the *Employment Trend Survey* (ETS; 1993–1998). The ETS is an establishment survey conducted by the Ministry of Labor in Japan at the end of June and December in every year. It records changes in employment at private establishments with at least five employees.[8]

The ETS records the age composition of employees at the sampled establishments in its annual June survey. The ETS is not itself a panel, but it can be made into one using the census code for each establishment. These codes enable us to connect records collected on the same establishment in multiple ETS surveys. The result is a panel data set following 4,935 private establishments with thirty or more employees from 1996 and 1998.[9] Data showing yearly employee movements by age category for a given establishment enable us to capture job flows using the foregoing equations.

8. The ETS records changes in employment at establishments in all industries except agriculture, forestry, and fishing.
9. Establishments that did not respond to the question on the total number of regular employees in either the 1996 or 1998 surveys are excluded.

4.5 Basic Results

Table 4.2 shows calculated gross job flows from 1996 to 1998, by age category. The first row shows the net job growth rates defined by equation (2). Workers aged fifteen to nineteen, twenty to twenty-four, forty to forty-four, and forty-five to forty-nine all experienced negative job growth rates. The negative job growth was especially large for twenty- to twenty-four-year-olds.

It is important to note, however, that the job growth rate by age group includes movements across the age categories. In fact, most members of the first Japanese baby boom generation, born between 1947 and 1949, moved from the forty-five- to forty-nine-year-old age category to the fifty- to fifty-four-year-old age category in the period between 1996 and 1998. This diminished employment opportunities for forty-five- to forty-nine-year-olds. A similar influence may also have affected job opportunities for twenty- to twenty-four-year-olds because the second baby boom generation (born between 1971 and 1973) moved from the twenty- to twenty-four-year-old age group to the twenty-five- to twenty-nine-year-old age group during the sample period. To control for this, I simply subtract the labor force growth rate from the net job growth rate to compute the per capita job growth rate.[10]

The third column shows that twenty- to twenty-four-year-old employees have the lowest per capita job growth rate. While their labor force growth rate decreased 6.27 percent due to the delayed workforce entry of the second baby boom generation, their per capita job growth rate decreased by 8.35 percent. Negative per capita job growth rates are observed for all groups under age thirty-five.

By contrast, per capita job growth rates are still positive for older employees, such as those aged fifty to fifty-nine. As the first baby boomers moved into the fifty- to fifty-four-year-old category, the labor force growth rate of this category jumped to 9.77 percent. The overall job availability increased by 13.44 percent, yielding a per capita job growth rate of 3.67 percent. This figure indicates that the first baby boomers have more job security at fifty to fifty-four years of age than the previous generation had at that age. Although job growth rates for forty- to forty-four-year-old and forty-five- to forty-nine-year-old employees are negative, labor force growth rates also declined for these groups, so their per capita job growth rates are positive. Consequently, the per capita number of jobs increased for employees aged thirty-five to sixty-four. The only employees who experienced a decrease in per capita job opportunities were those under thirty-five or sixty-five and older.

---

10. The data on labor force growth rate come from the *Annual Report on the Labor Force Survey,* conducted by the Statistics Bureau, Management and Coordination Agency (1968–2001).

Table 4.2 Gross Job Flows in Private Establishments with Thirty or More Employees, 1996–1998

	Total	Age										
		15–19	20–24	25–29	30–34	35–39	40–44	45–49	50–54	55–59	60–64	65+
i. Job growth rate	1.23	−4.75	−14.61	2.41	5.23	4.17	−4.65	−1.79	13.44	12.73	5.18	5.41
ii. Labor force growth rate	1.22	−2.08	−6.27	5.39	5.71	2.77	−6.64	−6.62	9.77	6.25	3.29	6.59
iii. Per capita job growth rate	0.01	−2.66	−8.35	−2.98	−0.48	1.40	1.99	4.82	3.67	6.48	1.89	−1.19
Decomposition of i (= iv + v)												
iv. At continuing establishments	−1.91	−8.00	−16.46	0.48	2.76	1.47	−7.28	−5.99	7.80	8.37	2.84	0.13
v. Through demographic changes	3.14	3.26	1.84	1.93	2.47	2.70	2.63	4.19	5.63	4.35	2.34	5.27
Decomposition of iv (= vi + vii)												
vi. At expanding establishments	5.52	33.90	9.73	15.64	17.38	16.51	13.00	11.53	20.08	22.15	26.49	26.45
vii. At contributing establishments	−7.43	−41.90	−26.19	−15.16	−14.62	−15.04	−20.28	−17.52	−12.28	−13.78	−23.64	−26.31
Decomposition of v (= viii + ix)												
viii. Increases in establishments	11.90	9.64	9.26	11.35	12.69	12.04	10.94	12.09	14.75	13.30	12.15	13.98
ix. Decreases in establishments	−8.76	−6.38	−7.42	−9.42	−10.22	−9.34	−8.31	−7.90	−9.12	−8.94	−9.81	−8.71

Decomposing net job growth reveals the main influences on employment opportunities. Equation (3) separates net job flows into flows at continuing establishments and flows due to changes in the number of establishments. I find that the greatest decline in jobs for young employees occurred in continuing establishments, where the number of jobs decreased by 16.46 percent for twenty- to twenty-four-year-olds from 1996 to 1998. During the same period, the number of jobs decreased by 6 to 7 percent for forty- to forty-nine-year-olds and increased by 7 to 8 percent for fifty- to fifty-nine-year-olds. Positive job growth arising from changes in the number of establishments was spread unevenly across age categories. It was less than 2 percent for twenty- to twenty-nine-year-olds, but 4 to 6 percent for fifty- to fifty-nine-year-olds. Therefore, the increase in employment opportunities for those aged fifty to fifty-nine was due to a combination of increasing employment at continuing establishments and an increase in the number of establishments with large numbers of older employees.

According to equation (4), net job growth at continuing establishments may be further subdivided into gross job gains and losses. The gross rate of job gain relative to initial employment is 9.73 percent for twenty- to twenty-four-year-olds, which is substantially lower than that of other age categories. Further, job loss rates at continuing establishments are relatively high for those aged fifteen to nineteen, twenty to twenty-four, and sixty-five and over. The rates of gross job gains and losses caused by changes in the number of establishments (equation [5]) look relatively similar across age groups when compared to the trends for continuing establishments. The rate of job gain from increases in the number of establishments is still relatively low for those under twenty-five, however, and much higher for those aged fifty to fifty-nine.

To quantify the extent to which job opportunities declined during the 1996 to 1998 recession, I create a comparable ETS panel data set for the 1993–1995 period. Figure 4.6 compares per capita job growth rates during 1993–1995 and 1996–1998. In the former period, the per capita job growth rate was lowest for fifteen- to nineteen-year-old employees. The negative rate of 4.7 percent for those aged twenty to twenty-four means that per capita job opportunities drastically declined for this age group in the second half of the 1990s. The figure also shows that, although negative per capita job growth affected only those aged fifteen to twenty-four in the mid-1990s, later on the twenty-five- to thirty-four-year-old and sixty-five and over age categories were also affected.

From these results, we see that job opportunities for younger employees in the 1990s have significantly declined in several areas, particularly for those aged twenty to twenty-four. However, we should remember that these job growth changes were computed for establishments with thirty or more employees. The net employment growth rate over the same period in firms

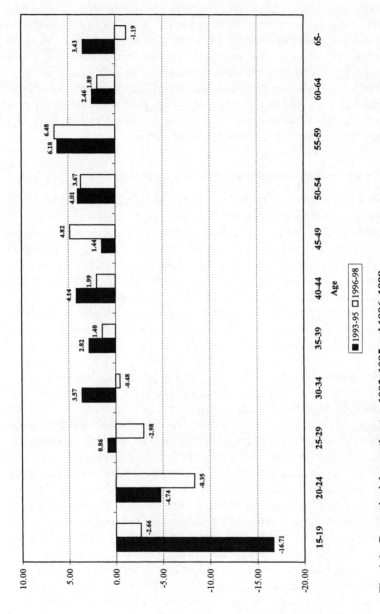

Fig. 4.6 Per capita job growth rates, 1993–1995 and 1996–1998
Source: Ministry of Labor (1993–1998).

with less than thirty employees, computed from the *Labor Force Survey,* was 4.5 percent for employees aged twenty to twenty-four. This was lower than their labor force growth rate. Therefore, per capita job opportunities for young employees were reduced across all firms. From the same data, I also compute the growth rate of self-employed and family workers in nonagricultural industries in that period to be –9.5 percent for twenty- to twenty-four-year-olds. On the other hand, their unemployment rate grew by 8.9 percent, and the growth in their labor force nonparticipation rate was –4.0 percent. Declines in employment opportunities for youth were therefore directly linked to an increase in unemployment rather than an increase in labor force nonparticipation or self-employment.

4.6   Results by Employment Status, Industry, and Firm Size

Table 4.3 presents job growth rates and grow rate decompositions by full-time and part-time employment status. The decline in the number of jobs available to those aged twenty to twenty-four was mainly the result of a 17.99 percent reduction in full-time employment opportunities at continuing establishments between 1996 and 1998. For twenty- to twenty-four-year-old workers, only part-time job opportunities increased in this period. In most cases, only part-time jobs are available to young workers when they attempt to find jobs. In contrast, full-time job opportunities for those aged fifty to fifty-four and fifty-five to fifty-nine increased because of job growth at continuing establishments and changes in the number of firms.

These results are consistent with full-time job displacement of young workers by middle-aged and older workers. A decrease in the number of part-time jobs available to thirty-five- to thirty-nine-year-old and forty- to forty-four-year-old workers may indicate that the decline in full-time job opportunities for young workers is forcing them to enter the part-time job market, thus depriving middle-aged workers of part-time jobs.

Table 4.4 shows job growth rates by industry and firm size for younger (fifteen- to nineteen-year-old and twenty- to twenty-four-year-old) and older (fifty- to fifty-four-year-old and fifty-five- to fifty-nine-year-old) workers. The job growth rates for the young were negative in all industries except the service industry. On the other hand, the job growth rates for the older group were positive in most industries. In particular, job opportunities in the manufacturing, finance, and insurance industries increased for older workers, whereas younger workers lost jobs in these industries.

Regardless of firm size, the job growth rate for twenty- to twenty-four-year-olds was negative. It was lowest in large firms with 1,000 or more employees. Conversely, the number of jobs available to those aged fifty to fifty-four and fifty-five to fifty-nine increased in large firms. The displacement effect seems to be quite strong in large firms.

Table 4.3   Job Growth Rates and Growth Rate Decompositions, 1996–1998

						Age						
	Total	15–19	20–24	25–29	30–34	35–39	40–44	45–49	50–54	55–59	60–64	65+
Full-time job growth rate	0.57	–9.24	–16.03	2.41	5.36	5.31	–4.06	–3.05	12.02	11.97	4.40	1.73
At continuing establishments	–2.93	–13.37	–17.99	0.46	2.55	2.04	–7.42	–7.53	6.32	7.02	–0.69	–4.70
Through demographic changes	3.50	4.13	1.96	1.94	2.81	3.27	3.35	4.48	5.70	4.95	5.09	6.42
Part-time job growth rate	7.01	19.66	10.48	2.44	3.31	–5.91	–8.47	6.10	23.60	18.78	7.99	16.19
At continuing establishments	7.10	21.17	10.69	0.82	5.73	–3.62	–6.41	3.72	18.49	19.22	15.52	14.30
Through demographic changes	–0.09	–1.51	–0.21	1.62	–2.42	–2.29	–2.06	2.37	5.10	–0.44	–7.53	1.88

Table 4.4   Job Growth Rates by Industry and Firm Size, 1996–1998

	Total	Age 15–19	20–24	50–54	55–59
Industry					
Mining	−8.24	−41.84	−30.95	8.57	−17.34
Construction	−2.36	−28.78	−15.52	3.98	0.49
Manufacturing	0.39	−4.18	−19.73	11.42	16.73
Electricity gas, heat, and water supply	7.95	−0.58	−5.05	−0.82	31.61
Transportation and communication	7.99	7.63	−8.31	26.56	8.34
Wholesale, retail trade, and restaurants	−10.01	−12.03	−22.37	8.62	5.77
Finance and insurance	3.31	41.07	−18.27	15.65	11.26
Real estate	13.89	37.36	−1.80	41.62	7.27
Services	8.57	5.52	0.89	15.62	15.46
Firm size (employees)					
1,000 or more	−0.07	0.45	−22.87	17.47	16.53
300–999	−1.27	−15.39	−13.85	5.44	7.50
100–299	2.06	3.21	−4.99	12.04	7.88
30–99	4.61	−10.73	−11.14	14.48	16.46

Long economic recessions and the progressive aging of the Japanese society have not necessarily reduced employment opportunities for middle-aged and older employees. The foregoing empirical results suggest instead that employment adjustment due to decreased labor demand has mainly affected younger workers in the late 1990s.

4.7   Determinants of Labor Flows in Large Establishments

The previous section showed that employment opportunities for young workers declined significantly in large firms. This is consistent with a displacement effect in which large firms with graying workforces decrease youth employment in order to be able to retain large numbers of middle-aged and older employees. In this section, I examine whether this effect exists in large establishments.

The ETS attempts to survey all large establishments (500 or more employees) every year.[11] More than 70 percent of these belong to firms with 1,000 or more workers. The ETS breaks down establishment-level employment changes into worker inflows and outflows, as shown in equation (1). This formula separately captures hirings, separations, worker movements across establishments within a firm (*haichi-tenkan*), and worker flows across different firms (*shukko*). We can estimate what determined the rates

11. According to the *Employment Maintenance Survey* conducted by the Statistics Bureau, there were 4,297 large-sized private establishments with 500 or more employees in Japan in 1994. In 1997, 2,904 large establishments were sampled in the ETS, or 67.6 percent of all these establishments.

of these annual worker flows in 1997 relative to the initial number of employees at the beginning of the year. I use human resource stock variables measured at the end of June 1997 as explanatory variables in the regression analysis. They include the ratios of middle-aged and older employees (forty-five and older), management and clerical workers, female employees, part-time employees, and employees contracted as *shukko*. All of these ratios are computed relative to the existing total number of employees in the establishment. One-digit industry dummies, a firm-size dummy, and a metropolitan-area dummy are also included as explanatory variables.[12]

I concentrate on large establishments in order to rule out an endogenous relationship between my labor-flow and labor-stock variables. I examine the effect of characteristics of the labor stock, especially the ratio of midlevel and senior workers, on labor inflows and outflows. Annual labor flows may affect the stock ratios in small and medium-sized establishments, where the human resource stock is small. If so, the flow and stock variables are mutually endogenous, and an ordinary regression may be seriously biased. Therefore, I limit my study to large establishments with large labor stocks that are mostly independent of current annual flows.

The forty-five or older ratio represents three aspects of establishment characteristics. First, a high ratio implies that the establishment has had high employment levels in the past. A firm usually has a higher ratio of employees forty-five or older in the 1990s because it hired large numbers of young workers in the rapid-growth era of the 1960s and early 1970s. These establishments with graying workforces face higher labor costs under seniority-based compensation schemes. Second, this high ratio also represents a sustained reduction in the hiring of young workers in the later period of slowed growth, a negative consequence of a long-term economic shock to labor demand.[13] Third, the high ratio of middle-aged and older workers presents difficulties for establishments wishing to deploy workers. In other words, it may be difficult to reduce the number of existing older employees in an establishment through separations, *haichi-tenkan,* or *shukko.* All three of these aspects might generate a displacement effect, decreasing the number of young workers.

Table 4.5 presents the regression results. The most important point is that the effect of the ratio of workers aged forty-five or older on any kind of inflow rate is always negative and statistically significant. As the ratio

12. The metropolitan area dummy equals one if the firm is located in Tokyo, Osaka, Aichi, or Kanagawa. These metropolitan areas host more than 50 percent of all the establishments. The firm size dummy equals one if the establishment is a middle-sized firm with 500 to 999 employees, and zero if it is a large firm with 1,000 employees or more. Manufacturing is the excluded industry dummy. Firms in the mining and real estate industries are excluded from the analysis because of their small sample sizes.

13. Genda (2001) shows that the persistence of job destruction is preserved in establishments with a higher proportion of graying workers, using the method of Davis, Haltiwanger, and Schuh (1996).

Table 4.5 Regression Estimates of Hiring and Separation Rates, 1997

	Hiring Rate				Separation Rate			
	Full-Time	Part-Time	Shukko	Haich-Tenkan	Full-Time	Part-Time	Shukko	Haich-Tenkan
Ratio of employees 45 or older	-0.0510	-0.0165	-0.0049	-0.0529	-0.0310	-0.0100	-0.0033	-0.0147
	(-5.64)	(-4.07)	(-4.17)	(-2.80)	(-1.76)	(-2.85)	(-3.09)	(-1.88)
Management and clerical worker ratio	-0.0337	-0.0094	0.0000	0.1287	0.0132	-0.0102	-0.0003	0.0941
	(-5.33)	(-3.30)	(0.02)	(9.71)	(1.07)	(-4.13)	(-0.49)	(17.07)
Female ratio	0.0718	-0.0124	-0.0014	-0.0329	0.0398	-0.0082	-0.0018	-0.0155
	(8.66)	(-3.35)	(-1.31)	(-1.89)	(2.46)	(-2.55)	(-1.90)	(-2.15)
Part-time ratio	-0.0656	0.3281	0.0013	0.0081	-0.0519	0.2836	0.0025	-0.0142
	(-5.11)	(56.98)	(0.78)	(0.30)	(-2.08)	(56.43)	(1.65)	(-1.27)
Shukko ratio	-0.0103	-0.0119	0.1502	-0.1392	-0.1070	-0.0051	0.1660	-0.1080
	(-0.29)	(-0.75)	(32.03)	(-1.87)	(-1.54)	(-0.36)	(39.48)	(-3.48)
500–999 employees dummy	0.0077	-0.0003	0.0006	-0.0281	0.0080	0.0005	0.0005	-0.0268
	(2.47)	(-0.25)	(1.47)	(-4.31)	(1.31)	(0.47)	(1.37)	(-9.88)
Major metropolitan area dummy	0.0060	0.0027	0.0011	0.0023	0.0124	0.0024	0.0008	0.0002
	(2.08)	(2.15)	(3.13)	(0.39)	(2.22)	(2.17)	(2.63)	(0.08)
Construction dummy	0.0025	0.0039	-0.0007	0.0025	-0.0109	0.0031	-0.0009	0.0127
	(0.35)	(1.23)	(-0.82)	(0.16)	(-0.78)	(1.12)	(-1.08)	(2.04)
Electricity, gas, heat, and water supply dummy	-0.0001	0.0032	-0.0014	0.0612	-0.0361	0.0035	-0.0019	0.0905
	(-0.005)	(0.53)	(-0.82)	(2.16)	(-1.37)	(0.66)	(-1.19)	(7.68)
Transportation and communication dummy	0.0361	0.0067	0.0002	0.1310	0.0776	0.0035	0.0010	0.0954
	(5.97)	(2.48)	(0.26)	(10.33)	(6.59)	(1.49)	(1.53)	(18.09)
Wholesale, retail trade, and restaurants dummy	-0.0035	0.0074	-0.0006	-0.0066	0.0061	0.0031	-0.0005	0.0007
	(-0.63)	(2.99)	(-0.55)	(-0.57)	(0.56)	(1.43)	(-0.82)	(0.15)
Finance and insurance dummy	0.0115	0.0085	-0.0006	0.0093	0.0026	0.0075	-0.0007	0.0203
	(1.38)	(2.28)	(-0.55)	(0.53)	(0.16)	(2.30)	(-0.73)	(2.80)
Services dummy	0.0265	0.0062	-0.0005	0.0055	0.0164	0.0050	0.0003	0.0029
	(6.08)	(3.18)	(-0.94)	(0.61)	(1.93)	(2.93)	(0.76)	(0.77)
Constant	0.0666	0.0077	0.0024	0.0286	0.0672	0.0057	0.0019	0.0237
	(14.64)	(3.77)	(4.06)	(3.00)	(7.58)	(3.20)	(3.70)	(5.98)
N	2,904	2,904	2,904	2,904	2,904	2,904	2,904	2,904
F-statistic	33.09	355.74	85.17	29.29	7.15	353.66	127.40	105.41
Adj. R^2	0.125	0.613	0.273	0.112	0.026	0.612	0.361	0.318

Notes: t-values are in parentheses. Shukko is transfers and returns across firms. Haich-tenkan is transfers across establishments within a firm.

of middle-aged and older employees increases, the hiring of full-time and part-time workers, as well as inflows through *shukko* and *haichi-tenkan,* is decreased relative to initial employment. At the same time, labor outflows are also restrained, and separation rates are significantly lowered. Consequently, there is less labor turnover at establishments with a larger share of older employees. This is consistent with a displacement effect.

Other findings show that the hiring rate of full-time workers is significantly lower at large firms (1,000 or more employees) with high shares of male white-collar employees. Therefore, I find that the hiring of full-time workers is further restricted when middle-aged and older workers in large firms are mostly white-collar males. On the other hand, table 4.5 shows that there is no tendency toward high separation rates in such firms. These findings directly contradict claims of job insecurity among middle-aged and older white-collar workers. Hirings and separations of part-time and full-time workers fall with the ratio of employees forty-five and older. There is almost no evidence that establishments with a larger number of graying workers hire part-time workers to replace decreasing numbers of full-time workers. No such simple relationship of substitutability between full-time and part-time workers is observed.

4.8   Determinants of the Hiring of New Graduates

Next, I focus on employees who graduated from school and entered the full-time job market for the first time in 1996.[14] Table 4.6 shows the results. The hiring rate of new graduates relative to the initial number of employees is significantly lower at establishments with a higher share of employees aged forty-five or older. In particular, high school graduates had greater difficulty finding full-time jobs in large establishments with a higher share of older employees. There were also fewer college graduates recruited by these establishments. Those with nonscientific majors (*bunkei* in Japanese) were least likely to be hired. The regression model can be applied to data from 1991 to 1996, and the negative and significant coefficient on the middle-aged and older employee ratio is observed in every year. In this sense, the depressed rate of new-graduate hiring observed throughout the 1990s in establishments with graying workforces is not a temporary phenomenon, but a long-term problem.

The previous regression analysis presumes that labor flows have little effect on the current composition of the labor stock, such as the forty-five or older ratio in large establishments. It is possible, however, that substantial labor flows would change this composition. In addition, some establishments with a greater number of middle-aged and older employees may face serious labor supply constraints. Due to regional or industry conditions, they may experience a shortage of young job applicants. Then the

14. There are no questions in the ETS relating to the hiring of new graduates after 1996.

Table 4.6   Regression Estimates of the Ratio of New Graduates to Initial Employees, 1996

	All New Graduates	High School Graduates	Special School Graduates	Junior College Graduates	College Graduates	University Graduates (Non-Science)	University Graduates (Science)
Ratio of employees 45 or older	-0.0276	-0.0141	-0.0024	-0.0021	-0.0088	-0.0051	-0.0037
	(-4.12)	(-4.20)	(-1.61)	(-1.35)	(-2.43)	(-2.12)	(-1.95)
Management and clerical worker ratio	0.0618	0.0097	-0.0017	0.0084	0.0453	0.0247	0.0206
	(12.75)	(3.99)	(-1.59)	(7.26)	(17.19)	(14.17)	(14.85)
Female ratio	0.0305	-0.0021	0.0249	0.0068	0.0008	-0.0036	0.0044
	(4.97)	(-0.70)	(18.30)	(4.64)	(0.26)	(-1.63)	(2.54)
Part-time ratio	-0.0340	0.0046	-0.0258	-0.0071	-0.0056	-0.0002	-0.0053
	(-3.58)	(0.98)	(-12.26)	(-3.14)	(-1.09)	(-0.06)	(-1.98)
Shukko ratio	-0.0085	0.0088	-0.0128	-0.0027	-0.0017	-0.0064	0.0047
	(-0.40)	(0.84)	(-2.76)	(-0.55)	(-0.15)	(-0.86)	(0.78)
500–999 employees dummy	0.0019	0.0036	-0.0001	-0.0009	-0.0013	-0.0001	-0.0011
	(0.86)	(3.11)	(-0.39)	(-0.17)	(-1.05)	(-0.23)	(-1.71)
Major metropolitan area dummy	0.0026	-0.0007	0.0003	-0.0006	0.0035	0.0005	0.0030
	(1.22)	(-0.65)	(0.75)	(-1.21)	(3.08)	(0.72)	(4.94)
Construction dummy	0.0143	-0.0033	0.0017	0.0006	0.0152	0.0037	0.0114
	(2.76)	(-1.26)	(1.47)	(0.54)	(5.40)	(2.03)	(7.70)
Electricity, gas, heat, and water supply dummy	0.0263	0.0187	0.0011	0.0058	0.0005	-0.0013	0.0019
	(2.78)	(3.94)	(0.55)	(2.57)	(0.10)	(-0.40)	(0.70)
Transportation and communication dummy	-0.0007	0.0020	0.0028	0.0011	-0.0066	-0.0011	-0.0055
	(-0.15)	(0.91)	(2.79)	(1.01)	(-2.72)	(-0.67)	(-4.31)
Wholesale, retail trade, and restaurants dummy	-0.0055	-0.0050	-0.0035	0.0013	0.0016	0.0084	-0.0068
	(-1.40)	(-2.51)	(-3.98)	(1.38)	(0.75)	(5.94)	(-6.02)
Finance and insurance dummy	0.0301	-0.0112	-0.0020	0.0272	0.0160	0.0318	-0.0157
	(4.90)	(-3.64)	(-1.49)	(18.45)	(4.82)	(14.42)	(-8.94)
Services dummy	0.0110	-0.0052	0.0104	0.0031	0.0029	0.0040	-0.0010
	(3.51)	(-3.23)	(14.59)	(4.00)	(1.70)	(3.46)	(-1.10)
Constant	0.0077	0.0118	-0.0023	-0.0003	-0.0014	-0.0010	-0.0003
	(2.34)	(7.12)	(-3.14)	(-0.44)	(-0.78)	(-0.85)	(-0.41)
N	2,984	2,984	2,984	2,984	2,984	2,984	2,984
F-statistic	40.45	6.56	101.49	64.07	58.23	73.73	37.45
Adj. R^2	0.146	0.0236	0.304	0.215	0.199	0.240	0.137

*Notes: t-*values are in parentheses. "All New Graduates" does not include employees who had graduated from junior high school.

hiring rate of new graduates might be small in spite of a strong demand for young workers in these establishments.

In order to account for these issues, the labor demand for, instead of the actual hiring of, new graduates is estimated in an alternative model. The dependent variable is the ratio of job openings for new graduates in the upcoming year, rather than the actual number hired, to the initial number of employees. The coefficients on the labor stock variables are not affected in this specification, so labor demand is effectively independent of labor supply constraints.

All of the independent variables were measured at the end of June 1996. The dependent variable is calculated using job openings for workers who graduated in March 1997. Determinants of labor demand for the establishments, including those with no job openings, were estimated using a tobit model. Establishments that had not yet determined their number of job openings were eliminated. The results are shown in table 4.7. The estimated coefficient on the ratio of workers forty-five or older is negative and significant at each education level. Thus, I can confirm that establishments with more middle-aged and older workers have decreased their labor demand for new graduates.

4.9 Discussion

What is the background behind such a strong displacement effect in Japan? Several factors explain the slow pace of employment adjustment of middle-aged and older workers.

First, dismissals are considerably restricted in Japan. Unlike most European countries, restraints on dismissals are imposed by case law, not legislation. Employers have a judiciary duty either to verify just cause for dismissals or to attempt alternative measures to avoid them. Only when all four of the following reasonable causes for dismissal are satisfied are dismissals considered fair and allowable in court: (a) urgent business reasons for personnel reduction, such as closing establishments; (b) necessity of dismissals for reducing staff, in addition to depressing new hiring, when there is no possibility of *haichi-tenkan* and *shukko;* (c) the criteria for selecting staff for dismissal are reasonable; and (d) procedures such as notifying employees in advance and consulting trade union or employee representatives are reasonably followed.

The dismissal case law, which protects regular workers from dismissal in Japan, places the most stringent restrictions on dismissals among the advanced countries. The Organization for Economic Co-operation and Development (OECD) *Employment Outlook* 1999 gives the OECD ranking by country in terms of the regulation of employment protection. Japan, Norway, and Portugal stand out as offering the highest employment protection, as measured by the summary indicator "difficulty of dismissal," while

Table 4.7   Tobit Estimates of Job Openings for March 1997 New Graduates, or *Shinsotsu-kyujin*.

	High School Graduates	Special School Graduates	Junior College Graduates	College Graduates	University Graduates (Non-Science)	University Graduates (Science)
Ratio of employees 45 or older	-0.0300	-0.0367	-0.0210	-0.0447	-0.0377	-0.0268
	(-4.71)	(-2.91)	(-3.08)	(-3.16)	(-3.26)	(-3.23)
Management and clerical worker ratio	0.0102	0.0189	0.0245	0.0895	0.0536	0.0495
	(1.89)	(2.13)	(5.53)	(9.73)	(7.81)	(9.23)
Female ratio	-0.0055	0.0213	-0.0032	-0.0145	-0.0268	0.0038
	(-0.79)	(1.83)	(-0.46)	(-0.99)	(-2.21)	(0.44)
Part-time ratio	0.0005	-0.0498	-0.0081	-0.0082	0.0099	-0.0229
	(0.05)	(-2.94)	(-0.79)	(-0.38)	(0.60)	(-1.69)
Shukko ratio	0.0065	-0.0623	-0.0347	-0.0337	-0.0931	-0.0078
	(0.32)	(-1.43)	(-1.44)	(-0.91)	(-2.06)	(-0.38)
500–999 employees dummy	0.0048	-0.0055	-0.0013	-0.0005	0.0039	-0.0018
	(2.30)	(-1.23)	(-0.62)	(-0.01)	(1.13)	(-0.76)
Major metropolitan area dummy	0.0027	0.0092	0.0014	0.0062	0.0022	0.0073
	(1.37)	(2.21)	(0.74)	(1.45)	(0.64)	(2.90)
Construction dummy	0.0023	0.0100	-0.0017	0.0150	0.0002	0.0158
	(0.38)	(1.12)	(-0.35)	(1.73)	(0.64)	(3.31)
Electricity, gas, heat, and water supply dummy	0.0331	0.0083	0.0050	-0.0018	-0.0007	-0.0024
	(3.87)	(0.45)	(0.72)	(-0.09)	(-0.05)	(-0.22)
Transportation and communication dummy	0.0208	0.0165	0.0095	-0.0038	0.0024	-0.0096
	(3.67)	(1.52)	(1.58)	(-0.30)	(0.27)	(-1.15)
Wholesale, retail trade, and restaurants dummy	-0.0042	-0.0117	0.0076	0.0106	0.0255	-0.0150
	(-0.97)	(-1.43)	(2.28)	(1.45)	(4.66)	(-3.22)
Finance and insurance dummy	-0.0154	-0.0104	0.0312	-0.0129	0.0208	-0.0374
	(-1.85)	(-0.88)	(6.09)	(-1.19)	(2.65)	(-5.57)
Services dummy	-0.0101	0.0287	0.0060	0.0067	0.0135	-0.0013
	(-2.52)	(5.16)	(1.82)	(1.02)	(2.56)	(-0.33)
Constant	0.0191	-0.0151	-0.0007	-0.0043	-0.0043	-0.0022
	(5.87)	(-2.42)	(-0.22)	(-0.60)	(-0.73)	(-0.54)
N	1,095	403	731	933	783	856
LR Chi² (13)	78.68	86.65	173.15	174.52	168.73	176.55
Prob > Chi²	0.0000	0.0000	0.0000	0.0000	0.0000	0.0000
Pseudo R^2	-0.0246	-0.2256	-0.0917	-0.1120	-0.1105	-0.0850

Notes: t-values are in parentheses. The dependent variables are measured relative to the number of employees working at the beginning of 1996. 237 firms reported no demand for March 1997 new graduates and were included in the regression as zero values of the dependent variable.

the United States and the United Kingdom offer the lowest level of protection (OECD 1999, 58).[15]

This strong protection of employed workers results in most employment being adjusted through changes in the hiring of young workers, who consequently face a change in labor demand. Although labor costs rise with the age of an employee, employers cannot adjust existing employment until after the mandatory retirement of these employees. Therefore, I predict that depressed hiring of young workers in Japan will continue until most of the first baby boomers, born between 1947 and 1949, reach the mandatory retirement age near 2010.

New legislation that modifies current case law, not deregulation of enacted laws, will be required to relax the social norms concerning dismissals that were established in the rapid-growth era. At present, however, such legislation is not being considered (Araki 1997). However, the modification is necessary, because it would allow employers suffering a business downturn to freely adjust large numbers of middle-aged and older employees.

It is not only legal restraints that raise the cost of dismissal for Japanese firms, but also economic rationalizations. A distinctly Japanese labor practice is to give large proportions of workers a wide range of problem-solving skills through on-the-job training (Koike 1988). Although this is common for white-collar employees both in Japan and in other developed countries, Japan is the only country in which blue-collar workers in large firms also accumulate a wide variety of skills. As a result, most middle-aged and older employees of large firms have acquired both skills and experience. This accumulated skill system encourages employers to retain experienced employees, in whom they have sunk a specific human capital investment, when facing a business downturn.

Further, "reputation effects," or fears that large-scale employment adjustment might lower a firm's social reputation to the detriment of the firm's future ability to find competent labor, are a strong constraint on Japanese firms. Consequently, it is rational from an economic point of view for firms to keep current workers in their jobs, in spite of rising labor costs.

Labor demand of large firms, whose jobs traditionally come with opportunities for intensive skill accumulation, declined in the 1990s. Youth entry into these large firms is decreasing, resulting in a smaller proportion of young workers' being able to secure jobs with long-term employment prospects. This may lead to a smaller proportion of employees' having a wide range of problem-solving skills than in the past.

4.10   Conclusion

Young workers are more likely than middle-aged and older workers to have difficulty finding full-time jobs in the aging Japanese society. How-

15. For details of the ranking procedures, see chapter 2 in OECD (1999).

ever, the serious decline in youth employment in Japan has never been properly addressed. In contrast, many labor policies intended to increase the job opportunities of middle-aged and older employees have been enacted, although the number of job openings for this group has historically been relatively stable. Case law in Japan, which severely restricts dismissals, also decreases the chances for the young to find jobs offering long-term skill accumulation.

An increase in youth joblessness may cause social problems in Japan. The youth crime rate is closely linked to labor market conditions (Ohtake and Okamura 2000). The failure to transfer skills from older generations to younger generations might seriously affect future productivity in the Japanese economy.

Because of the declining birthrate, a permanent shortage of young workers has been predicted. However, the decline in youth labor demand has been much more drastic than the slow decrease in labor supply. Declining youth employment has been due not to a labor supply shock, but to a labor demand shock. Moreover, that demand shock is not temporary, but persistent.

The movement to prohibit mandatory retirement, extending employment up to age sixty-five, will certainly accelerate in the near future. Then job opportunities for youth will further decrease without a compensatory readjustment of wages, revision of the legal criteria relating to dismissals, or increase in the number of young and middle-aged self-employed workers.[16] In order to pursue both efficiency and equity in the labor market, it is important to create a market structure that provides equal opportunities for skill accumulation and career development, regardless of age.

References

Araki, Takashi. 1997. Changing Japanese labor law in light of deregulation drives: A comparative analysis. *Japan Labor Bulletin* 36 (5): 5–10.
Blanchflower, David G., and Richard B. Freeman. 2000. *Youth employment and joblessness in advanced countries.* Chicago: University of Chicago Press.
Chuma, Hiroyuki. 1997. Keizai Kankyo no Henka to Chu-konenso no Choki-kinzokuka (The changes in economic circumstances and tendency of long-term employment among middle-aged and older workers). In *Koyo Kanko no Henka to Josei Rodo,* ed. H. Chuma and T. Suruga, 47–82. Tokyo: Tokyo University Press.
Davis, Steven J., and John C. Haltiwanger. 1999. Gross job flows. In *Handbook of*

16. Japan is one of the few advanced countries in which the number of self-employed, nonagricultural workers decreased in the 1980s and 1990s. The decline in self-employment was particularly large for the middle-aged. There were 1.12 million forty- to forty-four-year-old self-employed workers in 1991, but only 0.56 million in 1998.

labor economics, vol. 3B, ed. Orley C. Ashenfelter and David Card, 2711–805. Amsterdam: Elsevier.

Davis, Steven J., John C. Haltiwanger, and Scott Schuh. 1996. *Job creation and destruction.* Cambridge: MIT Press.

Genda, Yuji. 1998. Japan: Wage differentials and changes since the 1980s. In *Wage differentials: An international comparison,* ed. T. Tachibanaki, 35–71. London: Macmillan.

———. 2001. *Uncertainty and jobs.* Tokyo: Chuo-koron-shinsha.

Hashimoto, Masanori, and John Raisian. 1985. Employment tenure and earnings profiles in Japan and the United States. *American Economic Review* 82:346–54.

Ishikawa, Tsuneo. 2001. *Income and wealth.* Oxford: Oxford University Press.

Koike, Kazuo. 1988. *Understanding industrial relations in modern Japan.* New York: St. Martin's.

Ministry of Labor. 1984. *Basic survey on wage structure.* Tokyo: Ministry of Labor.

———. 1991. *Basic survey on wage structure.* Tokyo: Ministry of Labor.

———. 1993–1998. *Employment trend survey.* Tokyo: Ministry of Labor.

———. 1997. *Survey on employment insurance.* Tokyo: Ministry of Labor.

———. 1998. *Basic survey on wage structure.* Tokyo: Ministry of Labor.

Muraki, Taro, Asao Mizuno, Yukiko Abe, and Soichi Ohta. 1999. Heisei 11 nenban Rodo Hakusho wo megutte (The dialogue of the white paper on labor 1999). *Monthly Journal of the Japanese Institute of Labour* 41 (9): 66–81.

Ohtake, Fumio, and Kazuaki Okamura. 2000. Shonen Hanzai to Rodo Shijo: Jikeiretsu oyobi Todofuken Panel Bunseki (Youth crime and labor market: Analyses using time-series and panel data). Nihon Keizai Kenkyu, Japan Center for Economic Research.

Organization for Economic Cooperation and Development (OECD). 1999. *Employment outlook.* Paris: OECD.

Statistics Bureau. 1968–2001. *Annual report on the Labor Force Survey.* Tokyo: Management and Coordination Agency.

———. 1984–2001. *Report on the Special Survey of the Labor Force.* Tokyo: Management and Coordination Agency.

———. 1998. *Report on the Job-Seeking Situation Survey.* Tokyo: Management and Coordination Agency.

———. 1999. *Monthly report on the Labor Force Survey.* Tokyo: Management and Coordination Agency.

Tachibanaki, Toshiaki. 1984. Jyakunen ni okeru Shitsugyo Mondai ni tsuite (The youth unemployment problems in Japan). *Monthly Journal of the Japan Institute of Labour* 26 (12): 12–22.

U.S. Department of Labor, Bureau of Labor Statistics. 1999. *Current population survey.* Prepared by the U.S. Bureau of the Census for the Bureau of Labor Statistics. Washington, D.C.

Yamada, Masahiro. 1998. *Days of the parasite single.* Tokyo: Chikuma-shobo.

5

Total Labor Costs and the Employment Adjustment Behavior of Large Japanese Firms

Yoshifumi Nakata and Ryoji Takehiro

5.1 Introduction

Employment instability has recently become a prominent social issue in Japan. It is widely believed that Japanese firms, particularly large firms, are committed to stable employment even in the face of unfavorable economic conditions. If firms are unable to absorb demand fluctuations by adjusting working hours, they adjust employment levels by restricting the inflow of new workers and encouraging older workers to retire early, rather than by laying off employees. Increasingly, however, this employment practice is being criticized as the major cause of the prolonged recession.

In response to the growing interest in this topic, a number of recent studies have investigated employment instability in large Japanese firms. These studies, which employ newly available firm-level panel data sets, include Suruga (1997), Noda (1998), Noda and Urasaka (2001), Okui (2000), and Nakata and Takehiro (2001). Typically, some type of partial adjustment model is used to examine the mechanisms through which employment adjusts. These studies find that a firm's size and elements of its governance structure, such as type of ownership and industrial relations policies, are important in explaining its employment adjustment behavior.

However, the methodology of these types of partial adjustment models has been questioned. Hamermesh (1989), for example, showed that fixed cost considerations are necessary for explaining large, lumpy changes in plant-level employment in his sample of manufacturing firms. Partial adjustment models, which assume a smooth, quadratic adjustment cost func-

Yoshifumi Nakata is dean and professor of management in Doshisha Management School. Ryoji Takehiro is associate professor of economics, Doshisha University.

tion, are therefore not suitable for analyzing lumpy employment adjustment that occurs at the plant level.

All of the above studies analyze samples of manufacturing firms only,[1] and, with the exception of Suruga (1997), they all apply the partial adjustment model without investigating the implications thereof. In addition, the current literature fails to address two important empirical facts. First, it is well established that Japanese firms make extensive use of their ability to adjust individual work hours. Indeed, overtime work is regularly observed even in periods of low demand.[2] Second, with the exception of Okui (2000), there is a complete lack of nonwage labor cost data in the Japanese literature.[3] However, there are reasons to expect Japanese employers to consider fringe benefit costs in addition to wage costs when choosing their optimal labor demand. For example, the rapid aging of the Japanese population has increased employers' social security contributions in the last decade, and this trend is expected to continue through the current decade. It is impossible to properly evaluate the employment adjustment behavior of Japanese employers without taking all of these considerations into account.

We construct a firm-level panel data set of total labor costs and hours worked over a period of twenty-five years. The data cover firms in nonmanufacturing industries as well as automobile assembly firms, which were chosen as representative of the manufacturing industry. This new data set enables us to analyze the employment adjustment behavior of Japanese firms from a broader perspective.

Specifically, our analysis consists of the following:

1. We construct a firm-level panel data set of thirty-three major Japanese firms over twenty-five years. This data set is rare in that it includes consistent employment data over the entire time period. By studying the frequency and magnitude of large-scale employment adjustment in this data, we examine the commonly held view that large Japanese firms are committed to employment stability.

2. We expand the scope of investigation beyond the manufacturing industry by including department stores and supermarkets in the dataset. This allows us to compare employment adjustment patterns across industries as well as within industries.

3. We use total labor costs per capita rather than average monthly salary to measure the factor price when estimating the partial adjustment model.

---

1. Although there are numerous studies that examine interindustry differences in employment adjustment, they all use aggregate data, such as Kurosaka (1988). We only review studies using firm/establishment-level panel data.

2. Muramatsu (1983) is the first Japanese economist to examine this issue in detail. The sixth chapter of his book (Eichner, McClellan, and Wise) contains an exhaustive treatment of both the theoretical and empirical aspects of this topic.

3. Smith and Karlson (1991) incorporate nonwage cost data in examining the automobile industry, an industry we also study, in England.

We then compare the relative suitability of the two measures within the context of the model.

4. We use information on hours worked, available for the subset of eleven automobile firms, to construct a measure of total labor input. This makes it possible for us to examine whether fluctuations in total labor input can be explained by the partial adjustment model.

We conclude by summarizing and interpreting our findings and discussing opportunities for future research.

5.2   Employment Adjustment

It is commonly believed that Japanese firms, particularly large firms, do not adjust their employment levels through layoffs unless they are faced with an extraordinary situation, such as bankruptcy. Rather, they adjust employment inflows, an easier margin to adjust than employment outflows. Given this limited adjustment leverage, it is very unlikely that a Japanese firm could trim its workforce, particularly its regular workforce, more than 5 percent per year.[4] It is inconceivable for a firm to adjust employment in this way by more than 10 percent per year.

5.2.1   Employment Data

We examine this belief by looking at employment data for thirty-three major Japanese firms in the automobile assembly, department store, and supermarket sectors. The data come from two sources. One is an economic activities report, called *Yukashouken Hokokusyo Soran* (literally, "comprehensive report of valued commercial papers"), submitted by each of these firms to the Ministry of Finance at the end of every fiscal year. The other source is labor union reports on union members' working conditions. Summary statistics of each of the variables are presented separately by sector in table 5.1. The sample includes nearly all of the leading firms in these industries in Japan. Thus, the data are suitable for examining the employment adjustment behavior of major Japanese firms.

5.2.2   Employment Adjustment Trends

Table 5.2 presents a summary of employment changes of regular workers in the sample from 1975 to 1997. The following observations are noteworthy:

1. It is not uncommon for major firms in all three industries to reduce employment by more than 5 percent in a single fiscal year. In fact, only six of the thirty-three firms have never experienced such a large employment

---

4. Five percent is the average annual turnover rate of regular workers among large Japanese firms.

Table 5.1   Summary Statistics by Industry

	N	Mean	Standard Deviation	Minimum	Maximum
Automobile Assembly Firms					
Regular workers: total number	12	22,442	18,448.84	4,942	70,524
Regular workers: % female	12	6.73	2.38	3.44	11.94
Average age: male workers	12	39.27	1.79	36.3	43.00
Average age: female workers	12	29.58	2.07	25.7	32.50
Average tenure: male workers	12	17.01	3.39	7.90	21.20
Average tenure: female workers	12	8.94	1.60	5.70	11.80
Sales per capita (million yen)	12	78.03	18.40	58.01	110.17
Ordinary profit per capita (million yen)	12	2.25	2.95	−0.80	8.87
Average monthly wage (yen)	12	381,541	30,803	345,676	444,599
Bonus over average monthly wage (monthly)	11	4.18	0.41	3.51	4.88
Employment cost per capita (million yen)	12	8.06	1.46	5.82	11.46
Department Stores					
Regular workers: total number	11	5,087.18	3,672.59	1,061	12,029
Regular workers: % female	11	49.76	6.58	40.00	62.39
Average age: male workers	11	42.17	1.89	38.80	44.90
Average age: female workers	11	31.24	2.02	27.30	34.50
Average tenure: male workers	11	20.33	2.88	13.60	24.30
Average tenure: female workers	11	10.54	1.41	8.10	13.30
Sales per capita (million yen)	11	73.60	9.74	56.27	91.24
Ordinary profit per capita (million yen)	11	0.70	0.63	0.13	2.43
Average monthly wage (yen)	11	346,696	43,398	257,162	413,101
Bonus over average monthly wage (monthly)	9	4.25	0.56	3.55	5.27
Employment cost per capita (million yen)	11	7.52	0.96	6.32	9.05
Supermarkets					
Regular workers: total number	10	7,495	5,736	431	16,686
Regular workers: % female	10	34.49	11.71	8.61	51.75
Average age: male workers	10	37.93	2.42	34.20	41.50
Average age: female workers	10	28.81	3.33	24.80	35.70
Average tenure: male workers	10	14.79	2.63	9.60	18.00
Average tenure: female workers	10	7.88	2.27	5.40	11.90
Sales per capita (million yen)	10	121.07	32.44	93.78	200.93
Ordinary profit per capita (million yen)	10	1.40	1.79	−1.55	4.66
Average monthly wage (yen)	10	323,029	21,991	297,079	350,208
Bonus over average monthly wage (monthly)	9	3.81	0.71	2.70	4.90
Employment cost per capita (million yen)	10	10.65	1.74	6.94	12.55

reduction, and most firms have experienced it more than once. A majority of our sample, twenty firms, has undergone such reductions at least twice in the last twenty-five years.

2. Most firms have experienced employment reductions *much* larger than 5 percent. Eleven of the thirty-three firms have trimmed their workforce in a given year by more than 10 percent. The average maximum one-year reductions are 7.42 percent, 10.50 percent, and 14.37 percent in the automobile assembly, department store, and supermarket sectors respec-

Table 5.2 Annual Employment Change of Regular Workers

	N	Absolute Value of % Change		% Change		% Change		No. Years for Which Change ≥ 5%	No. Years for Which Change ≤ −5%
		Mean	Standard Deviation	Maximum	Year	Minimum	Year		
Automobile Assembly Firms									
Hino	25	2.43	1.96	7.19	1975	−4.50	1988	3	0
Honda	25	3.40	2.88	9.90	1981	−5.41	1996	5	1
Isuzu	25	4.21	4.02	13.85	1994	−14.36	1987	5	2
Mitsubishi	11	1.96	1.45	4.28	1993	−2.10	1999	0	0
Mazda	25	2.65	2.19	3.52	1991	−6.31	1995	0	5
Nissan	25	3.19	2.12	4.77	1990	−8.94	1996	0	4
Subaru	25	1.81	1.16	3.26	1988	−4.95	1975	0	0
Suzuki	25	3.16	2.61	9.48	1983	−6.88	1976	6	1
Yamaha	19	4.67	5.18	15.74	1981	−18.62	1984	3	1
Daihatsu	25	3.22	2.43	9.34	1981	−5.19	1976	4	1
Toyota	25	2.83	2.54	13.35	1983	−2.95	1993	1	0
Nissan Diesel	25	4.74	3.71	14.14	1975	−8.85	1999	6	5
Department Stores									
Hanshin	25	3.21	2.50	6.78	1976	−8.45	1977	1	5
Matsuzakaya	25	3.42	4.34	20.76	1975	−6.94	1996	2	5
Hankyu	25	3.65	2.53	8.79	1978	−5.30	1997	8	1
Daimaru	25	3.56	3.03	5.32	1984	−15.18	1999	2	2
Izutsuya	25	3.85	4.07	5.60	1977	−20.33	1996	1	6
Isetan	25	3.22	2.09	8.00	1981	−7.74	1977	1	2
Sogo	25	4.01	3.48	5.99	1991	−16.43	1996	3	4
Takashimaya	25	5.46	9.32	44.30	1996	−8.44	1977	3	4
Mitsukoshi	25	2.69	1.79	3.92	1993	−6.57	1998	0	3
Matsuya	25	3.77	3.14	4.29	1986	−11.71	1978	0	6
Tokyu	25	4.53	5.07	21.64	1975	−8.40	1998	4	5

(*continued*)

Table 5.2   (continued)

	Absolute Value of % Change			% Change		% Change		No. Years for Which	No. Years for Which
	N	Mean	Standard Deviation	Maximum	Year	Minimum	Year	Change ≥ 5%	Change ≤ −5%
Supermarkets									
Daiei	25	4.77	5.27	13.82	1995	−22.64	1996	3	5
Inageya	20	7.39	6.98	28.24	1982	−6.48	1996	9	1
Ito Yokado	25	4.84	4.92	15.16	1975	−1.43	1986	9	0
Jujiya	25	8.45	9.61	5.80	1998	−41.91	1997	1	10
Izumiya	21	2.50	1.46	5.38	1985	−4.25	1998	1	0
Mycal	25	6.42	4.70	13.28	1977	−19.69	1996	5	10
Nagasakiya	25	6.41	6.60	31.02	1990	−15.33	1986	1	10
Yuni	23	3.21	1.90	7.89	1981	−6.64	1996	2	2
Seiyu	25	5.53	5.44	22.05	1989	−17.64	1996	5	5
Jasco	25	3.80	3.05	13.76	1977	−7.67	1975	5	1

Source: Yukashouken Hokokusyo Soran (various years)

tively. This magnitude of employment reduction is unattainable through scaling back new recruitment alone, even if new recruitment were stopped entirely.

3. Large employment reductions are not confined to a single industry or time period. At least two firms in each industry have trimmed employment by more than 10 percent in a single year, and these large reductions are spread over the twenty-five years.

4. Large employment increases are as common as large employment decreases. The automobile assembly, department store, and supermarket companies in our sample experienced twenty-two, twenty-five, and forty-one single-year increases in employment of 5 percent or more, and twenty, forty-three, and forty-four single-year reductions in employment of 5 percent or more, respectively. Therefore, most firms experienced large-scale employment increases and decreases with roughly the same frequency.

These findings show that large employment reductions are common at leading Japanese firms, yet it is still widely believed that layoffs are very rare at these firms. We now proceed to analyze the employment adjustment of our sample firms in the context of a partial employment adjustment model.

5.3   The Partial Employment Adjustment Model

In order to understand the employment adjustment behavior of major Japanese firms, we use a partial employment adjustment model to estimate both a partial adjustment parameter and the elasticities of employment with respect to output and the relative wage.

5.3.1   Discussion of Alternative Specifications

The model is based on the assumption that a firm maximizes its expected future profit stream by minimizing a quadratic employment adjustment cost function. As previously mentioned, this specific form of the adjustment cost function has been criticized in the literature. The chief critique is that there is a fixed cost of employment adjustment that cannot be captured by the model's quadratic form. Labor economists agree that some fixed costs are incurred regardless of the magnitude of employment adjustment. We claim that for the large firms we investigate, fixed costs are small enough relative to variable costs that we can ignore this criticism. In other words, we assume that the quadratic cost function can reasonably approximate the actual costs of these firms. Final judgment regarding the appropriateness of our assumption rests with the reader.

Another criticism of this type of adjustment cost specification is that it treats the costs of both an increase and a decrease in employment levels symmetrically. It is difficult to say a priori that employment adjustment in one direction is always more costly than employment adjustment in the other direction. This is an empirical question to be answered by the data. We test this cost asymmetry hypothesis by examining whether the partial adjustment parameter differs with the direction of the employment change. We omit a detailed presentation of the results for the sake of brevity and simply report here that our data reject the asymmetric adjustment cost hypothesis. The following analysis assumes a symmetric cost structure.

A final qualification regarding our model concerns the choice of the labor cost variable. It is common to use wage or salary data to measure the relative price of labor. We run our estimation using both this conventional measure and the factor-price measure that we prefer, total labor costs. We can then compare the results, although we have strong reservations about the appropriateness of the conventional measure for our specific analysis. We again omit a detailed presentation of these results for the sake of brevity and simply note that the two specifications yield similar results. However, the overall fit of the model is *much* better when total labor costs are used as the factor price of labor.

5.3.2   Estimation of the Model Using Total Labor Costs

It is sensible for firms to consider nonwage employment expenses, such as compulsory and noncompulsory benefits, when making hiring decisions. This is particularly true given that these costs as a share of total employment costs have increased in recent years. For example, by 1995 the share of nonwage benefits in total employment costs in the manufacturing industry as a whole was 14.5 percent (Okui 2000, figs. 1 and 2).

We therefore replace wages with total labor costs as a measure of the factor price of labor and estimate the following partial employment adjustment model for the entire sample of thirty-three firms.

(1) $\Delta \ln N_t = \lambda a_1 + \lambda \ln (N_{t-1}) + \lambda a_2 \ln (X_t) + \lambda a_3 \ln \left(\frac{W_t}{P_t} \right) + \lambda a_4 T + v$

(2) $\ln N_t^* = a_1 + a_2 \ln (X_t) + a_3 \ln \left(\frac{W_t}{P_t} \right) + a_4 T$

where N is actual employment, N^* is desired employment, X is output,[5] W is total labor cost, P is output price,[6] T is time (year), and λ is the partial adjustment parameter.

The results are summarized in table 5.3. Each column corresponds to a particular firm, and each row contains parameter estimates and t-values for a specific explanatory variable. The results are quite striking given the rather poor performance of the model when the conventional wage variable is used as the measure of the factor price. From equations (1) and (2),

5. Sale value in yen is used for estimation.
6. Industry gross domestic product (GDP) deflator is used for estimation.

Table 5.3 Results of the Partial Adjustment Model Using Total Labor Cost

Automobile Assembly Firms

Variables	Daihatsu	Suzuki	Nissan Diesel	Mitsubishi	Mazda	Isuzu	Hino	Honda	Yamaha	Toyota	Nissan	Subaru
Constant	2.807 (1.81)	3.542 (2.62)	1.955 (1.53)	5.253 (1.37)	-0.090 (-0.04)	8.147 (3.51)	5.707 (3.79)	6.123 (4.02)	6.505 (2.42)	4.326 (3.20)	0.675 (0.51)	2.857 (1.43)
N_{t-1}	0.487 (2.16)	0.622 (3.26)	0.346 (2.67)	0.671 (2.22)	0.119 (0.61)	0.907 (3.83)	0.688 (4.65)	0.747 (4.32)	0.888 (4.61)	0.650 (4.13)	0.360 (1.57)	0.346 (1.68)
X_t	0.352 (2.18)	0.549 (3.12)	0.361 (2.51)	0.393 (3.92)	0.110 (1.26)	0.5073 (2.84)	0.254 (3.52)	0.422 (4.79)	0.535 (5.13)	0.354 (4.30)	0.379 (1.49)	0.040 (0.45)
W_t/P_t	-0.343 (-1.85)	-0.610 (-2.82)	-0.422 (-2.33)	-0.487 (-2.75)	-0.027 (-0.16)	-0.768 (-3.05)	-0.341 (-4.71)	-0.564 (-0.41)	-0.688 (-4.63)	-0.323 (-2.92)	-0.283 (-1.02)	-0.011 (-0.09)
T	-0.208E-02 (-0.70)	-0.692E-02 (-1.65)	0.541E-02 (1.05)	0.187E-02 (0.36)	-0.373E-02 (-2.25)	0.011 (1.94)	0.011 (4.42)	0.020 (3.12)	0.029 (3.62)	0.829E-02 (2.05)	-0.507E-02 (-1.34)	0.877E-03 (0.39)
R^2	0.517	0.445	0.457	0.828	0.760	0.513	0.659	0.739	0.785	0.684	0.588	0.236
Adjusted R^2	0.397	0.306	0.321	0.656	0.700	0.391	0.574	0.674	0.714	0.606	0.485	0.045
Durbin-Watson	1.433	0.873	1.232	2.630	1.650	1.039	1.793	1.362	1.258	2.056	1.216	1.835
Sum of Squared Residuals	0.013	0.013	0.027	0.803E-03	0.444E-02	0.033	0.513E-02	0.956E-02	0.019	0.693E-02	0.014	0.605E-02
Log-likelihood	47.573	47.602	39.941	29.188	59.059	37.848	57.533	50.999	33.476	54.375	46.991	55.803

Department Stores

Variables	Daimaru	Matsuzakaya	Isetan	Mitsukoshi	Matsuya	Tokyu	Takashimaya	Hanshin	Izutsuya	Sogo	Hankyu
Constant	9.793 (3.46)	7.562 (4.05)	9.081 (10.57)	-2.186 (-1.09)	4.583 (1.65)	5.760 (3.19)	1.576 (0.83)	10.285 (4.88)	-1.555 (-0.43)	5.159 (2.95)	10.901 (7.00)
N_{t-1}	1.028 (4.61)	0.744 (5.62)	0.711 (11.49)	0.024 (0.18)	0.666 (3.26)	0.571 (4.75)	0.582 (5.89)	0.871 (5.99)	0.271 (0.93)	0.651 (3.80)	1.200 (8.62)
X_t	0.336 (2.65)	0.505 (6.22)	0.253 (6.57)	0.167 (1.20)	0.427 (3.31)	0.542 (7.57)	0.813 (6.50)	0.257 (2.11)	0.418 (1.29)	0.513 (6.04)	0.606 (5.74)
W_t/P_t	-0.578 (-4.11)	-0.890 (-5.59)	-0.722 (-14.10)	0.023 (0.09)	-0.533 (-1.80)	-0.927 (-5.33)	-0.822 (-4.76)	-0.818 (-5.18)	-0.131 (-0.41)	-0.744 (-4.38)	-1.016 (-8.05)
T	-0.944E-03 (-0.34)	0.7946E-02 (3.19)	0.408E-02 (3.13)	-0.331E-02 (-0.84)	-0.309E-02 (-0.79)	0.474E-02 (1.82)	-0.971E-04 (-0.01)	0.012 (3.54)	-0.557E-02 (-0.91)	0.498E-02 (2.11)	0.025 (8.16)
R^2	0.622	0.769	0.935	0.440	0.517	0.830	0.821	0.743	0.397	0.791	0.858
Adjusted R^2	0.528	0.712	0.919	0.300	0.396	0.788	0.777	0.679	0.247	0.739	0.822
Durbin-Watson	0.955	0.870	1.987	1.173	0.643	1.434	1.271	0.979	1.212	1.587	1.430
Sum of Squared Residuals	0.805E-02	0.425E-02	0.211E-02	0.816E-02	0.015	0.923E-02	0.036	0.524E-02	0.038	0.0129	0.493E-02
Log-likelihood	52.795	59.505	66.885	52.665	45.978	51.362	37.158	57.317	36.486	47.869	57.942

(continued)

Table 5.3 (continued)

					Supermarkets						
	Daiei	Ito Yokado	Nagasakiya	Mycal	Seiyu	Izumiya	Yuni	Jasco	Jujiya	Inageya	Tobu Store
Constant	-1.962	8.337	-2.533	12.056	3.471	3.198	8.943	8.421	-2.757	-0.881	6.577
	(-0.72)	(12.19)	(-0.85)	(2.17)	(1.22)	(2.83)	(2.45)	(3.79)	(-1.08)	(-0.21)	(2.07)
N_{t-1}	0.772	0.825	0.427	0.605	0.628	0.974	0.742	0.712	0.500	0.510	0.578
	(6.45)	(13.52)	(2.93)	(2.10)	(3.71)	(5.26)	(3.04)	(3.59)	(3.96)	(3.60)	(3.18)
X_t	1.146	0.414	0.828	-0.181	0.639	0.541	0.351	0.050	1.504	0.899	0.200
	(4.48)	(7.91)	(5.36)	(-0.84)	(3.53)	(5.32)	(1.68)	(0.39)	(7.50)	(3.04)	(0.85)
W_t/P_t	-0.770	-0.769	-0.495	-0.506	-0.742	-0.234	-0.828	-0.336	-1.343	-0.646	-0.582
	(-6.16)	(-10.26)	(-2.25)	(-1.73)	(-2.79)	(-3.41)	(-2.88)	(-2.93)	(-5.32)	(-2.44)	(-1.71)
T	-0.015	0.032	-0.012	0.021	0.265E-02	0.212E-02	0.023	0.032	0.043	-0.015	0.013
	(-1.53)	(9.73)	(-2.13)	(1.43)	(0.32)	(0.80)	(2.15)	(3.59)	(3.62)	(-0.92)	(0.96)
R^2	0.791	0.954	0.680	0.337	0.630	0.726	0.450	0.584	0.827	0.782	0.478
Adjusted R^2	0.738	0.942	0.600	0.172	0.538	0.653	0.312	0.480	0.784	0.715	0.348
Durbin-Watson	1.662	1.674	1.408	0.613	0.540	1.953	0.480	1.039	0.064	0.023	0.062
Sum of Squared Residuals	0.027	0.214E-02	0.055	0.092	0.048	0.446E-02	0.017	0.790E-02	0.064	0.023	0.062
Log-likelihood	40.167	66.706	32.587	27.279	33.973	55.711	45.020	52.995	31.063	34.347	31.445

Note: Dependent variables $\Delta \ln N_t$.

we know that the coefficients of N_{t-1}, X_t, and W_t/P_t represent a partial adjustment parameter (λ), a short-term output elasticity (λa_2), and a short-run wage elasticity (λa_3), respectively. Therefore, we expect

$$0 \le \lambda \le 1, 0 < \lambda a_2, 0 < -\lambda a_3.$$

These three parameters have the expected signs and are statistically significant for almost every firm. In addition, the model's ability to explain the variation in employment changes is dramatically improved by use of our factor price measure. The adjusted R-squared exceeds 0.5 in most cases, which is almost twice that of the model using the conventional wage measure. Simply put, the partial employment adjustment model can explain much of the employment adjustment behavior of leading Japanese firms. This casts significant doubt on the conventional wisdom that large Japanese firms have abided by a noneconomic commitment to employment stability for their regular employees.

5.4   Estimation Results

5.4.1   Interindustry Analysis

We reorganized the estimation results in table 5.3 to produce table 5.4, which shows partial adjustment coefficients, long-run output elasticities, and long-run wage elasticities. We now investigate interindustry variation in employment adjustment behavior by comparing industry average of adjustment coefficients. The estimates of the employment adjustment coefficient, λ, do not differ much across industries. They range from 0.569 for automobile assembly firms to only 0.670 for supermarkets. This range of only 0.10 does not change when we look at the means of only the statistically significant coefficients. This new range of estimates is virtually the same, varying from 0.667 for automobile assembly firms to 0.780 for department stores. These adjustment coefficients are much larger than those estimated by macrodata, which is consistent with the findings in table 5.2.

By contrast, the industry means of the long-run elasticities, particularly the output elasticity, diverge somewhat. The industry means of the wage elasticity range from 0.670 for automobile firms to 1.089 for supermarkets, although the range shrinks to 0.300 when only statistically significant elasticities are included. Similarly, the industry-specific means of the output elasticities vary from 0.665 for automobile firms to 1.319 for department stores. The range of these means increases when we include only the statistically significant elasticities. However, the industry order for the means remains the same. Automobile assembly firms have the smallest mean, followed by department stores and then supermarkets.

We test whether the industry differences in elasticities are statistically significant by pooling the data and running the employment adjustment

Table 5.4 Estimated Partial Employment Adjustment Coefficients: Output Elasticities and the Relative Wage Elasticities

	Employment Adjustment Coefficient (N_{t-1})	t-value	Output Elasticity (X_t)	t-value	Wage Elasticity (W_t/P_t)	t-value	Adjusted R^2
Automobile Assembly Firms							
Toyota	0.650	4.13	0.544	4.3	0.496	2.92***	0.606
Suzuki	0.622	3.26	0.883	3.12	0.981	2.82***	0.306
Nissan Diesel	0.346	2.67***	1.043	2.51***	1.221	2.33***	0.321
Honda	0.747	4.32	0.565	4.79	0.755	4.07	0.674
Yamaha	0.888	4.61	0.603	5.13	0.774	4.63	0.714
Isuzu	0.907	3.83	0.559	2.84	0.846	3.05***	0.391
Hino	0.688	4.65	0.369	3.52	0.495	4.71	0.574
Daihatsu	0.487	2.16***	0.723	2.18***	0.704	1.85**	0.397
Mitsubishi	0.671	2.22**	0.585	3.92***	0.725	2.75**	0.656
Mazda	0.119	0.61**	0.929	1.26**	0.228	0.16**	0.700
Nissan	0.360	1.57**	1.055	1.49**	0.787	1.02**	0.485
Subaru	0.346	1.68**	0.116	0.45**	0.030	0.09**	0.045
Average	0.569		0.665		0.670		
Sig. average	0.667		0.653		0.796		
Sig. S.D.	0.190		0.202		0.258		
Sig. CV	0.284		0.309		0.324		
Department Stores							
Daimaru	1.028	4.61	0.326	2.65	0.562	4.11	0.528
Matsuzakaya	0.744	5.62	0.678	6.22	1.196	5.59	0.712
Isetan	0.711	11.49	0.356	6.57	1.017	14.10	0.919
Sogo	0.651	3.80	0.788	6.04	1.143	4.38	0.739
Hankyu	1.200	8.62	0.505	5.74	0.846	8.05	0.822
Tokyu	0.571	4.75	0.949	7.57	1.623	5.33	0.788
Takashimaya	0.582	5.89	1.396	6.50	1.411	4.76	0.777
Hanshin	0.871	5.99	0.295	2.11**	0.940	5.18	0.679

Matsuya	0.666	3.26	0.641	3.31	0.801	1.80**	0.396
Izutsuya	0.271	0.93**	1.544	1.29**	0.483	0.41**	0.247
Mitsukoshi	0.024	0.18**	7.030	1.20**	-0.970	-0.09**	0.300
Average	0.665		1.319		0.823		
Sig. Average	0.780		0.705		1.092		
Sig. S.D.	0.214		0.349		0.331		
Sig. CV	0.274		0.496		0.303		
Supermarkets							
Daiei	0.772	6.45	1.484	4.48	0.997	6.16	0.738
Ito Yokado	0.825	13.52	0.502	7.91	0.933	10.26	0.942
Jujiya	0.500	3.96	3.008	7.50	2.687	5.32	0.784
Izumiya	0.974	5.26	0.555	5.32	0.240	3.41	0.653
Seiyu	0.628	3.71	1.017	3.53	1.181	2.79***	0.538
Nagasakiya	0.427	2.93***	1.942	5.36	1.159	2.25***	0.600
Inageya	0.510	3.60	1.763	3.04	1.267	2.44***	0.715
Yuni	0.742	3.04	0.474	1.68**	1.116	2.88***	0.312
Jasco	0.712	3.59	0.070	0.39**	0.472	2.93***	0.480
Mycal	0.605	2.10**	-0.299	-0.84**	0.836	1.73**	0.172
Average	0.670		1.051		1.089		
Sig. average	0.677		1.467		1.117		
Sig. S.D.	0.176		0.881		0.683		
Sig. CV	0.261		0.600		0.611		

Notes: We confirm the employment adjustment coefficients between extensive phases, and reducible ones are indifferent significantly. Sig. Average, Sig. S.D., and Sig. CV mean that all those statistics are calculated by statistically significant parameter estimates. S.D. = standard deviation. CV = coefficient of variations.

***Not significant at the 1 percent level.

**Not significant even at the 5 percent level.

equations with industry dummies. We perform three pairwise comparisons (one for each pair of industries) and a tri-industry comparison. The results, shown in table 5.5, confirm the results of table 5.4. The adjustment speed, λ, is not statistically different between automobile firms and department stores or automobile firms and supermarkets.[7] It is, however, significantly different between department stores and supermarkets. The two elasticities, on the other hand, are significantly different for all three pairs—automobile firms versus department stores, automobile firms versus supermarkets, and department stores versus supermarkets. We therefore conclude that the two elasticities, which represent production specificity, differ across industries. Industries are not so different, however, in their speed of employment adjustment. This suggests that there are similarities in the employment practices of leading Japanese firms across industries.

5.4.2   Intraindustry Analysis

The first thing to notice is the low variation in the estimated coefficients across firms. The coefficient of variations (CV) of the respective parameter estimates, shown at the bottom of the panels in table 5.4, are calculated by the statistically significant coefficients only. The CVs for adjustment parameters lie between 0.26 and 0.29. This relatively small variation in the estimated adjustment parameters further supports our interpretation of the interindustry adjustment parameters. The interfirm similarity of the employment adjustment parameters suggests that employment practices are similar, this time across leading Japanese firms within an industry.

The second thing to notice is the differences among supermarket companies in the two long-run elasticities. The CVs of the two elasticities exceed 0.6. In contrast, the CVs of the two elasticities for automobile assemblers are barely larger than that of the adjustment parameter. The CVs of the elasticities for department stores fall between the other two sectors: There are some differences in the long-run output elasticities, but the relative wage elasticities are very similar. These results suggest that the production frontiers of manufacturing firms, which produce similar products, are similar. There are much greater differences in the production frontiers of retail firms, which likely reflect the numerous choices retail managers must make when deciding how to sell their products.

The third thing to notice is that the relationship between the two elasticities is striking. Panel A of figure 5.1 plots both elasticities for each firm. There is clearly a positive relationship: A firm with a large output elasticity tends to have a large wage elasticity as well. Similarly, a firm with a small output elasticity tends to have a small wage elasticity. This positive relationship is observed for each industry as well as for the three industries as a group. The correlation coefficients of the elasticities are 0.917, 0.790,

---

7. It is noteworthy that the adjustment speed is much slower than those in table 5.4.

Table 5.5   Tests for Coefficient Difference by Industry

Base	Adjustment Coefficient (N_{t-1})	t-value	Output Elasticity (X_t)	t-value	Wage Elasticity (W_t/P_t)	t-value	Adjusted R^2
Automobile assembly firms	0.249	8.24	0.678	8.78	0.601	6.34	0.414
Dummy = department stores	0.078	1.77**	2.265	5.35	2.045	4.08	
Dummy = supermarkets	0.220	5.25	0.71	6.18	0.490	3.20	0.408
	0.099	1.93**	2.703	5.48	2.725	5.73	
Dummy = department stores and supermarkets	0.239	6.28	0.700	6.86	0.563	4.61	0.423
	0.074	1.33**	2.330	4.14	1.864	2.84	
	0.082	1.76**	3.120	5.72	3.290	6.23	
Department Stores	0.110	6.39	0.830	8.57	0.411	3.38	0.348
Dummy = supermarkets	0.209	6.52	1.609	8.80	1.612	9.38	

**Not significant at the 5 percent level.

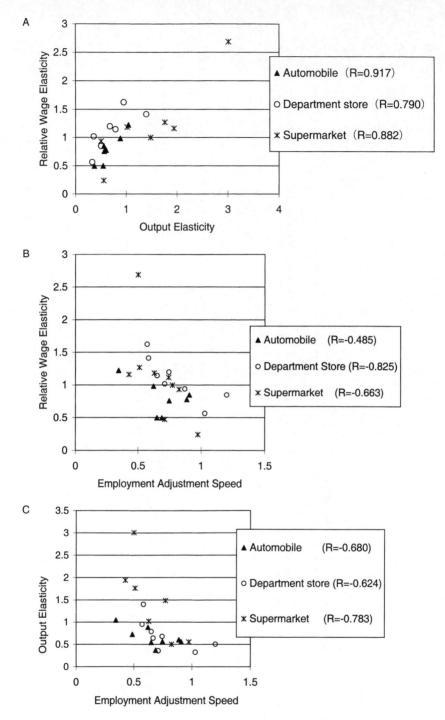

Fig. 5.1 **Within-industry correlations:** *A,* **Correlation between wage and output elasticities;** *B,* **Correlation between wage elasticity and employment adjustment speed;** *C,* **Correlation between output elasticity and employment adjustment speed**

and 0.882 for automobile assembly firms, department stores, and super-markets, respectively.

The last point is that the adjustment parameter has a negative relation-ship with the two elasticities. Panels B and C of figure 5.1 show that a firm with a large wage or output elasticity tends to have a small adjustment pa-rameter. This relationship is observed for each industry, although the rela-tionship is stronger when all three industries are pooled together. If we take the production frontier or its factor demand revelation in the two elastici-ties as given, we can interpret this negative relationship as the firm's com-pensating for the slow long-run adjustment of labor demand to relative wage or output changes by speeding up the short-run employment adjust-ment. If this interpretation is accurate, there is a complementarity between the industry's technology frontier and its labor management practices. We believe that this possibility merits further investigation.

5.5 The Partial Adjustment Model Using Total Labor Input

5.5.1 The Necessity of Total Labor Input Analysis

Our final task in this paper is to examine the applicability of the partial employment adjustment model to total labor input fluctuations in our sample firms. We have two motivations for this extension.

The first is that total labor input is a better measure of a firm's labor us-age than are employment levels. It is reasonable to assume that there will be periods during which a given number of employees work longer or shorter hours as firms produce more or less output, respectively. Thus, la-bor input is best captured using work hours. Figure 5.2 shows both the change in sales and the change in total labor input at Nissan. The parallel movements of these two series suggest that this is indeed true.

The second is that, as figure 5.2 reveals, there are huge fluctuations in ac-tual work hours in our sample. Thus, it is inaccurate to assume that em-ployment levels fully capture a firm's total labor input. Average actual annual work hours of Federation of Japan Automobile Workers Unions (JAW) members at all eleven sample automobile firms were obtained thanks to the generosity of the JAW. Their understanding of the signifi-cance of our research is greatly appreciated.

5.5.2 Estimation Results

Table 5.6 presents the results of a modified partial adjustment analysis of total labor input. We substituted our total labor input variable, which is the product of employment and JAW work hours, for the typically used employment variable. We also replaced average annual total labor costs with hourly values.

The results again show an improvement in the overall fit of the employ-

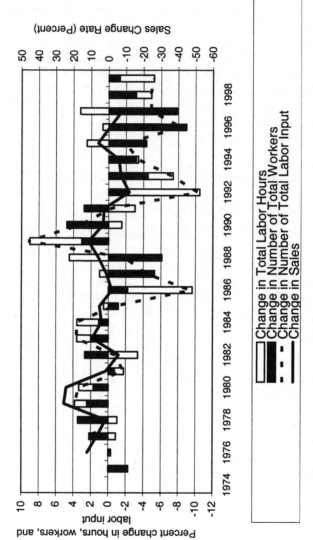

Fig. 5.2 Decomposition of total labor input: Nissan

Legend:
Change in Total Labor Hours
Change in Number of Total Workers
Change in Number of Total Labor Input
Change in Sales

Sales Change Rate (Percent)

Percent change in hours, workers, and labor input

Table 5.6   Results of the Partial Adjustment Model using Total Labor Input

Variable	Pooled Result[a]	Automobile Assembly Firms										
		Daihatsu	Suzuki	Mitsubishi	Mazda	Isuzu	Hino	Honda	Yamaha	Toyota	Nissan	Subaru
Constant		6.487	3.697	11.087	7.775	8.646	7.030	7.860	6.958	7.143	2.769	3.731
		(4.40)	(2.65)	(3.56)	(4.18)	(4.21)	(2.88)	(4.49)	(2.08)	(3.80)	(1.10)	(1.41)
$N_{t-1}H_{t-1}$	0.336	0.765	0.676	0.799	0.702	0.889	0.719	0.756	0.813	0.747	0.673	0.351
	(8.84)	(5.06)	(4.37)	(4.71)	(4.80)	(5.65)	(4.90)	(4.83)	(3.99)	(4.25)	(4.52)	(1.89)
X_t	0.196	0.523	0.618	0.236	0.363	0.526	0.407	0.408	0.522	0.458	0.682	0.188
	(8.20)	(4.80)	(4.13)	(5.94)	(3.45)	(4.56)	(3.85)	(4.99)	(5.77)	(4.10)	(3.61)	(1.49)
W/P_t	-0.136	-0.494	-0.697	-0.216	-0.465	-0.711	-0.483	-0.507	-0.587	-0.429	-0.568	-0.225
	(-4.40)	(-4.52)	(-3.48)	(-3.06)	(-2.05)	(-3.97)	(-4.47)	(-4.55)	(-3.82)	(-3.00)	(-2.08)	(-1.31)
T	-0.305E-02	-0.190E-02	-0.085E-02	-0.345E-02	-0.224E-02	0.747E-02	0.012	0.017	0.022	0.700E-02	-0.404E-02	-0.148E-02
	(-2.81)	(-0.89)	(-2.65)	(-3.85)	(-0.65)	(1.25)	(4.09)	(3.41)	(2.71)	(1.58)	(-0.57)	(-0.62)
R^2	0.403	0.742	0.587	0.947	0.728	0.6977	0.710	0.793	0.786	0.645	0.705	0.253
Adjusted R^2	0.362	0.677	0.484	0.894	0.660	0.622	0.638	0.741	0.714	0.557	0.631	0.066
Durbin-Watson	1.399	2.120	0.831	1.774	1.731	1.181	1.746	1.634	1.548	1.404	1.576	1.076
Sum of Squared Residuals	0.299	0.908E-02	0.013	0.78E-04	0.010	0.031	0.013	0.616E-02	0.015	0.015	0.016	0.014
Log-likelihood		51.548	47.812	39.657	50.076	38.601	47.610	55.605	35.548	46.534	45.878	46.657

Note: Dependent variables $\Delta \ln N_t$.

[a] Pool result is obtained by within-model calculations to find the fixed effects. Therefore, there is no common constant in the result.

ment adjustment model for most firms when they are compared to those in table 5.3. The adjusted R-squared increases for eight of the eleven firms. The number of statistically significant parameters increases. Also, there is an increase in the partial adjustment parameter of most firms. The average partial adjustment parameter exceeds 0.7, and the incremental increase serves to bring each firm's parameter closer to 1. Again, these findings support our contention that leading Japanese firms follow conventional employment adjustment practices. They adjust both employment levels and work hours in response to fluctuations in output and the relative price of labor.

5.6 Conclusion

This paper investigates employment adjustment in leading Japanese firms. Specifically, we accomplish the following four tasks:

1. We construct a twenty-five-year, firm-level panel data set for thirty-three major Japanese firms in three industries: automobile manufacturing, department stores, and supermarkets. The data set includes consistent employment data on regular full-time workers. We use this data set to examine the accuracy of the commonly held belief that large Japanese firms make an employment commitment to their workers. By studying the frequency and magnitude of employment adjustments, we find that large-scale employment adjustment is not at all uncommon among these firms and that the conventional wisdom is not supported by empirical evidence.

2. We use a partial employment adjustment model to explain the observed employment fluctuations. We use per capita total labor costs in place of average monthly salary as a measure of the factor price of labor. This model explains the employment adjustment behavior of leading Japanese firms very well.

3. We find negative relationships between the adjustment parameter and the output and wage elasticities of employment for each industry separately and as well as for all three industries together. We interpret this negative relationship as evidence that firms compensate for slow long-run adjustment of labor demand to changes in relative wage or output by speeding up short-run employment adjustment. If this interpretation is accurate, there is a complementarity between an industry's technology frontier and its labor management practices in the three industries we study.

4. We use information on work hours, available for eleven automobile firms, to construct total labor input data. This enables us to apply the partial adjustment model to fluctuations in total labor input. The results show an improvement in the overall fit of the employment adjustment model for most firms.

In conclusion, our findings suggest that the employment adjustment practices of leading Japanese firms reflect basic economic principles. Firms adjust employment levels and work hours in response to fluctuations in output and the relative price of labor.

References

Hamermesh, Daniel. 1989. Labor demand and the structure of adjustment costs. *American Economic Review* 79 (4): 674–89.

Kurosaka, Yoshiou. 1988. *Makuro keizaigaku to Nihon no roudou shijyo* (Macro economics and the Japanese labor market). Tokyo: Keizai Shinposya.

Ministry of Finance. Various years. Yukashouken hokusyo soran. Tokyo: Ministry of Finance.

Muramatsu, Kuramitsu. 1983. *Nihon no roudou shijyo bunseki* (An analysis of the Japanese labor market). Tokyo: Hakuto Syobou.

Nakata, Yoshifumi, and Ryoji Takehiro. 2001. Joint accounting system and human resource management by company group. *Japan Labor Bulletin* 40 (10): 5–11.

Noda, Tomohiko. 1998. Rodokumiai to koyochosei—Kigyo panel data ni yoru bunseki. (Labor union and employment adjustment—An analysis of firm panel data). *Kenzai Kenkyu* 49 (4): 317–326.

Noda, Tomohiko, and Junko Urasaka. 2001. Kigyotouchi to koyochousei (The effect of corporate governance on employment adjustment in Japanese manufacturing firms). *Japanese Journal of Labour Studies* 488:52–63.

Okui, Megumi. 2000. Jyoujyou kigyo no koyouchouseikeisuu no suitei. (Estimation of employment adjustment coefficient for those whose stocks are listed in the Japanese stock exchange markets). Kanazawa Gakuin University, Business Administration and Information Science Department. Mimeograph.

Smith, David J., and Stephen Karlson. 1991. The effect of fringe benefits on employment fluctuations in U.S. automobile manufacturing. *Review of Economics and Statistics* 73 (1): 40–49.

Suruga, Terukazu. 1997. Nihon kigyo no koyochosei. (Employment adjustment of Japanese firms). In *Koyokanko no Henkato Jyosei Roudou,* ed. Hiroyuki Chuma and Terukazu Suruga, 13–46. Tokyo: Tokyo Daigaku Syuppan Kai.

6

Individual Expenditures and Medical Saving Accounts
Can They Work?

Matthew J. Eichner, Mark B. McClellan,
and David A. Wise

6.1 Introduction

Only a couple of decades ago a large fraction of private insurance plans paid for care on a fee-for-service basis, with any incentives for limiting expenditures provided through typically small co-payments and deductibles. The rising cost of medical care encouraged a progression to managed care plans and today a large proportion of plan participants are enrolled in plans that to some extent limit cost through supply-side restrictions on the care that is provided. For a few years, it appeared as though the introduction of managed care arrangements was indeed reducing the rate of increase in the cost of medical care. There is substantial anecdotal evidence, however, that the ability of managed care plans to limit cost increases may be coming to an end. Patients' rights legislation and the move to "turn decisions back to doctors," for example, suggest that strict supply limits on care are increasingly coming under attack. The efficient provision of medical care remains a critical economic concern.

In this paper, we return to consideration of demand-side plan provisions that may help to control cost and to provide care more efficiently. The plan we consider is the medical saving account (MSA). MSAs have recently received considerable policy attention as an alternative approach to improving the efficiency of individual spending decisions for health care. The 1996

Matthew J. Eichner was assistant professor of economics and finance at the Columbia University Graduate School of Business and a research associate of the National Bureau of Economic Research when this work was conducted. Mark B. McClellan is professor of economics at Stanford University and a research associate of the National Bureau of Economic Research. David A. Wise is the John F. Stambaugh Professor of Political Economy at the Kennedy School of Government, Harvard University, and director of the program on the economics of aging at the National Bureau of Economic Research.

"Kennedy-Kassebaum" Health Insurance Portability and Availability Act (HIPAA) includes specific tax incentives to support the use of MSAs on a limited basis beginning in 1997.[1] The inclusion of MSAs in the HIPAA perhaps reflects the recent consideration by economists and legislators of tax reforms to encourage "demand-side" incentives to reduce medical expenditures. The MSA relies on catastrophic health insurance—which, since Arrow (1963), has been thought to be the most efficient way to provide health insurance—in conjunction with a saving plan dedicated to medical expenditures.

Notwithstanding the efficiency benefits of catastrophic health insurance, the practical use of such plans has been limited by the low saving rate of most Americans. Even rather small unexpected medical costs could be greater than the liquid saving of a large fraction of American families. Poterba, Venti, and Wise (1998), for example, find that even the median level of liquid financial assets of American families with heads aged fifty-five to sixty-four is only about $3,000.[2] The median for all families is much smaller. Eichner and Wise (1999) show that the median of family liquid assets is a paltry $1,900. For families with heads under forty-five, the median is much smaller, and it is only $300 for families with heads under twenty-five. Large firms are more likely than small firms to offer medical insurance. Among single people and families in which either spouse works in a firm with over 500 employees, the median is $1,800. Among families in which either spouse is covered by an employer- or union-provided health insurance plan, the median is somewhat higher, but still only $2,700. Even if other financial assets are counted, it is clear that a large fraction of families have saved very little. Thus it is evident that a large proportion of households, having chosen not to save, have also virtually assured that they will be "risk averse" with respect to unanticipated expenditures and—perhaps ironically—willing to pay for generous health insurance. Indeed, too much health insurance may be a companion to too little saving. A person who doesn't save may also find himself spending too much for health insurance to cover the risky situation in which no saving has placed him.

The fact that a very large fraction of families has almost no liquid savings and would find it hard to make even small out-of-pocket payments for medical care presents a practical argument against catastrophic insurance. An MSA is a way to address this concern. An MSA is, in our conception, a combination of a catastrophic health insurance plan with a significant deductible established in conjunction with a medical saving account. By

1. House resolution 3103 in the 104th Congress, which was renamed the Health Insurance Portability and Availability Act, was signed by President Clinton in August 1996.

2. Based on 1991 *Surveys of Income and Program Participation* (SIPP) data and excluding individual retirement account (IRA), 401(k), and any other personal retirement plans. *Survey of Consumer Finance* data, tabulated for us by Andrew Samwick, show higher but still very low medians.

providing a saving account that could be used to pay for substantial medical costs, without causing major short-term disruptions in family budgets, the MSA is intended to make insurance plans with high deductibles and copayments practical for a larger number of Americans. The typical plan would allow tax-free contributions to an MSA. At retirement, the MSA balance could be used for support in retirement, with taxes paid upon withdrawal of funds.

Low saving rates, however, may not be the only reason for the limited market for catastrophic health insurance. The current tax treatment of health insurance favors low-deductible plans. Employer-provided health insurance is financed with pretax dollars, so that individuals are likely to choose more coverage than they would if they faced the full price of insurance. Moreover, because out-of-pocket payments for medical care are only deductible if they exceed 7.5 percent of income, tax law favors plans that minimize out-of-pocket payments. Favorable federal tax treatment of MSAs would tend to counteract these obstacles to the purchase of health insurance with substantial out-of-pocket payments.[3]

Because a larger share of their actual medical expenditures would be financed from their own savings, individuals covered by an MSA would be more sensitive to costs of treatment over a broader range of expenditures. An MSA thus combines the desirable features of catastrophic coverage for reducing medical expenditures with a mechanism that creates a reserve for paying individual expenses. Thus an MSA coupled with a catastrophic insurance plan may reduce medical expenditures and encourage saving. To the extent that catastrophic insurance costs less than more generous plans, the MSA will also induce lower insurance costs.

Still, there remain important impediments to the feasibility of such plans. Perhaps the most important of these is the extent to which individual medical expenditures persist for long periods of time. A person who incurs high expenditures every year over a lifetime would essentially be self-insured and would accumulate no assets in the medical saving account. On the other hand, a person who is never sick would have a tax-free saving account.

In an earlier paper (Eichner, McClellan, and Wise 1998) we considered the persistence of the medical expenditures of members of a large Fortune 500 firm health insurance plan. We concluded that persistence in expenditures seemed not to pose an overriding impediment to the implementation of an MSA. In another paper (Eichner, McClellan, and Wise 1997), we discussed the attributes of such plans in a larger context, again focusing on the

---

3. At least thirteen states have already enacted tax breaks for MSAs, but these reforms have involved much lower state marginal tax rates. Existing federal law also allows employers to establish "flexible spending accounts," which permit employees to use pretax dollars for out-of-pocket medical expenditures. However, balances not spent at the end of the year are lost, so that employees tend to rely on them in a limited way for predictable expenses only.

crucial equity consideration: the extent to which the feasibility of MSAs is limited by the persistence of medical expenditures over an individual's working life. The broad implications of such tax incentives for insurance and health care purchasing decisions are also reviewed in this paper, and we discuss the key behavioral issues that are important in evaluating such plans. In particular, the analysis illustrates how the MSAs envisioned in the Kennedy-Kassebaum legislation would work in practice, describing the important features of MSA tax incentives and considering how these incentives might affect individual behavior.

We continue the analysis of MSAs in this paper, focusing again on the implications of persistence in individual expenditures. Two important improvements in recently available data prompt us to revisit this question: One is that we now have access to a six-year panel of individual medical expenditures in a large firm, whereas the prior analysis was based only on a three-year panel. The persistence in expenditures can be much more accurately gauged with the six-year panel. The second reason is that the new data allow more accurate identification of plan enrollees who do not use care in a given year. In our prior work we were in some instances unable to distinguish persons who left the firm from those who simply had no medical expenditures in a year. With the current data, we can identify all persons covered by the plan, even if they have no medical expenditure in a given year. In addition, in this paper we give more careful attention to the potentially important saving effects of MSAs. In particular, we consider the accumulation in the MSA account, based on how the funds are invested.

In the next section we describe the Fortune 500 firm data used in this analysis. In section 6.3, we present summary data on the persistence in expenditures and on the proportion of plan members who have high expenditures in successive years. In section 6.4, we describe the method that we use to project the lifetime expenditures of plan members under an MSA. The goal is to approximate the distribution of medical expenditures over a working lifetime in a large firm. We estimate a model that captures the pattern of expenditures among employees and then use the model to simulate the lifetime distribution of expenditures. Particular attention is given to two issues: One is the extent of persistence, the expected expenditure in one year conditional on expenditure in prior years. The second is the "unexplained" residual variance, or "shock" in expenditures, conditional on expenditure in prior years. An important aspect of the data is that this unexplained variance is very large and, much more than persistence, determines the lifetime distributions of expenditures. Moreover, these shocks are not approximated well by any analytic distribution. Thus our simulation procedure depends heavily on nonparametric analysis based on the empirical distribution of conditional expenditures.

The key results are in the form of simulations based on the estimated models. Under the illustrative plan we have simulated, most employees would approach retirement with a substantial proportion of MSA contributions remaining in the account. Only a small fraction would approach retirement with very small balances. Based on our illustrative plan, if investment of MSA assets were in equities, more than 50 percent of employees would have MSA balances greater than 300 percent of lifetime contributions to the MSA. Only about 10 percent of men would retain less than 200 percent of contributions and only about 10 percent of women would retain less than 125 percent of contributions. If investment were in bonds, balances would be much lower. In this case about 10 percent of both men and women would retain less than 50 percent of contributions. Thus we believe that persistence of medical expenditures does not present an overriding obstacle to the adaption of MSA plans.

6.2   The Data

The data are medical claims of employees in a large Fortune 500 manufacturing firm. The analysis is based on all fee-for-service insurance claims over the six-year period 1990 through 1995. Over this period approximately 500,000 employees and their dependents were covered through these insurance plans. All reported inpatient and outpatient medical expenditures for this population are included in our analysis.[4]

The firm has two fee-for-service plans, one for hourly and another for salaried employees. The hourly plan, with benefits negotiated in union contracts, provides "first-dollar" coverage for virtually all health care. Because of this virtually unlimited coverage, hourly employees have no financial incentives to join managed-care or health maintenance organization (HMO) plans, although specific provider relationships and location considerations may provide some nonfinancial incentives. The salaried plan has an annual deductible of $200 per individual and $250 per family, a 20 percent coinsurance rate for all expenses, and an out-of-pocket annual limit (including the deductible) of $500 per family. Routine physical examinations are not covered. Both plans incorporate limited case management for certain high-cost medical conditions and concurrent review of hospital stays. The hourly plan includes preadmission certification requirements for certain elective admissions; patients who elect admission despite precertification denial are responsible for 20 percent copayments up to $750 per individual

---

4. We do not include dental services, vision care, or outpatient pharmaceuticals, which account for approximately 15 percent of medical expenditures. Because these expenditures are relatively less concentrated in particular individuals than other inpatient and outpatient services, incorporating them would be unlikely to lead to a more concentrated distribution of medical expenditures in this population. Indeed, to the extent that such expenditures are not covered by traditional plans, their eligibility for MSA coverage would reduce individuals' net out-of-pocket medical expenses.

and $1,500 per family. Both plans also require second opinions for sixteen elective surgical procedures, although the procedures are covered regardless of the second-opinion finding. Both plans have very generous hospital stay limits: 365 days per stay, renewable after 60 days out of the hospital.

As emphasized in the introduction, there are two important features of the new data used in this analysis: One is the longer panel, and the other is the "enrollment" data that allow us to track employees who are plan members but have no medical expenditures in a given year. The enrollment data are available, however, only for the last three years of the panel. For the first three years, we must estimate whether a person who has zero expenditure is still enrolled in the plan. We do this by using the relationship between enrollment on the one hand and personal expenditure and other attributes on the other hand, based on the last three years of the panel. In this way, we create a synthetic data file that contains reported expenditures of all enrollees for the last three years; for the first three years positive expenditures are as reported, but zero expenditures are simulated. For example, suppose a person has no expenditure in year three. Based on the estimated probability that the person is still enrolled in the plan—a probability based on the enrollment data for the last three years—the person is randomly maintained in the file with zero expenditure, or removed from the sample.

6.3   Summary Descriptions of Persistence

Do employees who have high expenditures in one year also have high expenditures in subsequent years as well? To begin to answer this question, we have divided plan enrollees into annual expenditure deciles. Panel A of figure 6.1 shows average annual expenditures in each of the years 1990 through 1995 for two groups of enrollees: those who were in the top expenditure decile in 1990, and those who were in the top expenditure decile in 1995. Consider the first group: In 1990, their average expenditure was $10,295. In the next year, their average expenditure was $4,329; two years later, in 1992, they spent an average of $3,804; and so forth. By 1995, their average expenditure had fallen to $3,636. For comparison, the figure also shows the average expenditures for all enrollees over these three years, which was $1,293 in 1990 and increased 27 percent to $1,646 by 1995. Because of the overall "inflation" in expenditure, it is perhaps more informative to consider expenditure relative to the average, as shown in panel B of figure 6.1. Persons in the 10th decile in 1990 spent eight times as much as the average in that year. But six years later, in 1995, they spent just over twice the average.

Thus these data show two important regularities: Employees in the top decile continue to have expenditures above the average over the next five years, but there is also a substantial, almost fourfold, decline in expenditures—relative to the overall average—over these six years. Rather than considering the subsequent expenditures of employees conditional on ex-

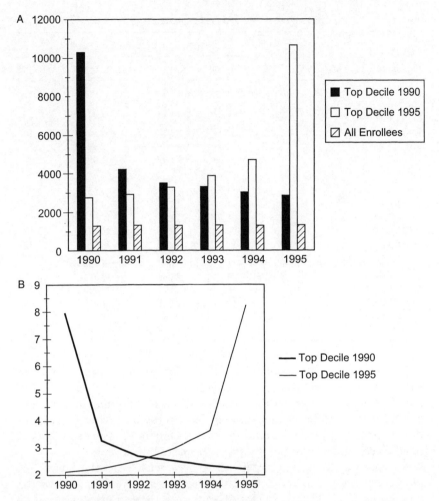

Fig. 6.1   Expenditure for top 1990 and 1995 deciles: *A*, Mean annual expenditure; *B*, Relative annual expenditure

penditure level in 1990, an alternative is to consider previous expenditure conditional on expenditures in 1995. What were the prior expenditures of employees in the top decile in 1995? Did they also have higher-than-average expenditures in the previous five years? Yes, but whereas the expenditures of employees in the top decile in 1995 were over eight times the average in that year, five years prior to that their average expenditure was only about two times the average, as shown in panel B of figure 6.1. Thus the subsequent expenditure pattern of persons in the top decile in 1990 is almost a mirror image of the prior expenditure pattern of persons who were in the top decile in 1995.

Table 6.1   Distribution of 1993 and 1995 Expenditures (%)

			Expenditure Interval in 1995		
Expenditure Interval in 1993	$0	$1–300	$301–1,000	$1,001–5,000	>$5,000
Joint Distribution of 1993 and 1995 Expenditures					
$0	32.18	6.02	2.98	2.02	1.24
$1–$300	8.76	7.37	3.76	2.53	1.30
$301–$1000	3.53	3.55	3.18	2.46	1.18
$1001–$5000	2.44	2.37	2.39	2.90	1.53
>$5000	1.27	1.09	1.02	1.49	1.44
Distribution of 1995 Expenditures Conditional on 1993 Expenditures					
$0	72.41	13.54	6.70	4.55	2.80
$1–$300	36.92	31.09	15.87	10.65	5.47
$301–$1000	25.41	25.53	22.85	17.69	8.52
$1001–$5000	20.96	20.39	20.54	24.94	13.17
>$5000	20.13	17.30	16.20	23.56	22.82
Distribution of 1993 Expenditures Conditional on 1995 Expenditures					
$0	66.79	29.50	22.34	17.73	18.56
$1–$300	18.18	36.14	28.25	22.17	19.36
$301–$1000	7.33	17.39	23.82	21.58	17.68
$1001–$5000	5.05	11.61	17.90	25.43	22.84
>$5000	2.64	5.36	7.69	13.09	21.56

On the other hand, employees with the lowest expenditures in 1990, which are not shown, had higher expenditures in the next six years. For example, those in the bottom three deciles, who spent nothing in 1990, had expenditures near the average six years later in 1995. In all deciles, expenditures tend to gravitate toward the mean. Only in the top decile do expenditures remain substantially above the mean for six years.

Another way to view persistence is to consider the distribution of employee expenditure intervals for two different years. Table 6.1 shows the distribution for 1993 and 1995 for all employees. Expenditures in each year are divided into five intervals, and three versions of the distribution are shown. The first panel shows the joint distributions of expenditures in the two years. For example, 7.37 percent of employees had expenditures between $1 and $300 in both years, and 8.76 percent had expenditures between $0 and $300 in 1993 and zero expenditures in 1995 (the percentages sum to 100 over all cells). The most important part of this panel pertains to the fraction of employees who had high expenditures in both years. Only about 7.4 percent had expenditures above $1,000 in both years, and only 1.44 percent had expenditures above $5,000 in both years. Thus only a very small proportion of employees have high expenditures in one year as well as two years later, or two years earlier.

The data also show persistence, consistent with the data in panels A and B of figure 6.1. The second panel of table 6.2 shows the distribution of 1995

Table 6.2   **Distribution of 1990 and 1995 Expenditures (%)**

		Expenditure Interval in 1995			
Expenditure Interval in 1990	$0	$1–300	$301–1,000	$1,001–5,000	>$5,000
Joint Distribution of 1993 and 1995 Expenditures					
$0	21.46	7.27	4.02	3.08	1.78
$1–$300	12.22	6.99	4.09	2.95	1.62
$301–$1000	5.30	3.65	3.12	2.65	1.36
$1001–$5000	3.58	2.42	2.21	2.59	1.49
>$5000	1.86	1.10	0.90	1.19	1.10
Distribution of 1995 Expenditures Conditional on 1990 Expenditures					
$0	57.05	19.33	10.69	8.19	4.74
$1–$300	43.85	25.07	14.66	10.59	5.82
$301–$1000	32.97	22.71	19.42	16.47	8.43
$1001–$5000	29.14	19.71	17.95	21.08	12.12
>$5000	30.18	17.82	14.70	19.36	17.93
Distribution of 1990 Expenditures Conditional on 1995 Expenditures					
$0	48.30	33.93	28.03	24.71	24.23
$1–$300	27.51	32.61	28.50	23.68	22.08
$301–$1000	11.94	17.04	21.77	21.26	18.43
$1001–$5000	8.07	11.31	15.39	20.80	20.27
>$5000	4.18	5.11	6.30	9.55	14.99

expenditures conditional on the expenditure interval in 1989. For example, 22.82 percent of persons who spent more than $5,000 in 1993 also spent more than $5,000 in 1995, whereas only 2.80 percent of persons who had no expenditures in 1989 spent more than $5,000 in 1991. Rather than looking forward, as in the second panel, the third panel of table 6.2 looks backward; it shows the distribution of 1993 expenditures conditional on the expenditure interval in 1995. Although only a small proportion of employees with expenditures above $5,000 in 1995 also had high expenditures two years earlier in 1993, these employees are more likely to have had high expenditures two years earlier than were persons who had low expenditures in 1991. For example, 21.56 percent of employees who spent more than $5,000 in 1995 had also spent more than $5,000 two years earlier, whereas only 2.64 percent of employees who spent nothing in 1995 had spent more than $5,000 two years prior.

Table 6.2 is just like table 6.1 except that it considers the distribution of expenditures five years apart, in 1990 and 1995. Again, the key fact is that only a very small fraction of enrollees have high expenditures in successive years; just 1.10 percent had expenditures above $5,000 in both 1990 and 1995. Only 6.37 percent had expenditures above $1,000 in both years.

These data may at first appear to be inconsistent with the known high concentration of medical expenditures among a small fraction of enrollees in any given year. In fact, they are consistent with those data. Although only a very small proportion of employees has high expenditures in the first and third years, for example, the mean expenditure among the top percentile is very large. Thus in any one year, about 20 percent of enrollees in our sample account for about 90 percent of total health care costs. What our data allow, in contrast to cross-sectional data sources, is the analysis of individual expenditures over time. Even over a longer period of time, a small proportion of enrollees accounts for the bulk of expenditures. But they are not the same employees from one year to the next. Again, even over an extended period of time only a small proportion of enrollees has large expenditures, and thus the few that do account for a large fraction of the cost.

6.4   A Semiparametric Model of Expenditures

We use the same basic model that we have used in our previous papers. The goal is a formal description of medical expenditures that will allow us to simulate the pattern of expenditures over the working life, based, in this paper, on the expenditure observed over six years. We begin with a description of the model and its use to predict expenditures and then give. A critical feature of the model is the extent to which it captures actual expenditure patterns.

6.4.1   The Model

A useful way to think about the problem is to assume that large medical expenditures arise as random shocks, which in practice are infrequent. But when they do occur, they may persist for several years. Thus, there are two critical aspects of health care expenditures that the model must capture. One is the relationship between expenditures in successive years, the persistence in expenditures. The other is the random shocks in health care expenditures that are not predicted by prior expenditures or individual demographic characteristics. No matter what the expenditures of employees in prior years, there is an enormous variation in expenditures the next year. Thus enrollees with no expenditure in one year stand some chance of having very high expenditure in the next year. Likewise, enrollees with very high expenditures in one year stand a good chance of having very low expenditures in the next year. Indeed, the lifetime distribution of expenditures is determined much more by these random shocks than by persistent expenditures that are predictable based on prior expenditures or demographic characteristics.

Because a large fraction of employees have no expenditures in a given year, it is useful to consider explicitly the expected value of expenditures in year tM_t, given by

(1) $E(M_t) = \Pr[M_t = 0] \times 0 + \Pr[M_t > 0] \times E(M_t \mid M_t > 0)$

We estimate the two components of this equation—$\Pr[M_t > 0]$ and $E(M_t \mid M_t > 0)$—separately. The probability of nonzero expenditures is estimated using a linear probability specification, and the level of expenditures given that expenditures are positive is estimated using a log-linear regression. In both cases, the estimated relationship is of the form

(2) $$M_t = \alpha + \beta D + \gamma M_{\text{lag}} + \varepsilon,$$

where medical expenditures in year t, M_t, are predicted by three factors: (a) demographic characteristics, denoted by D, and which include age, sex, and employment status (hourly or salaried); (b) past health care expenditures M_{lag} which include expenditures in years $t-1, t-2, \ldots, t-5$; and (c) random shocks, ε.

The critical part of our analysis is the use of the resulting estimates to predict future expenditures. The fit of these predictions depends not only on our ability to model expected expenditures given an individual's characteristics, but also on the distribution of shocks to expenditures. We want the distribution that is used in prediction to match the actual distribution as closely as possible, and this distribution is extremely skewed within any given cell of expenditures. We model this critical "error" component non-parametrically: Instead of assuming a particular distribution for the random shocks ε, we use the actual distribution of expenditure errors, given demographic characteristics and past expenditures. For example, consider the prediction of expenditures in the third year, given expenditures in the prior two years. The sample is divided into groups determined by age, sex, and employee status (hourly or salaried). Then, within each of these groups the sample is further divided into expenditure groups defined by expenditures in prior years. Now the prediction of expenditure in year six, for example, has two parts. First, the parameters estimated in equation (2) are used to predict mean expenditures in year six. This "systematic" part would show, for example, that enrollees with high expenditures in year one tended on average to have much lower expenditures five years later, as revealed in figure 6.1. Second, a random shock is added to this systematic component. Within each cell, the random component is selected randomly from the actual distribution of residuals within that cell. Suppose that the prediction is for enrollees who had high expenditures in years one through five. This method assures that if a given proportion of persons in this high-expenditure cell have high expenditures in the sixth year, then our predictions will also show this same proportion (on average) to have high expenditures in the sixth year.

Thus, the method captures not only the average relationship between expenditures over time, but if high expenditures persist for some proportion of persons with a given set of demographic and past expenditure characteristics, then the model will also capture the proportion with high persistence. Predictions for years beyond six are obtained by repeated applications of this procedure.

The predictions based on the analysis here should be more accurate than those presented in our previous papers, for two reasons: One is the longer panel and the other is that we take account of the departure of enrollees from the firm. There remains an additional limitation that even this longer panel may not capture. Suppose that expenditure twenty years hence is related to current expenditure. A six-year panel cannot capture the effect of any such long lag effects. We could augment our model with information from other sources on the relationship between medical care use over very long time periods. For example, are heart problems at age fifty preceded by high health care expenditures at age thirty? No available panel of medical claims information can be used to determine directly whether such a relationship exists. However, we can observe expenditures in the next five years of persons who had high expenditures at age thirty, as in the descriptive statistics in table 6.2, for example. Additionally, going to older ages and looking backwards, we can observe the expenditures in the previous five years of persons who had high expenditures at age fifty. Both of these approaches suggest that, for the most part, very high expenditures do not persist. Thus we believe that our predictions provide a good approximation to the distributions that would be observed in very long panels. We do not show parameter estimates in this paper, but parameter estimates based on the three-year panel are discussed in Eichner, McClellan, and Wise (1998).

6.4.2 Fit

In our previous work (Eichner, McClellan, and Wise 1998), we gave considerable attention to the fit of the model and found that the specification fit the data very well. In particular, the simulated distribution of expenditures at various ages matched the actual distributions very closely. Here we present only a few indicators of fit. Because predicting nonzero expenditure is an important component of prediction, we show estimates of the predicted proportion of enrollees with positive expenditure, conditional on demographic characteristics and expenditures in the prior two periods. Table 6.3 shows the actual and predicted percent with positive expenditures in 1995, conditional on expenditures in 1993 ($t-2$) and 1994 ($t-1$). The data are grouped by expenditure interval in the prior two periods. The simulated and actual percents are very close.

Figure 6.2 shows projections three years ahead, based on the prior three years of data, compared to actual data. The projections are by age, gender, and employee group. For example, data for persons when they were aged twenty-five, twenty-six, and twenty-seven are used to predict the proportion with positive expenditures at age thirty. The match between simulated and actual proportions is quite close.

Finally, figure 6.3 shows simulated proportions with positive expenditures over a "working life." These simulated proportions are determined as follows: Begin with a sample of 1,000 employees age twenty-five, for each

Table 6.3   **Actual Versus Simulated 1995 Expenditures, Conditional on Expenditures in 1993 and 1994 (%)**

	1993 Expenditure				
1994 Expenditure	$0	$0–300	$300–1,000	$1,000–5,000	$5,000+
$0					
Actual	22.94	42.50	45.22	48.29	44.47
Simulated	22.75	41.84	48.28	46.38	47.11
$0–$300					
Actual	51.32	66.62	69.85	71.77	69.16
Simulated	50.25	68.10	70.62	71.37	69.39
$300–$1000					
Actual	55.79	73.35	79.49	79.97	81.14
Simulated	56.68	74.93	78.26	78.72	78.00
$1000–$5000					
Actual	61.73	74.63	83.73	85.51	84.63
Simulated	60.27	72.27	83.05	85.69	83.75
$5000+					
Actual	66.03	74.88	76.70	85.57	90.00
Simulated	62.82	77.65	77.67	85.74	90.19

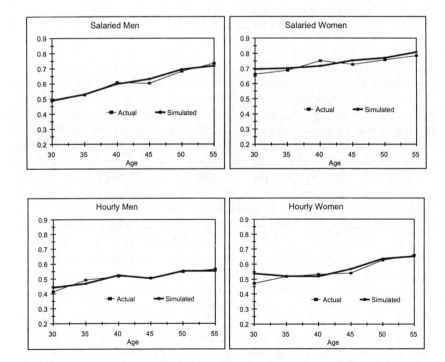

Fig. 6.2   **Three-year-ahead projections, by age, gender, and employee group**

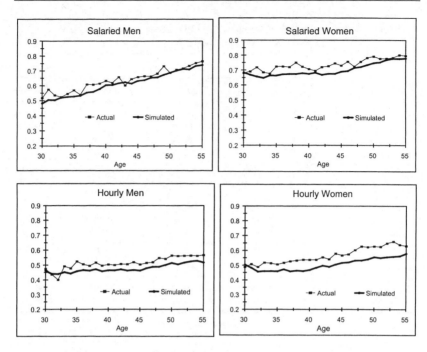

Fig. 6.3   **Projections of positive expenditures over a working life of salaried men, salaried women, hourly men, and hourly women**

gender and employee group. Then apply equations (1) and (2) repeatedly, producing a stream of expenditures for each person through age fifty-five. The simulated proportions at a given age are the proportion of enrollees simulated to have positive expenditures. The actual proportions are the actual proportions of enrollees at a given age with positive expenditures. Although the match for salaried men and women is quite close, for salaried enrollees the simulated proportions are somewhat lower than the actual proportions—thus exaggerating to some extent the proportions of enrollees for zero expenditures. Overall, though, we conclude that simulated expenditures compare closely with actual expenditure patterns.

The descriptive data above suggest that persistence is not as prevalent as might be thought. We would like to know, however, how the MSA accumulations of plan enrollees over a working life would vary among enrollees. Would a large number spend all contributions for medical expenditures, while others spent little or nothing? Or would the distribution of MSA balances tend to be much less extreme?

To answer this question, we have simulated lifetime expenditures. The simulations are based on a model of individual expenditures over time, which in turn is based on the pattern of expenditures over the six years of observed data. Here, we explain only the key features of the model. A useful way to think about expenditures is to assume that large medical expenditures arise as random shocks, which in practice are infrequent. But when they do occur, they may persist for several years. Thus, there are two critical aspects of health care expenditures that the model must capture. One is the relationship between expenditures in successive years, the persistence in expenditures. The other is the random shocks in health care expenditures that are not predicted by prior expenditures or by demographic variables. No matter what the expenditures of employees in prior years, there is an enormous variation in expenditures the next year. Thus enrollees with no expenditure in one year stand some chance of having very high expenditure in the next year. Likewise, enrollees with very high expenditures in one year stand a good chance of having very low expenditures in the next year. Indeed, the lifetime distribution of expenditures is determined much more by these random shocks than by persistent expenditures that are predictable based on prior expenditures or demographic characteristics. Extensive evaluation of actual versus predicted medical spending shows that the model predicts actual expenditure patterns quite well.[5] Importantly, the method captures not only the average relationship between expenditures over time, but if high expenditures persist for some proportion of persons with a given set of demographic and past expenditure characteristics, then the model also captures the proportion with high persistence.

Using the model, we have simulated the lifetime expenditures of 1,000 employees who begin work at age twenty-five and retire at sixty. To predict expenditures at age twenty-six, for example, we consider age, sex, employee group, and any expenditures over the prior six years. To predict for age twenty-seven, we use age twenty-six predicted expenditures plus the earlier five years of actual expenditures, and so forth. We realize that few, if any, persons, would work for the same firm over an entire working life, but it is the expenditure pattern that we want to capture, assuming that employees continue to use a similar MSA plan.

The cumulative distribution of (i.e., the common logarithm of) lifetime expenditures for men and for women through age sixty is shown in figure 6.4. Translating to dollars, over a working lifetime, expenditures of both men and women vary from about $10,000 (about 10 percent of employees) to over $100,000 (about 10 percent of employees). The median is about $32,000.

Given the distribution of expenditures, how might an MSA plan work? We consider this plan:

- The employer puts $2,000 in each employee's MSA at the beginning of each year.[6] For illustration, we assume that MSA assets are invested

5. For details of the model and tests of predictive validity see Eichner, McClellan, and Wise (1997, 1998).
6. We assume that employees do not withdraw from their MSA balances for other purposes or contribute less than the full $2,000 in each year. This allows us to focus on the maximum variation in accumulation that is likely to result with this MSA plan.

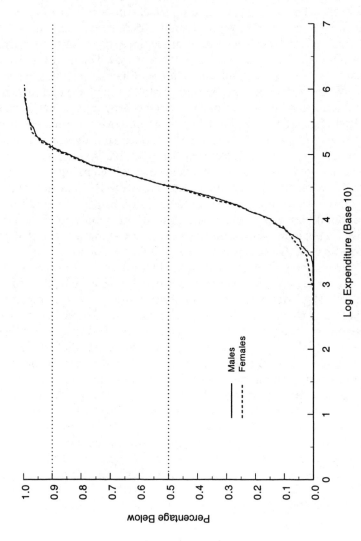

Fig. 6.4   Cumulative expenditures, ages 26–60

either in a bond fund or in a Standard & Poor's 500 index (S&P 500) market index fund. The real return on the bond fund is assumed to be equal to 2.5 percent, the average real return on high-grade long-term corporate bonds between 1926 and 1995, and the return on the market index fund equal to 7.7 percent, the average real return on large company stocks between 1926 and 1995 (see Ibbotson Associates 1998).

• The health insurance plan has a $4,000 annual deductible, with expenses below the deductible paid by the employee (out of the MSA) and 100 percent of expenditures above the deductible covered by the health insurance plan. If the MSA balance goes to zero, all expenses are paid by the insurance plan.

By assuming a real rate of return in the MSA we are in effect assuming that health care costs increase at the same rate as the consumer price index. Sensitivity analysis could of course be conducted for any number of other assumptions.

Under these assumptions, the distribution of MSA balances at age sixty are shown in panels A and B of figure 6.5. After a working lifetime, most employees are left with a substantial accumulation. With investment in stocks, the median balance for men is about $250,000. About 90 percent of the salaried men have a balance at age sixty that exceeds $150,000. For women, the median is somewhat less than $250,000. About 90 percent of women have balances that exceed $100,000. The balance with bond investment is much smaller: the median for both men is somewhat over and for women somewhat less than $100,000.

Perhaps an easier way to understand the plan implications is to consider the ending balance in the MSA relative to the sum of the $2,000 annual contributions to the MSA. The distribution of this ratio at age sixty is shown in panels A and B of figure 6.6. At retirement, the median balance for men with investment in stocks is about 350 percent of total contributions to the MSA; the median balance for women is about 325 percent of contributions. For only 10 percent of men is the balance less than 200 percent of contributions; for only 10 percent of women the balance is less than about 125 percent of total contributions. For 10 percent of men the balance is greater than about 450 percent of contributions, and for 10 percent of women the balance is over 450 percent of contributions.

It is clear that the typical employee would accumulate substantial balances in an MSA such as the one illustrated here.[7] Thus, with no counter-

---

7. The accumulation is, in fact, underestimated a bit. For technical reasons, simulated expenditures as a person ages are predicted two years at a time, assuming that the employee would pay all expenditures up to $8,000 over the two-year period, rather than up to $4,000 in any single year. This exaggerates a bit the actual employee expenditure under our plan. In addition, the investment return is assumed to apply to the balance remaining at the end of each two-year period—(balance)$(1 + r)(1 + r)$—which produces lower accumulation than a return applied continuously or at the end of each year.

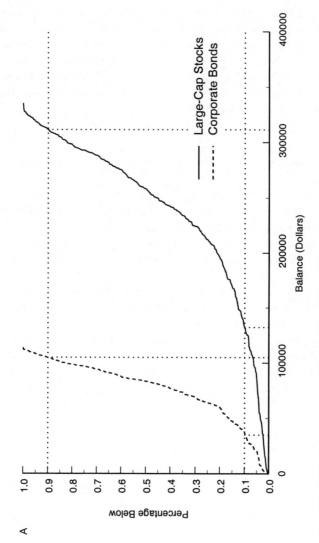

Fig. 6.5 MSA balances at age 60: *A*, Males; *B*, Females

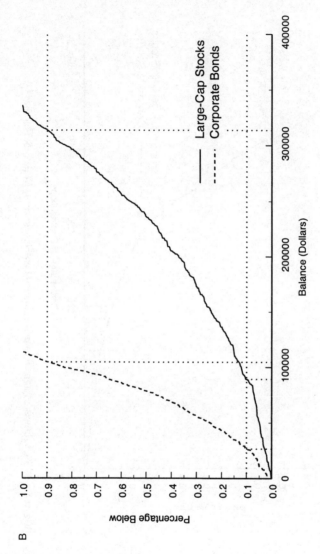

Fig. 6.5 (cont.)

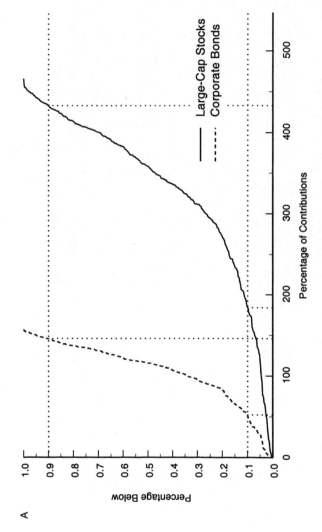

Fig. 6.6 MSA balances at age 60 as percentage of contributions: *A*, Males; *B*, Females

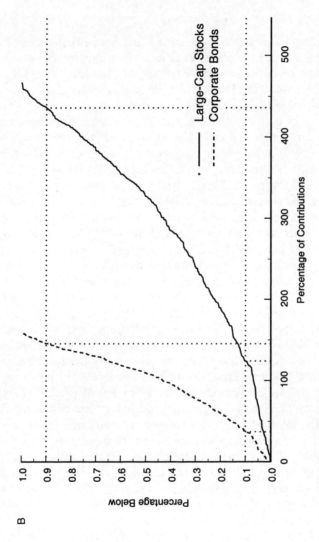

B

Large-Cap Stocks
Corporate Bonds

Percentage of Contributions

Percentage Below

Fig. 6.6 (cont.)

balancing changes, the typical employee would see a substantial increase in assets at retirement. It is also clear that the accumulation depends critically on the level of annual contributions to the MSA.

6.5   Summary and Further Discussion

Low household saving in the United States essentially makes catastrophic health insurance plans infeasible, since most households would find it difficult to pay even modestly large medical expenditures. MSAs are a way to accumulate a fund from which medical expenses could be paid under a catastrophic health insurance plan, thus—over a broad range of treatment—making individuals responsible for determining whether the benefit of the treatment is worth the price of care. But there is an additional potential obstacle to such an arrangement. If some persons have consistently high medical expenditures whereas others have consistently low expenditure, an MSA plan would essentially be self-insurance for the former and a tax-free saving account for the latter group. Thus we have considered whether the pattern of individual medical expenditures over time would present an important limit on the feasibility of MSAs. We find that although there is some persistence, the prospect of participants with consistently high medical expenditures is rare. This work follows our prior work in this area but relies on a longer panel data file than was available before and uses a data file that allows persons with zero expenditures to be distinguished from those who may have left the firm.

Under the illustrative plan we have simulated, most employees would approach retirement with a substantial proportion of MSA contributions remaining in the account. Only a small fraction would approach retirement with very small balances. Based on the illustrative plan we simulated, if investment of MSA assets were in equities, more than 50 percent of employees would have MSA balances greater than 300 percent of lifetime contributions to the MSA. Only about 10 percent of men would retain less than 200 percent of contributions and only about 10 percent of women would retain less than 125 percent of contributions. If investment were in bonds, balances would be much lower. In this case about 10 percent of both men and women would retain less than 50 percent of contributions. Thus we believe that persistence of medical expenditures does not present an overriding obstacle to the adaption of MSA plans.

The simulations do not incorporate any behavioral response and thus consider neither the reduction in medical expenditures that would likely result from such a plan, nor the ensuing reduction in medical insurance premiums that such a plan would allow. It is reasonable to assume that expenditures below the $4,000 deductible would be reduced. According to price elasticity estimates obtained by Eichner (1997), which are based on analysis of price response in another Fortune 500 firm, expenditure below the deductible would be reduced by about perhaps 35 percent. Since very high-cost treatments account for a large fraction of medical expenditures, the reduction in total cost would depend importantly on the size of the catastrophic insurance deductible.

It might well be, of course, that expenditures above the deductible would also be affected.

Such a plan would also add to individual "risk," increasing the variance in expected individual lifetime medical expenditures. The increased variance, however, must be evaluated in the context of increased saving, which would likely result from the MSA. Essentially all participants would accumulate more retirement assets than they otherwise would have. The risk is that the amount of the addition to saving is uncertain: Some would accumulate more than others.[8]

Plans like our illustrative MSA arrangement could have substantial implications for the composition of employee compensation, and possibly for the total level as well. A $2,000 MSA contribution when combined with any realistic reduced health insurance premium would still "cost" more than the current health plan. However, "forced savings" is perhaps a better characterization than "increased cost." Rough estimates suggest that the overall cost of the current firm plan is about $1,400 per participant (including spouses and children). With no behavioral effects, the MSA plan would reduce firm insurance costs by half, to about $700. With an MSA contribution of $2,000 and no reduction in other benefits, the net increase in the benefit portion of employee compensation due to the IHA package is $1,300. Employee health care expenditures are increased by about $700 because the decrease in the firm's insurance cost is due to the employee payments from the MSA balances. Thus, net benefits are increased by about $1,300.

We have not considered the tax implications of an MSA plan. The actual additional cost that must be divided between the firm and its employees may be substantially lessened by the favorable tax treatment accorded contributions to 401(k) and similar accounts. Nor have we considered the feasibility of combining it with a retirement plan such as a 401(k). (Many 401[k] plans were established with no apparent reduction in other pension benefits.[9]) Now, both the insurance premium and the MSA contribution, if it were treated like a retirement saving plan, would be tax deductible. In contrast, employee out-of-pocket health care expenses at present would typically not be tax deductible. Nor have we considered here the important adverse-selection problems that plague all health care systems with choice among a menu of plans. These issues remain to be explored.

8. We show the simulated distribution of asset accumulation. We do this to illustrate the risk of low (or high) accumulation. We do not assign a given utility function to the distributions. A small chance of a small accumulation could have a substantial affect on the overall utility attached to a distribution of outcomes.

9. See Poterba, Venti, and Wise (1996, 1998), for example.

In addition, small changes in the structure of the plan, can change substantially the way the numbers look. For example, if the MSA contribution is made at the end of the year—and thus is not available to fund expenditures in that year—accumulated MSA balances at retirement would be larger. The results would also look quite different if the MSA contribution were $1,000, say, instead of $2,000. This sensitivity suggests that a contribution could be set so that, taking into account the tax implication, for example, the MSA package would not increase health care costs.

Private retirement saving is now dominated by personal retirement saving—401(k)s and IRAs—and current trends suggest even greater reliance on personal retirement accounts in the future, as shown by Poterba, Venti, and Wise (2000). In particular, 401(k) plans established by employers are likely to expand further. Such plans place greater reliance on individual choice, perhaps engender greater self-reliance, and will almost surely lead to substantial increases in household assets at retirement. The market risk associated with such plans may also increase the risk faced by individuals, but, like the MSA risk, such risk must also be evaluated in the light of much greater accumulation of retirement assets. Many current proposals for Social Security reform also suggest the establishment of individual accounts, which place further choice in the hands of individuals and would also likely increase individual and national saving. The "medical saving account" portion of the MSA would likely have a similar effect. And it is natural to consider MSAs combined with 401(k) plans. In addition, the MSA holds the prospect of providing medical care more efficiently and reducing medical care expenditures. It does this by relying on individuals to decide whether the care they receive is worth the price they pay for it.

References

Arrow, K. 1963. Uncertainty and the welfare economics of medical care. *American Economic Review* 53:941–73.
Eichner, M. 1997. Incentives, price expectations, and medical expenditures. *Medical Expenditures and Major Risk Health Insurance* 1 (May).
———. 1998. The impact of intra-family correlations on the viability of catastrophic insurance. In *Frontiers in the economics of aging*, ed. D. Wise, 275–300. Chicago: University of Chicago Press.
Eichner, M., M. McClellan, and D. Wise. 1997. Health persistence and the feasibility of medical savings accounts. In *Tax policy and the economy*, ed. J. M. Poterba, 91–128. Cambridge: MIT Press.
———. 1998. Insurance or self-insurance? Variation, persistence, and individual health accounts. In *Inquiries in the economics of aging*, ed. D. Wise, 19–50. Chicago: University of Chicago Press.
———. 1999. Little saving and too much medical insurance: Medical saving ac-

counts could help. In *Personal saving personal choice,* ed. D. Wise. Stanford, Calif.: Hoover Institution Press.

Feldstein, M. F., and J. Gruber. 1995. A major risk approach to health insurance reform. In *Tax policy and the economy.* Vol. 9, ed. James M. Poterba, 103–130. Cambridge, Mass.: MIT Press.

Ibbotson Associates. 1998. *Stocks, bonds, bills, and inflation: 1998 yearbook.* Chicago: Ibbotson Associates.

Poterba, J. M., S. F. Venti, and D. A. Wise. 1996. How retirement saving programs increase saving. *Journal of Economic Perspectives* 10 (Fall): 91–112.

———. 1998. Personal retirement savings programs and asset accumulation: Reconciling the evidence. In *Frontiers in the economics of aging,* ed. D. Wise, 23–124. Chicago: University of Chicago Press.

———. 2000. Saver behavior and 401(k) retirement wealth. *American Economic Review, Papers and Proceedings* 90 (2): 297–302.

Supplementing Public Insurance Coverage with Private Coverage
Implications for Medical Care Systems

David M. Cutler

7.1 Introduction

A central question for governments running medical care systems is whether to allow people to supplement the public insurance policy. All developed countries insure a significant part of the population through public insurance. But not all services are covered publicly, or the services covered may not be of the highest quality. Governments thus need to decide whether people are allowed to purchase additional insurance to supplement the basic package and, if so, under what restrictions.

Supplemental health insurance may be of three types. The first, and most straightforward, is for services that are not covered under the public system. An example of such coverage is outpatient prescription drugs, which are omitted from Medicare in the United States and Canada. The second type of supplemental insurance is for the cost sharing required in public insurance systems. Medical systems frequently require beneficiaries to pay for part of the cost of their medical care utilization. If it is allowed, recipients of public insurance may purchase secondary insurance to reduce this cost sharing. The third type of insurance is for services that are covered under the public plan but for which private provision might be preferred to public provision. Because of tight budget constraints on service availability, some countries have waiting lines for access to specialty services. Some

This paper was prepared for the United States–Japan Conference on the Economics of Aging. I am grateful to the U.S. National Institute on Aging and the Japan Foundation Center for Global Partnership for research support.

David M. Cutler is professor of economics in the Department of Economics and Kennedy School of Government, Harvard University, and a research associate of the National Bureau of Economic Research.

people purchase private insurance to see providers outside of the public system, in effect jumping the public queue.

These three roles for supplemental insurance are very different, and thus their economic implications are different. Insurance for noncovered services is the least controversial. In most countries, the public sector allows or encourages such insurance. Such insurance may still have implications for the public sector, however. There are two ways this may occur. First, covered services may be complementary or substitutable for uncovered services. As the price of uncovered services changes, therefore, the demand for covered services may change as well. Second, the possession of private insurance might reduce poverty, reducing enrollment in other public health and income support programs.

Insurance for cost sharing required in the public system is more complex. On the one hand, allowing people to purchase such insurance reduces their exposure to financial risk, thereby increasing welfare. On the other hand, insurance for cost sharing creates a moral hazard, much of which is paid for by the public system. Because these public costs are not passed back to individuals purchasing private insurance, insurance to reduce cost sharing is in effect subsidized by the public sector. Whether supplemental policies to reduce cost sharing on net are welfare improving or decreasing depends on how the public system by itself compares to the optimal policy, and what the losses are from increased moral hazard.

Supplemental insurance for queue-jumping is perhaps the most controversial type of supplemental insurance. Some countries, such as Canada, prohibit physicians from accepting payment for services that are covered by the public sector. The government is concerned that if such payments are possible, the rich will buy increased access at the expense of the poor. But both rich and poor may benefit from this insurance, if increased demand by those with supplemental insurance leads to increased supply of medical resources.

This paper discusses these three types of supplemental insurance and presents empirical evidence on the effects of the first two. The empirical analysis focuses on the Medicare program in the United States, where supplemental insurance is extremely common—about 85 percent of Medicare recipients have additional coverage beyond the basic Medicare package. This insurance is used to insure uncovered services (primarily outpatient prescription drugs) and to reduce the cost sharing in the Medicare plan. In the United States, queue jumping is not important (because supply is essentially unlimited). I estimate that people with supplemental insurance coverage paying for Medicare cost sharing spend about 35 percent more on Medicare services than people without supplemental insurance coverage. However, supplemental insurance also limits poverty among the elderly. Keeping incomes high and thus keeping people off of other programs offsets nearly half of the moral hazard effect. In total, allowing supple-

Table 7.1   **Use of Supplemental Insurance in G7 Countries**

Country	Use of Supplemental Insurance
Canada	Uncovered services (prescription drugs)
France	Cost sharing
Germany	Uncovered services (amenities)
Italy	Queue jumping
Japan	Uncovered services (amenities)
United Kingdom	Queue jumping
United States	Uncovered services (prescription drugs); cost sharing

Notes: See Cutler (1999) for additional description. The United States row is for Medicare.

mental insurance leads to substantial cost increases for the public sector, but is not without benefits.

The next section of the paper discusses the three types of supplemental coverage theoretically. The third section presents basic information about supplemental insurance in the United States, and the fourth section estimates the impact of such coverage on medical care costs. The last section concludes.

7.2   Interactions Between Public and Private Insurance

Imagine a situation in which the government is providing health insurance to all or a portion of the population. The government has a benefit package that covers some services but not others. For example, the government might cover acute services but not long-term care services, or it might require substantial cost sharing under the basic insurance plan. Beneficiaries of the public program may want to supplement the public insurance plan with private insurance. Three types of supplemental insurance policies could be allowed.

7.2.1   Uncovered Services

The first type of supplemental insurance is for services that are not covered under the public insurance program. Table 7.1 shows countries that allow supplemental insurance for this purpose.[1] Among the Group of Seven (G7) countries, Canada, Germany, Japan, and the United States have supplemental insurance for this purpose. In Canada and the United States, the uncovered service is largely outpatient prescription drugs. In Germany and Japan, uncovered services include amenities, such as private hospital rooms, or minor services, such as eye and ear exams.

The public sector would appear, at first glance, to be indifferent to whether this insurance is provided. But insurance for noncovered services

---

1. The entry for the United States is for the Medicare program.

will affect the public sector in two ways. The first link results from service complementarity or substitutability. Supplementary insurance lowers the price of the services it covers. This price reduction will increase use of those services. This will in turn affect use of covered services, either positively (if covered and uncovered services are complements) or negatively (if covered and uncovered services are substitutes).

An example of this substitution is provided by the Medicare program in the United States. As noted above, Medicare does not cover outpatient prescription drugs. Some people who value coverage for prescription drugs will obtain private insurance for it. Coverage for prescription drugs may increase or decrease use of hospital and physician services, which are covered by Medicare. If prescription drugs keep people out of the hospital (for example, antihypertensive medication that prevents strokes), people with private insurance coverage for prescription drugs will spend less on hospital care than will people without coverage for prescription drugs. If prescription drugs are associated with increased doctor visits, however (for example, for monitoring of antihypertensive medication), private coverage might raise the costs of the public program.

Supplementary insurance for uncovered services also affects the public sector by altering eligibility for other public programs. In most countries, low-income people are exempt from the cost sharing in public insurance systems. In the United States, for example, Medicaid covers the cost of medical care for low-income elderly with high medical expenses. Such people may also receive additional income support or assistance with in-kind goods such as housing and food. People who have coverage for supplementary services are less likely to spend a large share of income on medical care, and are thus less likely to fall below the income threshold. As a result, having supplemental insurance coverage may reduce spending on other public programs.

7.2.2   Cost Sharing

The second type of supplemental insurance is for cost sharing required under the public insurance plan. When the public insurance plan requires some cost sharing, people may be allowed to purchase insurance that pays for these out-of-pocket costs. Supplemental insurance to reduce cost sharing is common in France and the United States.

Allowing such policies reduces the financial risk that people bear. If public insurance systems are insufficiently generous, this is a welfare gain. But such policies also have a clear moral hazard effect. People who have insured their cost sharing will use more services than people who have not. For example, they may be more likely to visit doctors for routine care, or to be hospitalized in precautionary situations. Some of this additional utilization will be paid for by the private insurance, but other costs will be paid

Healthy

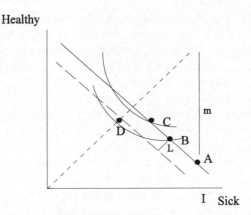

I   Sick

Fig. 7.1   The decision to purchase Medigap coverage

for under the public insurance policy. This will increase public spending on medical care.

Imagine, for example, that a person has a hospital deductible of $500. This deductible is sufficiently high that when the person has pneumonia he or she chooses to stay at home rather than entering the hospital. Now suppose the person buys private insurance that covers the $500 deductible. With no cost sharing required for a hospital stay, the person enters the hospital for pneumonia. The first $500 of this hospital stay is covered by the private insurance policy, but the rest is covered by the public policy. If the hospital stay costs $2,000, the cost to the public sector will be $1,500. In effect, the private insurance policy has induced moral hazard that is partly paid for by the public sector.

The moral hazard effect means that private insurance is implicitly subsidized by the public sector. The cost of the private policy is the expected cost of the $500 deductible, but the benefit of the policy is the expectation of the full $2,000 of medical services that it allows the individual to consume. Three-quarters of the cost of supplemental insurance is paid for by the public sector.

In such a situation, it is possible that increasing the generosity of the public program may actually *reduce* overall spending on the public program. I demonstrate this issue in figure 7.1.[2] Imagine an individual facing two possible health states: healthy and sick. Income is I in both states. An uninsured person who is sick would spend m on medical care. Thus, in the absence of insurance, the person will have consumption given by point A in figure 7.1: I when healthy and I-m when sick. The solid line passing through point A is the set of transfers that an insurance company can offer

---

2. The figure is based on the familiar Rothschild and Stiglitz (1976) analysis.

the person while not losing money. In the absence of moral hazard, the line would have slope equal to the negative of the inverse of the probability of being sick.[3] With moral hazard, the line has a flatter slope, reflecting the fact that medical and nonmedical consumption is diminished because of the additional medical care utilization.

Imagine that public insurance is incomplete. For example, the public sector might offer point B in the figure—income is smoothed, but there are still substantial liabilities when sick. The indifference curve associated with this insurance is also shown in the figure.

Suppose the person has access to a private insurance policy that provides full insurance, but at some administrative cost. If a person pays amount L, he can buy insurance to pay for the cost sharing in the public program. In figure 7.1, the consumer will choose to purchase the supplemental policy. Paying the transactions cost L allows the consumer to reach point D, which has higher utility than point B. The reason for the higher utility is that the value of increased risk sharing is greater than the administrative cost required to purchase the policy.

If the public insurance policy were made more generous, however, the supplemental policy would be less attractive. Imagine that the public policy were increased in generosity to point C. Utility at point C is higher than at point D, even though point D offers better insurance. The additional insurance is valuable, but not worth enough to overcome the transactions cost. Thus, when the policy is made more generous, fewer people buy the supplemental policy. Total medical spending will be lower at C than at D.

Even public-sector costs may fall, depending on how much of the increased costs of policy D are borne by the public sector. For example, if reducing the deductible to $250 would cause people not to purchase supplemental insurance but would lead to only half of the people with pneumonia entering the hospital, public-sector costs could decline by making the program more generous.

7.2.3   Queue Jumping

The third type of supplemental insurance is to finance services paid for by the public sector but in a more timely manner. In countries with supply-side constraints on medical service provision, as in most countries outside of the United States, there are frequently waiting lines to access medical services. Although emergency cases are often treated immediately, less urgent cases might have to wait a year or longer for treatment. People who place a high value on medical services might want to jump to the front of the line.

3. Suppose the person pays a premium I independent of health state and receives m of medical services when sick. The insurance company's profit is given by $\pi = I - pm$. In a zero-profit equilibrium, the amount of money received when sick is $m = -1/p$ per dollar of insurance purchased.

Imagine a situation in which a person has injured his or her hip and is waiting for a hip replacement operation. Receiving the operation involves two steps: consulting an orthopedist and then having surgery. In a supply-rationed system, the wait for the orthopedist might be six months to a year, followed by another half-year wait for surgery. A person who does not want to wait in line may use private insurance to pay for a visit to an orthopedist. In countries that allow it, orthopedists will see patients outside of the public system in a much shorter period of time—perhaps a week or two. From there, the individual can join the waiting list for surgery in the public hospital, just as if he or she saw the orthopedist under the public system; or, in an extreme case, the insurance might pay for the cost of surgery. At minimum, private insurance can, at little cost, reduce the waiting time for surgery by half or more, without necessarily paying for the entire course of treatment.

Rich people can afford supplemental insurance more than poor people and may value shorter waits more highly. The fear that queue jumping is a device for the rich to get better medical care than the poor has led some countries to ban this form of insurance and even ban out-of-pocket payments for services covered by the public sector. In Canada, for example, doctors are not allowed to charge privately for services that are covered by the public sector.

But the poor are not necessarily worse off. The reason for this is that when people use supplemental insurance, some resources are freed up, and total supply may rise at the same public expense. Imagine in the example above that orthopedist appointments last one hour and that with no supplemental payments, the orthopedist works from 9 A.M. to 5 P.M. When supplemental payments are allowed, the orthopedist might still see publicly insured patients from 9 A.M. to 5 P.M. and then see privately insured patients after 5 P.M. Privately insured patients are better off, since they see the doctor sooner. Patients with public insurance are better off as well, since the doctor allocates the same time as he did previously but has fewer patients to see. Publicly insured patients do not have as significant a reduction in waiting times as privately insured patients, but they are still better off.

Even if no individual doctor works more hours, publicly insured patients might be made better off. When the rich opt to purchase services privately, there are more funds left in the public budget, and thus a greater ability of the public sector to expand total resource supply. If orthopedists see public patients only from 9 A.M. to 4 P.M., the public sector can pay 12 percent less (one out of every eight hours) for seeing public patients. With the money that is saved, more orthopedists can be hired. Indeed, the public sector can hire the equivalent of an additional hour for each orthopedist, making it as if each doctor worked an hour more.

The case where publicly insured patients are worse off is when total resource supply remains the same but the rich get served more rapidly. For example, if physicians are paid on a salary basis and cut their time allotment to the public sector, without a reduction in salary, patients left in the public insurance plan will be worse off.

Of course, such an issue involves ethics as well as economics. One of the rationales for government provision of medical services is that countries do not want inequality in the provision of medical services (Cutler 2002). If inequality of medical care resources is bad inherently, supplemental insurance may be viewed adversely, even if the poor also receive more services.

7.3   Supplemental Insurance in the United States

I now turn to an empirical examination of the impact of supplemental insurance on the public sector. My analysis is focused on the Medicare program in the United States. Supplemental insurance for Medicare is available for uncovered services and cost sharing. I describe this insurance in this section and discuss its likely effects. In the next section, I examine the impact of supplemental insurance on public spending.

Medicare is the program that serves the aged and disabled population. Ninety percent of Medicare recipients are over age sixty-four; 10 percent qualify because of a disability. Most Medicare beneficiaries (about 85 percent) are enrolled in the traditional fee-for-service insurance plan. This plan, which is run by the federal government, has two types of benefits. Part A of the program provides inpatient benefits, including acute care services in inpatient hospitals and long-term care services, provided that they are related to an acute episode of care. Part B of the program covers outpatient services, including physician visits and laboratory services.

Table 7.2 shows information on payments for medical care services used by Medicare beneficiaries in 1995, taken from the *Medicare Current Beneficiary Survey* (MCBS). The top row shows that total spending for medical services for Medicare beneficiaries was $8,500 per person. Two-thirds of this amount ($5,697) was for acute care services, and one-third ($2,587) was for long-term care services.

As the next row shows, Medicare pays for only about half of medical services used by the elderly ($4,407). There are three reasons why the Medicare share is so low. First, Medicare requires substantial cost sharing. There is a large deductible for use of hospital care equal to the cost of one day in the hospital—$788 in 1998. Furthermore, the beneficiary pays for cost sharing for long-term hospital stays (above sixty days). For part B services, there is an annual deductible of $100, with a 20 percent coinsurance rate above that amount. There is no overall cap on beneficiary liability for Medicare.

This cost sharing is substantially greater than policies sold to the non-Medicare population. In 1999, for example, the average private fee-for-service policy for an individual had an annual deductible of $245. The coin-

Table 7.2   **Medical Spending for Medicare Beneficiaries, 1995**

	Total ($)
Total	8,463
Public	
Medicare	4,407
Medicaid	1,065
VA	66
Private—insured	
Employer	423
Individual	249
HMO	88
Unknown	46
Private—direct	
Out-of-pocket	1,605
Other	411

Source: Medicare Current Beneficiary Survey.

Note: Dental spending is not included in either acute or long-term care services. VA = Veterans' Administration

surance rate was typically 20 percent, with a maximum out-of-pocket payment by the individual of $1,500 or $2,000 (Kaiser Family Foundation 2000).

The second reason why Medicare's share of coverage is so low is that Medicare does not cover outpatient prescription drugs. Prescription drugs provided in a hospital are reimbursed as part of Medicare's payment to the hospital, but drugs taken on an outpatient basis are not covered by Medicare. The lack of prescription drug coverage is a reflection of when the program was enacted. In 1965, outpatient prescription drug coverage was not standard, and thus Medicare omitted this benefit. The program has not been changed to incorporate this coverage, even though essentially all private insurance coverage includes outpatient drugs. Medicare beneficiaries spend $568 annually on outpatient prescription drugs—half of which is paid for out of pocket. The biggest item in out-of-pocket spending for the elderly is outpatient prescription drugs.

The third reason why Medicare's share of costs is low is that Medicare's coverage of long-term care services is limited. Medicare pays for long-term care services only if the service is immediately related to an acute care episode. For example, a nursing home stay to recover functional mobility after a hip fracture would be covered by part A of Medicare, but a nursing home stay related to general aging and lack of functional capacity would not be covered. Long-term care provision in acute settings is a small part of total long-term care utilization: Medicare pays for less than 20 percent of total long-term care service use by the elderly.

7.3.1 Supplemental Coverage for Medicare Beneficiaries

For these and other reasons, many Medicare beneficiaries acquire insurance to supplement the Medicare package. This insurance is provided through one of four mechanisms. The first source of supplementary insurance coverage is from Medicaid. Medicare beneficiaries who are sufficiently poor, or whose medical costs leave them with sufficiently low income, will be covered by the Medicaid program. Medicaid pays for the cost sharing required under Medicare, outpatient prescription drugs, and long-term care services, making it the most complete form of supplemental insurance coverage. As figure 7.2 shows, about 13 percent of Medicare recipients are also covered by Medicaid.

Second, some employers provide coverage for services that Medicare does not cover. Employment-based supplementary insurance is a combination of insurance for cost sharing and insurance for uncovered services: It generally pays for the cost sharing required by Medicare and typically outpatient prescription drugs, but not long-term care services. About one-third of Medicare beneficiaries have supplemental insurance from a current or former employer.

Third, individuals can join a health maintenance organization (HMO) serving the Medicare population. HMOs contracting with the federal government agree to provide at least the Medicare package for an amount roughly equal to 90 percent of average spending in the fee-for-service program in that area. In practice, most HMOs have very low cost sharing for service use—$10 per visit or less. Because HMOs enroll healthier people than average, their costs are below those in the fee-for-service program. To attract enrollees, HMOs offer additional benefits, including coverage of outpatient prescription drugs. Nearly 15 percent of Medicare beneficiaries are enrolled in an HMO, and about half of those have coverage for outpatient prescription drugs.

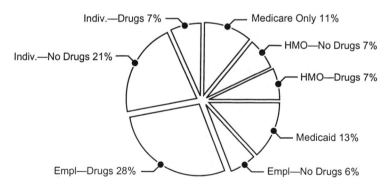

Fig. 7.2   Insurance coverage for Medicare beneficiaries
Source: MCBS (1995).

Table 7.3   **Description of Medigap Plans**

	A	B	C	D	E	F	G	H	I	J
Basic	X	X	X	X	X	X	X	X	X	X
Hospital deductible		X	X	X	X	X	X	X	X	X
SNF coinsurance			X	X	X	X	X	X	X	X
Part B deductible			X			X				X
Physician balance billing						X	X[a]		X	X
Emergency care outside										
United States			X	X	X	X	X	X	X	X
At-home recovery				X			X		X	X
Preventive care					X					X
Basic drug coverage								X	X	
Extended drug coverage										X
Price range ($)										
Low	639	900	775	1,236	1,284	1,176	1,416	1,860	2,172	2,172
High	1,665	2,001	1,271	1,395	1,284	2,449	1,436	1,896	2,987	3,144

Notes: Basic coverage pays for coinsurance for long-duration hospital stays and coinsurance for part B services. The at-home recovery benefit is for cost sharing for long-term care services related to an acute episode. Preventive care is up to $120 per year if ordered by a doctor. Basic drug coverage is 50 percent coverage after a $250 deductible, up to a maximum benefit of $1,250. Extended drug coverage has a maximum of $3,000. Prices are for a male, aged 65, living in Los Angeles County, and were obtained from quotesmith.com.

[a]Pays for 80 percent of balance billing.

Fourth, individuals can purchase private insurance coverage that supplements Medicare, termed "Medigap" insurance. About one-third of Medicare beneficiaries purchase Medigap insurance. The individual Medigap insurance market is highly regulated. Since 1990, there have been ten standard Medigap plans, the details of which are shown in table 7.3. The most common policies are plans C and F, which cover cost sharing required under Medicare and, in the case of plan F, balance billing charged by the physician.[4] The premium for these plans ranges from $1,000 to about $2,500.

Three of the Medigap plans offer some coverage for outpatient prescription drugs, but these plans are not very popular. This unpopularity largely reflects adverse selection. Plans with drug coverage cost about $700 more than the plans without drug coverage, even with a maximum payment for drug benefits of $1,250 to $3,000. As a result of this adverse selection, most people with individual supplemental insurance do not have coverage for outpatient prescription drugs. Furthermore, long-term care services are not covered by Medigap policies. Although there is some insurance for long-term care, it is not very widespread (Cutler 2002): Only about 4 per-

---

4. Medicare calculates patient cost sharing on the basis of its fee schedule. Physicians can, in some circumstances, charge more than the fee schedule. The entire amount of this excess billing, or balance billing, is charged to the patient.

cent of the elderly have long-term care insurance. Most elderly people rely on the Medicaid program as their implicit long-term care insurance policy. Effectively, individual Medigap insurance serves as supplementary coverage to reduce Medicare cost sharing.

As figure 7.2 shows, in total nearly 90 percent of Medicare beneficiaries have some form of supplemental insurance coverage. Supplemental insurance coverage varies substantially with income, although the relationship is not linear. Figure 7.3 shows the share of the elderly with different forms of supplemental insurance coverage by income. About 40 percent of the poorest elderly (those with income below $10,000 per year) have supplemental coverage through Medicaid. Only 10 percent have employer-based insurance, and 25 percent purchase insurance individually. At more moderate income levels (between $10,000 and $15,000), individual insurance predominates, with Medicaid coverage being relatively unimportant. Finally, at higher incomes (about $15,000 and particularly above $30,000), most supplemental insurance is from employer-sponsored plans, with a residual share for individual coverage.

As a result of these offsetting trends, the share of the elderly with any supplemental insurance does not rise particularly rapidly with income—ranging only from 85 to 95 percent. What does change, however, is the probability that an individual has coverage for the most important omitted category in Medicare—outpatient prescription drugs. As figure 7.4 shows, the poorest and richest elderly are more likely to have prescription drug coverage than are the lower-middle-income group. This lack of prescription drug coverage for the nearly poor has raised substantial policy concern (McClellan 2000).

7.4   Moral Hazard and Service Substitution

The question for economic research is how the presence of supplemental insurance affects the costs of the Medicare program and the welfare of Medicare beneficiaries. Queue jumping is not a concern in the United States (supply is effectively unlimited), but moral hazard and service substitution are. I thus examine how the presence of supplemental insurance affects medical care spending, taking account of both service substitution and moral hazard effects.

To test the impact of insurance for cost sharing on Medicare spending, I relate Medicare spending for each individual to indicators for whether the person has supplemental insurance coverage that pays for the cost sharing required in Medicare. The moral hazard theory suggests that each of Medicaid, individual Medigap, and employer Medigap insurance should raise Medicare spending. To test whether coverage for prescription drugs affects spending on covered services, I include a separate dummy variable for whether the person has prescription drug coverage. This effect may be

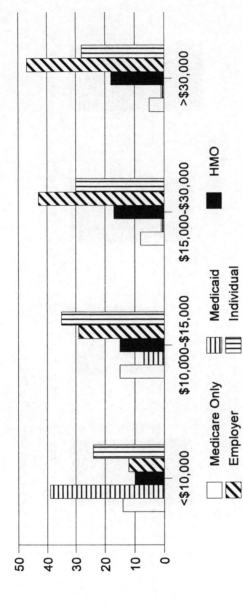

Fig. 7.3 Supplementary insurance coverage by income
Source: MCBS (1995).

Legend:
- Medicare Only
- Employer
- Medicaid
- Individual
- HMO

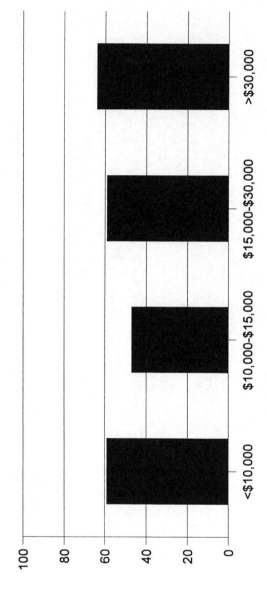

Fig. 7.4 Prescription drug coverage by income

positive or negative, depending on whether drug coverage is complementary or substitutable for the services covered by Medicare.

The regressions are of the following form:

(1)   Medicare Spending $= \alpha_1 \cdot$ Medicaid $+ \alpha_2 \cdot$ Individual Medigap

$$+ \alpha_3 \cdot \text{Employer Medigap}$$

$$+ \alpha_4 \cdot \text{Drug Coverage} + X\gamma + \varepsilon.$$

One could, in principle, include HMO coverage in equation (1), but data on medical care spending are not reported for people in HMOs. Thus, this group is omitted from the regression model.

The central difficulty of estimating equation (1) is the possibility of adverse selection. If people who are sicker are more likely to obtain supplemental insurance, then it will appear as if insurance drives up medical spending when in fact this is not the case. This is particularly important in the case of Medicaid, where people enroll in the system because they are sick. But the converse may also be true: Since richer people are more likely to have private supplemental insurance than are poorer people, and richer people are on average in better health than poorer people, supplemental insurance may appear not to affect Medicare spending when it might in practice do so.

The selection problem is likely to be most severe for the Medicaid population, since eligibility for Medicaid is largely determined on the basis of high medical costs. I thus focus the analysis principally on private supplemental insurance. Even with this focus, the issue of selection remains. Without an instrumental variable that is correlated with insurance purchase but not with health status, there is no good solution to this problem. I do not have such an instrument. Instead, I control for selection by including a number of measures of health status in the X variables. If I can adequately control for the factors about health status that predict insurance choice, I will be able to estimate the moral hazard and substitution components of supplemental insurance. The MCBS (1995) includes an extremely wide range of health measures, including self-reported health status (excellent, very good, good, fair, or poor); trouble with hearing and vision (none, some, a lot, or deafness or blindness); whether health limits the person's social life (never, some of time, most of time, all of time); the number of impairments in activities of daily living (ADLs) and instrumental activities of daily living (IADLs)[5] (no impairments, IADL limitations only, one to two ADL impairments, three to four ADL impairments, five or more ADL impairments); whether the person ever or currently smokes; whether the person has trouble eating solid foods; whether the person has

---

5. ADLs are physical measures, such as the ability to bathe oneself. IADLs are functional measures, such as the ability to manage money and cook.

had a hysterectomy; and whether the person has been told by a doctor that he or she has any of a number of chronic conditions (hardening of the arteries, hypertension, angina pectoris, other heart conditions, stroke, skin cancer, other cancer, diabetes, rheumatoid arthritis, arthritis, mental retardation, Alzheimer's disease, mental disorders, osteoporosis, broken hip, Parkinson's disease, emphysema, and partial paralysis). I include dummy variables for all of these measures.

In addition, I control for demographic characteristics of the individual, including age (in five-year age groups), sex, race (black, other), and the logarithm of family income.

Since medical care spending is skewed, there is a question about the appropriate specification of the dependent variable in equation (1). Sophisticated models of spending use a two-part framework: a model for the use of any services combined with a model for spending conditional on use of services. For simplicity, I estimate only linear models of medical spending. For the type of effects I am interested in, this specification seems appropriate.

The first two columns of table 7.4 report estimates of equation (1). Column (1) does not include any of the health status measures: They are included in the second column. Comparing the columns is an indication of how important health-based selection into supplemental insurance is in explaining Medicare spending.

The estimates on individual insurance and employer-based insurance are generally similar in the first two columns. Supplemental individual or employer-based insurance raises Medicare spending by about $1,500 without health controls and $1,800 with health controls. In each case, the effects are statistically significantly different from zero. In both equations, I cannot reject the hypothesis that the coefficients on individual and employer-based coverage are the same. Since selection into these two types of insurance is likely to be very different, these results lend some confidence to the idea that selection is not a particular problem in these results. Furthermore, the coefficients on both variables are remarkably similar with and without the control variables. This further suggests that selection is not a concern. Indeed, the increase in the coefficients between columns (1) and (2) indicate that selection into supplemental insurance coverage is favorable: The correlation between income, average health, and purchase of insurance is stronger than the selection into insurance by sicker people within any income group.

I find that, consistent with the concern about the endogeneity of Medicaid, controlling for health status substantially reduces the coefficient on this variable. In the second column, it suggests roughly the same moral hazard as employer and individual insurance.

The magnitude of moral hazard implied by the estimates for employer and individual supplemental insurance is high. Medicare spending is about

Table 7.4   Regression Models for Medical Care Spending

Independent Variable	Medicare Spending		Prescription Drug Spending	
	(1)	(2)	(3)	(4)
Supplemental insurance (base = none)				
Individual Medigap	1443**	1777**	121**	92**
	(352)	(346)	(22)	(20)
Employer Medigap	1697**	1799**	191**	146**
	(444)	(433)	(27)	(25)
Medicaid	4584**	2799**	14	−62*
	(575)	(568)	(35)	(36)
Prescription drug coverage	−447	−194	117**	130**
	(385)	(372)	(24)	(22)
Self-reported health status (base = excellent)				
Very good	—	49	—	63**
		(411)		(24)
Good	—	790**	—	154**
		(415)		(24)
Fair	—	837*	—	215**
		(503)		(29)
Poor	—	1730**	—	195**
		(703)		(41)
Activity limitations (base = none)				
IADLs only	—	−210	—	9
		(446)		(26)
1–2 ADLs	—	2024**	—	90**
		(370)		(22)
3–4 ADLs	—	1580**	—	27
		(542)		(32)
5+ ADLs	—	3889**	—	1
		(627)		(37)
Health limit social life (base = none of time)				
Some of time	—	953**	—	83**
		(371)		(22)
Most of time	—	1948**	—	114**
		(544)		(32)
All of time	—	5140**	—	124**
		(640)		(37)
Smoking Status				
Ever smoked	—	837**	—	36**
		(309)		(18)
Current smoker	—	508	—	−54**
		(427)		(25)
Trouble eating solid foods	—	111	—	38*
		(397)		(23)
Ever had hysterectomy	—	287	—	56**
		(385)		(23)
Ever had cataract	—	708*	—	67**
		(343)		(20)

(continued)

Table 7.4   (continued)

Independent Variable	Medicare Spending		Prescription Drug Spending	
	(1)	(2)	(3)	(4)
Diagnosed conditions				
Hardening of arteries	—	–126	—	54**
		(405)		(24)
Hypertension	—	–236	—	183**
		(274)		(16)
Heart Attack	—	783*	—	112**
		(417)		(24)
Coronary heart disease	—	853**	—	146**
		(413)		(24)
Other heart disease	—	1046**	—	85**
		(321)		(19)
Stroke	—	488	—	8
		(449)		(26)
Skin cancer	—	–329	—	22
		(363)		(21)
Other cancer	—	694**	—	55**
		(345)		(20)
Diabetes	—	3149**	—	210**
		(365)		(21)
Rheumatoid arthritis	—	–253	—	79**
		(419)		(25)
Arthritis	—	–555**	—	74**
		(278)		(16)
Mental retardation	—	–1719	—	–150
		(1671)		(98)
Alzheimer's	—	–1948**	—	–309**
		(692)		(40)
Mental disorders	—	334	—	27
		(657)		(38)
Osteoporosis	—	62	—	57**
		(453)		(27)
Broken hip	—	914	—	–73**
		(612)		(36)
Parkinson's	—	548	—	326**
		(1065)		(62)
Emphysema	—	1498**	—	216**
		(356)		(23)
Partial paralysis	—	604	—	–70**
		(601)		(35)
Trouble with vision (base = no trouble)				
Little trouble	—	–764	—	–9
		(1673)		(98)
Lots of trouble	—	33	—	–4
		(300)		(18)
Blind	—	19	—	3
		(481)		(28)

(*continued*)

Table 7.4   (continued)

	Medicare Spending		Prescription Drug Spending	
Independent Variable	(1)	(2)	(3)	(4)
Trouble with hearing (base = no trouble)				
Little trouble	—	–1806	—	–301*
		(2842)		(166)
Lots of trouble	—	–714**	—	–12
		(287)		(17)
Deaf	—	–469	—	4
		(518)		(30)
Demographics	Yes	Yes	Yes	Yes
N	8,100	8,100	8,100	8,100
R^2	.022	.095	.031	.193

Source: Data are from the 1995 MCBS.

Note: The sample is elderly people who are not enrolled in an HMO.

**Statistically significant at the 5 percent level. Dashes indicate that information was not included in the model.

*Statistically significant at the 10 percent level.

$5,000 per person for this population. Thus, the increase in spending resulting from supplemental insurance is about 35 percent. Other estimates in the literature suggest that Medigap insurance raises Medicare spending by about one-quarter. The higher estimates in these data may reflect an inability to adequately control for selection, but the similarity of the coefficients between the first and second columns argues against this explanation. The large coefficients in comparison to previous estimates may alternatively indicate that the degree of moral hazard has increased over time.

The coefficient on drug coverage does not suggest any clear effect of this variable on spending for covered services. Having drug coverage lowers spending on covered services by $200 per person, but this effect is not statistically significant. I therefore conclude that lowering the price of prescription drugs to the elderly does not materially affect their use of Medicare-covered services.

The coefficients on the health status measures are generally along the lines one would predict. Worse health is associated with increased spending. This is particularly true for self-reported health status (poor health adds $1,700 per year); health limiting one's social life (substantial limitation adds $5,100 to spending); ADL limitations ($2,000 to $4,000 more); smoking (smokers spend $800 more), heart disease ($1,000 more), diabetes ($3,100 more), and emphysema ($1,500 more).

As an additional test of whether insurance is accurately capturing incentive effects and not just omitted health status, the last two columns of the table report models for prescription drug spending. The theory suggests that people with supplemental drug coverage should spend more on prescription drugs than people who do not have such coverage.

The estimates confirm this theory. People with supplemental drug coverage spend about $130 more on prescription drugs per year. The effect is similar with and without the controls for health status. The moral hazard implied by this estimate is also large. Average spending on prescription drugs is about $550 per person. Compared to this, the additional use for people with employer insurance is about 25 percent.

Conditional on prescription drug coverage, people with employer and individual insurance spend more on drugs than those with Medicare coverage alone. Again, the coefficients are similar on these two variables. This is consistent with acute care and pharmaceutical use being complementary; encouraging people to visit the doctor more results in more prescribed medications.[6] Finally, Medicaid recipients consume fewer prescription drugs, given their health state and their coverage for prescription medications.

There is an additional path through which supplemental coverage may influence public-sector medical spending. If people with supplemental insurance are less likely to incur high medical spending for out-of-pocket needs, they may be less likely to enroll in Medicaid. This could reduce public spending on medical care and other social services.

To examine this issue, I relate receipt of Medicaid to coverage for prescription drugs. The equations are of the following form:

(2) Medicaid Coverage $= \beta_1 \cdot$ Medicaid $+ \beta_2 \cdot$ Individual Medigap

$+ \beta_3 \cdot$ Employer Medigap

$+ \beta_4 \cdot$ Private Drug Coverage $+ X\delta + \varepsilon.$

A negative coefficient on supplemental coverage would indicate that such coverage prevents people from spending down onto Medicaid.

Table 7.5 shows the estimates of equation (2). As with the earlier equations, I include a variety of health status controls to control for selection. Recall also that income is also included in the regression, so that the link between supplemental coverage and Medicaid coverage is not a result of differences in coverage by income group. Supplemental insurance is associated with a significant decrease in the probability of enrolling in Medicaid. People with insurance for Medicare cost sharing (employer or individual) are about 25 percentage points less likely to enroll in Medicaid than

---

6. Because these are uncompensated substitution effects and not compensated substitution effects, the effect of drug prices on other acute spending need not equal the effect of other acute prices on drug spending if the income effects differ. Having coverage for other acute costs raises income sufficiently to induce additional drug spending. The additional income from having prescription drug coverage does not lead to any increase in use of other services, however.

Table 7.5   **Impact of Supplemental Insurance Coverage on Medicaid Coverage**

Variable	Coefficient
Supplemental insurance (base = none)	
Individual Medigap	−.271**
	(.008)
Employer Medigap	−.244**
	(.010)
Private drug coverage	−.014
	(.009)
Health status controls	Yes
Demographics	Yes
N	8,100
R^2	.430

Note: Regressions are for people aged 65 and older.
**Statistically significant at the 5 percent level.
*Statistically significant at the 10 percent level.

are those without such coverage. Private drug coverage is associated with a 1.4 percentage point reduction in the probability of Medicaid coverage (statistically significant at the 11 percent level).

The implications of these changes are large. Consider the experiment of giving everyone without supplemental insurance coverage a policy equivalent to the average individual policy currently chosen, along with prescription drug coverage. The estimates in table 7.4 indicate that spending on Medicare covered services would increase by $473 per beneficiary. At the same time, the estimates in table 7.5 indicate that this change would reduce the probability of Medicaid coverage by 8 percentage points. Since Medicaid increases spending by about $2,800 per person (table 7.4), the savings from reduced Medicaid utilization would be about $224 per beneficiary. Thus, nearly half of the cost of supplemental insurance in higher Medicare spending would be offset by health savings in the Medicaid program. In addition, there would be savings in reduced income payments and potentially other transfers as well, such as food stamps. The net effect could be even smaller.

As a result, encouraging people to purchase supplemental insurance coverage privately—as Medicare's implicit subsidy to first-dollar coverage does—costs less than the static moral hazard analysis suggests. And tailoring such policies to the group most likely to go on Medicaid may actually save money.

7.5   Discussion

The most important role of supplemental health insurance among Medicare beneficiaries in the United States is to reduce cost sharing in the

Medicare program. My estimates suggest that Medicare spending is increased by about 35 percent for people with supplemental insurance coverage over equivalent people without supplemental coverage. This estimate may be somewhat high, because of omitted measures of health status, but even a coefficient half this size would imply significant moral hazard.

Coverage for uncovered services does not have a direct effect on public spending. People with supplemental insurance that covers outpatient prescription drugs spend no more or less on Medicare than do people without such coverage. But supplemental insurance reduces spending through other mechanisms by reducing eligibility for the Medicaid program. The "Medicaid offset" implies that the net cost of supplemental insurance coverage is perhaps half of the gross cost, taking account only of Medicaid spending on Medicare-covered services. Savings in other programs could be large as well.

In some countries, although not the United States, there is a further role of supplemental insurance in allowing people to jump to the front of waiting lines. Because this role is not important in the United States, I do not analyze it empirically. It would be worthwhile to consider this in future work focused on other countries.

This research highlights the critical importance of the design of basic benefit packages. One reason why supplemental insurance policies are so popular is that the Medicare benefit package leaves substantial cost sharing to the individual. It may be efficiency-enhancing to reduce the cost sharing facing beneficiaries and thus reduce the financial risk facing Medicare beneficiaries without supplemental coverage. Estimating what such cost sharing would optimally be and how it would interact with supplemental insurance coverage is an important research priority.

References

Cutler, David M. 2002. Equality, efficiency, and market fundamentals: The dynamics of international medical care reform. *Journal of Economic Literature* 40 (3): 881–906.

Kaiser Family Foundation. 2000. *Employer health benefits: 1999 annual survey.* Menlo Park, Calif.: Kaiser Family Foundation.

McClellan, Mark. 2000. Medicare reform: Fundamental problems, incremental steps. *Journal of Economic Perspectives.* 14 (2): 21–44.

Medicare Current Beneficiary Survey (MCBS). 1995. Access to Care and Cost and Use Files. Sponsored by the Centers for Medicare & Medicaid Services, Baltimore, Md.

Rothschild, Michael, and Joseph E. Stiglitz. 1976. Equilibrium in competitive insurance markets: An essay on the economics of imperfect information. *Quarterly Journal of Economics* 90:629–50.

Option Value Estimation with Health and Retirement Study Data

Andrew Samwick and David A. Wise

8.1 Introduction

The relationship between retirement and the provisions of Social Security and employer-provided pension plans has been widely studied, and analyses have been based on many different methods. Recently, considerable work has been based on the "option value" model developed by Stock and Wise (1990a,b). In this paper, we move toward an option value analysis based on data from the new Health and Retirement Study (HRS).

Both public and private retirement benefits often accrue unevenly, with large jumps in benefit entitlement for working an additional year at some ages, small increases at other ages, and very often a loss in benefits for working beyond certain ages. Employer-provided defined benefit plans in the United States provide a good example.[1] Specific provisions vary widely across firms so that the accrual patterns also vary greatly as well. Thus, to study the effects of plan provisions on retirement it is critical to know the

Andrew Samwick is professor of economics at Dartmouth College and a research associate of the National Bureau of Economic Research. David A. Wise is the John F. Stambaugh Professor of Political Economy at the John F. Kennedy School of Government, Harvard University, and the director for health and retirement programs at the National Bureau of Economic Research.

We are grateful to the National Institute on Aging for financial support and to Bob Peticolas for assistance with the pension provider software and data. We thank Yukiko Abe, Alan Gustman, and participants at the joint Japan Center for Economic Research–National Bureau of Economic Research conference on "Labor Markets and Firm Benefit Policies in Japan and the United States" for helpful comments. Any errors are our own.

1. The strong relationship between retirement plan provisions and retirement is not limited to defined benefit pension plans in the United States. The striking relationship between public retirement plans and labor force departure rates in many countries is described in a coordinated collection of country analyses. The results in eleven countries are summarized by Gruber and Wise (1998).

precise provisions of the plan that determine a person's benefits. In addition, benefits under defined benefit plans are typically determined by past wage rates. Although some surveys have obtained earnings histories, until the advent of the HRS, plan provisions have not been available in surveys that obtain information on retirement.

The incentive effects inherent in plan provisions were first described by Bulow (1981) and emphasized by Lazear (1983). Kotlikoff and Wise (1985, 1987, 1989b) used data from the Bureau of Labor Statistics—which provided information on the precise provisions of a large sample of employer-provided plans—to describe the incentive effects over a broad range of plans and emphasized the enormous variation across plans. These data, however, contained no information on the retirement decisions of individuals covered by the plans. To obtain plan provisions together with retirement data, they turned their attention to firm personnel records. These data included information on individuals' retirement decisions as well as information on their earnings histories, in addition to a precise description of their firm pension plan provisions. Kotlikoff and Wise (1989a) used such data to describe the striking relationship between pension plan provisions in a firm and retirement from that firm.

These firm data were then used by Stock and Wise (1990a,b) in the development and estimation of the option value model. The central feature of this method is recognition of the future accrual pattern of pension benefits. Subsequent analyses by Lumsdaine, Stock, and Wise (1992) of the option value model in comparison with a stochastic dynamic programming specification were based on additional firm data. Several additional papers by Lumsdaine, Stock, and Wise (1990, 1991, 1993) compared results from several different firms, for men and women, and for different types of employees. The substantial similarity of parameter estimates across different firms and for different groups of employees suggested a rather strong behavioral interpretation of the model estimates. This was confirmed through external "out-of-sample" checks of predictive validity, by considering how well the model predicted the effect on retirement of unanticipated and temporary changes in pension plan provisions, occasioned by early retirement window plans. Such tests were emphasized by Lumsdaine, Stock, and Wise (1990, 1991, 1992). The option value model was also used by Ausink (1991) and Ausink and Wise (1996) to explain retirement from the U.S. Air Force.

This series of analyses demonstrated the very strong pension plan incentives to retire and actual firm departures. The firm data, however, typically provide individual data only on information used to calculate pension benefits—earnings history, age, and years of service—and limited demographic data, like gender and sometimes worker type (e.g., salaried or hourly wage, white-collar versus production). Other individual attributes that are likely to affect retirement are not available in firm personnel record files. There is no measure of health status, for example. Nor is there information on nonpension assets. Additionally, the particular firms from which the personnel records are obtained are not necessarily representative of the entire population of workers covered by pensions.

Samwick (1998) made the first attempt to integrate all of these individual attributes into an option value analysis, using data from the 1983 *Survey of Consumer Finances* (SCF). The SCF 1983 was the first nationally representative data set to contain a companion *Pension Provider Survey* (PPS) of several hundred plans. Using parameters from the Stock and Wise (1990b) literature, he showed that a calculated option value of continued work was a significant predictor of retirement and performed better in estimation and simulation than a simpler one-year retirement wealth accrual. The results extended and generalized the results of two previous literatures: estimates of the effect of Social Security that failed to account for pensions, and option value estimates of the effect of pensions on firm-level, rather than population, data. However, there were several shortcomings of the analysis, including a small sample size, a limited panel dimension, and the lack of comprehensive wage histories.

A central goal of the HRS was to obtain information on individual attributes that would be likely to affect retirement in conjunction with precise descriptions of the provisions of pension plans under which employees were entitled to benefits. The HRS combines a PPS with detailed wage histories and has been conducted every other year since 1992. It therefore provides new opportunities to examine retirement in a very comprehensive setting. Coile and Gruber (2000, 2001), Coile (1999), and Harris (2001) have recently estimated variants of the option value model using HRS data.

In this paper, we describe initial exploratory work that will lead to an option value analysis based on the HRS data. There are three goals. The first is to describe the critical content of the HRS and confirm that these new data are important components of comprehensive analysis of retirement. The second is to make preliminary calculations of pension incentives and to estimate their effect on the probability of retirement. We choose a reduced-form framework that allows nonpension characteristics to be easily incorporated. The third goal, by way of the first two, is to provide guidance that we hope will help analysts in other countries who may wish to conduct such analyses and indeed may wish to develop HRS-like surveys.

8.2 Descriptive Data

In this section, we begin by describing the important features of the HRS that facilitate analyses of retirement. The first is the self-reported information on pension plans and expected entitlements. Pensions are organized as defined benefit (DB), in which future benefits paid by the employer are based on a set of formulas that depend on age, years of service, and earnings levels, or as defined contribution (DC), in which employers and sometimes employees make specified contributions to an account that accumulates until the employee leaves the firm. Employees may be covered by a DB plan, a DC plan, or both. Employees without pensions of any kind are covered only by Social Security. A second feature is health status. The HRS contains several different measures of health status, including information on important changes in health between survey waves. There is also information on health insurance coverage, for both workers and retirees. The third feature is wealth other than pensions, which may also be an important determinant of retirement, especially as it interacts with health and the availability of pensions immediately upon retirement. A fourth feature is the definition of retirement. The effect of pensions on the decision to leave a particular firm differs substantially from their effect on the decision to leave the labor force entirely. Depending on the context, either of these decisions could be the appropriate definition of retirement.

The HRS sample includes people between the ages of fifty-one and sixty-one who are at many different stages of their working careers. Table 8.1 gives a breakdown of the sample by labor force status and gender. The sample includes all age-eligible respondents for whom wealth and self-reported pension data are available in wave 1 and whose labor force status could be obtained in wave 2. The top two rows show that 70.17 percent of the sample is working, with 57.01 percent employed and 13.16 percent self-employed. Since pensions are disproportionately a phenomenon of employees, our subsequent analysis will focus on this group. Employment probabilities differ by gender, with 80.16 percent of men and 61.16 percent

Table 8.1   **Labor Force Status of Health and Retirement Study in Wave 1**

	Men	Women	Total
Working			
Employed	61.59	52.87	57.01
Self-employed	18.57	8.29	13.16
Not working			
Unemployed	3.69	2.75	3.20
Laid off	0.32	0.34	0.33
Disabled	8.60	8.11	8.34
Retired	6.89	5.88	6.36
Homemaker	0.06	20.87	11.01
Other	0.29	0.88	0.60
N	4,026	4,466	8,492

Notes: Each cell contains the percent of each column in the specified labor force status group. Percentages are weighted by person-level weights. The sample includes all age-eligible respondents to the HRS Wave 1 for whom wealth and self-reported pension data are available in Wave 1 and whose labor force status could be obtained in Wave 2.

of women working. About 10 percentage points of this disparity are due to self-employment, with the remaining 8.72 percentage points due to employment.

The rest of the table describes the subsample that is not working. For men, about 8.60 percent report that they are disabled, with another 6.89 percent retired and 4.01 percent unemployed or laid off. For women, the corresponding percentages are lower by up to 1 percentage point in each of these categories. The final categories, "homemakers" and "other" responses, comprise 21.75 percent of the sample of women and a negligible proportion of the sample of men.

Table 8.2 provides a breakdown of the working sample based on self-reported pension coverage. We distinguish four groups (excluding the very small number of workers who did not report the type of pension plan they had): no pension, DC only, DB only, and both DB and DC. The first row of the table shows that approximately one-third of the sample is not covered by an employer-provided pension plan. Employers are under no obligation to offer pension plans to their workers, although there are many regulations that require employers not discriminate among classes of workers if they sponsor a plan for any of their workers. The coverage rates differ by gender, with women having a 40 percent chance of not being covered compared to 28 percent for men. This group of workers depends on Social Security for much of their retirement income. The incentive effects of Social Security on retirement are similar to those of DB pensions, described presently. A recent exposition using HRS data can be found in Coile and Gruber (2001).

As previously noted, there are two primary types of pension plans. A DC plan is organized as a fund into which the employer and employee may make contributions. The contributions are invested, often with employee discretion, and accumulated until the employee leaves the firm. At that time, the employee can generally take the benefits as a lump sum, an annu-

Table 8.2   **Pension Coverage of Employed Workers in HRS Wave 1**

	Men	Women	Total
No pension	27.87	39.91	33.74
DC pension only	20.11	20.19	20.15
DB pension only	29.09	26.45	27.80
DB and DC pensions	22.93	13.46	18.31
N	2,450	2,334	4,784

Notes: Each cell contains the percent of each column with the specified type of pension. Percentages are weighted by person-level weights. The sample includes all age-eligible respondents to the HRS Wave 1 for whom wealth and self-reported pension data are available in Wave 1 and whose labor force status could be obtained in Wave 2. Only respondents who are working but not self-employed are included.

ity, or as a rollover into another retirement account. In general, DC pensions do not have important incentive effects regarding the timing of retirement. Their main incentive effects typically occur early in the employee's tenure, as vesting provisions encourage employees to stay with the firm for a specified period of time in order to receive their employers' contributions. The next row of the table shows that roughly 20 percent of both men and women in the HRS are covered only by DC pensions.

A DB plan is organized around one or more formulas that specify a benefit payment as a function of the employee's retirement age, years of participation in the plan, and earnings while covered by the plan. The benefits from a DB plan are usually paid as an annuity. The benefit levels may change over time due to cost-of-living adjustments (formally through the plan provisions or informally through the employer's discretionary increases). Benefit formulas are often integrated with Social Security benefit levels or early and normal retirement ages. The next two rows of the table show that 29.09 percent of men are covered only by a DB plan, with another 22.93 covered by a plan with features of both a DB and a DC plan or by at least one plan of each type. Over half of male workers are therefore covered by a plan with DB characteristics. For women, approximately 40 percent have a plan with DB characteristics, with 26.45 percent having a DB only and 13.46 having both types of plan.

The critical feature of DB plans for the study of retirement behavior is the very strong incentives they provide to workers to retire at specific ages. Two factors are generally at work in providing incentives to stay with the firm. The first is that when final pay is computed, earnings are typically specified in nominal amounts. Thus, an extra year of work indexes the initial benefit to nominal wage growth. This is very important early in the career, when nominal wage growth is high, and less important later in the career, when wage growth is less rapid. The second is the actuarial reduction factor applied to initial benefit ages that are less than the plan's normal retirement age (NRA). The NRA is the age at which the worker is entitled to the full amount of the benefits implied by the appropriate pension formula. If the worker leaves before the early retirement age (ERA), then benefits are usually payable at the ERA with a full actuarial reduction for each year of extra benefit receipt relative to the NRA. If the worker stays until he or she qualifies for early retirement benefits, then the reduction factor is typically more advantageous than an actuarially fair rate. Such features provide a strong incentive to stay with the firm at least until the ERA. In contrast, benefits are not as generously increased for delaying initial receipt of benefits beyond the NRA—the upward revision is often less than actuarially fair.

These incentives can be easily quantified by considering the financial incentives to delay retirement by a single year. We compute this "pension wealth accrual" as the difference in the actuarial present value of the pay-

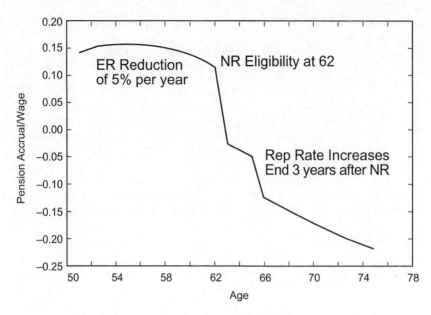

Fig. 8.1   Pension accrual profile, for worker hired at age 40

ments from the pension if retirement occurred next year instead of this year. Figure 8.1 graphs the pension wealth accrual for a hypothetical worker in a large plan in the HRS sample. The plan's normal retirement age is sixty-two, but all workers with ten years of work at the firm qualify for early retirement at a favorable reduction rate. Alternatively, workers can qualify for normal retirement as soon as they have worked thirty years at the firm. Benefits are equal to 1.6 percent of final average pay—defined as the average of the last five years of wages—for every year worked. Workers can increase this percentage slightly by working up to three years after first qualifying for normal retirement benefits. The graph depicts the ratio of the pension accrual to the wage for a hypothetical worker who was hired at age forty. The vertical height of each point on the graph is the pension accrual received by working to that age instead of leaving at the previous age.

The idiosyncrasies of the plan's benefit and eligibility formulas are reflected in the shape of the graph. Since the worker was hired at forty, she will qualify for normal retirement benefits at age sixty-two. In years prior to that, the pension accrual is at approximately 15 percent of the contemporaneous wage. This amount is quite substantial on an annual basis, and it is by no means atypical of DB plans. It reflects the extra year of earnings, the additional year closer to the NRA, and the higher level of final average pay. At the NRA of sixty-two, there are no more increments for reaching the NRA, so the accrual falls to zero and then below. For the next three years, accruals stay above –10 percent. After the replacement rate adjust-

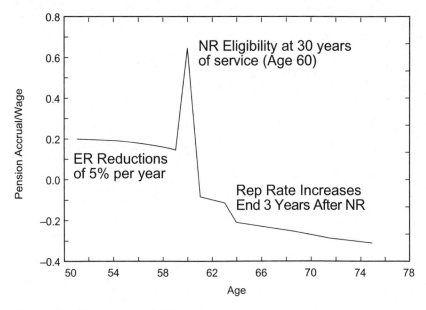

Fig. 8.2 Pension accrual profile, for worker hired at age 30

ments stop, the pension accrual is quite negative, as the worker is simply giving up additional years of benefits with little upward revision to the benefit amount. In such a graph, positive values reflect a financial incentive to stay at the firm, and negative values provide a financial incentive to leave the firm.

As an illustration of the sensitivity of pension accrual calculations to age and years of work, figure 8.2 shows the pension accrual for the same worker, assuming she was hired at age thirty rather than age forty. The main change in the profile is that the worker reaches thirty years of service at age sixty and can retire with full benefits at that time. Prior to that age, accruals are approximately 20 percent of the contemporaneous wage. At that age, the present value of the two fewer years worth of benefit reductions due to early retirement generates a considerable spike in the profile, equal to about 70 percent of earnings that year.[2] The accruals then turn negative, particularly after the three years of replacement rate increases are exhausted. Clearly, if this worker is observed to retire at age fifty-nine, right before this spike, then we would reasonably conclude that financial incentives can have little to do with retirement decisions.

Several conclusions can be drawn from these graphs. The first is that

2. Large pension accruals are also common at the earliest possible ERA, due to the sudden switch to an actuarially favorable reduction rate for benefits taken before the NRA. In this plan, the ERA occurs ten years after hire. A worker hired at age forty-six would have a large accrual at age fifty-six under this plan.

there is considerable heterogeneity in the financial incentives from pension plans. These incentives will vary across plans and, importantly, across workers in the same plan based on age and years of service. The second is that the types of incentives provided by DB pension plans may change over a worker's career. At younger ages, the prospect of large accruals for continued work provides financial incentives to delay retirement until the early retirement age. After the early retirement age, benefit adjustments for continued work are typically not enough to compensate for the lost year of benefit receipt, and the pension incentives encourage departure from the firm. Social Security and pension formulas may differ in which type of incentive is more pronounced. The third conclusion is that the data requirements to calculate pension accruals are considerable and exacting. Missing the date of birth by a year could place the large spike at sixty-one instead of sixty. We might observe a worker stay through age sixty and then retire. If we have missed the date by only a year, then this worker will retire after actually getting the large increment to wealth but appear to retire just before it. The problem is even more severe when the possible mistakes pertain to the date of hire. In the original Stock and Wise (1990b) literature, personnel records from a handful of firms could identify this date precisely. In a household survey, even with Social Security earnings histories, mismeasurement is more likely to be a source of noise.

We distinguish two different stages of retirement between the first two waves of the HRS. We denote "full retirement" as a transition in labor force status from working to retirement, as indicated by the individual. However, the payment of pension benefits is conditional not on complete withdrawal from the labor force but only on separation from the employer. We denote "firm retirement" as any departure from the employer indicated in the first wave of the survey, regardless of what the worker did after that. The option value literature, because it utilizes personnel records, is generally constrained to analyzing only firm retirement. Samwick's (1998) analysis considers both definitions of retirement and finds a significant effect of the calculated option value in both cases.[3]

Figure 8.3 shows the hazard rate for full retirement between the first two waves of the HRS. The hazard rate is the probability of retiring at a given age, conditional on not having retired before that age.[4] The graph contains separate hazard rates for each of the four pension coverage groups identified in table 8.2. As there are approximately two years between the waves of the HRS, the probabilities in the table reflect the probability of retiring at any point during that time interval. In general, there is an upward-sloping pattern to the retirement hazards, indicating a strong effect of age on re-

---

3. See Ruhm (1990) for an analysis of partial retirement and the role of "bridge" jobs.
4. It is important to note that in what follows we are examining retirement probabilities for those who are working in the first wave. This ignores the contribution of those who have already retired before the first wave on the calculation of the hazard rate.

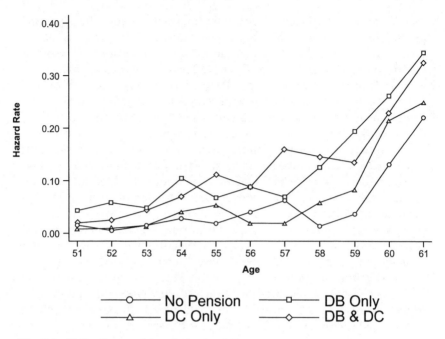

Fig. 8.3   Full retirement hazards, by pension type

tirement. The particularly large increases for ages sixty and sixty-one are
due to the ERA for Social Security of sixty-two. Although the level of the
hazards is comparable across the four groups, workers without pensions
tend to have the lowest retirement probabilities, and those with DB or DB
and DC pension tend to have the highest probabilities. There are noticeable upturns in the DB pension groups at ages fifty-four and fifty-five, ow-
ing to the ERA of fifty-five in many plans.

Figure 8.4 shows the analogous graph for firm retirement. The striking
feature of this graph is the very high departure rate for workers without
pensions. At all ages, approximately 40 percent of the workers without
pensions leave their employers during the two years between the first two
waves of the HRS. Because the level of this graph differs substantially from
the full retirement hazard, we can infer that most of the departures result
in a job at a different employer or any of the other nonretirement categories
of labor force status shown in table 8.1. The hazard rates for workers with
pensions do not approach 40 percent until the ages immediately prior to
sixty-two. Hazard rates for workers with pensions show the same increasing pattern as in the full retirement graph.

There are two likely explanations for the higher hazard rates for workers
without pensions. The first is that jobs that offer pensions are simply better jobs than jobs without pensions. In that case, workers are generally

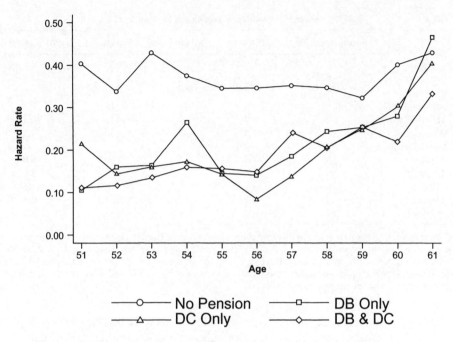

Fig. 8.4   Firm retirement hazards, by pension type

happier with their employers and, for that reason, less inclined to leave. This type of unobserved heterogeneity is not present in option value models based on a single firm, in which all workers have the same job and the same pension. The second explanation is based on the fact that most of the strong pension incentives are to delay retirement at these ages. As a result, we should see lower retirement probabilities when workers have pensions. The pension signals the likelihood of a large accrual of wealth at some point in the future with continued work.

In either case, the impact on a cross-sectional retirement model is clear. Since accruals are positive on average, variation in financial incentives between pension-covered and uncovered workers introduces a negative correlation between accruals and retirement, even if it were the case that among workers with pensions, higher accruals have no effect on the timing of retirement. As a precaution against this possibility, we condition on pension coverage in the tabulations in the remainder of this section and examine only workers with pensions in the econometric estimates in the next section.

The purpose of pensions is to provide resources to support consumption in retirement. Workers can also provide these resources by saving on their own. Other things being equal, workers with more wealth may choose to retire earlier. This could be true for exogenous reasons, such as receiving

Table 8.3   Full Retirement Probabilities by Wealth and Pension Type

	Bottom Quartile	2nd Quartile	3rd Quartile	Top Quartile	All Quartiles
Net worth					
No pension	2.7	6.5	4.5	7.8	5.0
DC only	1.7	4.7	7.2	9.4	5.9
DB only	7.6	7.8	11.4	18.9	11.5
DB and DC	4.0	8.7	10.8	13.5	10.5
All types	3.8	6.9	8.5	12.7	8.0
Financial assets					
No pension	2.5	5.5	4.4	9.7	5.0
DC only	3.0	4.5	6.5	9.2	5.9
DB only	4.8	8.9	15.1	16.7	11.5
DB and DC	5.4	6.0	7.4	17.3	10.5
All types	3.3	6.4	8.6	17.9	8.0

Notes: Each cell contains the probability that the employee retired from the labor force (full retirement) between the first two waves of the HRS. Probabilities are weighted by person-level weights. The sample includes all age-eligible respondents to the HRS Wave 1 for whom wealth and self-reported pension data are available in Wave 1 and whose labor force status could be obtained in Wave 2. Only respondents who are working but not self-employed are included.

an inheritance. It may also be true for endogenous reasons—workers who have a strong preference for consuming resources during retirement will save more while working to facilitate an earlier retirement date.[5] As a first step, we tabulate the probability of retirement for workers in the four quartiles of the wealth distribution, controlling for pension coverage. We make separate calculations for total household net worth and financial assets. The quartiles for the net worth distribution are $42,500, $111,540, and $224,150. Financial assets include liquid assets such as bank and money market accounts, certificates of deposit, stocks, bonds, mutual funds, and individual retirement accounts (IRAs). The quartiles of the financial asset distribution are $2,500, $18,500, and $62,000.

Table 8.3 presents the results for full retirement. The bottom row of the top panel shows that retirement probabilities increase with the level of wealth, with the largest increase coming for the top quartile of the distribution. The other rows in that panel show that this holds true in each of the pension groups as well. The bottom panel of the table shows that the same qualitative results hold for the quartiles of the financial asset distribution as well.

The analogous calculations for firm retirement are presented in table 8.4. There are several interesting patterns in the relationship between wealth and retirement. First, for the whole sample of workers, firm retirement probabilities are highest for the top and bottom quartiles than in the

5. See Gustman and Steinmeier (1999) for a recent study of retirement saving using the HRS.

Table 8.4   Firm Retirement Probabilities by Wealth and Pension Type

	Bottom Quartile	2nd Quartile	3rd Quartile	Top Quartile	All Quartiles
Net worth					
No pension	39.5	34.1	33.9	38.9	37.0
DC only	14.1	15.9	20.5	25.3	19.1
DB only	19.2	18.3	18.7	26.6	20.7
DB and DC	22.1	14.7	18.2	16.9	17.4
All types	28.8	22.3	22.9	27.2	25.3
Financial assets					
No pension	39.2	36.8	31.2	39.3	37.0
DC only	14.3	18.7	18.1	24.7	19.1
DB only	18.8	17.0	22.8	24.6	20.7
DB and DC	18.0	13.9	17.5	19.6	17.4
All types	28.1	23.1	22.9	27.1	25.3

Notes: Each cell contains the probability that the employee left the Wave 1 employer (firm retirement) between the first two waves of the HRS. Probabilities are weighted by person-level weights. The sample includes all age-eligible respondents to the HRS Wave 1 for whom wealth and self-reported pension data are available in Wave 1 and whose labor force status could be obtained in Wave 2. Only respondents who are working but not self-employed are included.

middle two quartiles. This is largely due to the presence of this pattern in the set of workers without pensions. Second, for the subsample of workers with DC only or DB only pensions, firm retirement probabilities are much higher for the top wealth quartile than for lower quartiles. This is the same pattern from the full retirement probabilities in table 8.3. Third, for workers with DB and DC pensions, workers in the 2nd quartile of the distribution have unusually low firm retirement probabilities. Wealth is clearly an important factor to incorporate into the analysis of retirement.

An important feature of the HRS is the thorough information that is provided on respondents' health and their resources available in the event of the onset of failing health. Studies have already been conducted using the data on important changes in health between surveys. In our preliminary investigations, we focus on self-reported health status and the availability of health insurance both while working and during retirement.

Table 8.5 breaks down the probability of retirement by the interaction of health status and various health insurance characteristics. The top row shows the fraction of the sample that reports each of the five possible answers. Only 2 percent report poor health. This very select group of workers has the highest rate of firm retirement and the lowest rate of full retirement. This holds true for almost all of the insurance categories. These workers tend to leave by way of disability, and such transitions are not included in our measure of self-reported full retirement status. Another 9.3 percent of the sample reports fair health, and the remainder of the sample is split into excellent (27.7 percent), very good (33.3 percent), or good (27.7 percent) health.

Table 8.5   Retirement Probabilities by Health Status and Health Insurance Coverage

	Excellent	Very Good	Good	Fair	Poor	All Types
Percentage	27.7	33.3	27.7	9.3	2.0	
Full retirement						
No insurance through employer	7.3	6.6	8.7	7.0	6.6	7.4
Employer provided health insurance	8.2	8.2	8.3	9.0	6.7	8.2
Any retiree health insurance	8.6	9.7	10.7	13.3	9.1	9.9
Insurance "locked"	6.0	3.4	3.2	2.9	0.0	3.9
All workers	7.9	7.7	8.4	8.1	6.7	8.0
Firm retirement						
No insurance through employer	27.2	30.2	33.1	50.6	50.3	33.0
Employer provided health insurance	19.6	21.2	20.2	25.7	40.6	21.2
Any retiree health insurance	19.9	21.6	24.4	30.8	43.3	22.9
Insurance "locked"	19.2	22.6	16.8	24.5	37.7	20.8
All workers	22.1	24.2	24.7	37.3	44.3	25.3

Notes: Each cell contains the probability that the employee retired from the labor force (full retirement) or left the Wave 1 employer (firm retirement) between the first two waves of the HRS. Probabilities are weighted by person-level weights. The sample includes all age-eligible respondents to the HRS Wave 1 for whom wealth and self-reported pension data are available in Wave 1 and whose labor force status could be obtained in Wave 2. Only respondents who are working but not self-employed are included.

The first two categories of insurance split the sample based on whether the worker receives health insurance coverage through her employer. For all health statuses, workers are more likely to leave their employers if they do not have employer-provided health insurance than if they do. However, the opposite is generally true for full retirement—probabilities are lower if there is no employer-provided health insurance. This difference suggests that the relationship for firm retirement is the result of other differences across jobs that are correlated with the availability of health insurance.

The next two categories relate to the availability of any form of retiree health insurance (whether through the employer or not). The third row tabulates retirement probabilities for workers with retiree health insurance. As in the case of employee health insurance, having retiree health insurance is associated with higher probabilities of full retirement and lower probabilities of firm retirement. The fourth row attempts to measure the extent to which health insurance coverage may be "locking" workers into their jobs. These workers have employer-provided health insurance but no retiree health insurance (from any source). For this group, both full and firm retirement probabilities are lower than average, especially for workers who are in very good or excellent health. It is clearly important to control for health insurance availability when analyzing retirement (e.g., see Gruber and Madrian 1996).

8.3   The Distribution of Pension Wealth and Accruals

We now turn to the distribution of pension wealth and accruals in the subsample of workers for whom detailed pension data are available. For workers who reported being covered by a pension in the first wave of the HRS, an attempt was made to contact the pension provider and obtain the summary plan description. Building on earlier work with the PPS for the 1983 SCF, the HRS staff has developed software to calculate pension entitlements based on the plan descriptions. The latest documentation of the software is Lamkin and Peticolas (1998). As noted above, calculating pension entitlements requires considerable precision in the household data. It also requires that the plan provisions be specified exactly.

Not all of the pensions are represented in the PPS. Approximately two-thirds of the workers who reported having a pension in the HRS have their pensions in the PPS. For workers who reported a DB plan or DB and DC plans, the proportion of plans found is about 75 percent. For workers with DC only, the proportion is just over 50 percent. The difference is related to employer size. Defined benefit plans are disproportionately offered by large employers, both private and public. They are therefore easier to track down and more likely to have the relevant documents accessible to complete the survey. Our PPS sample includes 2,097 workers for whom we can calculate pension entitlements.

The proportion of workers whose self-reported pension types match the set of plans found in the PPS on their behalf is surprisingly low. The percentages getting the match exactly right are 60.10, 47.86, and 40.91 for the self-reported DB only, DC only, and DB-DC groups, respectively. Of particular concern are the 11.99 percent of the respondents who report DB only but actually have DC only, as well as the 28.16 percent who report DC only but actually have DB only. Such disparities illustrate why a comprehensive PPS is needed, but they also raise questions about whether workers should be expected to respond to the incentives they think they have or to the incentives they actually have.[6] It is important to note that problems of misclassification are more likely to affect an HRS sample than the firm-based samples of Stock and Wise (1990a), since there is now a cross-section of plans in addition to people.

The derivation of the option value model of Stock and Wise (1990b) begins with an assumed indirect utility function:

---

6. See Gustman and Steinmeier (1999) for a comparison of the self-reported pension data and the PPS data in the HRS.

$$(1) \qquad V_t(R) = \sum_{s=t}^{R-1} \beta^{s-t} \pi(s \mid t) E_t(y_s^\gamma) + \sum_{s=R}^{T} \beta^{s-t} \pi(s \mid t) E_t[k \cdot B_s(R)^\gamma]$$

The variables and parameters in this equation are as follows:

t: current age
R: age of retirement
T: maximum possible age
$\pi(s \mid t)$: probability of surviving to age s conditional on surviving to age t
y_s: wages at age s
$B_s(R)$: pension benefits at age s conditional on retirement at age R
β: discount factor (parameter)
k: relative value of income during retirement (parameter)
γ: risk aversion (parameter)

The first term in the expression on the right side is the indirect utility while working, and the second term is the indirect utility while retired. Stock and Wise (1990b) defined the option value of continued work to be $V_t(R^*) - V_t(t)$, where R^* is the retirement age in $(t + 1, \ldots, T)$ that maximizes that difference:

$$(2) \qquad OV_t(R^*) = \sum_{s=t}^{R^*-1} \beta^{s-t} \pi(s \mid t) E_t(y_s^\gamma) + \sum_{s=R^*}^{T} \beta^{s-t} \pi(s \mid t) E_t[k \cdot B_s(R^*)^\gamma]$$
$$- \sum_{s=t}^{T} \beta^{s-t} \pi(s \mid t) E_t[k \cdot B_s(t)^\gamma]$$

Stock and Wise (1990a) note that the probability that a worker retires at age t is simply the probability that the option value is negative. They estimate the parameters of the model using maximum likelihood. In later work, Samwick (1998) specifies values for the utility function parameters to calculate the option value and includes that measure as an explanatory variable in a probit equation for retirement. In more recent work with the HRS, Coile and Gruber (1999a,b, 2000, 2001) and Coile (1999) use a variant of the option value that they call the "peak value" of retirement in similar reduced-form models:

$$(3) \qquad PKV_t(R^*) = \sum_{s=R^*}^{T} \beta^{s-t} \pi(s \mid t) E_t[B_s(R^*)] - \sum_{s=t}^{T} \beta^{s-t} \pi(s \mid t) E_t[B_s(t)]$$

As discussed in Samwick (2001), the peak value is the same as the option value under the assumptions that future wages do not affect the optimal retirement age, workers are not risk averse ($\gamma = 1$), and income in retirement has the same utility value as income before retirement ($k = 1$). What these assumptions sacrifice in realism, they make up in analytical and computational convenience. The peak value is denominated in dollars, rather than measures of utility. The peak value chooses the retirement age that maximizes the value of the following measure, which we denote as the "multiyear accrual":

(4) $$ACC_t(R) = \sum_{s=R}^{T} \beta^{s-t}\pi(s \mid t)E_t[B_s(R)] - \sum_{s=t}^{T} \beta^{s-t}\pi(s \mid t)E_t[B_s(t)]$$

We use this measure directly in our reduced-form estimation. We vary the chosen retirement date over a range of possibilities. The importance of choosing a high value of R is indicated by figure 8.2. The value of $ACC_{50}(R)$ for R less than 58 does not incorporate the large pension accrual that comes as a result of reaching thirty years of service and hence an earlier age for normal retirement. For illustrative purposes, we choose values of R equal to $t + 1$, $t + 2$, 62, and 65 in our empirical work. For horizons beyond a year, we scale the multiyear accrual by the length of the horizon (i.e., $R - t$) in order to have an annualized measure of pension accruals. Our economic assumptions include a 3 percent inflation rate, a 2 percent real interest rate (so that $\beta = 1/[1.03 \cdot 1.02]$), a 1 percent economywide wage increase, and a quadratic age-earnings profile around that aggregate such that nominal wage growth is 4.1 percent at age fifty and 3.2 percent at age seventy-five. Survival probabilities are given by the 1936 cohort life table.

Descriptive statistics for the pension and wage data are presented in table 8.6. The top panel is denominated in units of $10,000. As a reference point, the mean wage in this sample is $35,100, and the median is $31,000. The next line shows the present value of pension benefits. The mean value of pension wealth is $129,800, compared to a median of $58,300. Pension

Table 8.6   **Descriptive Statistics for Wage and Pension Variables**

	Mean	Standard Deviation	25th Percentile	Median	75th Percentile
Pension and Wage Variables ($10,000s)					
Wage	3.51	2.32	2.08	3.10	4.40
Pension variables					
Present value	12.98	20.38	1.44	5.83	17.01
Accrual, 1 year	1.14	2.55	0.21	0.60	1.36
Accrual, 2 year	1.13	1.80	0.24	0.64	1.45
Accrual, age 62	1.05	1.25	0.31	0.73	1.42
Accrual, age 65	0.92	1.07	0.32	0.66	1.22
Pension Variables as Ratios to Wages					
Pension variables					
Present value	3.18	3.42	0.63	2.01	4.57
Accrual, 1 year	0.30	0.50	0.09	0.20	0.37
Accrual, 2 year	0.31	0.43	0.10	0.22	0.40
Accrual, age 62	0.29	0.25	0.14	0.26	0.39
Accrual, age 65	0.25	0.18	0.13	0.24	0.35

Notes: The sample includes all age-eligible respondents to the HRS Wave 1 for whom wealth and self-reported pension data are available in Wave 1, whose labor force status could be obtained in Wave 2, who are working but not self-employed, and whose pension information is reported in the Pension Provider Survey (2,097 observations). Pension and wage variables are denominated in units of $10,000, expressed in constant 1992 dollars. Ratios are to the wage level in the *first wave* of the survey. Accruals are annual averages over the specified horizon.

wealth is more concentrated than wages, in large part because pension plans that cover higher-income workers tend to have higher replacement rates. The next four rows give the *annualized* values of the multiyear pension accruals defined above. Over the next year of the sample, the workers can expect pension wealth to increase by a mean of $11,400 and a median of $6,000. These numbers are sizable fractions of earnings. Over the next two years of the sample, the workers can expect pension wealth increments of $11,300 at the mean and $6,400 at the median *in each year.* Extending the horizon to age sixty-two increases the mean and median values to $10,500 and $7,300 per year.

During the age range when workers cannot retire and immediately begin collecting Social Security benefits, multiyear accruals decrease in mean and standard deviation and rise in median values. The reductions in the mean and standard deviation suggest that once a pension gives a large single-year accrual, it is less likely to offer another large accrual to the same worker. The increase in the median with the number of years indicates an increasing probability of having at least one large single-year accrual during the multiyear period. Further extending the horizon to age sixty-five reduces both the mean and median values (to $9,200 and $6,600, respectively), suggesting that a large fraction of workers begin to see net reductions in pension wealth for delaying retirement until that age. The bottom panel of the table presents the distribution of pension wealth and accruals, normalized by the worker's wage. This normalization reduces the dispersion of the pension distribution, but it does not change the general pattern of increasing median multiyear accruals through age sixty-two, followed by a slight decline between ages sixty-two and sixty-five.

The HRS also allows for precise calculations of the analogous incentive measures for Social Security, as in Coile and Gruber (2001). These calculations are facilitated by a supplemental data set of Social Security earnings histories. We have not yet incorporated the earnings histories into our analysis. As a result, most of the variation in Social Security incentives is unavailable to us. The remaining variation in incentives is largely a function of age, marital status, and the wage in the survey year. At present, we control for those factors directly in our econometric estimates.

8.4   Reduced Form Estimates

In this section, we estimate reduced form models of the effect of pension wealth and accruals on the probability of retirement using a probit specification. We include the level of pension wealth, the accrual of pension wealth, and the wage to capture the main features of the worker's budget constraint. We use each of the four accrual measures summarized in table 8.6 in separate equations. We also control for a number of other potentially important factors: net worth, health status, health insurance, union status, gender, marital status, education, and age. The key predictions to be tested are for a positive effect of pension wealth on the probability of retirement and a negative effect of the pension wealth accrual and the wage on the probability of retirement.

Table 8.7 reports the results using full retirement as the dependent variable. The coefficients from the probit have been transformed into the marginal effects of the variables, evaluated at the sample means of the independent variables.[7] The four columns correspond to different horizons for the pension accrual variable, with the one-year accrual in the first column and the average multiyear accrual to age sixty-five in the fourth column. The estimates for variables other than the pension and wage variables do not change in a substantive way as the horizon on the retirement incentives variable is increased.

The results on the key variables are mixed in this set of estimates. The present value of pension wealth is positive and significant in every specification, as predicted. Using the fourth column, an increase of $100,000 in pension wealth (about one-half of a standard deviation) would increase the probability of retirement by 1.9 percentage points. This increase represents 18 percent of the baseline probability of full retirement of 10.54 percentage points.[8] The pension accrual is positive and insignificant in the specifications that use one or two years as the horizon. It has a negative effect when measured over longer horizons. In the fourth column, it is statistically significant. The point estimate for the marginal effect is −0.0198, suggesting that a $10,000 increase in the average accrual (roughly one standard deviation) would reduce the probability of full retirement over the two-year interval between the waves of the survey by 1.98 percentage points, or 19 percent of the baseline retirement probability.

Based on the examples in figures 8.1 and 8.2, it is not surprising that measures of pension accruals that incorporate more years are more significantly related to retirement. Another insight as to the difference between the pension accrual measures is reflected in the marginal effects for the wage. The wage is estimated to have a negative effect in all specifications, as predicted. The effect is on the order of −0.01, with larger and more significant results occurring for the shorter horizon measures. This pattern is consistent with the extra information in the longer horizon relative to the one-year horizon being correlated with the wage, and this accounts for the changes in the marginal effects with the horizon length.

The effects of the other control variables are consistent with the cross-tabulations presented in tables 8.3 through 8.5. Higher net worth is associ-

---

7. For dummy variables, the marginal effect is evaluated as the difference in the probabilities when the dummy equals 1 compared to 0.

8. This differs from the probability of 8 percent in table 8.3 because the sample here includes only those workers with pensions in the PPS. For firm retirement, the baseline probability of retirement is 18.93 percent, compared to 25.3 percent in table 8.4.

Table 8.7   **Marginal Effects Probits for Full Retirement, Using Detailed Pension Data**

	Accrual Period for Pension Incentives			
	One Year	Two Year	Until Age 62	Until Age 65
Pension present value	0.0017	0.0017	0.0019	0.0019
	(0.0004)	(0.0004)	(0.0004)	(0.0004)
Pension accrual	0.0021	0.0020	−0.0093	−0.0198
	(0.0022)	(0.0039)	(0.0074)	(0.0081)
Wage	−0.0098	−0.0096	−0.0057	−0.0024
	(0.0045)	(0.0044)	(0.0043)	(0.0055)
Net worth 2nd quartile	0.0234	0.0234	0.0225	0.0211
	(0.0208)	(0.0208)	(0.0207)	(0.0205)
Net worth 3rd quartile	0.0728	0.0733	0.0729	0.0703
	(0.0259)	(0.0259)	(0.0258)	(0.0256)
Net worth 4th quartile	0.1214	0.1214	0.1213	0.1200
	((0.0310)	(0.0310)	(0.0308)	(0.0306)
Health status very good	0.0104	0.0105	0.0104	0.0096
	(0.0148)	(0.0148)	(0.0148)	(0.0147)
Health status good	0.0220	0.0226	0.0224	0.0209
	(0.0167)	(0.0167)	(0.0167)	(0.0165)
Health status fair	0.0710	0.0709	0.0701	0.0695
	(0.0324)	(0.0324)	(0.0322)	(0.0320)
Health status poor	−0.0082	−0.0071	−0.0074	−0.0089
	(0.0494)	(0.0507)	(0.0516)	(0.0507)
Health insurance own employer	−0.0085	−0.0081	−0.0087	−0.0107
	(0.0171)	(0.0170)	(0.0171)	(0.0173)
Health insurance any retiree	0.0344	0.0347	0.0352	0.0355
	(0.0200)	(0.0200)	(0.0199)	(0.0197)
Health insurance "locked"	−0.0209	−0.0209	−0.0231	−0.0232
	(0.0254)	(0.0254)	(0.0248)	(0.0247)
Union member	0.0487	0.0491	0.0492	0.0479
	(0.0122)	(0.0123)	(0.0123)	(0.0123)
Male	0.0369	0.0368	0.0344	0.0307
	(0.0230)	(0.0230)	(0.0229)	(0.0229)
Married	−0.0169	−0.0168	−0.0179	−0.0192
	(0.0213)	(0.0213)	(0.0214)	(0.0215)
Married male	−0.0358	−0.0359	−0.0364	−0.0353
	(0.0268)	(0.0268)	(0.0268)	(0.0268)
High school diploma	0.0074	0.0073	0.0068	0.0071
	(0.0139)	(0.0139)	(0.0138)	(0.0137)
College degree	0.0072	0.0073	0.0056	0.0041
	(0.0175)	(0.0175)	(0.0171)	(0.0215)
Advanced degree	−0.0033	−0.0038	−0.0050	−0.0065
	(0.0190)	(0.0189)	(0.0187)	(0.0186)
Log-likelihood	−590.7896	−591.1238	−589.9275	−586.7828

Notes: Each cell contains the marginal effect on the probability that the employee retired from the labor force (full retirement) between the first two waves of the HRS. Standard errors are reported in parentheses beneath each coefficient. The sample includes all age-eligible respondents to the HRS Wave 1 for whom wealth and self-reported pension data are available in Wave 1, whose labor force status could be obtained in Wave 2, who are working but not self-employed, and whose pension information is reported in the Pension Provider Survey (2102 observations). Column headings indicate the type of pension accrual variable that is used. Dummy variables for each sample age are included, but coefficients are not reported.

ated with greater probabilities of full retirement. The effect at the highest quartile is particularly strong: Moving from the 3rd to the 4th quartile increases the probability of retirement by 5 percentage points. Worse health status is also associated with greater probabilities of full retirement in moving from excellent to fair health. Moving from good to fair health increases the retirement probability by about 5 percentage points. Moving from fair to poor health does not increase the probability of full retirement, because other exits from working, such as disability, compete with retirement. Having retirement health insurance available increases the probability of retirement by 3.5 percentage points. The coefficients on having insurance through the employer and "locked" into health insurance are negative but insignificant. Unionized workers are more likely to retire. Gender, marital status, and education levels are not statistically significant.

Table 8.8 presents the same specifications as table 8.7, but with firm retirement as the dependent variable. The same patterns emerge as in the previous table, with more significant results on both pension wealth and pension accruals. This is not surprising, as pension incentives apply directly to departures from the firm, even those that do not include full retirement. The marginal effect of pension wealth in the age sixty-five specification is 2.4 percentage points per \$100,000. This reflects 12.68 percent of the baseline probability of 18.93 in this sample. A \$10,000 increase in average pension accruals would generate firm retirement probabilities that were 3.30 percentage points lower, or 17.43 percent of the baseline probability of firm retirement.

8.5 Conclusion

Our analysis shows that financial incentives in employer-provided pension plans have important effects on retirement behavior. As a prelude to more structural modeling of retirement, we use a non-utility-based measure of the financial incentives to delay retirement that is similar to the option value of Stock and Wise (1990b) and the peak value of Coile and Gruber (2000, 2001). We show that when the financial incentives are calculated over a sufficiently long period, higher financial incentives to delay retirement predict lower retirement rates. Pensions have a far more robust effect on the decision to leave a particular firm than they do on the decision to leave the labor force entirely, as they do not condition benefit receipt on anything other than separating with the firm. This is in contrast to Social Security, which does not distinguish between the firms at which wages were earned but does condition benefit receipt on, for example, labor market earnings and adjusted gross income.

In contrast to past studies, (e.g., Samwick 1998) we find an important wealth effect of the present value of pension benefits on the decision to retire. This is mirrored in a strong effect of nonpension wealth on retirement,

Table 8.8   **Marginal Effects Probits for Firm Retirement, Using Detailed Pension Data**

	Accrual Period for Pension Incentives			
	One Year	Two Year	Until Age 62	Until Age 65
Pension present value	0.0020	0.0020	0.0023	0.0024
	(0.0006)	(0.0006)	(0.0006)	(0.0007)
Pension accrual	−0.0007	−0.0024	−0.0214	−0.0330
	(0.0042)	(0.0067)	(0.0108)	(0.0123)
Wage	−0.0125	−0.0121	−0.0062	−0.0031
	(0.0061)	(0.0061)	(0.0064)	(0.0066)
Net worth 2nd quartile	0.0024	0.0025	0.0013	0.0004
	(0.0261)	(0.0261)	(0.0260)	(0.0260)
Net worth 3rd quartile	0.0379	0.0381	0.0363	0.0343
	(0.0284)	(0.0284)	(0.0282)	(0.0282)
Net worth 4th quartile	0.1227	0.1229	0.1223	0.1222
	(0.0335)	(0.0335)	(0.0334)	(0.0334)
Health status very good	0.0355	0.0356	0.0349	0.0345
	(0.0234)	(0.0234)	(0.0234)	(0.0234)
Health status good	0.0436	0.0436	0.0429	0.0416
	(0.0251)	(0.0250)	(0.0250)	(0.0250)
Health status fair	0.1345	0.1347	0.1328	0.1329
	(0.0425)	(0.0425)	(0.0423)	(0.0423)
Health status poor	0.2947	0.2951	0.2936	0.2918
	(0.1064)	(0.1065)	(0.1064)	(0.1062)
Health insurance own employer	−0.0318	−0.0319	−0.0333	−0.0358
	(0.0269)	(0.0269)	(0.0270)	(0.0271)
Health insurance any retiree	−0.0156	−0.0157	−0.0136	−0.0127
	(0.0360)	(0.0359)	(0.0358)	(0.0356)
Health insurance "locked"	−0.0321	−0.0325	−0.0335	−0.0314
	(0.0388)	(0.0387)	(0.0386)	(0.0387)
Union member	0.0230	0.0234	0.0225	0.0211
	(0.0176)	(0.0176)	(0.0175)	(0.0175)
Male	0.0253	0.0250	0.0226	0.0194
	(0.0363)	(0.0363)	(0.0364)	(0.0364)
Married	−0.0719	−0.0720	−0.0734	−0.0747
	(0.0329)	(0.0329)	(0.0329)	(0.0330)
Married male	−0.0112	−0.0111	−0.0128	−0.0117
	(0.0420)	(0.0420)	(0.0420)	(0.0420)
High school diploma	0.0446	0.0445	0.0439	0.0446
	(0.0216)	(0.0216)	(0.0216)	(0.0216)
College degree	0.0319	0.0318	0.0312	0.0309
	(0.0272)	(0.0272)	(0.0271)	(0.0271)
Advanced degree	−0.0713	−0.0711	−0.0730	−0.7042
	(0.0245)	(0.0245)	(0.0244)	(0.0243)
Log-likelihood	−943.4425	−943.3694	−941.0250	−939.4280

Notes: Each cell contains the marginal effect on the probability that the employee left the Wave 1 employer (firm retirement) between the first two waves of the HRS. Standard errors are reported in parentheses beneath each coefficient. The sample includes all age-eligible respondents to the HRS Wave 1 for whom wealth and self-reported pension data are available in Wave 1, whose labor force status could be obtained in Wave 2, who are working but not self-employed, and whose pension information is reported in the Pension Provider Survey (2102 observations). Column headings indicate the type of pension accrual variable that is used. Dummy variables for each sample age are included, but coefficients are not reported.

especially in the distinction between the top quartile and the rest of the wealth distribution. As expected, there is also a strong effect of health status on retirement probabilities, particularly for the roughly 10 percent of the sample reporting fair or poor health.

Our current analysis suggests several areas for future research. First, the measures of retirement incentives can be expanded to include Social Security wealth and accruals, making full use of the Social Security earnings histories that are available with the HRS. Second, the sample can be extended to include subsequent waves of the survey to observe additional retirements and postretirement behavior. Third, the structural parameters of the option value model can be estimated. Fourth, the effects of wealth, health, and other job characteristics can be integrated more formally into the calculation and estimation of the option value of retirement.

References

Ausink, J. 1991. *The effect of changes in compensation on a pilot's decision to leave the air force.* Ph.D. Diss. Harvard University, John F. Kennedy School of Government, Cambridge, Mass.

Ausink, J., and D. Wise. 1996. The military pension, compensation, and retirement of U.S. Air Force pilots. In *Advances in the Economics of Aging,* ed. D. Wise, 83–109. Chicago: University of Chicago Press.

Bulow, J. 1981. Early retirement pension benefits. NBER Working Paper no. 654. Cambridge, Mass.: National Bureau of Economic Research, April.

Coile, C. 1999. Social security, pensions, and the retirement decisions of couples. MIT, Department of Economics.

Coile, C., and J. Gruber. 2000. Social security and retirement. NBER Working Paper no. 7830. Cambridge, Mass.: National Bureau of Economic Research, August.

Coile, C., and J. Gruber. 2001. Social security incentives for retirement. In *Themes in the Economics of Aging,* ed. D. Wise, 311–341. Chicago: University of Chicago Press.

Gruber, J., and B. Madrian. 1996. Health insurance and early retirement: Evidence from the availability of continuation coverage. In *Advances in the Economics of Aging,* ed. D. Wise, 115–43. Chicago: University of Chicago Press.

Gruber, J., and D. Wise. 1998. Introduction and summary of papers. In *Social security programs and retirement around the world,* ed. J. Gruber and D. Wise, 1–35. Chicago: University of Chicago Press.

Gustman, A., and T. Steinmeier. 1999. Effects of pensions on saving: Analysis with data from the Health and Retirement Study. *Carnegie-Rochester Conference Series* 50 (July): 271–326.

Harris, A. 2001. The effects of social security on retirement behavior: A test of the option-value model using the Health and Retirement Study. Congressional Budget Office, Manuscript, February.

Kotlikoff, L., and D. Wise. 1985. Labor compensation and the structure of private pension plans: Evidence for contractual versus spot labor markets. In *Pensions, labor, and individual choice,* ed. D. Wise. Chicago: University of Chicago Press.

————. 1987. The incentive effects of private pension plans. In *Issues in Pension Economics,* ed. Z. Bodie, J. Shoven, and D. Wise, 283–336. Chicago: University of Chicago Press.

————. 1989a. Employee retirement and a firm's pension plan. In *Economics of Aging,* ed. D. Wise, 279–330. Chicago: University of Chicago Press.

————. 1989b. *The wage carrot and the pension stick: Retirement benefits and labor force participation.* Upjohn Institute for Employment Research.

Lamkin, J., and B. Peticolas. 1998. Pension estimation program documentation (Richard Curtin): Modified for use with PCs. University of Michigan, Survey Research Center. Mimeograph.

Lazear, E. 1983. Pensions as severance pay. In *Financial Aspects of the United States Pension System,* ed. Z. Bodie and J. Shoven, 57–85. Chicago: University of Chicago Press.

Lumsdaine, R., J. Stock, and D. Wise. 1990. Efficient windows and labor force reduction. *Journal of Public Economics* 43 (2): 131–59.

————. 1991. Fenêtres et retraites (Windows and retirement), *Annales d'Economie et de Statistique* 20/21:219–42.

————. 1992. Three models of retirement: Computational complexity versus predictive validity. In *Topics in the economics of aging,* ed. D. Wise, 21–60. Chicago: University of Chicago Press.

————. 1993. Pension plan provisions and retirement: Men & women, Medicare, and models. In *The economics of aging,* ed. D. Wise, 183–212. Chicago: University of Chicago Press.

Ruhm, C. 1990. Bridge jobs and partial retirement. *Journal of Labor Economics* 8:482–501.

Samwick, A. 1998. New evidence on pensions, social security, and the timing of retirement. *Journal of Public Economics* 70:207–36.

————. 2001. Comment on Coile and Gruber: Social security incentives for retirement. In *Themes in the Economics of Aging,* ed. D. Wise, 341–54. Chicago: University of Chicago Press.

Stock, J., and D. Wise. 1990a. The pension inducement to retire: An option value analysis. In *Issues in the Economics of Aging,* ed. D. Wise, 205–24. Chicago: University of Chicago Press.

————. 1990b. Pensions, the option value of work, and retirement. *Econometrica* 58 (5): 1151–80.

9

Why Do the Japanese Spend So Much on Drugs?

Seiritsu Ogura and Takehiko Hagino

9.1 Introduction

In Japan, drugs account for an enormous proportion of health care costs. Of the five major developed countries listed in table 9.1, Japan and France have the highest absolute per-patient cost of drugs, spending three times as much as England, twice as much as the United States, and one and a half times as much as Germany. Japan consistently ranks at the top in terms of the share of drugs in total health care costs, spending more than 20 percent on drugs according to the Organization for Economic Cooperation and Development (OECD) Health Data (1998, table 9.2).

According to the 1996 *Survey on Socialized Medicine* (Ministry of Health and Welfare 1994–1996)[1] injections account for as great a share of inpatient costs as do surgeries (9.5 percent and 9.4 percent, respectively), while drugs and injections together consume 39.6 percent of outpatient health care costs. Although drugs are a very important component of total health care expenditures in Japan, their importance seems to be heavily concentrated in the outpatient care of elderly patients. In inpatient care, drugs account for only 12.8 percent of the difference in average costs between the elderly and the rest of the population. In outpatient care, drugs account for 56 percent of this difference. Given the rapid aging of the Japanese population, it is clear that if we do not find some way to control

Seiritsu Ogura is professor of economics at Hosei University in Tokyo. Takehiko Hagino was an economist at the Japan Center for Economic Research when this paper was written.

The authors wish to thank the Japan Center for Global Partnership and the Toyota Foundation for financial support, and Mark McClellan for helpful comments. This paper is a revised version of the Ogura-Hagino report (in Japanese) contained in Takayama (1999).

1. This survey, based on approximately 300,000 reimbursement claims submitted by health care providers, is published annually by the Ministry of Health and Welfare.

Table 9.1   International Health Care and Drug Expenditures, 1993

	National Health Care Expenditures (yen per capita)	Outpatient Drug Expenditures (yen per patient)	Inpatient Drug Expenditures (yen per patient)	Share of All Drugs in National Health Care Expenditure (%)
France	253,680	43,375	50,375	19.9
Germany	224,420	32,195	38,283	17.1
England	110,625	16,341	18,153	16.4
United States	312,755	23,076	35,418	11.3
Japan	195,217	43,533	57,589	29.5

Source: Illustrated White Paper on Health Insurance (1998).
Note: Data for England are from 1992. Exchange rates: 23 yen/franc, 79 yen/deutsche mark, 231 yen/pound, and 122 yen/dollar.

Table 9.2   Share of Drugs in National Health Care Costs, 1990–1998 (%)

	1990	1991	1992	1993	1994	1995	1996	1997
France	16.7	16.7	16.6	16.8	16.6	16.7	17.0	16.7
Germany	14.2	14.3	14.2	12.4	12.3	12.3	12.7	12.6
England	13.8	14.0	14.5	15.3	15.3	15.9	16.5	17.3
United States	8.6	8.5	8.5	8.4	8.4	8.6	8.8	7.8
Japan	21.4	22.8	21.9	22.1	20.9	20.2	20.8	20.0

Source: 1998 OECD Health Data

the cost of drugs, we will not be able to control health care expenditures in the twenty-first century.

Why do we spend so much on drugs? The first place to look for an answer is in the enormous distortions generated by drug price regulations during the last five decades. Although the entire health care sector lies outside the realm of the market economy (the government sets comprehensive reimbursement prices for individual health care services in an attempt to control every possible aspect of health care service delivery), these regulations on drug prices are very peculiar. Regulated drug prices vary by brand name even if they are chemically identical. In general, when the government purchases any other good or service it must observe a set of very stringent procurement procedures designed to assure the lowest possible price. With drugs, physicians are allowed to use more expensive brand-name drugs when cheaper alternatives are available, even though they are supposed to be acting as agents of the government.

Second, the government sets reimbursement (retail) prices on the basis of market (wholesale) prices from almost eighteen months earlier, and these retail prices are then fixed for the following two years. If the market functioned normally, such regulation would be a source of enormous risk for health care providers. In other words, the market structure must be very peculiar for such a system to have functioned without driving a large number of providers to bankruptcy.

Third, drug markets are very tightly regulated and protected by extremely high barriers to new entry. The regulations concerning the introduction of new drugs work as prohibitive barriers to entry, as they are both very time consuming and costly. At the same time, these high barriers make it easy for insiders to set noncompetitive prices and to build cozy relationships with regulators.

In this paper, we present evidence regarding the effects of price distortions on resource allocation in the health care sector. Our estimates indicate that the magnitude of these effects exceeds 20 percent, and may be as high as 50 percent, of drug costs. We then show that the government's attempts to control drug prices directly are at best ineffective, as they have been offset by drug-switching effects in most drug groups. These drug-switching effects are in turn induced by the built-in profit margins for "new" drugs, which are generously priced by regulators. We base our conclusions on statistical analyses of the first comprehensive microdata set compiled in Japan.

The rest of the paper proceeds as follows: In section 9.2, we review the drug price controls of the last decade and classify the economic inefficiencies associated with these controls; in section 9.3, we analyze the drug selection behavior of physicians; in section 9.4, we present a decomposition analysis of drug costs; in section 9.5, we discuss various reform proposals currently under consideration; section 9.6 concludes.

9.2   Drug Pricing in the Japanese Health Care System

As all drugs are privately produced, health care service providers must purchase all necessary drugs through the market. Trading is free for almost all drugs, and market prices are formed on the basis of reimbursement prices. In effect, the reimbursement prices are the drugs' retail prices and market prices are the drugs' wholesale prices, generating profit margins for each drug.

9.2.1   Formula for Drug Price Revisions

The Ministry of Health and Welfare (MHW) updates the list of reimbursement prices for individual drugs approximately every two years using its *Survey of Drug Prices.*[2] The current list of drugs contains almost 14,000

---

2. In the *Survey of Drug Prices,* the government collects data on the actual purchase prices of individual drugs from health care providers. The survey's objectivity, however, is somewhat weakened because it is announced well in advance and data are collected for just one month (usually September).

different drugs. For nearly ten years, the government has been using the following formula to revise the reimbursement prices:[3]

(1) $$Y_t = X_{t-1} + r_t Y_{t-1},$$

where

Y_t: New drug price,
X_{t-1}: Average market price in the *Survey of Drug Prices,*
r_t: Reasonable zone factor $(0 < r_t < 1)$, and
Y_{t-1}: Old drug price.

Once a new price is set, it is fixed for the next two years. Hence, at least in theory, providers take on the considerable risk of market price variation in drug prices. In the last ten years of practice, however, once the new prices are announced almost all market prices have continuously declined. As a result, providers enjoy positive profit margins on almost all drugs and so have an economic incentive to sell as many drugs as possible to their patients. There are two reasons for this: the reasonable zone factor and the generous price setting for "new" drugs.

9.2.2   Drug Pricing Rules

If we subtract old drug prices from both sides of equation (1), we obtain

(2) $$Y_t - Y_{t-1} = -(Y_{t-1} - X_{t-1}) + r_t Y_{t-1}.$$

By dividing both sides by old drug prices, we obtain the revision formula in proportion terms

(3) $$y_{t-1} = -\pi_{t-1} + r_t,$$

where y_{t-1} is the rate of change of the reimbursement price of the drug and π_{t-1} is the discount rate the firm offered to providers in the previous period.

(4) $$y_{t-1} = \frac{(Y_t - Y_{t-1})}{Y_{t-1}}$$

(5) $$\pi_{t-1} = \frac{(Y_{t-1} - X_{t-1})}{Y_{t-1}}$$

In the absence of the reasonable zone factor, equation (5) implies that if a firm offers a discount to promote the sale of a drug, that drug's price is permanently lowered. Such a prospect should make the firm hesitant to offer a discount. With the reasonable zone factor, however, the firm can offer price discounts without endangering future profitability, provided that the discount rate remains within the range of the reasonable zone factor.

---

3. Strictly speaking, this formula has only been adopted for all drugs since 1992. Prior to that time, "bulk-line" formulas were used.

Recently, however, the government has been forced to rapidly reduce both drug prices[4] and reasonable zone factors in an attempt to control health care costs, particularly those of the elderly. The zone factor dropped from 15 percent in 1992 to 13 percent in 1994, 11 percent in 1996, 10 percent in 1997, and 5 percent in 1998. Starting in 1997, an even lower rate was applied to "new" drugs with chemical components similar to existing drugs: 8 percent in 1997 and 2 percent in 1998.

9.2.3 Assessing Price Regulations: Decomposition of the Variation in the Cost of Drugs

As we have shown, Japanese drug price regulation has a built-in price reduction mechanism. If there were no change in quantity used, price would change at exactly the same rate as cost. The overall cost of drugs in public health insurance, however, follows two-year cycles, showing decreases in the years of price revisions and increases in the years following price revisions (table 9.3). Many (Ikegami et al. 1998; Ogura 1996, 1998) believe that this pattern is explained by the combination of two trends working against the cut in drug prices: increasing reliance on multiple drugs and overall switching to more expensive drugs. Some add a third trend of switching to *new* expensive drugs. As far as we know, however, no one has quantified these trends using comprehensive drug-usage data.

Five-Factor Decomposition

We decompose the variation in drug costs using the following five factors: (a) prescription probability factor; (b) drug-switching factor; (c) price regulation factor; (d) daily quantity factor; and (e) number of days prescribed factor. All drugs are classified at the three-digit level. The per-patient average cost of drugs in group k in period t is denoted $v_k(t)$; $v_k(t)$ is the product of $\Gamma_k(t)$, the probability that any drug in group k is prescribed; and $\Omega_k(t)$ is the per-patient cost of drugs in group k (given that at least one drug in the group has been prescribed). Therefore, we have

$$V(t) = \sum_{k=1}^{n} v_k(t)$$

$$v_k(t) = \Gamma_k(t)\Omega_k(t).$$

The per-patient cost, $\Omega_k(t)$, is in turn the product of four factors (summed over all i): $s_i(t)$, the probability of selecting drug i in group k; $p_i(t)$, the reimbursement price of drug i; $x_i(t)$, the daily quantity of drug i; and $d_i(t)$, the number of days that drug i is used. Or,

$$\Omega_k(t) = \sum_{i} s_i(t)p_i(t)x_i(t)d_i(t).$$

4. For the officially announced changes in drug prices, see table 9.3.

Table 9.3   Changes in Drug Prices, 1990–1996

Year	Change in Drug Prices (%)	Drug Spending, All Patients (yen)				Drug Spending, Outpatients Only (yen)			
		Drugs	Injections	Total	Change (%)	Drugs	Injections	Total	Change (%)
1990	−9.2	5,359	2,027	7,386	−5.7	4,945	634	5,579	−1.8
1991		5,839	2,100	7,939	7.5	5,405	688	6,093	9.2
1992	−8.1	5,760	2,074	7,834	−1.3	5,380	688	6,068	−0.4
1993		5,863	2,084	7,947	1.4	5,493	805	6,298	3.8
1994	−6.6	5,564	1,789	7,353	−7.5	5,255	689	5,944	−5.6
1995		5,841	1,903	7,745	5.3	5,546	758	6,304	6.1
1996	−6.8	5,433	1,823	7,256	−6.3	5,156	760	5,916	−6.2
1989–1996	−30.7				4.1				7.9

Source: Survey of National Medical Care Insurance Services 1990–1996 (MHW 1994–1996)

Note that the sum of the $s_i(t)$ terms, each of which represents the probability of selecting drug i conditional on prescribing some drug in group k, equals one.

Given the above formulation, the variation in $v_k(t)$ is determined by the variation in the five component variables. The proportional rate of change in $v_k(t)$ is given by

$$\frac{\Delta v_k(t)}{v_k(t)} = \frac{\Delta \Gamma_k(t)}{\Gamma_k(t)} + \frac{\Delta \Omega_k(t)}{\Omega_k(t)} = \frac{\Delta \Gamma_k(t)}{\Gamma_k(t)} + \frac{\sum_i \Delta s_i(t) p_i(t) x_i(t) d_i(t)}{\sum_i s_i(t) p_i(t) x_i(t) d_i(t)}$$

$$+ \frac{\sum_i s_i(t) \Delta p_i(t) x_i(t) d_i(t)}{\sum_i s_i(t) p_i(t) x_i(t) d_i(t)} + \frac{\sum_i s_i(t) p_i(t) \Delta x_i(t) d_i(t)}{\sum_i s_i(t) p_i(t) x_i(t) d_i(t)}$$

$$+ \frac{\sum_i s_i(t) p_i(t) x_i(t) \Delta d_i(t)}{\sum_i s_i(t) p_i(t) x_i(t) d_i(t)}.$$

In words, we offer the following explanation:

1. The first term is the rate of change in the probability of prescribing drugs in group k. The trend toward relying on more groups of drugs is found by summing the first term over all the drug groups.

2. The second term is the drug-switching effect within group k, or the rate of change in the per-patient cost of drugs as a result of changes in drug selection. The trend of switching to expensive drugs is observed directly in the second term.

3. The third term is the price regulation effect in group k, or the rate of change in the per-patient cost of drugs as a result of changes in regulated drug prices. This is the government's control variable, and the sum of the third term over all the drug groups should be close to the rate the government announces.

4. The fourth term is the rate of change in the per-patient cost of drugs as a result of changes in daily quantities.

5. The fifth term is the rate of change in the per-patient cost of drugs as a result of changes in the number of days for which drugs are prescribed.

Data: Modification and Errors

We use the 1994, 1995, and 1996 *Survey of Drugs* for our analysis (MHW). The data are described in detail in section 9.3.2. There are two groups of claims that are dropped from the original data sets. First, we exclude all claims submitted by drug stores because they do not include patient identification numbers. Second, we exclude observations above the 99th percentile in each three-digit group in terms of daily quantities. We make this exclusion because of the extremely large variance in daily quantities for some groups. The descriptive statistics for our sample are given in table 9.4.

Table 9.4　Drug Data Descriptive Statistics, by Three Digit Group

Group	Sample Size			Weighted Sample Size			Number of Drugs			Cost Share			Average Number of Days Taken			Average Cost per Day (yen)		
	1994	1995	1996	1994	1995	1996	1994	1995	1996	1994	1995	1996	1994	1995	1996	1994	1995	1996
114	31,577	25,259	23,105	3,655,202	3,407,630	3,186,121	177	169	174	1.97	1.88	1.75	7.8	8.0	7.6	147	158	157
117	8,977	7,889	7,399	624,664	613,802	626,488	168	160	181	1.16	1.01	1.12	37.3	37.7	40.9	107	100	95
119	10,547	8,937	7,450	804,231	815,196	723,704	16	16	20	3.06	3.04	2.68	26.9	28.6	28.7	304	301	278
131	20,384	17,359	17,521	2,943,641	2,913,736	2,936,797	141	138	154	2.22	2.23	2.59	2.4	2.5	2.5	688	717	765
212	4,893	4,045	3,700	616,395	574,248	595,687	71	74	83	1.65	1.48	1.67	27.1	27.3	27.9	213	218	216
214	9,478	8,486	8,165	1,177,132	1,283,977	1,303,849	121	120	145	2.57	2.77	3.03	31.4	33.3	33.2	150	149	151
217	16,474	14,555	13,808	1,722,539	1,779,782	1,740,082	93	95	105	3.04	3.03	3.06	27.3	27.7	26.4	139	142	143
218	10,435	9,622	7,860	1,522,350	1,676,518	1,396,209	32	32	34	3.88	4.15	3.70	26.6	27.7	27.6	205	206	207
219	16,483	13,413	10,495	1,407,114	1,305,332	1,013,397	95	95	109	4.00	3.80	3.33	27.8	28.8	28.2	219	233	251
232	29,016	24,270	20,800	3,143,325	3,117,989	2,661,715	111	108	132	4.14	3.95	3.20	26.1	25.7	25.0	108	113	104
239	10,709	9,066	8,284	1,092,362	1,067,588	1,022,061	41	42	52	0.97	1.04	0.90	13.6	12.4	12.5	139	183	152
241	757	396	463	61,739	43,055	50,419	19	19	18	1.05	1.24	1.27	2.7	2.1	2.0	13,582	32,402	26,989
249	5,329	4,410	3,852	589,651	568,551	485,626	51	44	49	1.93	1.98	2.27	12.5	11.7	9.7	561	686	1,036
259	4,664	4,662	4,886	380,981	465,509	491,760	20	20	26	1.23	1.54	1.66	24.4	27.0	27.4	285	282	265
264	64,118	55,264	54,666	7,828,626	7,903,908	7,735,899	155	149	169	4.85	4.59	4.56	2.5	2.4	2.4	536	554	527
325	4,777	3,930	4,037	249,848	259,122	267,570	76	72	80	1.82	1.67	2.19	14.0	13.9	15.8	1,116	1,072	1,122
331	30,507	26,147	27,181	1,993,999	2,189,348	2,317,219	79	78	84	1.73	1.90	2.01	7.0	7.5	7.3	265	266	257
339	6,589	5,380	6,171	681,982	645,230	797,465	22	21	27	4.13	3.42	4.48	27.5	27.3	28.4	473	447	426
399	15,234	13,124	12,696	1,249,896	1,287,442	1,352,312	69	71	83	6.89	7.48	7.58	10.1	10.0	9.6	1,172	1,331	1,258
422	1,844	1,541	1,369	229,891	236,293	195,668	56	51	49	3.80	3.71	2.90	22.6	23.5	22.4	1,568	1,539	1,423
429	809	796	842	84,001	96,666	92,219	28	29	41	1.34	1.46	1.32	16.4	16.1	17.5	2,088	2,156	1,762
430	854	788	659	57,497	62,287	55,247	43	39	43	1.48	1.20	0.86	1.6	1.6	1.5	33,418	27,812	22,932
449	8,446	6,869	7,971	1,173,619	1,150,464	1,339,759	31	31	44	2.45	2.30	3.08	16.1	17.0	18.0	278	271	275
520	6,134	5,211	4,244	690,171	714,314	639,812	203	188	199	2.12	2.10	1.82	21.8	22.4	22.2	302	303	276
613	30,053	26,448	25,291	3,724,928	4,246,507	3,814,287	205	202	250	7.27	7.56	7.28	5.3	5.3	5.3	792	768	770
624	10,375	9,225	9,371	1,303,008	1,481,840	1,517,252	26	26	31	2.12	2.49	2.47	5.8	6.0	6.2	598	641	561
634	1,829	1,557	1,477	96,557	92,083	83,259	76	65	70	3.28	3.40	3.32	3.6	3.9	3.9	20,428	21,781	21,843
639	1,430	1,031	843	180,229	176,196	127,060	28	24	29	0.84	1.46	1.50	2.3	2.4	2.9	4,310	8,032	8,735
721	6,998	6,077	4,864	618,810	632,830	517,710	89	84	101	3.58	3.46	2.47	1.7	1.7	1.7	7,119	7,364	6,165

Source: Authors' computations based on surveys on drugs (MHW 1994–1996).

Notes: The cumulative share of drugs in the listed drug groups is 80 percent. Data include drugs used in injections. One shot is a "day" for injections.

We still have to deal with two problems that plague any attempt to use indexes: what to do with drugs introduced into and removed from our sample. Drugs that are introduced for the first time in period t do not have data in period $t - 1$, including price data. Drugs that are removed in period t do not have data in period $t + 1$, including price data. If we exclude both of them, we lose a significant part of total drug costs from our analysis, but if we include them we will no longer have an identity.

In the end, we have chosen inclusion with some modification. For the prescription factor and the drug-switching factor terms, we include both introduced and removed drugs. For the price regulation factor, daily quantity factor, and number of days prescribed factor terms, we include neither. This is the main reason for the nonnegligible residuals obtained in the decomposition analysis in certain cases.

Results

The decomposition analyses have been carried out for all three-digit groups. Table 9.5 reports aggregated results (the sum of all drugs) with breakdowns for some provider and regional characteristics.

Results for All Drugs. Between 1994 and 1995, when there were no revisions of drug prices, the average cost of drugs increased by 5.1 percent. According to our decomposition, changes in the prescription probability increased the cost of drugs by 1.7 percent. The drug-switching effect increased the cost of drugs by 5.4 percent, while changes in daily quantities decreased the cost of drugs by 0.7 percent. Finally, changes in the number of days prescribed increased the cost of drugs by 1.5 percent. The errors therefore amount to –2.8 percent.

Between 1995 and 1996, when drug prices were revised, average drug costs fell by 9.7 percent. The reduction in drug prices decreased the cost of drugs by 7.7 percent, and changes in the prescription probability decreased the cost of drugs another 7.0 percent. The drug-switching effect increased the cost of drugs by 7.1 percent, changes in daily quantity increased the cost of drugs by 0.2 percent, and changes in the number of days prescribed decreased the cost of drugs by 0.1 percent.

Price Controls and Drug-switching Effects. The magnitudes of drug-switching effects are particularly important as an indicator of the effectiveness of drug price regulation. In table 9.6 we report the percentage changes in price in 1996 for ten major three-digit groups, as well as the drug-switching effects in 1995 and 1996. Our ten major groups account for almost 40 percent of the cost of drugs in 1995, and changes in their prices were enough to drive drug costs down by 3.3 percent. However, the drug-switching effects in these groups in 1995 and 1996 together drove drug costs

Table 9.5   **Drug Cost Variation Decompositions, 1994–1995 and 1995–1996 (%)**

	Change in Total Drug Costs	Change in Prescription Probability	Drug Switching Effect	Change in Drug Prices	Change in Daily Quantity	Change in Number of Days Taken	Error
1994–1995							
Total	5.1	1.7	5.4		−0.7	1.5	−2.8
Inpatient care	5.1	0.8	5.4		−1.5	1.9	−1.6
Outpatient care	5.1	1.5	8.3		0.9	1.4	−7.0
Ownership							
National/public	4.9	4.7	4.4		2.7	3.1	−9.9
Private	4.2	2.5	6.8		5.1	1.5	−11.6
University	−11.3	9.9	22.3		−0.8	−1.5	−41.2
Clinic with beds	0.8	−1.6	4.4		−1.4	7.3	−8.0
Clinic without beds	6.8	4.3	6.3		9.1	3.6	−16.5
Number of beds							
0	4.2	3.8	6.1		5.9	2.3	−14.0
<200	5.4	3.4	3.0		−2.6	10.9	−9.3
>200	1.7	2.4	7.2		10.7	0.2	−18.9
Number of patients per physician							
<100	0.7	−0.9	2.0		15.4	2.1	−17.9
100–200	7.9	6.3	13.4		1.0	1.5	−14.4
>200 and <400	16.3	10.9	4.1		−0.2	6.5	−5.0
>400	9.0	12.4	51.7		−3.1	−0.9	51.1
Region							
Hokkaido	−0.2	14.1	9.0		−3.5	3.7	−23.6
Tohoku	8.1	8.9	13.0		−1.0	−1.4	−11.4
Kanto	−7.3	2.6	1.1		12.9	−3.3	−20.7
Hokuriku	−24.9	−6.4	27.5		−1.4	3.4	−48.0
Chubu-Tokai	8.2	4.4	28.4		−3.1	3.6	−25.3
Kinki	12.1	3.0	11.2		24.8	3.2	−30.1
Chugoku	−6.6	−0.8	8.3		−0.1	5.3	−19.2
Sikoku	10.2	18.3	13.6		−1.0	23.1	−43.8
Kyosyu	14.3	13.4	3.3		−3.5	7.6	−6.5
1995–1996							
Total	−9.7	−7.0	7.0	−7.7	0.2	−0.1	−2.2
Inpatient care	−9.8	−6.1	5.3	−7.2	−0.2	0.0	−1.6
Outpatient care	−9.6	−5.2	7.1	−7.9	1.0	−0.1	−4.5
Ownership							
National/public	−5.2	1.1	16.8	−7.2	−2.4	0.0	−13.6
Private	−16.8	−9.9	8.7	−8.1	0.7	0.4	−8.5
University	9.2	11.0	30.4	−5.4	−2.6	4.2	−28.4
Clinic with beds	−8.2	−3.7	10.6	−8.8	2.5	−1.2	−7.5
Clinic without beds	−13.8	−7.2	6.3	−8.6	2.2	−1.5	−5.0
Number of beds							
0	−14.5	−7.1	7.0	−8.6	1.1	−1.9	−5.0
<200	−5.9	−5.9	46.8	−8.7	2.3	−1.8	−38.6
>200	−3.7	2.8	6.7	−7.0	−4.6	4.4	−6.0

Table 9.5   (continued)

	Change in Total Drug Costs	Change in Prescription Probability	Drug Switching Effect	Change in Drug Prices	Change in Daily Quantity	Change in Number of Days Taken	Error
Number of patients per physician							
<100	−7.3	−3.2	10.8	−7.4	−1.4	5.6	−11.7
100–200	−9.5	−1.2	8.8	−7.7	1.1	−1.0	−9.5
>200 and <400	−9.2	−4.2	6.8	−8.2	2.3	−0.3	−5.4
>400	−11.8	−4.5	4.2	−8.8	1.0	4.1	−7.7
Region							
Hokkaido	0.8	−0.2	15.6	−8.2	2.2	2.6	−11.2
Tohoku	−16.9	16.0	4.7	−7.9	−0.6	4.7	−33.8
Kanto	−2.4	27.2	18.2	−7.5	−0.8	4.8	−44.3
Hokuriku	5.3	461.3	9.5	−8.2	1.1	3.1	−461.5
Chubu-Tokai	−16.8	−7.0	2.7	−8.5	0.6	−0.8	−3.8
Kinki	−13.2	−2.3	9.1	−8.0	−1.1	4.0	−14.8
Chugoku	−5.3	3.4	5.4	−7.8	−1.0	0.7	−6.0
Sikoku	−1.9	13.1	44.4	−9.9	−2.9	2.0	−48.5
Kyusyu	−15.7	0.3	22.6	−7.7	−2.3	−0.7	−27.9

Source: Authors' computations based on surveys on drugs (MHW 1994–1996).

Table 9.6   **Price Changes and Switching Effects for Selected Drug Groups (%)**

			Switching Effect		
Three-Digit Group	1995 Cost Share	1996 Price Change	1995	1996	Total
131	2.2	−3.9	4.52	12.01	16.53
214	2.8	−6.7	3.56	5.95	9.51
217	3.0	−7.9	5.55	9.28	14.83
218	4.2	−2.8	2.95	−0.91	2.04
219	3.4	−8.8	5.55	10.54	16.09
232	4.0	−9.4	5.22	2.52	7.74
264	4.6	−11.7	1.94	2.93	4.87
422	3.7	−5.6	−1.19	5.79	4.6
613	7.6	−11.4	−0.14	9.64	9.5
721	3.5	−11.7	14.96	−7.04	7.92
Total	38.83	−3.30	1.44	1.93	3.40

Source: Authors' computations based on surveys on drugs (MHW 1994–1996).

up by 3.4 percent. The relative magnitudes of the price changes and the switching effects vary widely across drug groups, but in the aggregate they are almost equal.

Observations. We offer the following conjectures based on these three years of data:

1. The drug-switching effects work to increase the cost of drugs at an annual rate of somewhere between 5 percent and 7 percent.

2. When there is no reduction in drug prices, the trend toward more prescriptions pushes up total drug costs by nearly 2 percent, but when drug prices are reduced, the trend is reversed and prescription probabilities contribute to a 7 percent decline in drug costs.

3. During the 1994–1996 period, the reduction in drug prices and prescription probability together barely offset the drug-switching effect.

9.3   Economic Incentives in Drug Choice

Many physicians strongly deny that their drug choices are affected in any way by economic incentives. Are their decisions purely based on medicine and truly free from economics? In this section we examine physician selection behavior using a formal model to analyze a comprehensive dataset on drugs chosen by physicians.

9.3.1   Selection Functions

Assume that a physician selects a drug out of J possible drugs using the following selection function:

$$u_{ik} = \beta'_k \mathbf{x}_i + \gamma'_k \mathbf{z}_k + \varepsilon_{ik},$$

where $\mathbf{x}$ is a vector of patient and provider characteristics, $\mathbf{z}$ is a vector of drug characteristics, and ε is the error term. The drug's profit margin is included as one of the elements of $\mathbf{z}$, and the corresponding coefficient in γ gives the direction and size of the influence of the profit margin on the physician's selection. The physician selects drug j for patient i if and only if

$$u_{ij} \geq u_{ik}, k = 1, \ldots, J.$$

If the error terms ε_{ik} is independently and identically distributed as an extreme value,[5] then

$$\text{Prob}(y_i = j) = \frac{e^{\beta'_j x_i + \gamma'_j z_j}}{\sum_{k=1}^{J} e^{\beta'_k x_i + \gamma'_k z_k}},$$

where y_i is the drug selected by the physician. By fitting a multinomial logit model we obtain estimates of the parameters of the criterion function.

As usual, because the choice model is estimated using data from patients who were given at least one of the J possible drugs, only $J-1$ criterion functions can be estimated and only the differences in coefficients between the $J-1$ drugs and the base drug can be determined.

5. See chapter 5 of Ben-Akiva and Lerman (1985) for derivations.

9.3.2   Data and Empirical Strategy

The MHW collects data for the *Survey of Drugs* from the same source used to compile the *Survey on Socialized Medicine:* reimbursement claims submitted by clinics and hospitals. The drug data contain drug identification codes, quantities prescribed, and the cost of drugs to individual patients. We have limited access to the 1994, 1995, and 1996 *Surveys of Drugs* (MHW). The limitation is that the drug data contain only partial identification codes. The full drug identification code consists of twelve alphanumeric characters, of which we have access to only the first four. The first (and broadest) classification category uses the first three digits, and the second category uses the first four digits. If the price of a particular drug is unique within its four-digit group, we can identify the drug using its quantity and cost information, but if there are two or more drugs that have an identical list price, exact identification of individual drugs is impossible. A data set on individual drug names and full chemical components has been purchased separately from a commercial source for 1995, and additional codes for the other years have been added manually.

In the drug data, each observation contains provider characteristics, patient characteristics (including sex, age bracket, and major disease), and drug characteristics (including estimated out-of-pocket cost, profit margin, and four-digit grouping). There are typically a large number of drugs classified in any four-digit group, and several four-digit groups are contained in each three-digit group (table 9.7).[6] Thus, some aggregation of individual drugs is inevitable.

Using data on patients who were prescribed any drug in a given three-digit group, we estimate two specifications of our multinomial logit model. In the first model, we use the four-digit groups as our dependent variable. The different drugs within a four-digit group provide variation in profit margins and out-of-pocket costs. Thus, in this model, a particular four-digit group may become a physician's favorite because it contains a very profitable drug. Whenever possible, we select the first four-digit group in a three-digit group as the base case because it usually has the smallest total drug costs of the four-digit groups.

In the second model, we use the quintiles of drug prices in a given three-digit group as our dependent variable. In addition to individual characteristics, provider characteristics, profit margins, and out-of-pocket costs, dummy variables for each of the four-digit groups are included as independent variables. Thus, this model tries to explain why expensive drugs

---

6. Our data set contains nine three-digit groups, twenty-nine four-digit groups, and 729 different drugs with a sufficient number of observations for fitting the selection models. See table 9.7 for details.

Table 9.7   1995 Survey of Drugs Summary Statistics

Three-Digit Group	N	Four-Digit Group	Pharmaceutical Code	Sample Size	Weighted Sample Size
Agents for ophthalmic use (131)	22,423	Mydriatics and preparations	1311	300	28,286
		Miotics and preparations	1312	448	35,734
		Local anesthetics for ophthalmic use	1313	195	14,524
		Antiseptics and astringents for ophthalmic use	1314	468	31,562
		Cortisone derivatives and preparations for ophthalmic use	1315	4,554	680,740
		Vasoconstrictors for ophthalmic use	1316	20	1,877
		Antibiotic and preparations for ophthalmic use	1317	846	103,419
		Alkaloids and preparations	1318	0	0
		Other agents for ophthalmic use	1319	15,592	1,900,333
Antihypertensives (214)	8,445	Ganglonic blocking agents; hexamethonium, etc.	2141	0	0
		Hydralazine and preparations	2142	112	20,149
		Rauwolfia and preparations	2143	83	13,858
		Angiotensin-converting enzyme inhibitors	2144	3,948	590,152
		Methyldopa and preparations	2145	110	17,228
		Alkaloids and preparations	2146	0	0
		Other antihypertensives	2149	4,192	573,011
Vasodilators (217)	10,356	Coronary vasodilators	2171	10,256	1,310,327
		Peripheral vasodilators	2172	99	8,099
		Other vasodilators	2179	1	2
Antihyperlipemia agents (218)	8,531	Linoleic acid and preparations	2181	0	0
		Lecithin and preparations	2182	2	150
		Clofibrate derivatives and preparations	2183	572	90,050
		Other antihyperlipemia agents	2189	7,957	1,530,655

Category	Total	Code	Subitem		
Agents for peptic ulcers (232)	18,833	2321	Methylmethionine derivatives and preparations	61	4,860
		2322	Glutammine and preparations	15	1,579
		2323	Azulene and preparations	153	27,022
		2324	Extract preparations of crude drugs	6	336
		2325	H2-recepter antagonists	3,486	554,789
		2329	Other agents for peptic ulcers	15,112	2,013,021
Analgesics, antipruritics, astringents, and anti-inflammatories (264)	57,061	2641	Methyl salicylate and preparations	2	280
		2642	Antihistaminic preparations for external use	177	12,628
		2643	Ammonia preparations	1	220
		2644	Lead compound and preparations; lead oxide, lead acetate, etc.	0	0
		2645	Peppermint-gum and camphor-peppermint preparations	15	1,179
		2646	Adrenocortical hormone preparations	11,334	1,359,440
		2647	Mixed preparations compounded of antibiotics and adreno-corticoals hormone preparations	3,435	474,236
		2649	Other analgesics, antipruritics, astringents, and anti-inflammatories	42,097	5,642,188
Antimetabolic agents (422)	826	4221	Mercaptopurine derivatives and preparations	0	0
		4222	Methotrexate derivatives and preparations	2	610
		4223	Fluorouracil derivatives and preparations	379	96,952
		4224	Cytosine derivatives and preparations	1	100
		4229	Other antimetabolic agents	444	98,052
Antibiotic preparations acting mainly on gram-positive bacteria (613)	12,516	6131	Penicillin derivatives and preparations	707	177,937
		6132	Cephem derivatives and preparations	11,485	3,028,090
		6135	Fosfomycin and preparations	232	54,405
		6139	Other antibiotic preparations acting mainly on gram-positive and gram-negative bacteria	92	26,994
X-ray contrast agents (721)	918	7211	Iodine compounds and preparations	54	8,084
		7214	Barium salts and preparations	63	10,055
		7219	Other X-ray contrast agents	801	170,401

Source: Authors' computations based on survey on drugs (MHW 1994–1996).

are chosen: Is it because of patient characteristics, provider characteristics, drug characteristics, or economic incentives? In order to maintain consistency with the first model, the base case has been set at the 1st quintile whenever possible.

One possible criticism of these estimations is that there is a considerable degree of arbitrariness in the Japanese pharmaceutical classification system. For example, within any three-digit group there is a large number of drugs whose fourth digits are nine, which denotes all "other agents" in the group. Typically these are drugs that could not be grouped with existing drugs when they were introduced. As a result, many of the most popular drugs in a group often belong to the "nine" category, although they may not be similar at all. Thus, the dummy variables for the four-digit groups may not be reliable, and we may be able to improve our estimation by using better drug classification systems in the selection function.

Fortunately, in an attempt to test the feasibility of a reference price system for Japan, a working group of MHW, consisting mainly of physicians and pharmacologists, has constructed more homogeneous groups of drugs for four categories: (a) peptic ulcers, (b) antihypertensives, (c) analgesics and others, and (d) antibiotics and others. In order to move from the official classification to these reference groups, we need to identify all drugs in a given group. We were unable to do this for (a), (b), and (c). However, we were able to identify most of the individual drugs in group (d) using price differences. Our data regarding the new homogeneous groupings within (d) are summarized in table 9.8. Since the first two groups have fewer than several hundred observations, we do not try to estimate their selection functions separately. We only estimate functions for the last three groups and for the antibiotic drugs group as a whole.

9.3.3   Results

First Model

Judging from the pseudo-R^2 values, the estimated model fits the data very well, with most of the explanatory power provided by the profit margin variable. Of the twenty four-digit group selection functions, this variable was significant in nineteen. An example of the estimated selection function is shown for antihypertensives in table 9.9. The sizes of the coefficients are not intuitive, however, because of the comparative or conditional nature of the estimated selection functions.

To interpret the estimated profit margin coefficients, we perform a simulation in which all profit margins are set equal to zero without changing prices. The result of the simulation is summarized in table 9.10. Although the results vary from one three-digit group to another, in two of the groups the reduction in total drug costs exceeds 30 percent. In three additional groups this reduction exceeds 20 percent, and in two other groups it ex-

Table 9.8 Antibiotics Reference Price Groups, 1998–1999

Chemical Components	Sample Size	Main Effect	Sample Size	Generic Name	Sample Size	Weighted Sample Size	Four-digit Pharmaceutical Code
Antibiotic preparations acting mainly on gram-positive bacteria	19	Cell wall synthesis obstruction	1	Penicillins	1	330	6111
				Glycopeptides	0	0	6113
		Protein synthesis obstruction	18	Tincomycin	18	7,664	6112
Antibiotic preparations acting mainly on gram-negative bacteria	349	Cell wall synthesis obstruction	117	Penicillins	25	2,145	6121
				Cephems	92	15,537	6129
		Cell membrane functional disturbance	5	Polypeptides	5	721	6125, 6126
		Protein synthesis obstruction	8	Aminoglycosides	8	2,745	6123
		Nucleic acid synthesis obstruction	219	Quinolones	219	39,516	6241
Antibiotic preparations acting mainly on gram-positive and gram-negative bacteria	12,391	Cell wall synthesis obstruction	12,373	Penicillins 1	279	78,435	6131
				Penicillins 2	428	93,293	6131
				Cephems 1	3,942	1,024,126	6132
				Cephems 2	7,492	1,908,932	6132
				Faropenem	0	0	6139
				Fosfomycin	232	53,601	6135
		Protein synthesis obstruction	2	Thiamphenicol	2	3	6249
		Folacin synthesis obstruction	16	Sulfa compounds	16	2,694	6212, 6213, 6219
Antibiotic preparations acting mainly on gram-positive bacteria and mycoplasma	1,827	Protein synthesis obstruction	1,827	Macrolides 1	95	26,227	6141
				Macrolides 2	1,476	392,654	6149
				Macrolides 3	191	46,373	6143, 6145, 6146
				Macrolides 4	65	16,585	6149
				Macrolides 5	0	0	6142
Antibiotic preparations acting mainly on gram-positive and gram-negative bacteria, rickettsia, and chlamydia	6,249	Protein synthesis obstruction	226	Chloramphenicol	1	260	6151
				Tetracyclines 1	11	2,991	6152
				Tetracyclines 2	214	55,104	6152
		Nucleic acid synthesis obstruction	6,023	Quinolones	6,023	1,248,396	6241

Source: MHW (1999).

Table 9.9   **Selection Function for Antihypertensives, Model 1 (multinomial regression)**

	Group 2144		Group 2149	
Variable	Coefficient	z	Coefficient	z
Profit margin	0.266	223.058	0.220	186.088
Out-of-pocket costs	0.004	3.851	0.010	8.927
Number of beds	0.000	8.800	0.000	7.598
Female	−0.218	−18.495	−0.171	−14.843
Age 0–19	13.699	0.083	14.766	0.090
Age 20–39	−0.440	−9.121	−0.677	−14.804
Age 40–59	0.112	5.989	0.301	16.380
Age 65–75	−0.340	−17.322	−0.023	−1.200
Age 76+	−0.207	−8.170	0.045	1.811
Circulatory diseases	0.115	9.415	0.168	14.057
Gm worker	−0.419	−18.241	0.021	0.925
Gm dependent	−0.647	−29.640	−0.722	−33.759
Gm elderly	0.245	7.486	0.193	6.082
Nh elderly	0.171	6.460	0.195	7.670
National	−0.291	−17.518	−0.115	−7.092
University	0.760	10.237	0.955	13.025
Clinic with beds	0.557	30.631	0.634	35.622
Clinic without beds	−0.707	−45.492	−0.910	−59.956
Constant	−1.571	−62.090	−0.800	−32.398
N	1,214,398			
Log-likelihood	−883,404.8			
LR χ^2 (36)	270,078.53			
Prob > χ^2	0.0000			
Pseudo R^2	0.1326			

Source: Authors' computations based on surveys on drugs (MHW 1994–1996).

Note: Outcome choice circulatory diseases = a dummy variable for patients with circulatory disease as their primary disease. Gm- = patients under government managed insurance. Nh- = patients under town- or city-managed national health insurance. National = patients of hospitals or clinics run by the Japanese government. University = patients of teaching hospitals.

ceeds 10 percent. Overall, the reduction amounts to almost 20 percent of drug costs.

Second Model

We estimate the selection functions for all nine groups, but we only report the results for antihypertensives (214; table 9.11). Roughly speaking, in the second model, the physician selects the cost of the drug. This straightforward model makes it very easy to interpret the results. The magnitudes of the coefficients on the profit margin variables are very stable, but their pattern of variation suggests that profit margins are relatively more important in inducing selection of higher-priced drugs. Also, by compar-

Table 9.10   Zero–Profit Simulation Results, Model 1

Drug Groups	Three-Digit Group	Four-Digit Group	Number of Drugs	Cost per Month (yen)	Profit per Month (yen)	Total Costs (millions of yen) Actual	Estimated	Simulated	Error (%)	Zero Profit Changes (%)
Agents for ophthalmic use	131	1310	4	534	68	9	9	19		
		1311	11	5,532	754	156	156	92		
		1312	9	907	121	32	32	36		
		1314	1	13	1	0	0	9		
		1315	25	503	90	343	343	315		
		1317	12	631	86	65	65	116		
		1319	64	1,691	261	3,210	3,210	2,090		
		Total	126	1,366	212	3,816	3,816	2,676	0.0	−29.9
Antihypertensives	214	2140	21	1,654	273	85	85	1,070		
		2144	23	5,523	983	3,260	3,260	695		
		2149	71	4,755	845	2,720	2,720	2,090		
		Total	115	4,997	888	6,065	6,065	3,855	0.0	−36.4
Vasodilators	217	2170	8	1,053	132	9	8	650		
		2171	63	3,378	678	4,430	4,430	739		
		Total	71	3,364	675	4,439	4,438	1,389	0.0	−68.7
Antihyperlipemia agents	218	2180	9	3,917	626	353	373	1,920		
		2189	22	5,843	807	8,910	8,910	6,600		
		Total	31	5,735	797	9,293	9,283	8,520	−0.1	−8.2
Agents for peptic ulcers	232	2320	12	463	92	16	16	49		
		2325	16	5,352	1,058	2,970	2,970	737		
		2329	63	2,031	450	4,090	4,090	4,790		
		Total	91	2,718	575	7,076	7,076	5,576	0.0	−21.2

(*continued*)

Table 9.10   (continued)

Drug Groups	Three-Digit Group	Four-Digit Group	Number of Drugs	Cost per Month (yen)	Profit per Month (yen)	Total Costs (millions of yen)			Error (%)	Zero Profit Changes (%)
						Actual	Estimated	Simulated		
Analgesics, antipruritics, astringents, and anti-inflammatory agents	264	2640	9	471	52	7	7	858		
		2646	65	1,141	234	1,550	1,550	862		
		2647	13	713	115	338	338	894		
		2649	62	1,443	342	8,140	8,140	5,280		
		Total	149	1,340	307	10,035	10,035	7,894	0.0	−21.3
Antimetabolic agents	422	4220	22	31,929	5,736	3,120	3,120	3,510		
		4229	3	43,910	6,870	4,310	4,310	3,770		
		Total	25	37,931	6,304	7,430	7,430	7,280	0.0	−2.0
Antibiotic preparations acting mainly on gram-positive and gram-negative bacteria	613	6130	11	1,265	311	118	103	1,760		
		6131	20	1,448	313	225	258	664		
		6132	47	1,799	427	5,450	5,450	2,590		
		Total	78	1,761	418	5,793	5,811	5,014	0.3	−13.7
X-ray contrast agents	721	7211	5	1,607	208	29	29	87		
		7214	5	20,777	4,885	3,540	3,540	2,790		
		Total	43	18,933	4,435	3,569	3,569	2,877	0.0	−19.4
Total			729	—	—	57,515	57,523	45,081	0.1	−18.8

Source: Authors' computations based on surveys on drugs (MHW 1994–1996).

Table 9.11   Selection Functions for Antihypertensives, Model 2 (multinomial logit regression)

| | Daily Cost Quintile | | | | | | | |
| | 1 | | 2 | | 3 | | 5 | |
Variable	Coefficient	z	Coefficient	z	Coefficient	z	Coefficient	z
Profits per day	-1.20	-180.15	-0.35	-247.45	-0.13	-243.29	0.01	28.10
Out-of-pocket costs	-0.30	-45.38	-0.16	-88.46	-0.05	-65.40	0.05	185.48
Number of beds	0.00	25.08	0.00	23.50	0.00	30.52	0.00	21.35
Female	-0.56	-23.48	-0.26	-21.93	-0.11	-18.52	0.14	28.06
2144 dummy	-74.08	0.00	-38.50	-496.15	-34.97	-470.42	-0.74	-48.89
2149 dummy	-35.82	-500.41	-34.95	-486.25	-33.47	-449.69	-0.17	-11.30
Age 0–19	-31.12	0.00	-0.11	-0.29	1.91	5.33	-6.75	-55.19
Age 20–39	2.41	15.59	-0.24	-2.57	-1.67	-28.67	-1.31	-39.03
Age 40–59	0.50	12.16	0.14	6.76	0.05	5.30	-0.21	-27.21
Age 65–75	-0.60	-13.35	0.55	24.66	0.08	7.71	-0.25	-27.00
Age 76+	0.08	1.48	0.66	24.50	0.16	11.70	-0.42	-35.67
Diseases of the eyes	-0.42	-17.15	-0.39	-30.17	0.04	5.78	0.10	18.53
Gm worker	-2.09	-36.84	-3.23	-97.68	-1.38	-70.89	1.94	155.09
Gm dependent	0.72	13.61	-0.91	-28.63	-0.56	-40.03	0.25	23.73
Gm elderly	-2.62	-31.38	-3.91	-81.66	-1.65	-56.81	2.76	147.20
Nh elderly	-3.30	-47.08	-4.08	-90.64	-1.61	-58.14	2.64	151.93
National	0.36	11.03	0.47	28.50	0.25	28.97	0.36	49.92
University	-3.02	-22.73	-0.64	-11.88	-0.84	-26.91	-0.52	-21.05
Clinic with beds	0.80	24.41	0.52	30.05	-0.06	-6.88	-0.39	-48.67
Clinic without beds	-0.26	-8.71	-0.11	-6.66	-0.31	-37.40	0.10	13.98
Constant	47.98		43.77	730.72	38.31	542.33	-2.88	

N 1,214.298
Log-likelihood   -1,029,430.2
LR χ^2(80)   1,229,246.58
Prob > χ^2 0.0000
Pseudo R^2 0.3738

Source: Authors' computations based on surveys on drugs (MHW 1994–1996).

Note: Outcome of 4th quintile for nonelderly male covered by national health insurance program treated in a private hospital is the comparison group. Gm- = patients under government managed insurance. Nh- = patients under town- or city-managed national health insurance. National = patients of hospitals or clinics run by the Japanese government. University = patients of teaching hospitals. Diseases of the eyes = a dummy variable for patients of ophthalmologists. Z statistics are in parentheses.

ing the dummy variables[7] for 2144 and 2149 we see that while 2144 is more popular, 2149 probably does not offer many products in the lower three price zones. Patient characteristics seem to be important in deciding which price zone to select: The elderly seem to be very important in accounting for the highest-priced drugs.

In order to give an idea of the interpretation of the size of the estimated profit margin coefficients, we carry out a simulation identical to that in the first model. The results of the simulation are summarized in table 9.12. In four groups the reduction in total drug costs exceeds 50 percent. In four additional groups this reduction exceeds 30 percent, and in the remaining group it exceeds 4 percent. Overall, the reduction amounts to 45 percent of drug costs.

Using Reference Price Group Information

Using the framework of the second model and the reference group information of the Working Committee of the MHW in 1998, we estimate selection functions for three individual reference groups and antibiotics (as a whole). Presumably, drugs within reference groups are close substitutes, but there seems to be important heterogeneity among them. For example, we have noticed that in some cases the most expensive drugs are not necessarily the most profitable, even though they are used most frequently and were introduced most recently. One can think of several reasons why this may happen:

1. Newer drugs may be preferred by physicians because they reflect technological innovation and hence are better in some sense, even though they may not be the most profitable drugs in the group.

2. Manufacturers may be more reluctant to offer large discounts for new drugs because doing so will shorten their economic life.

3. The government may have become more stringent in pricing new drugs in an attempt to control drug costs.

In order to capture these effects we add a new variable indicating the year each drug was introduced. There are two exceptions to this rule: (a) if the drug is a "me-too" drug, we chose the first year the particular chemical was approved; (b) if the drug had already been approved at the beginning of our sample we treat it as having been introduced in 1967.[8] If physicians prefer drugs that are more profitable, "new," or both, we expect the year variable to work in the same way as the profit margin variable.

Table 9.13 reports the results for the largest group, antibiotic agents for gram-negative and –positive bacteria. The estimation results are fairly con-

---

7. The base-case four-digit class is 2140 in this case.
8. Nihon-seiyaku-danntai-rengoukai, Hoken-yakka-kenkyu-iinkai (1997) includes data on drugs that were approved after 1967.

Table 9.12   Zero-Profit Simulation Results, Model 2

Drug Group Description	Three-Digit Code	Cost Quintile	Number of Drugs	Costs per Month	Profits per Month	Total Costs (million yen)			Error (%)	Zero Profit Changes (%)
						Actual	Estimated	Zero Profits		
Agents for ophthalmic use	131	1	26	97	23	44	44	73		
		2	26	330	57	99	99	160		
		3	26	524	82	397	397	526		
		4	24	1,064	150	640	640	506		
		5	24	3,859	602	2,640	2,640	337		
		Group total	126	1,366	212	3,820	3,820	1,602	0.0	−58.1
Antihypertensives	214	1	23	673	87	28	28	263		
		2	22	1,799	323	158	158	388		
		3	24	3,548	641	928	928	1,480		
		4	27	5,355	1,013	2,660	2,660	581		
		5	19	7,012	1,147	2,290	2,290	586		
		Group total	115	4,997	888	6,064	6,064	3,298	0.0	−45.6
Vasodilators	217	1	15	829	120	71	71	1,020		
		2	14	1,592	497	297	297	3		
		3	15	2,689	478	828	828	108		
		4	16	2,976	714	624	624	3		
		5	11	4,944	926	2,610	2,610	223		
		Group total	71	3,364	675	4,430	4,430	1,357	0.0	−69.4
Antihyperlipemia agents	218	1	6	594	78	3	3	146		
		2	6	946	114	9	9	319		
		3	7	1,466	370	67	67	62		
		4	5	2,731	478	209	209	2,290		
		5	7	6,069	833	9,010	9,010	951		
		Group total	31	5,735	797	9,298	9,298	3,768	0.0	−59.5
Agents for peptic ulcers	232	1	22	426	77	114	114	389		
		2	17	1,041	219	573	573	1,150		
		3	18	2,005	571	626	626	178		
		4	17	2,581	608	2,470	2,470	602		
		5	17	6,397	1,156	3,290	3,290	1,650		
		Group total	91	2,718	575	7,073	7,073	3,969	0.0	−43.9

(continued)

Table 9.12 (continued)

Drug Group Description	Three-Digit Code	Cost Quintile	Number of Drugs	Costs per Month	Profits per Month	Total Costs (million yen) Actual	Estimated	Zero Profits	Error (%)	Zero Profit Changes (%)
Analgesics, antipruritics, astringents, and anti-inflammatory agents	264	1	29	406	51	37	37	727		
		2	31	565	120	120	120	186		
		3	28	894	182	2,030	2,030	3,410		
		4	31	1,126	231	1,330	1,330	918		
		5	30	1,747	425	6,520	6,520	1,290		
		Group total	149	1,340	307	10,037	10,037	6,531	0.0	−34.9
Antimetabolic agents	422	1	5	7,897	2,203	43	43	57		
		2	5	11,864	822	89	89	1,660		
		3	4	17,998	3,559	191	191	204		
		4	6	30,388	5,554	857	857	627		
		5	5	43,354	7,091	6,240	6,240	730		
		Group total	25	37,931	6,304	7,419	7,419	3,278	0.0	−55.8
Antibiotic preparations acting mainly on gram-positive and gram-negative bacteria	613	1	16	579	157	26	26	170		
		2	15	871	210	72	72	301		
		3	15	1,389	356	446	446	243		
		4	16	1,553	418	1,220	1,220	107		
		5	16	1,960	441	4,030	4,030	4,710		
		Group total	78	1,761	418	5,793	5,793	5,531	0.0	−4.5
X-ray contrast agents	721	1	9	1,180	142	18	18	50		
		2	8	7,160	1,597	113	113	98		
		3	10	12,211	2,607	290	290	1,140		
		4	8	22,670	5,366	2,050	2,050	892		
		5	8	25,221	6,004	1,100	1,100	0		
		Group total	43	18,933	4,435	3,571	3,571	2,180	0.0	−39.0
		Total				57,504	57,504	31,513	0.0	−45.2

Source: Authors' computations based on surveys on drugs (MHW 1994–1996).

Table 9.13   **Selection Function for Antibiotic Agents for Gram-positive and Gram-negative Bacteria, Model 2**

Variable	Coefficient	z	Marginal Effect
Quintile 1			
Profit margin	−0.16	−212.57	−0.16
Year introduced	−0.57	−155.64	−0.88
Number of beds	0.00	−9.26	0.00
Female	−0.85	−37.84	−0.95
Age 0–19	−2.50	−46.14	−3.24
Age 20–39	0.21	3.99	0.33
Age 40–59	−0.96	−17.19	−0.95
Age 65–75	−2.21	−27.50	−2.23
Age 76+	−3.29	−25.35	−3.41
Circulatory diseases	1.66	30.23	1.70
Respiratory diseases	1.35	49.45	1.41
Gm worker	0.41	12.70	0.28
Gm dependent	−0.54	−20.11	−0.62
Gm elderly	0.23	1.71	0.22
Nh elderly	0.90	9.88	0.95
Public Hospital	0.04	0.61	0.02
University	−9.53	−0.07	−9.22
Clinic with beds	0.82	16.62	0.73
Clinic without beds	0.53	10.84	0.42
Constant	35.71	173.81	
Multinomial logit regression			
N	3,158,387		
Log-likelihood	−1,644,565.5		
LR χ^2 (76)	3,145,966.69		
Prob $> \chi^2$	0.0000		
Pseudo R^2	0.4889		
Quintile 2			
Profit margin	−0.10	−345.91	−0.10
Year introduced	−0.22	−152.29	−0.52
Number of beds	−0.01	−44.42	−0.01
Female	0.05	4.93	−0.04
Age 0–19	0.63	23.26	−0.11
Age 20–39	0.84	30.62	0.97
Age 40–59	−0.63	−20.36	−0.61
Age 65–75	−1.45	−35.47	−1.47
Age 76+	−1.27	−22.42	−1.39
Circulatory diseases	1.35	52.05	1.39
Respiratory diseases	0.76	58.66	0.82
Gm worker	−0.18	−10.78	−0.31
Gm dependent	−0.65	−51.95	−0.73
Gm elderly	0.36	6.19	0.35
Nh elderly	0.83	18.49	0.89
Public Hospital	0.27	10.31	0.26
University	−11.64	−0.07	−11.33
Clinic with beds	0.25	8.91	0.15
Clinic without beds	0.27	9.65	0.16
Constant	15.44	171.22	

(continued)

Table 9.13   (continued)

Variable	Coefficient	z	Marginal Effect
	Quintile 3		
Profit margin	−0.02	−169.93	−0.02
Year introduced	0.11	134.24	−0.19
Number of beds	0.00	−20.65	0.00
Female	−0.15	−28.11	−0.24
Age 0–19	2.06	126.79	1.32
Age 20–39	0.42	24.24	0.55
Age 40–59	0.24	13.29	0.25
Age 65–75	−0.04	−1.73	−0.06
Age 76+	0.26	8.05	0.14
Circulatory diseases	0.20	14.34	0.24
Respiratory diseases	0.06	8.93	0.11
Gm worker	−0.04	−3.83	−0.17
Gm dependent	−0.02	−4.01	−0.10
Gm elderly	0.06	1.72	0.06
Nh elderly	0.33	12.85	0.38
Public Hospital	0.19	14.38	0.18
University	−0.87	−10.09	−0.56
Clinic with beds	1.07	84.55	0.98
Clinic without beds	0.73	58.77	0.63
Constant	−8.70	−160.91	
	Quintile 4		
Profit margin	n.a.	0.00	
Year introduced	n.a.	−0.30	
Number of beds	n.a.	0.00	
Female	n.a.	−0.10	
Age 0–19	n.a.	−0.74	
Age 20–39	n.a.	0.12	
Age 40–59	n.a.	0.01	
Age 65–75	n.a.	−0.02	
Age 76+	n.a.	−0.12	
Circulatory diseases	n.a.	0.04	
Respiratory diseases	n.a.	0.05	
Gm worker	n.a.	−0.13	
Gm dependent	n.a.	−0.08	
Gm elderly	n.a.	−0.01	
Nh elderly	n.a.	0.05	
Public Hospital	n.a.	−0.01	
University	n.a.	0.31	
Clinic with beds	n.a.	−0.09	
Clinic without beds	n.a.	−0.11	
Constant	n.a.		

sistent with those from the other three groups. Larger profit margins and later introduction years increase the selection of more expensive drugs. The sensitivity is larger for more expensive drugs. In other words, physicians can be very easily persuaded to choose more expensive drugs if either their profit margins are larger or they are newer. They can also be very eas-

Table 9.13   (continued)

Variable	Coefficient	z	Marginal Effect
	Quintile 5		
Profit margin	0.00	55.15	0.00
Year introduced	0.74	870.17	0.44
Number of beds	0.00	23.74	0.00
Female	0.27	68.52	0.17
Age 0–19	1.46	175.51	0.72
Age 20–39	-0.40	-47.88	-0.27
Age 40–59	-0.08	-9.66	-0.07
Age 65–75	0.06	5.18	0.04
Age 76+	0.25	15.67	0.13
Circulatory diseases	-0.14	-17.27	-0.10
Respiratory diseases	-0.15	-33.27	-0.10
Gm worker	0.34	59.08	0.21
Gm dependent	0.21	41.95	0.13
Gm elderly	0.01	0.34	0.00
Nh elderly	-0.20	-16.24	-0.15
Public Hospital	-0.01	-0.75	-0.02
University	-0.58	-24.35	-0.27
Clinic with beds	0.02	3.23	-0.07
Clinic without beds	0.12	20.42	0.02
Constant	-46.97	-824.83	

Source: Authors' computations based on surveys on drugs (MHW 1994–1996).

Note: Outcome of 4th quintile for nonelderly male covered by a national health insurance program treated in a private hospital is the comparison group. "Gm" stands for a person covered by health insurance managed by government. "Nh" stands for a person covered by a national health insurance program. N.a. = not applicable.

ily persuaded not to use the least expensive drugs if either their profit margins are smaller or they are older. For antibiotic drugs as a whole the same tendencies are confirmed, but much more emphasis seems to be placed on recent introduction, particularly for the most expensive drugs.

Again, we have carried out simulations for the zero profit-margin case (table 9.14). For the first group, the reduction in total costs is about 30 percent. For the second group, this reduction is about 20 percent, and for the third group, it is computed to reach close to 70 percent, although this figure may be unrealistic.

9.4   Inefficiencies in the Japanese Drug Price System

9.4.1   Inefficiency in the Production of Health Care Services

Under the present drug-pricing policy, providers of health care services are subject to strong economic incentives to prescribe as many drugs as possible to their patients. The wrong economic incentives can distort providers' decisions in two ways. First, they may influence the physician's se-

Table 9.14   Summary of Zero Profit-Margin Simulations for Antibiotic Agents for Gram-positive and Gram-negative Bacteria

	Daily Cost Quintiles	Sample Size		Weighted Costs (Million Yen)			Change in Costs (%)	
		Unweighted	Weighted	Actual	Estimated	Zero Profit	Actual to Estimated	Estimated to Zero Profit
Gram-positive and gram-negative bacteria	1	105	24,517	12	12	194		
	2	295	85,731	74	74	1,360		
	3	702	191,093	258	258	151		
	4	5,132	1,289,103	2,100	2,100	324		
	5	6,139	1,567,943	3,300	3,300	1,840		
	Total	12,373	3,158,387	5,744	5,744	3,869	0.0	−32.6
Gram-positive bacteria and mycoplasma	1	22	3,884	2	2	9		
	2	56	15,721	11	11	2		
	3	193	48,051	53	53	72		
	4	77	20,619	29	29	268		
	5	1,479	393,564	938	938	478		
	Total	1,827	481,839	1,032	1,032	829	0.0	−19.7
Gram-positive and gram-negative bacteria, rickettsia, and chlamydia	1	17	6,792	2	2	23		
	2	176	48,782	45	45	822		
	3	648	117,068	273	273	562		
	4	1,833	386,980	1,180	1,180	251		
	5	3,575	747,669	3,600	3,600	69		
	Total	6,249	1,307,291	5,100	5,100	1,726	0.0	−66.2
General bacilus	1	151	34,650	14	14	246		
	2	582	162,809	134	134	1,970		
	3	1,956	512,459	721	721	740		
	4	10,830	2,717,233	5,260	5,260	786		
	5	7,316	1,591,721	5,930	5,930	4,110		
	Total	20,835	5,018,872	12,059	12,059	7,852	0.0	−34.9

Source: Authors' computations based on surveys on drugs (MHW 1994–1996).

lection decision among competing drugs, and second, they may influence the physician's selection decision between drugs and other factors of production, including physician services:

1. If providers are to produce their services efficiently, they must select the least-cost combination of production factors from all feasible combinations of inputs. If drug A and drug B have identical chemical compositions, the efficient provider must choose the one that costs less. But a system that gives differential profit margins across drugs tends to drive providers toward using the drug with the highest profit margin. This is usually the drug with the higher price. We have shown that this inefficiency can amount to as much as 30 percent of total expenditures on drugs.

2. In many realistic cases, moreover, there is a certain degree of substitutability between drugs and physicians' time (counseling). Under the present medical pricing system, in which physicians' time is not adequately reimbursed and profit margins are provided for drugs, it is certain that drugs are selected over other time-intensive procedures.

9.4.2   Substitution of New Drugs

If drug discounts had remained within the reasonable zones, drug prices could not have been continuously lowered throughout the 1990s. This is evidence that competition for larger shares among drug companies has been very effective in driving down prices. We should, however, also note that large numbers of drugs have been introduced simultaneously. In fact, as we have seen in the decomposition analysis, the drug companies seem to have been able to offset reductions in prices of existing drugs by introducing new drugs and setting their prices sufficiently high.

The introduction of new drugs, however, came at a cost. The drug companies have been engaged in some of the most intensive research and development activity in Japan's major industries. In 1995, for example, the industry spent 640 billion yen out of sales of 8 trillion yen, or 8 percent, on research and development (R&D). In contrast, one of the most competitive industries in Japan, the electronics and communications industry, spent only 5 percent of sales on R&D (figure 9.1). Such an intensive R&D effort in our drug industry may have been encouraged by several factors: (a) The costs of R&D for new drugs are taken into account when the government sets the reimbursement price for the first time; (b) high prices make it possible for firms to offer discounts to providers, thereby rapidly expanding sales and profitability; and (c) without new drugs, firms' profitability declines continuously as the prices of existing drugs are repeatedly cut by the government.

9.4.3   Dynamic Inefficiency

The Japanese drug industry, with the second largest domestic market in the world, has enjoyed very high profitability (figure 9.2). It is supported by

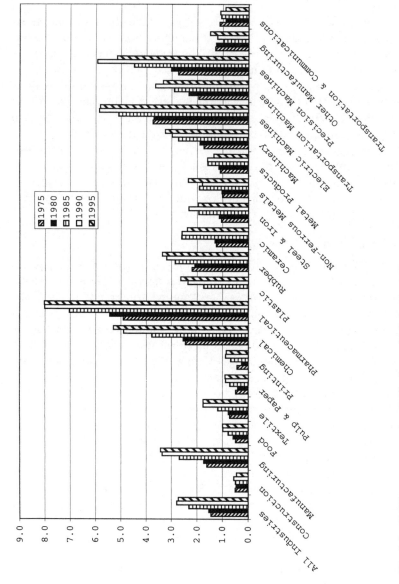

Fig. 9.1 R&D as a percentage of sales by major industry group

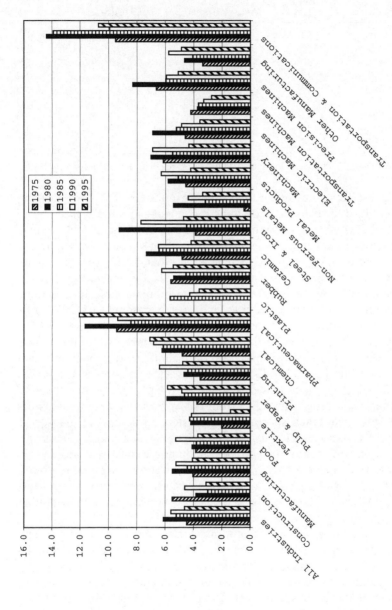

Fig. 9.2   Rate of profit (percent of sales) by major industry group

Table 9.15   Japanese Drug Imports and Exports (Billion Yen)

	Production	All Exports	Exports Asia	All Imports	Imports from the United States	Imports from Europe
1985	4,001	30	18	308	129	162
1986	4,280	30	19	330	122	193
1987	4,825	30	19	355	117	225
1988	5,059	28	21	376	118	242
1989	5,502	27	19	417	123	278
1990	5,595	36	18	469	133	322
1991	5,697	42	24	485	129	343
1992	5,574	49	26	588	129	433
1993	5,695	44	23	584	131	430

Source: MHW (1999), Yearbook of Production Statistics for the Pharmaceutical Industry 1999

the highest R&D rates among Japan's major industries. The story, however, may not lead to such a happy ending if one looks into the industry more closely. In fact, it is possible that these impressive R&D expenditures may have actually weakened the industry rather than strengthening it. To the extent that they were induced by regulation, these R&D expenditures are simply the costs of operating under this unproductive regulation.

The statistics on the international drug trade are our first clue that there is something very strange about the industry. According to MHW statistics, drug exports amount to less than one-tenth of drug imports. Furthermore, in terms of the regional pattern of trade, almost half of the exports go to countries in Asia, whereas most of the imports are from the United States and Europe (table 9.15). This indicates the presence of substantial technological gaps among these regions, with Japan in a middle position. An analysis of drug patent data from the world's 150 largest companies (Anegawa 1996) reaches a similar conclusion: 53 percent of the world's technological capital is found in the United States, 36.6 percent in Europe, and only 10.1 percent in Japan. These findings are consistent with the hypothesis that Japanese drug price controls have generated excess returns to "new" drugs, which are similar to existing drugs, or "me-too" drugs. Most of the R&D expenditure has been allocated to copycat development rather than to truly innovative drugs.

By its nature, investment in innovative drugs involves higher risk, and under the Japanese regulatory scheme, the lower-risk investment into developing "me-too" drugs has proved just as profitable. It is not surprising that one finds that most of the R&D funds of Japanese drug firms are allocated to these easier alternatives. The process of approving and pricing "new" drugs has long been notorious for its disregard of public accountability, scientific objectivity, and global standards.[9] In fact, there are a large

9. A new process, called good clinical practice (GCP), was adopted in 1998 as a result of foreign pressure.

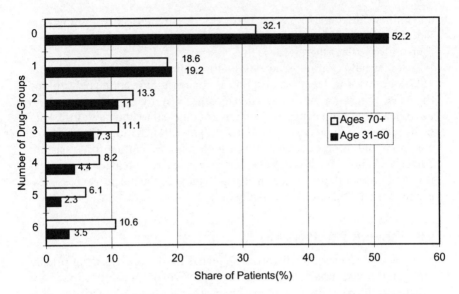

Fig. 9.3   Distribution of the number of drug groups given to outpatients with circulatory diseases
Source: Survey on Socialized Medicine (MHW 1994–1996).

number of drugs that are widely used in Japan but are not approved in the United States or Europe because their producers cannot offer sufficient evidence of increased effectiveness and superiority over existing drugs.[10]

9.4.4   External Diseconomies: Excessive Usage

The wrong economic incentives for the use of drugs may be generating very serious external diseconomies. Elderly patients are prescribed a particularly large number of drugs under the present system. According to the *Survey on Socialized Medicine* (MHW 1994–1996), the cost of drugs and injections for an elderly outpatient was 905 points[11] in 1996, almost twice the 477 points for the rest of the population. Using the new drug data compiled by the government,[12] we examine drug consumption more closely by selecting patients with circulatory diseases, the most prevalent diseases among the elderly.

Figure 9.3 illustrates that 25 percent of patients aged seventy and up received four or more groups of drugs, compared with 10.2 percent of patients aged thirty-one to sixty. Likewise, 10.6 percent of patients aged seventy and up consumed more than six groups of medicine. The risk of side effects tends to increase exponentially with the number of drugs consumed, and this is particularly acute among elderly patients with diminished liver

10. Recently, however, the MHW has changed its policy and started to remove some drugs widely used for cerebrovascular diseases due to lack of clinical effectiveness.
11. A point is 10 yen in government reimbursement schedule.
12. The drug data set is explained in detail in section 9.3.2.

and kidney functions. Moreover, many elderly patients utilize multiple providers, so the risks due to consumption of large numbers of drugs are neither controlled nor managed.

A somewhat separate issue exists with antibiotics. The distribution of antibiotics used in Japanese hospitals is concentrated very heavily among the latest generation of drugs, whereas other major countries continue to use older-generation drugs. In fact, it is not unusual to find new antibiotics being given to patients in outpatient settings with such mild afflictions as a common cold, a practice that runs a high risk of creating drug-resistant bacteria strains. This is another external diseconomy created by a regulatory system that deprives health care providers of the incentive to use less expensive, but still effective, existing drugs.

9.5   Various Reform Proposals

In view of the serious distortions created by the present drug-pricing policy, it is not surprising that a number of reform proposals have been advocated in the past three years. We review the merits and demerits of these proposals as reported by a government commission in January 1998.

9.5.1   Reimbursement of Actual Drug Costs (Liberal Democrats)

A body of ruling parties, including the Liberal Democrats, argue that the government should abandon drug price regulation altogether and move toward reimbursing providers the purchase costs of the drugs. The government commission objects to this plan on several grounds. First, patients will be charged differently from one provider to another. Second, patients will shop for better prices and choose large hospitals to get lower costs of drugs. Third, administrative costs will be huge for both insurers and providers. Fourth, providers may engage in such rent-seeking activities as utilizing extra middlemen to increase drug costs. The commission concludes that this plan should be modified at least to the extent that only the lesser of actual costs and list price is reimbursed.

9.5.2   Insurers Acting as Purchasing Agents

The second proposal the commission examined advocates a system in which drugs are purchased by insurers and supplied to providers as they are dispensed to their patients. Prices would be negotiated between manufacturers and insurers in the market. The commission asserts that although profit margins will vanish completely in this system, two problems will result: (a) Providers will have strong incentives to give excessive amounts of drugs to patients, as they lose track of drug costs; and (b) providers will have no incentive to use less expensive drugs. A variation on this was advocated by the Japan Medical Association (JMA) in a last-minute effort to abort the reference price system MHW was about to introduce. The JMA asked the government to purchase all drugs that providers need for patients with public health insurance.

9.5.3   Reference Price System of the MHW

Finding the other alternatives unacceptable, the commission considered the reference price system. In this system, first drug manufacturers announce list prices, and then the government sets a single reimbursement price for all drugs in a given homogeneous group. The reimbursement price would be set equal to a weighted average of the list prices in each group. The majority of commission members found this system to be the most desirable system, because it promotes price competition among substitutable drugs and allows manufacturers to price their own products. The member of the commission who represents JMA, however, opposed this plan strongly, presumably because JMA members would lose tremendous income by moving to this system. The JMA would agree to move to a different system only if it is allowed to recover its losses elsewhere in the fee schedule. Drug companies, particularly powerful drug companies, were not happy either. They feared that patients would not be willing to bear additional costs if they priced their products above the reimbursement prices, so they would lose part of their premium on higher-quality products. They also feared that the system would be open to considerable intervention by the MHW, as it depends critically on how broadly or how narrowly each reference group is defined. In view of this strong opposition, the ruling parties decided to mothball the plan just prior to the formation of the fiscal year (FY) 1999 government budget plan.

9.5.4   Removing Drug Costs from Public Health Insurance

Although no one has advocated this option so far, it is a logical alternative, given that the government will continue to regulate drug prices in one way or another as long as drugs are covered by public health insurance. It is hard to imagine, however, that a majority of Japanese will want to remove drug costs completely from the provisions of public health insurance. On the other hand, if options are offered to the public to retain drug coverage at full insurance charges or to give up the coverage for lower charges, there may be a substantial portion of the public who would be willing to take the risk or to buy private drug insurance.

9.6   Conclusions

We have presented empirical evidence to show that the periodic reductions in drug prices were mostly on paper and that they were largely offset by providers who switched to more expensive drugs and used a larger number of drugs for the same patients. Drug companies have continually introduced "new" drugs into the market to replace "old" drugs, and the government has approved these "new" drugs at considerably higher reimbursement rates than those of the drugs they replaced.

We have also shown that there is strong evidence that physician drug choice is influenced by drug profit margins. In fact, our results suggest that if the profit margins of drugs disappeared overnight, total drug costs would be reduced by 20 percent to 50 percent. This reduction is achieved even when the probability of using a given drug remains unchanged and drug prices are kept constant.[13]

In 1998, in an attempt to move away from the current price regulation system, the government commission in charge examined a number of alternative drug pricing schemes and chose the reference price system. Under this system, producers first set list prices, and then the government sets a maximum reimbursement price for what it defines as a homogeneous group of drugs. The adoption of the reference price system was blocked at the last minute by strong opposition from JMA and drug companies. Apparently the government is not yet ready to move to a free market for drugs, but any option retaining elements of regulation presents its own set of problems, some of which are fairly serious.

References

Anegawa, Tomofumi. 1996. Basic research on pharmaceutical firms—A comparative study of European, U.S. and Japanese firms using patient data. *Syakai-to-Iryou* 5 (4): 49–63.

Ikegami, Naoki, Shunya Ikeda, Seiritsu Ogura, and Hiroki Kawai. 1998. Why medical care costs in Japan have increased despite declining prices for pharmaceuticals. *PharmacoEconomics* 14:97–105.

Innami, Ichiro. 1996. Nihonno iyakuhin-sangyou ni taisuru kenkyu-kaihatsu-seisaku no kanouse (Towards a comprehensive R&D policy package for the Japanese pharmaceutical industry). *Syakai-to-Iryou* 6 (2): 59–75.

Iryokeizai-kenkyu-kikou (Institute for Health Economics and Policy). *Sizen-zou ni kansuru kenkyu* (Report on natural increase in health care costs). Tokyo: Iryokeizai-kenkyu-kikou.

Ministry of Health and Welfare (MHW). 1994–1996. *Shakai iryou shinryou koibetsu chosa* (Survey of national medical care insurance services). 2 vols. Tokyo: Kosei Shou.

———. 1994. *Survey of drugs.* Tokyo: MHW.

———. 1995. *Survey of drugs.* Tokyo: MHW.

———. 1996. *Survey of drugs.* Tokyo: MHW.

———. 1999. *Committee report.* Tokyo: MHW.

13. Although these numbers are large, they are not outrageous. For instance, after the public insurance program began making lump-sum payments to health care providers for long-term elderly inpatients, the cost of injections reportedly dropped by almost 50 percent and the cost of drugs by almost 35 percent. These providers are no longer subject to economic distortions that induce them to give more drugs and shots to their patients.

————. 1999. *Yakugi kogyo seisan dotai chosa tokei nenpo 1999* (Yearbook of production statistics of the pharmaceutical industry 1999). Tokyo: MHW.

Ben-Akiva, Moshe, and Steven Lerman. 1985. Discrete choice analysis: Theory and application to travel demand. Cambridge: MIT.

Nihon-seiyaku-danntai-rengoukai (Alliance of Pharmaceutical Manufacturers Association). 1997. *Shin-iyakuhin soudanhinmoku yakkakizyun syusai itiranhyou* (List of new drugs added to the drug price list through consultation). Tokyo: Nihon-seiyaku-dantai-rengoukai.

Ogura, Seiritsu, ed. 1996. *Seifukanshou-kenkou-hoken no iryoukidoukou-nada ni kansura chosa-kenkyu* (Analysis on the health care costs of health insurance managed by the government). Tokyo: Iroyokeisai-kenkyuu-kikou.

————. 1998. *Shizensou ni kansuru kenkyu houkokusyo* (Report on natural increase in health care costs). Tokyo: Iryokeisai-kenkyuu-kikou.

Organization for Economic Co-operation and Development (OECD). 1998. *OECD Health Data 1998.* Paris: OECD.

Takayama, Noriyuki, ed. 1999. *Koureika-syakai ni okeru koushi no yakuwari-buntan ni kansuru kenkyu houkokusyo* (Report on the roles of public and private sectors in an aging society). Kourei-fukusi-kenkyukai.

The Demand for Health Checkups under Uncertainty

Tadashi Yamada and Tetsuji Yamada

10.1 Introduction

Good health is by itself of great value. It enhances market earnings by increasing the number of healthy days an individual has available for work (Grossman 1972) and increases nonmarket productivity, allowing more time for household production (Becker 1976). Health checkups help to secure and maintain good health. However, the *1995 National Survey of Life* (*Kokumin Seikatsu Kiso Chosa* in Japanese; Statistics and Information 1998), administered by the Japanese government, shows that only about half of Japan's population undergoes health checkups. The reasons behind the low demand for health checkups, despite Japan's comprehensive health care system, are analyzed in this paper.

There are at least two additional benefits of health checkups that will be important in the analysis of demand for these checkups. First, a checkup will likely give an individual a more objective diagnostic health analysis, in addition to his or her own subjective evaluation of health, made under un-

Tadashi Yamada is professor of economics in the Institute of Policy and Planning Sciences at the University of Tsukuba. Tetsuji Yamada is professor in the Department of Economics–Camden College of Arts and Sciences at Rutgers, The State University of New Jersey.

The authors are grateful to the participants for their valuable comments. The authors also wish to thank Michael Grossman and Bernard Okun for their comments, and Jane C. Buenaventura for her research assistance. This research is supported by the Japan Center for Economic Research; the Japan Ministry of Education, Culture, Sports, Science and Technology (grant #11630034); the Japan Society for the Promotion of Science for Scientific Research (grant #14530042); and the Research Council Grant of Rutgers University. The views presented here are those of the authors and do not necessarily represent those of the funding agencies or affiliated institutions.

certainty. Second, health checkups lead to further demand for preventive medical care when necessary. Early medical care often curtails serious illness. In this respect, the demand for health checkups differs from the demand for health. The former is a derived demand, whereas the latter is a final demand. That is, health checkups appear in the demand for health, which in turn appears in the individual utility function. However, similar socioeconomic and demographic factors appear as determinants in both reduced-form demand functions (Grossman 2000).

In particular, individuals demand more health information as age increases (Kenkel 1990). Time costs are also major determinants of the demand for health checkups, which exhibits a larger time-price elasticity than the demand for other medical inputs (Phelps and Newhouse 1974; Coffey 1983). Income has a positive effect on the demand for preventive medical care (Kenkel 1994). A better knowledge of one's own health also increases the demand for preventive medical care (Hsieh and Lin 1997). However, better health gives individuals less incentive to collect health information. Furthermore, lack of knowledge about health leads individuals to adopt unhealthy consumption patterns (Kenkel 1991). Thus, uncertainty plays an important role in determining the demand for health checkups, as well as the demand for health itself (Arrow 1963).

This study focuses on the demand for health checkups rather than the demand for health. Its purpose is to clarify the reasons behind the low demand for health checkups in Japan. There are few empirical studies that analyze this issue using microdata from the *National Survey of Life* (Statistics and Information 1998). This study takes an original sample of about 630,000 observations from the twenty-to-sixty-four age group. Of this number, we focus on the thirty-to-sixty age group because this group is more homogeneous, consisting mainly of working people.

We find a gender differential in the demand for health checkups even after controlling for other socioeconomic and demographic characteristics. This differential tends to disappear as age increases. Age is a major factor in determining the demand for health checkups within the thirty-to-sixty age group, but it is less significant within smaller age groupings. The type of health insurance coverage and employer size are also robust factors that affect an individual's health checkup demand. Finally, we identify a strong negative correlation between the health checkup rate and the probability of becoming ill, as well as the duration of hospitalization.

This paper is organized as follows. Section 10.2 provides an overview of the health checkup system in Japan. Section 10.3 presents statistics on health checkups, based on the aforementioned survey. Section 10.4 presents a theoretical model with a comparative static analysis of the demand for health checkups and describes the variables of interest in this study. Section 10.5 reports the empirical results, and section 10.6 concludes.

10.2   An Overview of the Health Checkup System in Japan

Japan's medical insurance system is a comprehensive system covering the entire population through employees' health insurance, seamen's insurance, and national health insurance.[1] There are three types of employees' health insurance: (a) health insurance managed by associations (provided by employers with 700 employees or more);[2] (b) health insurance managed by the government (provided by employers with fewer than 700 employees); and (c) mutual aid associations insurance, covering public employees and teachers and personnel in private schools. Employees' health insurance covers 80 percent and 70 percent of medical costs for insured persons and their dependents, respectively. National health insurance (NHI) is a community-based insurance plan for local residents who are not covered by employees' health insurance. It pays for 70 percent of medical costs incurred by all insured persons.[3]

In March 2000, 15.2 million insured individuals and 16.5 million dependents were covered by health insurance managed by associations. An additional 19.5 million insured individuals and 17.3 million dependents were covered by health insurance managed by the government. The third and final employees' health insurance program, mutual aid associations insurance, insured 4.5 million individuals and 5.6 million dependents. There were 0.08 million individuals and 0.14 million dependents covered by seamen's insurance. Finally, 47.6 million persons were insured by NHI (Health and Welfare Statistics Association 2001).

Anybody can have a health checkup regardless of his or her type of health insurance. This service is provided for employees at their work sites or at hospitals and clinics in the vicinity of their workplace. Persons covered by NHI who are not in school receive notices about health checkups from their local governments. They can receive their health checkups at local health centers, hospitals, and clinics. Students in this program receive their health checkups at their school, college, or university.

There are three types of health checkups provided by firms: compulsory health checkups required by law, recommended health checkups, and discretionary health checkups. A general health checkup is usually compul-

1. In addition to these insurance systems, there is another system for individuals aged seventy and older, who receive medical care services at minimum cost. A detailed outline of Japan's Medical Care Security System is contained in the *Outline of Social Insurance in Japan 2000* (Social Insurance Agency, Government of Japan, 2001).
2. The number of employees is not rigid in practice.
3. The contribution rate levied on an employee's basic wages varies across types of health insurance. Employees covered by health insurance managed by associations are responsible for half the contribution rate (not to exceed 4.5 percent), of the set contribution range of 3.0 to 9.0 percent, with the remainder paid by their employers. Employers and employees evenly split the 8.5 percent contribution rate for health insurance managed by the government. National government employees, on the other hand, pay 4.05 percent of their 8.10 percent contribution rate (Social Insurance Agency, Government of Japan, 2001).

sory prior to the commencement of employment, and again once every year throughout the duration of employment. It includes the following items: (a) report of medical history; (b) self-evaluation and objective evaluation of medical symptoms; (c) measurement of height, weight, hearing, and vision; (d) chest x-ray radiography; (e) measurement of blood pressure; (f) urine examination; (g) anemia testing; (h) analysis of liver function; (i) testing of blood lipids; (j) testing of blood sugar; and (k) electrocardiogram.

Depending upon an employee's job type, employers must provide items in addition to this compulsory list. For example, employers must provide a health checkup once every six months to employees working at night, having health-hazardous jobs, or dealing with poisonous chemicals in the workplace. Employers must give the results of these health checkups to the district branch of the Labor Standards Inspections Office. In addition to these compulsory health checkups, firms often provide their employees with another type of health checkup as a fringe benefit: half-day, one-day, or two-day annual hospital checkups in order to promote the employee's health and to find sickness at an early stage.[4] This type of medical service for employees, called *Nin-gen Dock,* is not covered by employees' health insurance. According to *The Situations of Fringe Benefits* (Institute of Labor Administration 1998), 81 percent of 5,000 firms surveyed (sampled from all industries) subsidize 70 percent or more of the medical costs incurred from in-hospital comprehensive health checkups.[5] On average, employers pay $350 for such exams, but coverage ranges from $100 to $900.[6] This subsidy is provided by 89 percent of firms with 3,000 employees or more, 84 percent of firms with 1,000–2,999 employees, and 74 percent of firms with fewer than 1,000 employees.

Although employers are only legally required to contribute half of the insurance payments for their employees, the survey shows that firms often pay more. Although 84 percent of firms utilizing health insurance managed by the government pay half the rate, 86 percent of firms with health insurance managed by associations pay more than half the rate. Also, 95 percent of firms with more than 3,000 employees pay more than half of the contribution rate.

By law, an employer or establishment with more than 1,000 employees must have its own in-house industrial doctor. Employers dealing with

4. This health checkup benefit is often extended to the employee's spouse, parents, and children as well.
5. Institute of Labor Administration (1998, 278–85 and 334–47). The survey period was from 19 October to 28 December 1995.
6. All dollar values in this paper are calculated using an exchange rate of 1 dollar = 100 yen, for simplicity. Although a purchasing power parity (PPP) rate of $1 = ¥195.35 is used by the Organization for Economic Cooperation and Development (OECD; 1998), we do not believe that this rate reflects reality in Japan. Moreover, the dollar values given can be easily translated into PPP dollars if the values are halved.

health-hazardous or poisonous chemicals at the work site must provide an on-site doctor when 500 or more workers are employed. Firms with fifty or more employees must have a contracted medical practitioner or doctor that acts as an industrial doctor, overseeing the employees' health condition. Furthermore, firms must hire certified sanitary administrators (SAs). The number of SAs varies according to the size of the establishment: one SA for a firm of 50–200 employees, two SAs for a firm of 201–500 employees, three SAs for a firm of 501–1,000 employees, four SAs for a firm of 1,001–2,000 employees, five SAs for a firm of 2,001–3,000 employees, and six SAs for a firm of 3,001 or more employees. These regulations indicate that employees in larger firms enjoy better health benefits, including having health checkups at their place of work.

Similarly, NHI also provides various types of health checkups to local residents who are not covered by employees' health insurance or other types of health insurance.[7] Generally, the local government notifies residents about the schedules for health checkups. These health checkup periods are scattered throughout the year to accommodate the seasonal employment patterns of residents. Residents usually go to a local health center for their health checkups, but they must go to hospitals and clinics for some types of medical checkups. They pay the minimum fee according to the type of health checkup they have.

The types of health checkups provided by local governments are as follows: (a) group health checkups at local health centers and individual visits to hospitals or clinics, and (b) comprehensive medical health checkups in hospitals (i.e., the *Nin-gen Dock*). The former includes the basic health checkup items listed earlier for a fee of about $10 and tests for the following: gastric cancer ($8), carcinoma of the colon and rectum ($5), lung cancer (no fee; $5 for examination of sputum), tuberculosis (no fee), carcinoma cancer uteri ($6), osteoporosis ($5), breast cancer ($10), and other types of women's medical tests ($5).[8] The latter type of checkup includes the basic health checkup items plus other services depending on the length of hospital stay. The subsidies offered by local governments are, for example, $175 for a general medical examination (out-of-pocket expenses are about $190; that is, the total costs are about $365), $250 for a brain examination (out-of-pocket expenses are about $274), and $375 for a comprehensive examination (i.e., general plus brain examination; out-of-pocket expenses amount to about $410). The above-mentioned health checkups have age restrictions. For instance, the general medical examinations are for people aged thirty or higher, and the brain and comprehensive examinations are for those aged forty or higher. These examples also indicate that

7. Spouses of employees who are covered under employees' health insurance as dependents may receive this service by submitting a request to the corresponding local government.
8. The items included in the health checkup and the corresponding fees vary by locality, reflecting the budgetary constraints of local governments.

employees in larger firms enjoy better and more varied benefits than do those in smaller firms or the self-employed.

The next section provides a statistical overview of the health checkup program in Japan.

10.3 Health Checkup Statistics

In the preceding section, we discussed health checkups and coverage for these checkups under different types of health insurance. Clearly, the Japanese have adequate opportunity to undergo health checkups. Here we report on how many people aged twenty to sixty-four in Japan have health checkups, based on statistics from the *1995 National Survey of Life* (*Kokumin Seikatsu Kiso Chosa,* hereafter the Survey). The following summary of the Survey is quoted from the *Japan Statistical Yearbook 1999* (Statistics Bureau 1998).

> This Survey has been conducted by the Ministry of Health and Welfare every three years, since 1986. The Survey is a sampling survey covering all households and their household members within the stratified sample districts chosen at random from the enumeration districts of the 1990 Population Census, and is conducted by enumerator's interview method through the channels of prefectures, designated cities and health centers. The Survey was taken as of 1 June for about 270,000 households and about 800,000 household members in 5,100 districts, excluding one prefecture, Hyogo (616).

Table 10.1 gives the proportion of people reporting health checkups, by gender and age group. The total sample size is 449,051, of which 219,983 are male respondents and 229,068 are female respondents. These proportions reveal at least three noteworthy characteristics. First, the overall average proportion of individuals having health checkups is 0.557. Second, the overall proportion of males having health checkups is 0.607, which is about 10 percentage points above the 0.509 proportion of females. This difference narrows as age increases, excepting the thirty-to-thirty-nine age group (see fig. 10.1). Third, the health checkup rate peaks with the fifty-to-sixty age group for both males and females. A possible explanation for why the health checkup gender differential is widest in the thirty-to-thirty-nine

Table 10.1   **Health Checkup Rates by Gender and Age Group**

	N	Age					
		20–64	20–29	30–39	40–49	50–60	61–64
Total	449,051	0.557	0.457	0.521	0.597	0.620	0.585
Males	219,983	0.607	0.487	0.630	0.652	0.653	0.583
Females	229,068	0.509	0.429	0.415	0.543	0.590	0.587

Source: 1995 National Survey of Life, Statistics and Information (1998).

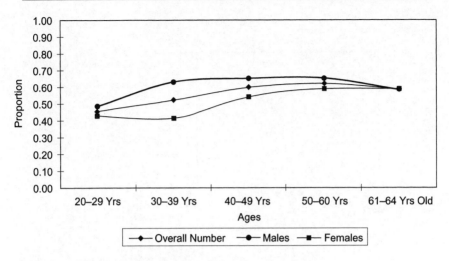

Fig. 10.1   Health checkup: Total number, age, and gender

Table 10.2   Health Checkup Rates by Type of Insurance Coverage

		Age					
	N	20–64	20–29	30–39	40–49	50–60	61–64
Health insurance managed by associations	106,593	0.647	0.550	0.610	0.704	0.733	0.666
Health insurance managed by the government	145,452	0.582	0.474	0.532	0.630	0.668	0.654
Mutual aid associations insurance	49,980	0.692	0.563	0.648	0.755	0.775	0.690
National health insurance	141,424	0.419	0.269	0.311	0.396	0.490	0.550
Seamen's insurance	1,515	0.576	0.443	0.517	0.568	0.682	0.500
Other health insurance	4,087	0.404	0.354	0.464	0.407	0.400	0.404

Source: 1995 National Survey of Life, Statistics and Information (1998).

age group is that females leave their place of employment to get married and start a family in this age range. Thus, they may have fewer opportunities to have their health checked. Most probably, the notification for the checkups now comes from their local government as opposed to from their workplace. A similar phenomenon occurs with males. There is an abrupt decline in the proportion of health checkups from the fifty-to-sixty to sixty-one-to-sixty-four age groups. This probably happens because sixty is the typical age of retirement. However, we still need to know why the proportion of health checkups increases as age increases. We attribute this phenomenon partially to the depreciation of health stock.

To examine whether there are differentials in the health checkup rate across types of health insurance, we show the checkup rate for each type of insurance coverage by age group in table 10.2 (graphed in fig. 10.2). In almost all age groups, the health checkup proportion is highest for mutual

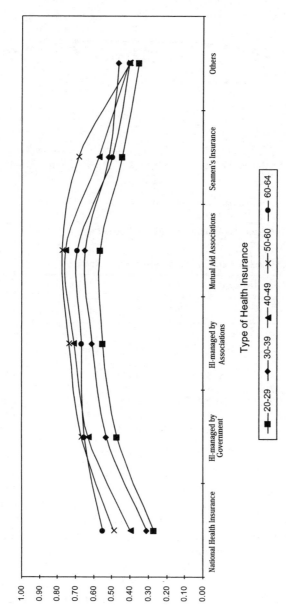

Fig. 10.2   Health checkup: Insurance coverage

aid associations insurance and second highest for health insurance managed by associations. A reason for these high health checkup rates is that employees covered by either of these health insurance plans enjoy more and better fringe benefits, and, with easier access to health checkups, they incur fewer costs. As noted in section 10.2, firms with 1,000 or more employees must have an industrial doctor and medical assistants such as nurses on site. By comparison, smaller firms may provide fewer medical facilities and services at their work sites, and they may not want employees to leave their jobs simply for health checkups. The employees themselves may face peer pressure not to take a day off for a health checkup. In response to this problem, branches of the Supervision of Labor Standards work to facilitate the provision of checkups, both by informing employers of their necessity and by parking medical vehicles with x-ray radiation equipment at or near work sites. As in table 10.1, the health checkup rate peaks in the fifty-to-sixty age range.

To confirm the existence of opportunities for health checkups among employees in relatively large establishments, we present health checkup rates by employment status in table 10.3. Again, we find that employees in larger

Table 10.3   Health Checkup Rates by Employment Status

		Age					
	N	20–64	20–29	30–39	40–49	50–60	61–64
Self-employed with employees	16,137	0.412	0.269	0.313	0.389	0.456	0.504
Self-employed without employees	25,831	0.447	0.256	0.309	0.412	0.481	0.555
Family workers	22,649	0.416	0.212	0.296	0.412	0.529	0.595
Company and association workers	15,325	0.617	0.463	0.540	0.608	0.682	0.689
Employed in a general enterprise with 1–4 employees	10,965	0.377	0.250	0325	0.427	0.477	0.492
Employed in a general enterprise with 5–29 employees	51,347	0.533	0.410	0.516	0.582	0.616	0.625
Employed in a general enterprise with 30–99 employees	45,075	0.660	0.549	0.650	0.705	0.735	0.726
Employed in a general enterprise with 100–499 employees	41,724	0.732	0.638	0.740	0.778	0.789	0.749
Employed in a general enterprise with 500–999 employees	13,063	0.750	0.661	0.748	0.814	0.815	0.748
Employed in a general enterprise with 1,000+ employees	63,248	0.803	0.709	0.810	0.853	0.862	0.811
Public employees	26,326	0.810	0.695	0.798	0.857	0.857	0.781
Monthly part-time workers	10,381	0.549	0.348	0.470	0.606	0.456	0.689
Daily part-time workers	2,980	0.448	0.262	0.352	0.492	0.529	0.602
Household workers	2,465	0.432	0.157	0.306	0.473	0.519	0.531
Others	5,470	0.459	0.285	0.388	0.501	0.561	0.575
Not working	123,065	0.409	0.265	0.286	0.424	0.528	0.552

Source: 1995 National Survey of Life, Statistics and Information (1998).

firms have very high health checkup rates. For example, employees in enterprises with over 1,000 workers have the highest rate among the general enterprises (that is, private firms); the proportion of workers having health checkups is 80 percent or more except for the twenty-to-twenty-nine age group. The overall rate for all age groups is highest for public employees (0.810). In addition, for most types of employees, the highest health checkup rates occur in the forty-to-forty-nine and fifty-to-sixty age groups, as shown in figure 10.3. However, among self-employed, part-time, and household workers, the proportion of health checkup recipients is largest for the sixty-one-to-sixty-four age group. In addition to facing a higher risk of sickness, older individuals may have more time available to go for checkups.

Table 10.4 and figure 10.4 show health checkup rates by industry and age group. Note that security employees have the highest overall health checkup rate: 0.752. This high rate reflects the occupational requirement mentioned earlier: People who work at night must have health checkups twice a year. Hence, the law enforcement industry is highly effective in encouraging its employees to have health checkups.

Finally, we examine the attitude of people who have symptoms of sickness or who are regularly visiting the hospital toward health checkups. We hypothesize a priori that these people, who are aware of their sickness or who are at high risk of becoming sick, are more likely to go for a checkup. Table 10.5 provides a summary of the evidence on this assumption. In the twenty-to-sixty-four age group, the overall difference in health checkup rates between people with no symptoms (symptom = 0) and people with symptoms (symptom = 1) is nearly 10 percentage points. The age subdivisions reveal that the differential increases with age.

In contrast, gender differences in health checkup rates for both the symptomatic and the symptom-free groups are virtually eliminated by age sixty-one to sixty-four. We cannot satisfactorily explain why the difference between the gender groups is so large regardless of whether symptoms are present. For instance, there is a 20 percentage point difference between males and females in the thirty-to-thirty-nine age group and a 10 percentage point difference in the forty-to-forty-nine age group. Females always have lower health checkup rates than males until the age of sixty. Attributing these gender differences solely to employment differences is both too hasty and too demanding of employment differences. At this point, it seems more reasonable to assume that men and women have different attitudes toward health risks. Similar results are obtained for hospital visits.[9]

The findings from this *National Survey of Life* sample of approximately 450,000 people, aged twenty to sixty-four, may be summarized as follows:

1. Males and females have distinctly different attitudes toward health checkups.

9. This similarity should be obvious since hospitals diagnose the symptoms.

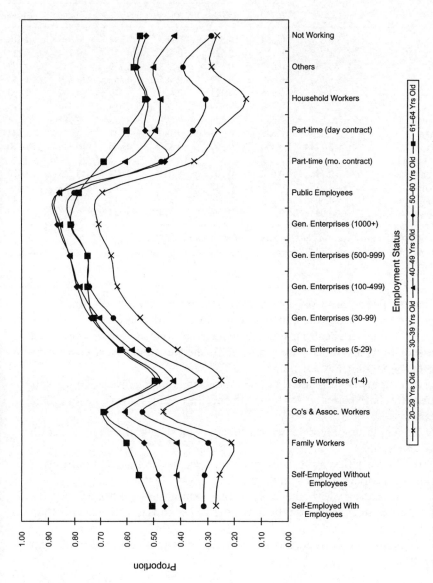

Fig. 10.3   Health checkup: Employment status (by age)

Table 10.4   Health Checkup Rates by Industry

	N	Age 20–64	20–29	30–39	40–49	50–60	61–64
Professional	49,819	0.659	0.594	0.665	0.693	0.696	0.610
Administrative	21,265	0.717	0.529	0.652	0.737	0.754	0.726
Clerical	55,745	0.657	0.590	0.683	0.729	0.745	0.707
Sales	36,534	0.517	0.452	0.505	0.541	0.549	0.550
Service	32,804	0.526	0.421	0.490	0.549	0.597	0.600
Security	3,757	0.752	0.639	0.745	0.818	0.774	0.715
Agriculture	13,811	0.567	0.316	0.391	0.533	0.617	0.634
Forestry	758	0.589	0.333	0.390	0.541	0.655	0.694
Fishery	2,174	0.453	0.307	0.328	0.446	0.544	0.500
Transportation and communication	10,796	0.653	0.503	0.633	0.679	0.733	0.680
Craftsmen[a]	83,173	0.602	0.528	0.588	0.623	0.642	0.614
None of the above	4,603	0.535	0.440	0.520	0.542	0.587	0.580
Unknown	133,994	0.423	0.286	0.314	0.445	0.524	0.560

Source: 1995 National Survey of Life, Statistics and Information (1998).

[a]Craftsmen include workers and laborers in mining, construction, and production processes as well as craftsmen.

2. As people grow older (e.g., from age group forty to forty-nine to age group sixty to sixty-four), they become more health conscious.

3. People with health insurance managed by associations or mutual aid associations insurance have more health checkups than those covered by other types of health insurance.

4. Employees in relatively large establishments (e.g., with 500 workers or more) have better access to health checkups. This is also true for public employees.

5. People employed in security-related jobs have the highest health checkup rate.

6. People with symptoms of illness undergo health checkups more often than do people without symptoms.

7. Regardless of whether they display symptoms of illnesses (visit the hospital or not), males usually have health checkups more frequently than do females.

These observations are incorporated in the theoretical model in the next section.

10.4   Theoretical Model

10.4.1   Model

As noted above, only 56 percent of twenty- to sixty-four-year-old Japanese had health checkups in 1995. Nearly half the population did not un-

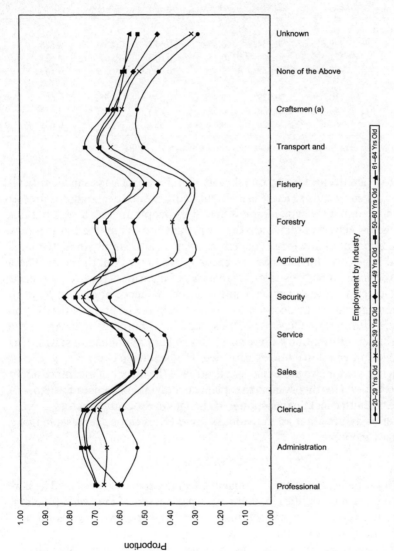

Fig. 10.4   Health checkup: Employment by industry and age

Table 10.5 **Health Checkup Rates by Symptoms and Gender**

		Age					
	N	20–64	20–29	30–39	40–49	50–60	61–64
Symptoms = 0							
Total	339,013	0.534	0.454	0.515	0.581	0.585	0.524
Males	171,577	0.586	0.481	0.622	0.636	0.621	0.524
Females	167,436	0.480	0.426	0.405	0.526	0.549	0.523
Symptoms = 1							
Total	110,038	0.629	0.476	0.549	0.652	0.685	0.655
Males	48,406	0.683	0.536	0.676	0.712	0.717	0.654
Females	61,632	0.586	0.444	0.456	0.599	0.658	0.655

Source: 1995 National Survey of Life, Statistics and Information (1998).

dergo a health checkup despite the fact that these checkups can identify illnesses at early stages. There are a number of possible explanations for this phenomenon. One explanation is that most people are risk lovers, but this seems unlikely. Another is that most people are risk averse but feel they have adequate knowledge concerning their health status; thus, the marginal benefits of having a health checkup are lower than the costs. There are too many other possible explanations to mention. However, it is clear that uncertainty about one's health and the incidence of disease plays an important role in the decision to have a checkup. Generally, a person can prevent future financial loss and psychological burdens by having more and better information with regard to his or her present health status. This kind of information could be provided by a health checkup.

In this section, we present an application of the theory of insurance under uncertainty. This theory aims to explain an individual's choice of whether to have a health checkup in response to changes in exogenous factors.

Let us assume that an individual's preferences can be represented by a utility function,

$$U = U(S_1, S_2; \pi_1, \pi_2). \tag{1}$$

Utility is defined over the contingent earning capacity (S_1, S_2).[10] The corresponding probabilities, π_1 and π_2, are parameters of the utility function, since the value of a state-contingent earning capacity depends on how likely the state is to occur.[11]

Suppose there is an event S_1 that an individual faces with probability π_1.

10. Wealth, rather than earning capacity, is typically used in uncertainty models (e.g., Silberberg 1990). However, since we apply the theory of household production to the model, the use of earning capacity is appropriate and can be assumed to reflect all monetary measures, including wealth.

11. This simple application of the theory of insurance under uncertainty is based on Pauly (1989, 309–19) and Silberberg (1990, 445–47).

If S_1 occurs, the individual maintains his initial health-related earnings endowment S_0 by incurring the cost of preventive activities h, which we take to be a health checkup.[12] In addition, the individual pays the insurance premium (or tax) P required by his type of health insurance, whose purpose is to protect him from a loss of his earnings endowment S_0 due to sudden illness. Thus, S_1 is defined as

$$(2) \qquad S_1 = S_0 - h - P.$$

The individual faces a second event S_2 with probability π_2, in which he suffers a loss L of his earnings capacity. We assume that the magnitude of the loss increases with the individual's age A. That is, the individual's opportunity costs increase (at a diminishing rate) as age increases.[13] In addition, the stock of health eventually depreciates with age. Finally, we also assume an additional factor H as an argument of L. The individual may engage in some health-promoting activities H to increase his health stock HS. Loss L is defined as follows:

$$(3) \qquad L = L(A, H), \frac{\partial L}{\partial A} > 0, \text{ and } \frac{\partial L}{\partial H} = \frac{\partial L}{\partial HS} \cdot \frac{\partial HS}{\partial H} > 0.$$

In equation (3), the size of L depends on the type of illness.[14] Different illnesses are associated with different measurable symptoms (with some overlap) such as high blood pressure, high cholesterol, proteinuria, and high white blood cell count. Each symptom s_j is associated with a particular illness and, hence, with a particular loss L_j. Having a health checkup is influenced by subjective or objective symptoms or both, so that

$$(4) \qquad h = h(s_j), j = 1, \ldots, n.$$

If symptoms have a probability distribution $\pi_j(s_j)$, then having a health checkup is an inverse function of symptoms,

$$(5) \qquad \pi_j^{-1}(h) = (s_j).$$

Therefore, the relationship between the health checkup h and loss L_j is

$$(6) \qquad \pi_j^*(h)L_j,$$

where π_j^* is probability associated with L_j. The expected loss due to illness can be expressed as

$$(7) \qquad \text{Expected Loss} = \pi^*(h)L(A, H) = \sum_{j=1}^{n} \pi_j^*(h)L_j(A, H).$$

12. For simplicity, we omit the individual subscript i and also assume the individual to be male.

13. The implicit assumption here is that health stock accumulates up to a certain age.

14. For example, the major diseases among fifty- to sixty-year-old Japanese are diseases of the digestive system, circulatory system, musculoskeletal system and connective tissue, and nervous system and sense organs (Statistics Bureau 1998, 670–71).

Finally, if event 2 occurs, the individual receives medical care, which has the effect of augmenting earnings capacity by M. However, obtaining medical care entails some costs, such as the discomfort associated with long waits in clinics and hospitals.[15] This "psychological burden" should be included in the cost calculation as $-gM$, where $0 < g < 1$. Now, event 2 can be defined in terms of costs and benefits in money-equivalent units:

(8) $\qquad S_2 = S_0 - h - P - \pi^*(h)L(A, H) + (1 - g)M$

Finally, π_1 and π_2, the probabilities attached to events 1 and 2, are functions of an individual's age A.[16] As an individual ages, he becomes more susceptible to illness. We express the individual's preferences over uncertain prospects using an expected utility function, or a Von Neumann-Morgenstern utility function, as follows:

(9) $\qquad EU = [1 - \pi(A)]U(S_0 - h - P)$

$$+ \pi(A)U[S_0 - h - P - \pi^*(h)L(A, H) + (1 - g)M]$$

The value of h that maximizes EU satisfies the following first-order condition:

(10) $[1 - \pi(A)]U_x(x) + \pi(A)U_y(y)[1 + \pi_h^*L(A, H)] = 0$, at $h > 0$,

or

(11) $\qquad -\dfrac{1}{1 + \pi_h^*L(A, H)} = \dfrac{\pi(A)U_y(y)}{[1 - \pi(A)]U_x(x)}$,

where

$x \equiv S_0 - h - P,$
$y \equiv S_0 - h - P - \pi^*(h)L(A, H) + (1 - g)M,$
$U_x = \partial U/\partial x > 0,$
$U_y = \partial U/\partial y > 0,$
$\pi_h^* = [\partial \pi^*(h)]/\partial h < 0.$

In equation (11), the expression on the left-hand side is the marginal productivity of the health checkup (Ehrlich and Becker 1972, 634).[17] The equi-

---

15. Approximately 49 percent of patients in large hospitals wait for at least an hour and a half, and 15 percent wait for more than three hours. By comparison, these rates are 44 percent and 17.2 percent for medium-sized hospitals, and 28 percent and 15.6 percent for small hospitals (Health and Welfare Statistics Association 1999, 84). However, medical examinations in hospitals are very quick; almost 64 percent of patients in large hospitals take only ten minutes or less for their examinations, and 18 percent take less than three minutes. About 61 percent and 57 percent of patients in medium-sized and small hospitals, respectively, take ten minutes or less for their medical examinations.
16. Here we drop the state subscripts so that $\pi = \pi_2$ and $1 - \pi = \pi_1$.
17. According to Ehrlich and Becker (1972), the left-hand side expression of equation (11) in this presentation is the slope of the production transformation curve, and the right-hand side is the slope of the indifference curve of S_1, S_2. Hence, both sides must be equal in equilibrium for $h > 0$.

librium condition requires $1 + \pi_h^* L(A, H) < 0$. That is, an additional dollar spent on health checkups must reduce the expected loss by more than a dollar.[18] In other words, if an individual does not expect the benefits from the reduction of his expected loss to be greater than the cost of the health checkup, he will not have the health checkup. Using equation (10) to restate this point, if the maximum EU occurs when $h = 0$, rather than when $h > 0$, then necessarily EU$' \leq 0$; hence, we will have a corner solution. Furthermore, even if $h > 0$ to start with, there may be some range of EU over which EU$' \leq 0$. This may be the case when $-1 \leq \pi_h^* L(A, H) \leq 0$. Then the individual will not have a health checkup, because EU($h = 0$) > EU($h > 0$). For example, when the individual already has adequate, positive information on his current health condition, it does not make any sense for him to see a medical doctor at the hospital for a slight cough.

The second-order condition of equation (10) requires

(12) $\qquad D = [1 - \pi(A)]U_{xx} + \pi(A)U_{yy}[1 + \pi_h^* L(A, H)]^2 < 0,$

where

$U_{xx} \quad = \partial U_x / \partial x < 0,$
$U_{yy} \quad = \partial U_y / \partial x < 0,$
$\partial \pi_h^* / \partial h = [\partial^2 \pi^*(h)] / \partial h^2 = 0$ (assumed without loss).

The effect of age on the demand for a health checkup h can be found by partially differentiating the first-order optimality condition, equation (10), with respect to A, as follows:

(13) $\quad \dfrac{\partial h}{\partial A} = \dfrac{1}{D}\{-\pi_A U_x + [1 + \pi_h^* L(A, H)][\pi_A U_y - \pi(A)\pi^*(h)U_{yy}L_A]$

$\qquad\qquad + \pi(A)\pi_h^* U_y L_A\} > 0$

where

$\pi_A = [\partial \pi(A)] / \partial A > 0,$
$L_A = [\partial L(A, H)] / \partial A > 0.$

The above suggests that as people grow older, they become more health conscious and hence go for their health checkups.

Let us now consider the case of an increase in the health insurance premium (or tax) P. That is, the relative coverage of medical care decreases in clinics and hospitals. The effect of an increase in P on health checkups is negative, as shown in the following equation:

(14) $\quad \dfrac{\partial h}{\partial P} = \dfrac{-1}{D}\{[1 - \pi(A)]U_{xx} + \pi(A)U_{yy}[1 + \pi_h^* L(A, H)]\} < 0,$

---

18. The reduction in this context might be due to "self-protection." In Ehrlich and Becker, "self-insurance [is] a reduction in the size of a loss, and self-protection [is] a reduction in the probability of a loss" (1972, 633).

since $[(1 - \pi(A))U_{xx} + \pi(A)U_{yy}(1 + \pi_h^*L(A, H))] < 0$ (see the appendix). In other words, as medical care coverage increases, an individual is more likely to have a health checkup.

The effect of an increase in an individual's initial endowment S_0 is positive, as shown in the following equation:

(15) $$\frac{\partial h}{\partial S_0} = \frac{1}{D}\{[1 - \pi(A)]U_{xx} + \pi(A)U_{yy}[1 + \pi_h^*L(A, H)]\} > 0.$$

This result in equation (15) shows that individuals with higher earning potential—for instance, those with larger stocks of human capital—are willing to have health checkups to secure against future earnings losses.

We now consider whether an individual who is willing to participate in health-stock-augmenting activities will have a health checkup. By partially differentiating the first-order optimality condition, we have

(16) $$\frac{\partial h}{\partial H} = \frac{1}{D}(\pi(A)L_H\{\pi_h^*U_y - \pi^*(h)U_{yy}[1 + \pi_h^*L(A, H)]\}) > 0,$$

$$L_H = \frac{\partial L(A, H)}{\partial H} > 0.$$

Hence, an increase in health-stock-augmenting activities, which raises earnings capacity through an increase in the individual's health stock, will tend to encourage the individual to have health checkups in order to avoid an earnings loss due to sudden illness.

We can also evaluate the effect of the psychological burden g, which is a burden incurred by an individual due to his illness. When an individual is sick and has to wait for many hours at a busy hospital, there are psychological costs, such as fatigue. In cases of severe illness, he may have to be hospitalized and medical treatment may take several hours or days. The effect of an increase in g on h is positive:

(17) $$\frac{\partial h}{\partial g} = \frac{1}{D}\{\pi(A)U_{yy}[1 + \pi_h^*L(A, H)](-M)\} > 0.$$

When an individual believes he is prone to some serious illness, perhaps through his job, he is more willing to have a health checkup in order to lessen the psychological burden should he fall ill.

On the other hand, the effect of an increase in medical benefits M is negative:

(18) $$\frac{\partial h}{\partial M} = \frac{1}{D}\{\pi(A)U_{yy}[1 + \pi_h^*L(A, H)](1 - g)\} < 0.$$

Hence, the individual becomes less self-protective as benefits increase, the classical moral hazard result.

Finally, we consider the effect of gender on health checkups. In equation

(7), the expected loss $\pi^*(h)L(A, H)$ can be computed separately by gender. Suppose

(19) $$\overline{L^f} = \pi^f(h)L^f(A, H) < \overline{L^m} = \pi^m(h)L^m(A, H),$$

where $\overline{L^i}$ is a gender-specific expected loss ($i = f, m$: $f =$ females, and $m =$ males). $\overline{L^i}$ is a positive function of both $\pi^i(h)$ and $L^i(A, H)$, and we assume $\pi^f(h) < \pi^m(h)$ and $L^f(A, H) < L^m(A, H)$.

The effect of an increase (or shift) in the probability distribution over health checkups is found to be

(20) $$\frac{\partial h}{\partial \pi^i(h)} = \frac{1}{D}\{\pi(A)U_{yy}[-L^i(A, H)][1 + \pi_h^*L(A, H)]\} > 0,$$

which follows from the assumption, $(\partial \pi_h^*)/[\partial \pi^i(h)] = 0$.

The above result indicates that individuals who are more prone to illness are more likely to have health checkups. The positive relationship can also be applied to $\overline{L^i}$; that is, $\partial h/\partial \overline{L^i} > 0$. Therefore, under the assumptions listed above, males are more likely to have health checkups than females.

These comparative static predictions must now be evaluated in an empirical setting. For the empirical specification, we assume that an individual's decision to have a health checkup depends on an unobservable utility index I_i, defined as

(21) $$I_i = \mathbf{X}_i\boldsymbol{\beta} + u_i,$$

where $\mathbf{X}_i$ is a $(1 \times k)$ row vector of explanatory variables that determine I_i, $\boldsymbol{\beta}$ is a $(k \times 1)$ column vector of parameters to be estimated, and u_i is a normally distributed random error term. The larger the value of the index I_i, the greater the probability an individual will have a health checkup.

We further assume that there is a critical level of the index I_i^*, such that if I_i exceeds I_i^*, the individual will have a health checkup, and otherwise he will not. In terms of the notation used above, $[1 + \pi_h^*L(A, H)] < 0$ and $\partial EU/\partial h = 0$ at $h > 0$ imply $I_i - I_i^* \geq 0$. Let $h = 1$ if the individual has a health checkup, and $h = 0$ if he does not. Since I_i, I_i^*, and $[1 + \pi_h^*L(A, H)]$ are not observable, we assume I_i and I_i^* to be normally distributed with the same mean and variance. Then, the probability that the individual has a health checkup can be expressed as

(22) $$\text{Prob}(h = 1) = \text{Prob}(I_h^* \leq I_i) = F(I_i) = \frac{1}{\sqrt{2\pi}} \int_{-\infty}^{X\beta} e^{-t/2}dt,$$

where $F(\cdot)$ is the cumulative distribution function, and t is a standardized normal variable—that is, $t \sim N(0, 1)$.[19] We estimate a probit model of the demand for health checkups and a tobit model for the length of hospital stay. The next section presents the explanatory variables used in these analyses.

19. The presentation of this probit model is from Gujarati (1995, 563–64).

Table 10.6   Distribution of Retirement Ages by Firm Size and Industry, 1997

	Retirement Age (%)				
	Under 55	56–59	60	61–64	65
Firm size					
30–99	5.7	6.6	78.4	0.9	8.3
100–299	2.7	2.5	88.1	2.9	3.8
300–999	1.9	2.3	91.9	2.0	1.9
1,000–4,999	0.1	0.4	96.8	1.7	1.0
5,000 and over	0.0	0.0	98.0	0.7	1.3
Industry					
Mining	5.8	8.3	76.7	3.3	5.8
Construction	3.6	1.7	69.6	0.9	23.9
Manufacturing	4.2	4.2	86.8	1.1	3.5
Electricity	3.1	4.7	89.8	1.6	0.8
Transportation and communication	3.6	9.4	76.3	5.2	5.6
Wholesale and retail	7.3	6.4	84.5	0.3	1.5
Finance and insurance	2.3	1.7	93.8	1.2	1.1
Real estate	1.7	2.8	89.2	0.8	5.5
Services	3.9	6.2	77.9	1.9	10.0

Source: Statistics Bureau (1998, 94).

Notes: Electricity includes gas, heat, and water as well as electricity. Wholesale and retail industry includes eating and drinking establishments.

10.4.2   Variables

Using the model outlined above, we examine the effects of several variables on the demand for health checkups. The dependent variable is a dummy variable that equals 1 if the individual has a health checkup and 0 otherwise.

A critical factor in explaining the variation in demand for medical health checkups is age. Theoretically, the relationship between age and medical health checkups should be positive and slowly increasing until the age of sixty, and declining thereafter. The reason for this decline is that the retirement age is sixty for those working in relatively large firms (see table 10.6).[20] Note, however, that new retirees are still eligible for a type of health insurance managed by associations or health insurance managed by the government for two years following retirement. Otherwise, these individuals purchase NHI.

Gender is another major explanatory variable used in this analysis. The male health checkup rate always exceeds the female rate in the twenty-to-sixty-four age range. This differential in health checkup rates certainly results from biological differences as well as socioeconomic and demo-

20. Employees covered by employees' health insurance obtain NHI after retirement.

graphic variables. We examine the effect of gender on the demand for health checkups, ceteris paribus.

In addition to the above demographic variables, another important explanatory variable is health insurance coverage. This includes health insurance managed by associations, health insurance managed by the government, and NHI. The former two types of insurance cover 80 percent of medical costs (70 percent for dependents), whereas the NHI covers 70 percent for everyone.

To examine the effect of an individual's initial endowment on health checkups, we use a dummy variable to indicate the household's highest income earner (the breadwinner) and include the household's monthly expenditure, which should have an income effect on the demand for health checkups. To account for nonreporting bias, we include a dummy variable for those records with missing income values.

To measure an individual's health-stock-augmenting activities, we use the frequency of daily practices such as eating regular meals, nutritiously balanced meals, and not-too-salty meals; eating in moderation; exercising; getting adequate sleep; and taking time to refresh oneself during the day. We hypothesize that the effect of this variable on the demand for health checkups is positive.

To evaluate the effect of the psychological burden associated with illness, the number of illnesses the individual reports is included as an explanatory variable. This number includes diseases of the circulatory system, respiratory system, digestive system, genitourinary system, and so forth. Although the illnesses of each system could be explanatory variables in the regression, we elect not to use this approach because of the difficulty in evaluating differences in the effects. Also, there are too many to be meaningful for our purposes. In addition to the illness variable, we include the number of stressful events the individual has had to face. These two explanatory variables are considered to be objective measures of health. To avoid specification error, the subjective evaluation of an individual's health condition should also be included in the regression analysis. To do this, we use three dummy variables indicating whether the individual feels he or she is in excellent, good, or fair health.

To capture the effect of medical benefits on the demand for health checkups, we use a life insurance variable as a proxy for benefits. There are various types of life insurance. Some provide coverage only for hospitalization costs and injuries.

To examine the effect of a change in the likelihood of illness on health checkups, we use a dummy variable for whether the individual has visited a clinic or hospital in the past year. If the individual did not visit either for an entire year, the individual is considered to be healthy, ceteris paribus. The probability that he or she falls ill is lower than that of someone who has visited these institutions in recent months.

In addition to the explanatory variables described above, variables measuring education, firm size, type of employment, population size, and regional dummies are also included in the regression models. The definitions and summary statistics of all of the variables are reported in table 10.7.[21] In the next section, we report the empirical results of the probit analysis.

10.5   Empirical Results

10.5.1   Health Checkup Results for the 20–64 and 30–60 Age Groups

Table 10.8 reports the results of probit and ordinary least squares (OLS; linear probability model) analyses for the twenty-to-sixty-four and thirty-to-sixty age groups. Table 10.9 reports the results of the thirty-to-sixty age group by gender. The overall results are quite similar in terms of the significance of the estimated coefficients, which are very robust. The OLS estimates are shown for comparative purposes. We will mainly discuss the results of the probit model in terms of the signs of the estimated coefficients.

First, MALE is significant and positive in both age groups, as expected (see table 10.8). After controlling for other socioeconomic and demographic variables (discussed in section 10.4), we do not reject the argument that males are more likely than females to have health checkups because their genetic and biological characteristics make them more prone to illness. The estimated coefficients on AGE and AGESQ (age[2]) are both highly significant. The positive estimated coefficient on AGE and the negative estimated coefficient on AGESQ for both age groups indicate that the profile of health checkups is concave in age. The probit estimate on AGE for the thirty-to-sixty age group is 0.083 and is about twice as large as that for the twenty-to-sixty-four age group, which is 0.037. This shows that the former is more concerned with their health than the latter. The changes in the health checkup rate as age increases, or the estimated coefficient on AGESQ, indicate that individuals lose health stock as they age.

As mentioned earlier, health checkups are time-consuming health inputs. Hence, the opportunity cost of lost work hours or days for the sake of a health checkup should be a major determinant of an individual's decision to have a health checkup. The sign of the wage rate (WAGE) is negative and highly significant. Again, the probit coefficient for the thirty-to-sixty age group (–0.259) is two times larger in absolute value than that for the twenty-to-sixty-four population (–0.139). The corresponding t-statistics also indicate stronger significance of the former than of the latter.[22] The es-

21. This study focuses on those aged thirty to sixty. However, statistics for the twenty-to-sixty-four age group are also reported. Gender-specific statistics are available from the authors upon request.
22. The results are the same for the OLS estimates.

Table 10.7   Description and Statistics (Year = 1995)

Variable	Description	Age 20–64 (N = 438,906) Mean	Age 20–64 (N = 438,906) Standard Deviation	Age 30–60 (N = 310,134) Mean	Age 30–60 (N = 310,134) Standard Deviation
HCHECKUP	If the individual has health checkup, HCHECKUP = 1; otherwise = 0.	0.557	0.497	0.584	0.493
MALE	If the individual is male, MALE = 1; otherwise = 0.	0.490	0.500	0.491	0.500
AGE	Age	42.314	12.737	45.250	8.576
AGESQ	Age squared.	1,952.690	1,076.338	2,121.134	777.190
MARRIED	If the individual is married, MARRIED = 1; otherwise = 0.	0.722	0.448	0.846	0.361
WAGE	Wage rate per hour (in 1,000 yen)[a]	1.490	0.454	1.613	0.467
BREADWIN	If the individual is the highest income earner in the household, BREADWIN = 1; otherwise = 0.	0.438	0.496	0.488	0.500
MONTHEXP	Monthly expenditures (in 10,000 yen)	28.910	38.096	29.581	38.240
MOEXPDUM	If monthly expenditures are not reported, MOEXPDUM = 1; otherwise = 0.	0.062	0.240	0.060	0.237
ASOCHI	If the individual has health insurance managed by associations, ASOCHI = 1; otherwise = 0.	0.237	0.425	0.237	0.425
GOVTHI	If the individual has health insurance managed by government, GOVTHI = 1; otherwise = 0.	0.324	0.468	0.326	0.469
MUTUHI	If the individual has mutual aid associations insurance, MUTUHI = 1; otherwise = 0.	0.111	0.315	0.124	0.329
NHI	If the individual has national health insurance, NHI = 1; otherwise = 0.	0.315	0.465	0.300	0.458
SIZE1000	If the individual is an employee of a firm with 1,000 employees or more, SIZE1000 = 1; otherwise = 0.	0.081	0.272	0.080	0.271
SIZE500	If the individual is an employee of a firm with 500–999 employees, SIZE500 = 1; otherwise = 0.	0.029	0.168	0.028	0.164
SIZE100	If the individual is an employee of a firm with 100–499 employees, SIZE100 = 1; otherwise = 0.	0.093	0.290	0.091	0.288

(continued)

Table 10.7 (continued)

Variable	Description	Age 20–64 (N = 438,906)		Age 30–60 (N = 310,134)	
		Mean	Standard Deviation	Mean	Standard Deviation
SIZE30	If the individual is an employee of a firm with 30–99 employees, SIZE30 = 1; otherwise = 0.	0.100	0.301	0.100	0.300
SIZE5	If the individual is an employee of a firm with 5–29 employees, SIZE5 = 1; otherwise = 0.	0.114	0.318	0.113	0.317
SIZE1	If the individual is an employee of a firm with 1–4 employees, SIZE1 = 1; otherwise = 0.	0.024	0.154	0.025	0.155
PUBEMPLY	If the individual is a public employee, PUBEMPLY = 1; otherwise = 0.	0.059	0.235	0.067	0.250
DOCTOR	The number of physicians per 100,000 population in a prefecture.	187.035	35.828	186.946	35.618
PROFES	If the individual is a professional such as engineer, PROFES = 1; otherwise = 0.	0.111	0.314	0.115	0.319
ADMINI	If the individual is an administrator, ADMINI = 1; otherwise = 0.	0.047	0.212	0.058	0.233
CLERIC	If the individual is a clerk, CLERIC = 1; otherwise = 0.	0.124	0.329	0.115	0.320
SALES	If the individual is a salesperson, SALES = 1; otherwise = 0.	0.081	0.273	0.085	0.279
SERVIC	If the individual is an employee of the service industry, SERVIC = 1; otherwise = 0.	0.073	0.260	0.076	0.265
SECURI	If the individual has a security-related job, SECURI = 1; otherwise = 0.	0.008	0.089	0.009	0.092
TRANSP	If the individual is an employee of the transportation industry, SERVIC = 1; otherwise = 0.	0.024	0.153	0.027	0.163
SICKNUMB	The number of injuries and illnesses.	0.366	0.792	0.372	0.791
STRESS	The number of stressful events that had been or are being experienced.	0.944	1.556	1.014	1.624
NOTVISIT	If the individual did not visit medical institutions for the past year, NOTVISIT = 1; otherwise = 0.	0.084	0.278	0.089	0.285
HLTHPRAC	The number of health-related daily practices.	2.507	1.901	2.545	1.878

Variable	Description				
HLTHEXCE	Self-evaluation of the individual's health: if excellent, HLTHEXCE = 1; otherwise = 0.	0.316	0.465	0.300	0.458
HLTHGOOD	Self-evaluation of the individual's health: if good, HLTHGOOD = 1; otherwise = 1.	0.175	0.380	0.175	0.380
HLTHFAIR	Self-evaluation of the individual's health: if fair, HLTHFAIR = 1; otherwise = 0.	0.385	0.487	0.399	0.490
EDU	The average proportion of high school graduates who went to either college or university in a prefecture.	0.369	0.100	0.368	0.100
LIFEINSU	The average amount of life insurance's contract (in 10,000 yen) in a prefecture.	780.724	64.988	779.765	64.886
POP1M	If the individual lives in a city with a population of about 1 million or more, POP1M = 1; otherwise = 0.	0.139	0.345	0.134	0.340
POP150	If the individual lives in a city with a population of more than 150,000 but less than 1 million, POP150 = 1; otherwise = 0.	0.268	0.443	0.264	0.441
POP50	If the individual lives in a city with a population of more than 50,000 but less than 150,000, POP50 = 1; otherwise = 0.	0.094	0.292	0.096	0.295
POPCUNTY	If the individual lives in a city or town with a population of less than 50,000, POPCUNTY = 1; otherwise = 0.	0.289	0.453	0.295	0.456
REGIOND1	Regional dummy: Hokkaido = 1; otherwise = 0.	0.021	0.144	0.022	0.145
REGIOND2	Regional dummy: Tohoku = 1; otherwise = 0.	0.139	0.346	0.142	0.349
REGIOND4	Regional dummy: KantoII = 1; otherwise = 0.	0.111	0.314	0.111	0.314
REGIOND5	Regional dummy: Hokuriku = 1; otherwise = 0.	0.087	0.282	0.088	0.283
REGIOND6	Regional dummy: Tokai = 1; otherwise = 0.	0.072	0.259	0.072	0.258
REGIOND7	Regional dummy: Kinki I = 1; otherwise = 0.	0.046	0.209	0.044	0.206
REGIOND8	Regional dummy: Kinki II = 1; otherwise = 0.	0.061	0.240	0.061	0.240
REGIOND9	Regional dummy: Cyugoku = 1; otherwise = 0.	0.103	0.305	0.104	0.306
REGIOND10	Regional dummy: Sikoku = 1; otherwise = 0.	0.076	0.265	0.077	0.267
REGIOND11	Regional dummy: Kita Kyusyu = 1; otherwise = 0.	0.090	0.286	0.090	0.286
REGIOND12	Regional dummy: Minami Kyusyu = 1; otherwise = 0.	0.075	0.263	0.076	0.265

[a]The wage rate is the gender-specific industry average wage rate for different age groups, namely, 20–24, 25–29, . . . , 55–59, and 60–64.

Table 10.8   **Probit and OLS Estimates of Health Checkup Probabilities**

	Age 20–64				Age 30–60			
	Probit		OLS		Probit		OLS	
Variable	Coefficient	t-statistic[a]	Coefficient	t-statistic[a]	Coefficient	t-statistic[a]	Coefficient	t-statistic[a]
C	-1.503	-29.110	-0.015	-0.846	-2.553	-28.704	-0.363	-12.216
MALE	0.041	4.260	0.016	4.981	0.163	12.015	0.060	13.161
AGE	0.037	22.557	0.013	23.561	0.083	23.775	0.029	24.467
AGESQ	-0.000	-11.723	-0.000	-12.283	-0.001	-18.185	-0.000	-18.730
MARRIED	0.004	0.789	-0.000	-0.010	0.075	10.645	0.024	10.090
WAGE	-0.139	-13.886	-0.056	-16.561	-0.259	-18.928	-0.097	-21.410
BREADWIN	0.095	16.362	0.032	16.105	0.061	8.029	0.020	7.793
MONTHEXP	0.000	6.193	0.000	6.081	0.000	4.328	0.000	4.369
MOEXPDUM	-0.080	-9.279	-0.028	-9.457	-0.088	-8.493	-0.030	-8.734
ASOCHI	0.305	16.495	0.106	16.793	0.320	14.609	0.111	15.008
GOVTHI	0.216	11.855	0.077	12.319	0.210	9.750	0.076	10.401
MUTUHI	0.295	15.062	0.102	15.214	0.283	12.291	0.099	12.686
NHI	-0.037	-2.008	-0.014	-2.181	-0.063	-2.938	-0.025	-3.365
SIZE1000	0.962	98.944	0.323	104.239	0.962	80.305	0.310	84.435
SIZE500	0.811	60.243	0.283	64.671	0.800	47.470	0.271	51.581
SIZE100	0.743	89.130	0.261	94.499	0.731	72.410	0.252	77.221
SIZE30	0.537	68.696	0.194	72.710	0.527	56.391	0.189	60.470
SIZE5	0.227	31.468	0.082	32.877	0.226	26.459	0.084	28.403
SIZE1	-0.085	-6.413	-0.033	-7.215	-0.075	-4.860	-0.030	-5.643
PUBEMPLY	0.821	63.152	0.275	65.890	0.842	55.552	0.271	57.303
DOCTOR	0.000	2.658	0.000	3.376	0.000	2.882	0.000	3.856
PROFES	0.111	15.188	0.040	16.321	0.118	13.636	0.042	14.807
ADMINI	0.226	21.206	0.072	20.898	0.232	19.730	0.073	19.561
CLERIC	0.147	20.486	0.052	21.521	0.170	19.237	0.057	19.971
SALES	-0.031	-3.994	-0.010	-3.705	-0.020	-2.181	-0.006	-1.886
SERVIC	-0.048	-5.855	-0.016	-5.893	-0.025	-2.577	-0.008	-2.434

	(1) Coef.	(1) t	(2) Coef.	(2) t	(3) Coef.	(3) t	(4) Coef.	(4) t
SECURI	0.132	5.259	0.048	6.096	0.124	4.198	0.047	5.218
TRANSP	0.027	1.948	0.011	2.272	0.037	2.327	0.014	2.752
SICKNUMB	0.138	48.575	0.046	48.973	0.140	41.478	0.046	41.860
STRESS	0.047	33.917	0.016	33.587	0.048	30.312	0.016	30.141
NOTVISIT	-0.162	-22.335	-0.057	-22.694	-0.184	-21.745	-0.063	-22.205
HLTHPRAC	0.081	71.211	0.027	71.785	0.080	58.508	0.027	58.724
HLTHEXCE	0.419	56.030	0.142	56.617	0.415	46.744	0.141	47.531
HLTHGOOD	0.481	60.929	0.163	61.568	0.481	51.441	0.162	52.226
HLTHFAIR	0.460	66.895	0.157	67.808	0.457	56.492	0.154	57.349
EDU	-0.651	-14.155	-0.232	-14.925	-0.779	-14.109	-0.279	-15.197
LIFEINSU	-0.000	-8.786	-0.000	-8.793	-0.000	-3.940	-0.000	-3.684
POP1M	-0.046	-5.819	-0.016	-5.862	-0.044	-4.540	-0.015	-4.535
POP150	-0.063	-10.574	-0.022	-10.859	-0.069	-9.643	-0.023	-9.848
POP50	0.097	12.075	0.034	12.427	0.115	12.118	0.039	12.359
POPCUNTY	0.224	37.968	0.077	38.813	0.238	33.798	0.080	34.507
REGIOND1	-0.257	-15.375	-0.092	-16.288	-0.312	-15.290	-0.112	-16.375
REGIOND2	0.046	4.034	0.012	3.148	-0.006	-0.408	-0.007	-1.572
REGIOND4	-0.011	-1.130	-0.006	-1.709	-0.037	-3.129	-0.015	-3.838
REGIOND5	0.053	4.937	0.016	4.502	0.022	1.649	0.005	1.053
REGIOND6	0.004	0.325	0.001	0.213	-0.005	-0.418	-0.002	-0.537
REGIOND7	-0.124	-10.085	-0.044	-10.546	-0.145	-9.666	-0.051	-10.186
REGIOND8	-0.186	-16.230	-0.064	-16.668	-0.207	-14.962	-0.071	-15.473
REGIOND9	-0.070	-6.059	-0.027	-6.837	-0.117	-8.111	-0.043	-9.030
REGIOND10	-0.234	-18.525	-0.084	-19.590	-0.288	-18.285	-0.103	-19.515
REGIOND11	-0.159	-13.356	-0.058	-14.436	-0.205	-13.590	-0.075	-14.865
REGIOND12	-0.123	-9.942	-0.047	-11.253	-0.199	-12.548	-0.075	-14.150
R^2	0.1767		0.1730		0.1806		0.1763	
Log-likelihood	-260,004		-273,960		-180,789		-190,634	
F-statistic	—		1,799.85		—		1,301.02	
N	438,906		438,906		310,134		310,134	

aCoefficients are significant at the 1 percent level, 5 percent level, and 10 percent level if the asymptotic t-statistics are greater than 2.576, 1.960, and 1.645, respectively.

Table 10.9   Profit and OLS Estimates of Health Checkup Probabilities by Gender

	Males Aged 30–60				Females Aged 30–60			
	Probit		OLS		Probit		OLS	
Variable	Coefficient	t-statistic[a]	Coefficient	t-statistic[a]	Coefficient	t-statistic[a]	Coefficient	t-statistic[a]
C	-1.580	-10.298	0.013	0.265	-2.998	-24.237	-0.525	-12.220
AGE	0.044	6.381	0.013	6.172	0.090	20.381	0.030	19.801
AGESQ	-0.000	-5.102	-0.000	-4.885	-0.001	-14.258	-0.000	-13.507
MARRIED	0.161	15.851	0.054	16.679	0.005	0.407	0.000	0.021
WAGE	-0.129	-5.130	-0.045	-5.816	-0.018	-0.737	-0.008	-0.961
BREADWIN	0.070	6.388	0.024	6.958	0.002	0.153	-0.002	-0.425
MONTHEXP	0.000	2.383	0.000	2.294	0.000	3.617	0.000	3.748
MOEXPDUM	-0.103	-6.887	-0.034	-7.236	-0.079	-5.470	-0.028	-5.449
ASOCHI	0.377	12.494	0.129	13.152	0.318	9.906	0.113	10.078
GOVTHI	0.224	7.627	0.083	8.668	0.211	6.640	0.076	6.825
MUTUHI	0.392	11.673	0.132	12.408	0.286	8.631	0.102	8.792
NHI	-0.203	-6.910	-0.079	-8.231	0.013	0.401	0.004	0.403
SIZE1000	0.781	49.536	0.240	50.789	0.987	42.214	0.331	44.747
SIZE500	0.650	30.909	0.211	33.539	0.795	25.589	0.275	27.166
SIZE100	0.611	43.205	0.202	45.746	0.703	45.019	0.247	47.200
SIZE30	0.425	31.656	0.147	33.992	0.510	36.807	0.185	38.638
SIZE5	0.134	10.890	0.046	11.239	0.232	18.350	0.087	19.355
SIZE1	-0.155	-7.067	-0.062	-8.599	-0.037	-1.694	-0.014	-1.782
PUBEMPLY	0.626	26.261	0.196	27.860	0.876	37.464	0.284	38.053
DOCTOR	0.000	0.909	0.000	1.136	-0.000	-0.130	-0.000	-0.028
PROFES	0.016	1.437	0.006	1.753	0.219	15.211	0.076	15.549

	(1)		(2)		(3)		(4)	
ADMINI	0.178	12.870	0.052	12.471	0.086	3.277	0.032	3.479
CLERIC	0.107	8.020	0.031	7.797	0.198	16.254	0.070	16.768
SALES	-0.094	-7.443	-0.033	-8.087	0.008	0.614	0.003	0.769
SERVIC	-0.090	-6.087	-0.031	-6.573	-0.006	-0.439	-0.001	-0.231
SECURI	0.060	1.843	0.024	2.524	0.239	2.879	0.085	2.997
TRANSP	-0.006	-0.351	-0.001	-0.267	0.048	0.770	0.019	0.904
SICKNUMB	0.143	27.225	0.044	27.782	0.133	30.195	0.045	30.249
STRESS	0.058	23.219	0.018	23.564	0.043	21.295	0.015	21.018
NOTVISIT	-0.167	-13.002	-0.054	-13.112	-0.194	-17.241	-0.069	-17.602
HLTHPRAC	0.078	39.020	0.024	39.365	0.083	43.831	0.029	44.264
HLTHEXCE	0.502	39.078	0.168	41.152	0.343	27.765	0.117	27.515
HLTHGOOD	0.579	42.275	0.191	44.302	0.402	31.224	0.138	31.094
HLTHFAIR	0.547	45.932	0.181	47.946	0.382	34.601	0.132	34.558
EDU	-0.629	-6.479	-0.188	-6.220	-0.826	-8.932	-0.290	-9.009
LIFEINSU	-0.000	-3.437	-0.000	-3.396	-0.000	-4.242	-0.000	-4.125
POP1M	-0.036	-2.507	-0.011	-2.600	-0.078	-5.778	-0.028	-5.987
POP150	-0.032	-3.074	-0.010	-3.158	-0.101	-10.391	-0.036	-10.543
POP50	0.066	4.706	0.022	4.922	0.157	12.025	0.055	12.112
POPCUNTY	0.163	15.829	0.053	16.401	0.301	31.205	0.106	31.462
R^2	0.1947		0.1901		0.1553		0.1522	
Log-likelihood	-83,533		-87,652		-96,228		-101,383	
F-statistic	—		714,883		—		566.706	
N	152,255		152,255		157,879		157,879	

Note: All regressions include the eleven regional dummies.

[a] Coefficients are significant at the 1 percent level, 5 percent level, and 10 percent level if the asymptotic t-statistics are greater than 2.576, 1.960, and 1.645, respectively.

timated coefficient on the variable BREADWIN is significantly positive, and the robust effect shows, as previously hypothesized, that the highest earner of a household is more willing to have health checkups to secure against the loss of earnings that would result from becoming ill. From the estimated coefficient on monthly household expenditures (MONTHEXP), we see that the income elasticity of the demand for health checkups is positive.

The individual's type of health insurance coverage is included as the policy variable in the model: ASOCHI, GOVTHI, MUTUHI, and NHI. As expected, the coefficients on the first three variables are positive, while that on NHI is negative. All estimates are statistically significant. Hence, the greater the coverage of medical care, the more likely the individual is to have a health checkup. If health checkups do constitute preventive medical care, individuals having health checkups will be less prone to illness.[23] As of 1995, life expectancy in Japan was 77.01 years for males and 83.59 years for females (Statistics Bureau 1998). The longevity of the Japanese may be attributed to the current health checkup program under the comprehensive health (medical) insurance system.

Normally, firms with a larger number of employees face more restrictions regarding employees' working conditions. Therefore, these firms usually provide more and better fringe benefits compared to firms with fewer employees. In our study, we use SIZE1000 for institutions with 1,000 employees or more, SIZE500 for those with 500–999 employees, SIZE100 for those with 100–499 employees, SIZE30 for those with 30–99 employees, SIZE5 for those with 5–29 employees, SIZE1 for those with 1–5 employees, and PUBEMPLY for public employees.[24] The estimated coefficients on the variables SIZE5 to SIZE1000 are highly significant and positive, as is that of PUBEMPLY. On the other hand, small institutions that fall within SIZE1 have a negative estimated coefficient. These results are indicative of the better working environments provided by larger firms.

We now turn to the effects of the individual's health condition on the demand for health checkups, holding constant the subjective evaluation of own health (HLTHEXCE, HLTHGOOD, and HLTHFAIR). First, the sign of the estimated coefficient on NOTVISIT is negative, while that on HLTHPRAC is positive. The former is a dummy variable that equals 1 if the individual did not visit any medical institutions during the past year. The latter is the number of health-related daily practices in which the individual engages (e.g., eating regular meals; eating low-salt, nutritionally balanced meals; getting adequate physical exercise and adequate hours of sleep; and so on). The signs of these variables conform to expectations. In

---

23. This issue will be discussed further when we present the empirical results on the probability of hospitalization.

24. The omitted dummy variable for firm size indicates the self-employed, family workers, part-time workers, and the unemployed.

other words, an individual with better health (or more health stock) is less likely to have a health checkup. On the other hand, a health-conscious person, that is, an individual who practices health-stock-augmenting activities, tends to have health checkups. For these health-conscious people, having a health checkup is another way of preventing health deterioration.

To evaluate the effect of the psychological burden of being ill, the variables SICKNUMB (the number of injuries and illnesses) and STRESS (the number of stressful events encountered) are included as explanatory variables. We hypothesized in the previous discussion that the psychological burdens of being ill and being in a queue at a hospital will provide incentives for the individual not to become ill. It is thus possible that the individual will go for health checkups to avoid becoming a patient. Both estimated coefficients on SICKNUMB and STRESS are positive and highly significant. The sizes of the coefficients for the twenty-to-sixty-four age group are almost identical to those of the thirty-to-sixty age group, ceteris paribus.

Finally, we examine the estimated coefficients on education (EDU) and life insurance (LIFEINSU). Education is usually considered to be a factor that increases the efficiency of health production. The variable normally has a positive effect on the demand for preventive medical care (Coffey 1983; Kenkel 1994; and Hsieh and Lin 1997, to name only a few). However, according to Grossman (1972), the coefficient on education depends on the elasticity of the MEC schedule, or the demand for health stock. The sign of an individual's education level is negative if the elasticity is less than 1 in absolute value. In this respect, the estimated negative coefficient is not necessarily wrong.[25] The estimated effect of LIFEINSU on the demand for health checkups is negative. That is, an individual with life insurance is less likely to have a health checkup. This result is similar to the canonical story of an individual who buys insurance, but also gambles (see Silberberg 1990, 453). One may also take the view that the significantly negative coefficient reflects the moral hazard inherent in the health checkup decision.

10.5.2   Other Health Checkup Results

This section highlights some results from breakdowns of the sample. Table 10.9 reports gender-specific results for the population aged thirty to sixty, and table 10.10 reports age group–specific results for ages thirty to thirty-nine, forty to forty-nine, and fifty to sixty.

First, concerning the gender-specific results in table 10.9, the age effect (AGE) is much stronger for females (0.090) than for males (0.044). After controlling for all other socioeconomic and demographic factors, females

---

25. However, the definitive sign analysis must await further study using microdata on education, since our survey data do not provide this variable. Therefore, we use a proxy variable (see EDU in table 10.7).

Table 10.10 **Probit Estimates of Health Checkup Probabilities by Age**

Variable	Age 30–39 Probit		Age 40–49 Probit		Age 50–60 Probit	
	Coefficient	t-statistic[a]	Coefficient	t-statistic[a]	Coefficient	t-statistic[a]
C	−1.568	−2.121	−1.364	−1.180	2.690	1.854
MALE	0.187	7.233	−0.016	−0.592	−0.157	−5.983
AGE	0.040	0.940	0.025	0.471	−0.132	−2.484
AGESQ	−0.000	−0.182	−0.000	−0.230	0.001	2.710
MARRIED	0.015	1.335	0.144	11.513	0.161	11.423
WAGE	−0.192	−4.724	−0.041	−1.436	0.017	0.728
BREADWIN	0.105	8.213	0.077	5.809	0.108	7.200
MONTHEXP	0.000	1.248	0.000	2.791	0.000	3.179
MOEXPDUM	−0.063	−3.088	−0.075	−4.397	−0.114	−6.643
ASOCHI	0.155	3.697	0.374	10.478	0.387	10.395
GOVTHI	0.037	0.886	0.262	7.469	0.281	7.732
MUTUHI	0.101	2.325	0.370	9.870	0.353	8.811
NHI	−0.220	−5.257	−0.062	−1.766	0.011	0.302
SIZE1000	1.042	49.837	0.921	47.915	0.834	35.867
SIZE500	0.857	30.132	0.800	29.196	0.671	20.424
SIZE100	0.863	47.605	0.690	42.490	0.589	31.465
SIZE30	0.632	36.406	0.501	33.330	0.432	25.812
SIZE5	0.332	20.545	0.211	15.371	0.135	8.954
SIZE1	−0.052	−1.788	−0.051	−2.137	−0.111	−3.921
PUBEMPLY	0.945	36.809	0.810	32.710	0.690	23.312
DOCTOR	0.000	2.172	0.000	0.238	0.000	−2.697
PROFES	0.157	10.364	0.109	7.850	0.053	3.176
ADMINI	0.259	9.698	0.233	12.349	0.212	11.552
CLERIC	0.215	14.240	0.151	10.708	0.106	5.974
SALES	0.010	0.603	−0.020	−1.420	−0.071	−4.587
SERVIC	−0.038	−1.980	−0.031	−2.009	−0.024	−1.462
SECURI	0.077	1.553	0.173	3.589	0.072	1.227
TRANSP	0.006	0.206	−0.010	−0.396	0.136	4.845
SICKNUMB	0.116	13.779	0.136	22.543	0.145	30.871
STRESS	0.035	12.853	0.049	19.166	0.065	21.517
NOTVISIT	−0.115	−7.001	−0.191	−14.560	−0.227	−15.178
HLTHPRAC	0.059	22.444	0.070	30.617	0.103	45.437
HLTHEXCE	0.307	17.221	0.425	28.466	0.460	31.930
HLTHGOOD	0.355	19.156	0.497	31.449	0.537	35.152
HLTHFAIR	0.345	20.310	0.451	32.998	0.510	40.665
EDU	−0.786	−7.632	−0.747	−8.132	−0.482	−5.057
LIFEINSU	−0.000	−3.053	−0.000	−3.502	−0.000	−3.860
POP1M	−0.049	−2.684	−0.062	−3.829	−0.078	−4.730
POP150	−0.074	−5.550	−0.073	−6.224	−0.065	−5.362
POP50	0.132	7.400	0.110	7.004	0.108	6.669
POPCUNTY	0.229	17.353	0.234	20.253	0.248	20.537
R^2	0.2111		0.1774		0.1566	
Log-likelihood	−51,588.9		−66,409.0		−61,864.5	
N	89,041		114,567		106,526	

Note: All regressions include the eleven regional dummies.

[a]Coefficients are significant at the 1 percent level, 5 percent level, and 10 percent level if the asymptotic t-statistics are greater than 2.576, 1.960, and 1.645, respectively.

are more likely to have health checkups than males as age increases. We are unable to satisfactorily justify why there exists a large difference in the estimates. However, we offer the following explanation. The health stock of a female is, for genetic and biological reasons, larger than that of a male. Ceteris paribus, females need more preventive health care. Therefore, they are more willing to have health checkups as they age.

Another noticeable difference is that the estimated coefficient on MARRIED is positive for males (0.161) and positive but very small for females (0.005). A married male bears more responsibility for his household than does a single unmarried male, and thus he must have health checkups to avoid health loss. The coefficient is not statistically significant for females.

The estimated coefficient on NHI is negative and statistically significant for males but positive and not significant for females. It is highly desirable from a policy perspective to motivate self-employed males, including farmers, to have health checkups. If the government is interested in promoting health checkups as a way to prevent illness, these men could be targeted with incentives.

With regard to the industry dummies, the estimates on SALES and SERVICES are negative and statistically significant for males. Therefore, for the same reasons mentioned for NHI, the government needs to be concerned about the working conditions that prevent employees in these industries from having health checkups. Males in the SALES and SERVICES industries could also be candidates for targeted incentives to encourage check-ups.

Turning to the age group results in table 10.10, the effect of MARRIED is not important for the youngest age group (thirty to thirty-nine) but is a dominant factor for the older groups. On the other hand, WAGE has a negative and significant coefficient for the youngest group, whereas it is negative and insignificant for the forty-to-forty-nine group and positive and insignificant for the fifty-to-sixty group. Therefore, in targeting the thirty-to-thirty-nine group, the high opportunity cost of hours spent to have health checkups must be considered by policymakers, especially for health checkups that take a full day. As mentioned earlier, the effect of NHI is significantly negative for both the thirty-to-thirty-nine and forty-to-forty-nine age groups and should be targeted in the promotion of health checkups. Similarly, those working in firms with four or fewer employees (SIZE1) should also be targeted by policymakers.

The results by type of individual health insurance, shown in table 10.11, reveal that males with ASOCHI, GOVTHI or MUTUHI—that is, those who have 80 percent coverage of medical costs—are more likely to have health checkups than are males with NHI (i.e., those with 70 percent coverage). Thus, medical cost coverage also plays a significant role in the health checkup decision. One may also take the view that those with health insurance other than NHI are more informed about health checkups and consequently have more opportunities to have them. When an individual

Table 10.11   Probit Estimates of Health Checkup Probabilities by Type of Health Insurance Coverage

Variable	ASOCHI Probit		GOVTHI Probit		MUTUHI Probit		NHI Probit	
	Coefficient	t-statistic[a]	Coefficient	t-statistic[a]	Coefficient	t-statistic[a]	Coefficient	t-statistic[a]
C	-3.326	-17.426	-2.582	-17.192	-3.810	-14.546	-1.671	-10.494
MALE	0.293	9.235	0.199	8.798	0.336	7.985	-0.021	-0.890
AGE	0.112	14.879	0.100	16.537	0.147	13.613	0.046	7.057
AGESQ	-0.001	-12.460	-0.001	-13.397	-0.001	-11.691	-0.000	-4.043
MARRIED	0.027	1.600	0.023	1.865	-0.029	-1.062	0.144	12.616
WAGE	-0.266	-9.012	-0.255	-10.714	-0.326	-7.781	-0.179	-7.382
BREADWIN	0.130	7.155	0.051	3.888	0.032	1.243	0.051	4.129
MONTHEXP	0.000	2.816	0.000	1.690	0.000	2.129	0.000	2.450
MOEXPDUM	-0.121	-5.339	-0.151	-8.086	-0.012	-0.333	-0.033	-1.925
SIZE1000	0.817	46.022	0.854	28.187	0.711	16.903	1.177	21.047
SIZE500	0.664	26.879	0.808	27.811	0.404	5.726	0.916	11.809
SIZE100	0.603	31.550	0.729	49.820	0.586	13.624	0.730	19.878
SIZE30	0.388	18.591	0.549	42.170	0.467	10.497	0.396	15.466
SIZE5	0.103	4.600	0.249	20.068	0.193	4.022	0.184	10.950
SIZE1	-0.214	-4.427	-0.091	-3.463	-0.188	-1.880	0.001	0.060
PUBEMPLY	0.692	9.208	0.833	11.668	0.698	25.861	0.618	4.819
DOCTOR	0.000	1.414	0.000	0.577	0.000	-0.646	0.000	1.745
PROFES	0.163	8.644	0.145	9.597	0.226	8.272	0.074	4.548
ADMINI	0.336	13.674	0.215	11.534	0.295	8.687	0.105	3.752
CLERIC	0.228	13.288	0.188	13.454	0.308	10.809	0.017	0.747

	(1)	(2)	(3)	(4)	(5)	(6)	(7)	(8)
SALES	0.151	7.381	-0.026	-1.703	0.139	2.573	-0.096	-6.785
SERVIC	0.070	3.115	-0.031	-1.904	0.195	4.630	-0.075	-4.918
SECURI	0.114	1.419	0.034	0.450	0.241	5.214	0.135	1.340
TRANSP	0.025	0.712	0.001	0.060	0.256	5.260	-0.030	-0.773
SICKNUMB	0.138	17.852	0.135	22.469	0.115	10.093	0.151	27.774
STRESS	0.063	18.830	0.046	16.525	0.054	11.411	0.039	13.991
NOTVISIT	-0.205	-11.197	-0.158	-10.896	-0.180	-6.731	-0.197	-13.393
HLTHPRAC	0.082	27.417	0.078	32.747	0.073	17.388	0.083	35.291
HLTHEXCE	0.535	28.039	0.408	26.103	0.444	16.339	0.343	22.397
HLTHGOOD	0.597	29.909	0.460	27.892	0.556	19.709	0.403	24.721
HLTHFAIR	0.579	33.009	0.449	31.458	0.520	20.788	0.369	26.848
EDU	-0.675	-5.248	-1.002	-10.785	-0.613	-3.760	-0.656	-6.692
LIFEINSU	0.000	1.912	-0.000	-1.449	0.000	1.684	-0.000	-6.191
POP1M	-0.045	-2.465	-0.082	-4.587	-0.058	-1.949	-0.007	-0.377
POP150	-0.051	-3.509	-0.074	-5.980	-0.070	-3.253	-0.081	-6.139
POP50	0.106	4.558	0.131	8.265	0.061	2.132	0.119	7.200
POPCUNTY	0.168	10.613	0.231	19.338	0.157	7.361	0.293	23.647
R^2	0.1810		0.1319		0.1877		0.1000	
Log-likelihood	-39,225.6		-60,556.9		-19,216.9		-58,513.5	
N	73,563		101,066		38,414		93,106	

Note: All regressions include the eleven regional dummies.

[a]Coefficients are significant at the 1 percent level, 5 percent level, and 10 percent level if the asymptotic t-statistics are greater than 2.576, 1.960, and 1.645, respectively.

is the breadwinner (BREADWIN) or the highest income earner in a household, he or she has a higher probability of having a health checkup, regardless of the type of health insurance held. This may arise because of the breadwinner's heavy responsibilities to the household.

People with NHI tend to be self-employed, farmers, part-time workers, professionals such as medical doctors and lawyers, who run their own offices, and the like. The estimates on the variables SIZE1000 to SIZE30 may be somewhat inconsistent in the NHI sample. It must be kept in mind, however, that there are quite a number of people working in large firms on a temporary basis. The statistically significant estimated coefficients for the SIZE variables in this subsample may be explained by the fact that workers in large firms have more opportunities to have checkups, regardless of their insurance coverage. In such cases, people with NHI are probably not using their health insurance to get checkups. Instead, most of the health checkup costs are borne by the employers, who run on-site medical offices. Thus, employees in large firms who are covered by NHI have greater accessibility to medical facilities for health checkups compared to those who are simply covered by NHI.

The estimated coefficient on LIFEINSU for the entire sample, reported in table 10.8, is significantly negative. Table 10.11 reveals, however, that it is significantly positive under ASOCHI (health insurance managed by associations for employees working in relatively large firms) and MUTUHI (Mutual aid associations for public employees and personnel in private schools).

Finally, we examine the demand for health checkups by size of institution, as shown in table 10.12. The sign of each explanatory variable is largely consistent across institution size, but the significance varies widely. On average, the results are more robust in institutions with ninety-nine or fewer employees. This may be due to the fact that employees in relatively small institutions have a greater ability to choose whether to have a health checkup. In other words, small institutions may not be providing adequate opportunities for their employees to obtain checkups, and they are not required to do so by law. Therefore, the health checkup decision is left largely to the employee's discretion.

10.5.3 Results for Patient Hospital Stays

The previous section focused on how individual characteristics affect the demand for health checkups. The regression results revealed that a large number of socioeconomic and demographic variables are significant in the health checkup decision. Here, we extend this analysis to explain the probability of being a patient in a hospital and, if admitted, the length of hospitalization. The dependent variables used in this section are PATIENT (a dummy variable indicating hospitalization) and HOSPITAL (length of

Table 10.12   **Dependent Variable: Health Checkup by Size of Enterprise**

Variable	1000+ Employees Probit		500–999 Employees Probit		100–499 Employees Probit		99 Employees or Less Probit	
	Coefficient	t-statistic[a]	Coefficient	t-statistic[a]	Coefficient	t-statistic[a]	Coefficient	t-statistic[a]
C	-2.039	-4.986	-1.744	-2.848	-1.531	-4.817	-1.106	-11.497
MALE	-0.046	-0.675	0.181	1.919	0.197	4.131	-0.040	-2.197
AGE	0.071	4.354	0.071	2.864	0.062	4.845	0.038	11.967
AGESQ	-0.001	-4.038	-0.001	-2.476	-0.001	-4.296	-0.000	-8.216
MARRIED	0.067	2.324	0.099	2.320	0.091	4.026	0.048	4.797
WAGE	0.008	0.135	-0.153	-1.685	-0.102	-2.119	-0.041	-2.127
BREADWIN	0.181	5.451	0.167	3.603	0.019	0.765	0.070	6.489
MONTHEXP	0.000	1.580	0.000	0.993	0.000	0.670	0.000	1.693
MOEXPDUM	-0.181	-4.332	-0.187	-2.831	-0.164	-4.422	-0.113	-6.291
ASOCHI	0.122	3.881	0.292	5.366	0.220	7.729	0.489	36.968
GOVTHI	-0.062	-1.507	0.181	3.161	0.140	5.158	0.393	39.573
DOCTOR	-0.000	-0.310	-0.000	-0.025	-0.001	-1.388	0.000	0.768
PROFES	0.053	1.756	0.051	1.055	0.084	3.113	0.143	10.760
ADMINI	0.179	4.303	0.118	1.710	0.173	4.098	0.180	6.375
CLERIC	0.104	3.550	0.028	0.621	0.115	4.649	0.104	8.463
SALES	0.073	1.861	0.065	1.099	-0.030	-0.0973	-0.120	-8.634
SERVIC	-0.022	-0.521	-0.011	-0.186	-0.115	-3.813	-0.139	-10.320
SECURI	-0.017	-0.150	-0.432	-2.220	0.091	0.775	0.093	1.368
TRANSP	0.044	0.928	-0.056	-0.672	-0.044	-1.066	0.011	0.523
SICKNUMB	0.130	7.844	0.148	5.678	0.144	10.768	0.131	20.537
STRESS	0.101	13.950	0.066	6.078	0.090	15.391	0.040	14.359
NOTVISIT	-0.162	-4.258	-0.074	-1.314	-0.139	-4.624	-0.119	-8.279

(continued)

Table 10.12   (continued)

Variable	1000+ Employees Probit		500–999 Employees Probit		100–499 Employees Probit		99 Employees or Less Probit	
	Coefficient	t-statistic[a]	Coefficient	t-statistic[a]	Coefficient	t-statistic[a]	Coefficient	t-statistic[a]
HLTHPRAC	0.095	16.261	0.082	8.843	0.087	17.673	0.072	31.265
HLTHEXCE	0.660	18.696	0.663	11.586	0.544	17.836	0.403	26.098
HLTHGOOD	0.758	20.502	0.719	11.900	0.613	18.935	0.447	27.338
HLTHFAIR	0.752	22.793	0.701	13.278	0.592	21.079	0.433	30.011
EDU	-0.626	-2.328	-0.027	-0.067	-0.338	-1.684	-0.826	-9.216
LIFEINSU	0.000	1.255	-0.000	-1.096	-0.000	-0.388	-0.001	-6.929
POP1M	0.018	0.513	-0.070	-1.188	-0.107	-3.141	-0.059	-3.453
POP150	0.004	0.148	0.008	0.174	-0.031	-1.262	-0.057	-4.786
POP50	0.137	2.836	0.068	0.980	0.078	2.322	0.084	5.527
POPCUNTY	0.095	3.096	0.126	2.660	0.130	5.351	0.195	16.948
R^2	0.0844		0.0765		0.0737		0.0959	
Log-likelihood	-10,053.3		-4,092.7		-14,434.2		-66,413.0	
N	24,787		8,589		28,375		104,840	

Note: All regressions include the eleven regional dummies.

[a] Coefficients are significant at the 1 percent level, 5 percent level, and 10 percent level if the asymptotic t-statistics are greater than 2.576, 1.960, and 1.645, respectively.

hospitalization in months).[26] The results shown in table 10.13 are from the second stage of a two-stage least squares (2SLS) regression. There are seven endogenous variables, from CHECKUP through CHEK1. For example, the variable CHEK1000 is the product of CHECKUP and SIZE1000.[27] In the discussion that follows, we focus on the estimated coefficients of these endogenous variables.

First, in the regressions using PATIENT as the dependent variable, the estimated coefficient on CHECKUP is highly significant and negative (−9.014).[28] The product terms are all negative, with CHEK1000, CHEK500, and CHEK5 being statistically significant. Thus, having a health checkup in an institution of one of these sizes reduces the probability of becoming ill and being hospitalized. On the other hand, individuals in institutions from SIZE1000 to SIZE30 who do not have a health checkup have a higher probability of becoming ill. Therefore, if institutions want to reduce their inpatient medical expenditures, they should encourage their employees to have health checkups on a regular basis. However, because the provision of health checkups does entail certain costs, the long-run cost-effectiveness of this policy is unknown.

Second, the effect of health checkups on HOSPITAL (tobit) is similar to that on PATIENT. CHECKUP is highly significant, and the negative sign indicates that individuals who have health checkups experience shorter hospital stays. The estimated coefficients on the product terms are all negative, and they are statistically significant for CHEK1000, CHEK5, and CHEK1. Combined with the positive estimated coefficients on SIZE1000 to SIZE5, these results suggest that, conditional on hospitalization, individuals who do not have health checkups will probably have longer hospital stays. To examine the robustness of the effect of CHECKUP on HOSPITAL, we estimate another HOSPITAL equation that takes into account the selection bias. The results obtained from the bias-corrected regression, HOSPITAL (OLS robust), are qualitatively quite similar to those obtained from HOSPITAL (tobit). The selectivity bias term (the estimated coefficient on the inverse Mills ratio variable) is −0.015 and highly statistically significant. The negative sign of the selectivity bias term indicates that individuals who have health checkups experience shorter lengths of hospitalization, on average, than those who do not.

The bottom of table 10.13 includes several additional statistics com-

26. For brevity, we do not report summary statistics for the independent variables in table 10.13. However, the mean, standard deviation, minimum, and maximum values of PATIENT are 0.005, 0.073, 0, and 1, respectively; for HOSPITAL, they are 3.088, 2.925, 0, and 12, respectively. Patients with hospital stays longer than one year are excluded from the sample. Including all inpatients would mean including an observation with a value of 687 months. The censored sample is more appropriate for this study.

27. The omitted variable under firm size is PUBEMPLY.

28. Since the endogenous variables are all predicted values from the first stage of the probit model for health checkups, the values are neither 0 nor 1, but decimal values.

Table 10.13   Probit, Tobit, and OLS Estimates of Patient Status (2SLS) and Hospital Status (2SLS)

Variable	PATIENT Age 30–60 Probit		HOSPITAL Age 30–60 Tobit		HOSPITAL Age 30–60 OLS (Robust)	
	Coefficient	t-statistic[a]	Coefficient	t-statistic[a]	Coefficient	t-statistic[a]
C	-2.580	-3.833	-26.959	-4.385	0.068	2.697
CHECKUP	-9.014	-23.727	-59.949	-15.021	-0.266	-8.402
CHEK1000	-2.060	-4.342	-13.913	-3.381	-0.091	-2.203
CHEK500	-1.133	-1.827	-8.052	-1.525	-0.006	-0.165
CHEK100	-0.544	-1.272	-2.509	-0.680	-0.037	-1.034
CHEK30	-0.518	-1.192	-4.331	-1.147	-0.014	-0.417
CHEK5	-1.086	-2.327	-7.092	-1.748	0.029	0.940
CHEK1	-1.164	-1.265	-24.867	-2.185	0.088	2.564
SIZE1000	3.339	10.652	22.284	7.816	0.114	3.285
SIZE500	1.992	5.063	13.729	4.039	0.029	0.911
SIZE100	1.445	5.595	8.774	3.841	0.050	1.743
SIZE30	0.630	2.569	4.498	2.103	0.012	0.469
SIZE5	-0.418	-1.789	-2.962	-1.458	-0.046	-1.948
SIZE1	-1.831	-5.973	-9.146	-2.998	-0.108	-4.447
PROFES	0.792	12.922	5.159	8.785	0.016	8.298
ADMINI	1.015	11.968	6.835	8.541	0.021	7.552
CLERIC	1.067	17.684	7.270	12.006	0.022	9.832
SALES	0.008	0.106	-0.422	-0.627	-0.004	-2.114
SERVIC	-0.041	-0.644	-0.635	-1.064	-0.004	-1.848
SECURI	1.318	8.683	8.886	6.457	0.035	4.687
TRANSP	0.394	5.402	3.166	5.023	0.007	2.200

	Coef.	t	Coef.	t	Coef.	t
MALE	0.542	7.716	3.065	4.913	0.006	2.529
AGE	0.186	7.753	1.422	6.327	0.004	5.274
AGESQ	-0.001	-4.219	-0.010	-3.984	-0.000	-2.503
MARRIED	0.213	4.609	1.641	3.845	0.006	3.332
MONTHEXP	0.001	2.923	0.009	2.545	0.000	1.530
MOEXPDUM	-0.368	-5.339	-3.026	-4.528	-0.009	-2.680
DOCTOR	-0.001	-1.100	-0.000	-0.030	-0.000	-0.122
EDU	-1.260	-3.014	-10.773	-2.902	-0.049	-3.259
LIFEINSU	-0.002	-5.454	-0.011	-3.270	-0.000	-2.859
POP1M	-0.290	-4.093	-2.134	-3.261	-0.004	-1.819
POP150	-0.297	-5.589	-1.694	-3.522	-0.004	-2.725
POP50	0.182	2.435	0.856	1.227	0.005	2.939
POPCUNTY	0.871	16.570	6.132	11.660	0.022	9.979
SIGMA	—	—	7.458	24.329	—	—
Inverse Mills ratio	—	—	—	—	-0.015	-15.175
R^2	0.092		—		0.01366	
F-Statistic	—		—		47.9938	
Log-likelihood	-2,938.20		-2,888.69		-8,161.42	
F-statistic, instrumented regression	1,545.66 (d.f. = 15,310081)		—		—	
Basmann F-Statistic	641.72 (d.f. = 8,156300)		129.86 (d.f. = 8,155942)		—	
Hausman Chi-square statistic	12,669.05 (d.f. = 8)		9,789.87 (d.f. = 8)		—	
Hausman F-Statistic	2,188.48 (d.f. = 7,156307)		243.53 (d.f. = 7,155949)		—	
N	156,352		155,994		155,994	

Note: All regressions include the eleven regional dummies.

[a] Coefficients are significant at the 1 percent level, 5 percent level, and 10 percent level if the asymptotic *t*-statistics are greater than 2.576, 1.960, and 1.645, respectively.

puted for these models. In the reduced form equation to estimate CHECKUP,[29] there are fifty-two instruments in total, thirty-seven of which (including the eleven regional dummies and the seven endogenous variables) are included in the structural model of PATIENT. Therefore, there are fifteen predetermined variables that do not appear in the structural model; health-related variables such as SICKNUMB to HLTHFAIR are excluded from the PATIENT model because their inclusion in the second stage would make the estimation singular.[30] The F-ratio (instrument) for the fifteen instruments under PATIENT is 1545.66 with d.f. = (15, 310081), which indicates that the instruments as a set are statistically significant.

Next, we test for the validity and relevance of the instruments. We use two types of tests: the Basmann test (1960) and the Hausman test (1983, 433). The regression results reported in table 10.13 pertain to employees working in establishments classified as SIZE1000 to SIZE1 or PUBEMPLY, with a sample size of 156,352. The statistics are Basmann F-ratio = 641.72 (d.f. = 8, 156300) and Hausman Chi-square = 12669.05 (d.f. = 8), both of which are statistically significant.[31] Hence, the fifteen omitted instruments are statistically valid in the first-stage estimation of health checkups.[32]

Finally, we test the exogeneity of the seven endogenous variables, CHECKUP to CHEK1, and determine whether they belong in the structural PATIENT model.[33] The Hausman F-ratio = 2188.48 (d.f. = 7, 156307) rejects the null hypothesis to exclude. The Hausman F-ratio = 243.53 (d.f. = 7, 155949) is also statistically significant for the HOSPITAL model.

To summarize, health checkups (CHECKUP) play an important role in both the PATIENT (the probability of being an inpatient) and HOSPITAL (the length of stay in hospital) models. An individual who undergoes health checkups has a much lower risk of being hospitalized than one who does not. Furthermore, hospital stays are shorter for individuals who have the checkups.

29. The sample size is 310,134 in the first stage, as shown for age thirty to sixty in table 10.8.

30. If the omitted variables are significantly correlated with other independent variables, there may be omitted variables bias. However, we are more concerned with the effects of the endogenous variables on the dependent variable PATIENT. By definition, the estimated values of endogenous variables are orthogonal to the residuals.

31. The degrees of freedom (8, 156300) for Basmann's test is obtained using the following formula: The numerator (i.e., 8) is the total number of excluded predetermined variables from the second-stage estimation (the PATIENT equation), minus the number of endogenous variables (i.e., 15 − 7), and the denominator (i.e., 156300) is the total number of observations in the second-stage estimation minus the total number of predetermined variables in the first-stage estimation (i.e., 156352 − 52).

32. The same processes are also applied to the estimation of the HOSPITAL equation in table 10.13.

33. This procedure is explained in Gujarati (1995, 672–73).

Table 10.14   **Marginal Effects of Health Checkups on Patient Status (Probit) and Hospital Status (Tobit)**

Variable	PATIENT Age 30–60 Probit	HOSPITAL Age 30–60 Tobit
CHECKUP	–0.084	–0.048
CHEK1000	–0.019	–0.011
CHEK500	–0.011	–0.006
CHEK100	–0.005	–0.002
CHEK30	–0.005	–0.003
CHEK5	–0.010	–0.006
CHEK1	–0.011	–0.020

Note: Results are from table 10.13.

10.5.4   The Marginal Effects of Health Checkups on the PATIENT and HOSPITAL Models

The marginal effects of a health checkup (CHECKUP) on PATIENT and HOSPITAL are reported in table 10.14. The marginal effect of a health checkup on PATIENT is –0.084, whereas that on HOSPITAL is –0.048.

The –0.084 value indicates that a 10 percentage point increase in the prevalence of health checkups (CHECKUP) will decrease the probability of hospitalization by 0.84 percentage points. This effect is averaged over all individuals aged thirty to sixty. In addition to this basic effect, if the individual is an employee in a firm of SIZE1000, SIZE500, or SIZE5, there is an additional reduction in the probability of hospitalization of 0.1 to 0.2 percentage points for a ten-percentage point change in CHECKUP.[34] In other words, the probability of hospitalization is 1 percent lower for an individual who has had a health checkup.[35] At first glance, this may appear to be a negligible value, but from the standpoint of a typical firm, one out of every 100 employees may avoid hospitalization.

The marginal effect of health checkups (CHECKUP) on HOSPITAL is –0.048. This implies a reduction in hospitalization of about 0.15 months for an individual aged thirty to sixty who stayed in the hospital less than one year.[36] The coefficients on the product terms, CHEK1000 through CHEK1, are all negative. The marginal effects of CHEK1000, CHEK5, and CHEK1 are statistically significant (see table 10.13). For example, the –0.011 on CHEK1000 is equivalent to a reduction in the length of hospital stay of about 0.03 months (0.011×3.1 months), or about one day.

---

34. The estimated coefficients of CHECK1000, CHECK500, and CHECK5 are statistically significant, as shown in table 10.13.

35. Here, the interpretation is in terms of percents rather than percentage points because the original value of CHECKUP in the reduced-form equation is either 1 or 0.

36. The average length of hospital stay is about 3.1 months for persons aged thirty to sixty who stayed in the hospital less than one year. The 0.15 month figure (4.5 days per month) is obtained by multiplying 0.048 by 3.1.

These reductions are substantial in light of hospital costs, opportunity costs, and psychological costs. Consider employed survey respondents who were hospitalized in May 1995 as an example. The average monthly out-of-pocket cost for individuals aged thirty to sixty is about $420 ($1 = 100 yen). Average monthly out-of-pocket cost for individuals aged thirty to sixty is approximately $1,100.[37] Since these individuals are employees in firms, they must be covered by health insurance managed by associations or health insurance managed by the government. Thus, the costs paid by the individuals reflect only 20 percent of total hospital costs. The other 80 percent is borne by the Social Insurance Medical Care Fee Payment Fund. Therefore, total hospital costs must be about $2,100 per month or $5,500 per month for thirty- to fifty-year-olds and thirty- to sixty-year-olds, respectively.

The reduction in the length of hospital stay due to health checkups translates into a reduction in hospital costs. On an individual basis, the reduction in hospitalization by 0.15 months, or 0.18 (= 0.15 + 0.03) months when firm size is taken into account, reduces hospital expenditures by $315 ($2,100 × 0.15) per case for a hospitalized individual aged thirty to fifty and $825 ($5,500 × 0.15) per case for a hospitalized individual aged thirty to sixty. About $70 to $190 may be added to these figures if the effect of the product term of health checkup and firm size, CHEK1000, is taken into consideration.[38]

In comparison to these costs, a thorough, in-hospital medical examination (i.e., a health checkup) costs only $365 (see section 10.2). Furthermore, an individual's out-of-pocket expenses for additional tests are minimal due to local government subsidies. These figures suggest that health checkups are highly cost-effective in the long run. Therefore, health checkups should be widely encouraged as a method of illness prevention.

10.6 Summary and Conclusion

This study investigates the demand for health checkups among the working population in Japan. According to the *1995 National Survey of Life* (Statistics and Information 1998), the health checkup rate of the twenty- to sixty-four-year-old population is about 56 percent. The analysis

37. The averages are from costs paid by individuals who were hospitalized during the month of May 1995. In terms of Japanese yen, the values are about 41,600 yen for individuals aged thirty to fifty and about 111,200 yen for those aged thirty to sixty.

38. The marginal effect of the product term of health checkup and firm size, CHEK1000, is –0.011. Therefore, savings can be calculated as $72 = (0.011 × 3.1 months × $2,100 per month) for thirty- to fifty-year-olds, and $188 = (0.011 × 3.1 months × $5,500 per month) for thirty- to sixty-year-olds. Patients with hospital stays longer than one year are excluded from the sample. Inclusion of all inpatients would mean including an observation with a value of 687 months. The censored sample is more appropriate for this study.

focuses on the thirty-to-sixty age group for two reasons: first, this age group is more homogeneous than the twenty-to-sixty-four age group; second, sixty is generally the retirement age for employees in Japan. The empirical results have direct policy implications for the prevention of illness among the working population. These results pinpoint specific policies that firms can implement to improve employee health and help contain growing medical expenditures.

The individual's health checkup decision is explored using a probit model, which is estimated separately by age group, gender, type of health insurance, and firm size. The major explanatory variables of interest include age, gender, wage rate, health insurance coverage, affiliated firm size, and objective evaluations of the individual's health condition. We also examine the effects of an individual's health checkup status on his or her probability of hospitalization and the subsequent length of hospital stay.

Most of the estimated coefficients of the aforementioned variables have the theoretically predicted signs and are highly significant determinants of the demand for health checkups. The estimated coefficients on age and age-squared are positive and negative, respectively, reflecting that the incentive to have a health checkup increases at a diminishing rate with stock of health. Because stock of health increases with age, as does earning ability, the incentives for having a health checkup also increase. Gender also plays an important role in the individual's decision to have a health checkup. Due to genetic and biological differences, males are more likely to have health checkups than females.

A health checkup is a time-consuming health input. For this reason, the opportunity cost of work hours or days is a major determinant of the health checkup decision. The sign of the individual's wage rate is negative and highly significant in the probit models, and the magnitude is largest for the thirty-to-thirty-nine age group. Given the negative effect of NHI on health checkup rates, the positive and significant effects of health insurance managed by associations, health insurance managed by the government, and mutual aid associations insurance reveal that individuals are more willing to have checkups when coverage is more generous. Furthermore, larger enterprises do more to encourage their employees to get health checkups than do smaller enterprises. Thus, in order to promote health checkups among employees and consequently in the population as a whole, a public policy that lowers the opportunity cost of health checkups for targeted groups of working people is desirable.

The estimated coefficients on the individual's objective health conditions are statistically robust. The more illness (and stress) an individual faces, the more likely he is to have a health checkup. On the other hand, if an individual has not visited clinics or hospitals for the past year, which we take to reflect a higher stock of health, he is less likely to have a health checkup, ceteris paribus. Therefore, promoting individuals' health stock, by providing better working conditions and reducing work stress, for instance, may help to contain the increase in medical expenditures.

In the short run, health checkups increase medical expenditures. These expenditures are offset, however, by reductions in the incidence and duration of hospitalization. Using 2SLS on the sample data, we find a significantly negative and robust health checkup effect on these measures. In other words, an individual who has had a health checkup has a much lower risk of being hospitalized than one who has not. Furthermore, if this individual is hospitalized, he is likely to have a shorter hospital stay. Thus, in the long run, checkups will reduce not only monetary expenditures but also psychological burdens associated with illness and hospitalization.

The point estimate of the effect of health checkups on the probability of hospitalization suggests that a 10 percentage point increase in the health checkup rate will reduce the probability of hospitalization by 0.8 percentage points. This is the base effect of an individual health checkup; the effect varies by firm size, and one important finding is that checkups may prevent hospitalization for one out of every 100 employees in large firms.

As for length of hospital stay, a 1 percentage point increase in the health checkup rate reduces stays by 0.15 months per year for the thirty-to-sixty age group. Adding in the effects associated with firm size reduces the average stay by an additional 0.03 months. Without the firm-size effects, these reductions translate into cost savings of $315 for individuals aged thirty to fifty and $825 for individuals aged thirty to sixty. The firm-size effects reduce costs further by $70 to $190 per month. These approximate monetary calculations are based solely on hospital costs paid by both the individual and the health insurance agency. If psychological and opportunity costs were incorporated into this analysis, total benefits would far surpass monetary savings.

To conclude, this paper finds that health checkups constitute a highly cost-effective means of illness prevention within the context of the current comprehensive system of national health care. We must increase the relatively low health checkup rate of 56 percent in the twenty-to-sixty-four-year-old population, if only because good health is, by itself, of great value.

Appendix

$$\{[1 - \pi(A)]U_{xx} + \pi(A)U_{yy}[1 + \pi_h^*L(A, H)]\) < 0.$$

From the first-order optimal condition of equation (11), we have

$$-[1 + \pi_h^*L(A, H)] = \frac{[1 - \pi(A)]U_x(x)}{\pi(A)U_y(y)}.$$

Since the right-side of the above equation shows the slope of the indifference curve (Ehrlich and Becker 1972, 626), we can express this as follows:

$$\text{MRS} = -\frac{[1 - \pi(A)]U_x(x)}{\pi(A)U_y(y)}.$$

By partially differentiating the optimal condition with respect to P, the results are found to be

$$\frac{\partial \text{MRS}}{\partial P} = -\frac{1}{[\pi(A)U_y(y)]^2}\{\pi(A)U_y(y)[1 - \pi(A)]U_{xx}$$

$$- [1 - \pi(A)]U_x\pi(A)U_{yy}\} > 0,$$

which implies

$$\left\{[1 - \pi(A)]U_{xx} - \frac{[1 - \pi(A)]U_x}{\pi(A)U_y(y)}\pi(A)U_{yy}\right\} < 0.$$

This is also expressed as

$$\{[1 - \pi(A)]U_{xx} + [1 + \pi_h^*L(A, H)]\pi(A)U_{yy}\} < 0.$$

Thus, we obtain

$$\{[1 - \pi(A)]U_{xx} + \pi(A)U_{yy}[1 + \pi_h^*L(A, H)]\} < 0.$$

References

Arrow, Kenneth J. 1963. Uncertainty and the welfare economics of medical care. *American Economic Review* 53 (5): 941–73.

Basmann, R. L. 1960. On finite sample distributions of generalized classical linear identifiability test statistics. *Journal of the American Statistical Association* 55 (289–92): 650–9.

Becker, Gary S., ed. 1976. A theory of the allocation of time. In *The economic approach to human behavior*, 89–114. Chicago: University of Chicago Press.

Coffey, Rosanna M. 1983. The effect of time price on the demand for medical-care services. *Journal of Human Resources* 18 (3): 407–24.

Ehrlich, Isaac, and Gary S. Becker. 1972. Market insurance, self-insurance, and self-protection. *Journal of Political Economy* 80 (4): 623–48.

Greene, William H. 2000. *Econometric analysis*. 4th ed. Upper Saddle River, N.J.: Prentice-Hall.

Grossman, Michael. 1972. On the concept of health capital and the demand for health. *Journal of Political Economy* 80 (2): 223–55.

———. 2000. The human capital model of the demand for health. In *Handbook of health economics*, vol. 14, ed. A. J. Culyer and J. P. Newhouse, 347–408. Amsterdam: Elsevier Science.

Gujarati, Damodar N. 1995. *Basic econometrics*. 3rd ed. New York: McGraw-Hill.

Hausman, Jerry A. 1983. Specification and estimation of simultaneous equation models. In *Handbook of econometrics*, vol. 1, ed. Zvi Griliches and Michael D. Intriligator, 391–448. Amsterdam: North-Holland Publishing.

Health and Welfare Statistics Association. 1999. *Movements in national sanitation* (Kokumin eisei no doko). Tokyo: Health and Welfare Statistics Association.

———. 2001. *Movements in health insurance and social security* (Hoken to nenkin no doko). Tokyo: Health and Welfare Statistics Association.

Hsieh, Chee-ruey, and Shin-jong Lin. 1997. Health information and the demand for preventive care among the elderly in Taiwan. *Journal of Human Resources* 32 (2): 308–33.

Institute of Labor Administration. 1998. Situations of fringe benefits (Fukuri kosei jijou). Tokyo: Institute of Labor Administration.

Kenkel, Donald S. 1990. Consumer health information and the demand for medical care. *Review of Economics and Statistics* 72 (3): 587–95.

———. 1991. Health behavior, health knowledge, and schooling. *Journal of Political Economy* 99 (2): 287–305.

———. 1994. The demand for preventive medical care. *Applied Economics* 26 (4): 313–25.

Organization for Economic Cooperation and Development (OECD). 1998. *Organization for economic co-operation and development health data 1998* (CD-ROM). Paris: OECD.

Pauly, Mark V. 1989. Overinsurance and public provision of insurance: The roles of moral hazard and adverse selection. In *Uncertainty in economics: Readings and exercises,* ed. Peter Diamond and Michael Rothschild, 44–54. London: Academic Press.

Phelps, Charles E., and Joseph P. Newhouse. 1974. Coinsurance, the price of time, and the demand for medical services. *Review of Economics and Statistics* 56 (3): 334–42.

Silberberg, Eugene. 1990. *The structure of economics: A mathematical analysis.* 2nd ed. New York: McGraw-Hill.

Social Insurance Agency, Government of Japan. 1999. *Outline of social insurance in Japan 1998.* Tokyo: Japan International Social Security Association.

———. 2001. *Outline of social insurance in Japan 2000.* Tokyo: Japan International Social Security Association.

Statistics Bureau, Management and Coordination Agency, Government of Japan. 1998. *Japan statistical yearbook 1999.* 48th ed. Tokyo: Japan Statistical Association.

Statistics and Information, Ministry of Health and Welfare, Government of Japan. 1998. *1995 National Survey of Life* (Kokumin seikatsu kiso chosa) in ASCII data file [data disk]. Tokyo: Government of Japan.

The Role of Firms in Welfare Provision

Toshiaki Tachibanaki

11.1 Introduction

Firms support welfare provision in various ways. First, firms help finance social security benefits by contributing to social insurance programs, such as public pensions, unemployment compensation, and medical care. Second, firms organize and manage their own systems of welfare provision for their employees. Typical examples are enterprise pensions (or occupational pensions) and health insurance systems. Third, firms provide their employees with housing services and other nonstatutory welfare services directly. The third form is typically observed in large Japanese firms.

The distinction between direct and indirect methods of welfare provision is particularly important. An indirect method implies that firms contribute to both employees and citizens who are anonymous from the firm's point of view. An example is a social insurance system, where firms are unable to identify who the actual beneficiaries are. Firms simply contribute to a social insurance fund. Of course, employees also contribute to social insurance systems. A direct method implies that firms contribute directly and exclusively to their own employees. Thus, firms can identify the actual beneficiaries of the welfare provision because they support only their employees. Typical examples are enterprise pensions, health insurance systems, and housing services. An interesting question is whether such direct and indirect methods have different effects on workers' behavior, welfare systems' management, or firms' economic performance.

In principle, there are three groups that finance welfare provision. They are (a) fellow citizens, like employees and the self-employed; (b) firms; and

Toshiaki Tachibanaki is professor of economics at the Faculty of Economics, Kyoto University.

Toshiaki Tachibanaki

(c) the public sector (i.e., general tax revenues). Fellow citizens and firms can contribute in various ways, as indicated previously for firms. The public sector can also contribute in various ways. Some countries, like Denmark, rely largely on general tax revenues to provide welfare services, whereas other countries, like Japan and the United States, do not rely heavily on general tax revenues. Why are there differences across countries?

11.2 International Comparisons

It is useful to review current international methods for providing social and welfare services, and in particular how welfare services are provided by the public sector. In other words, what is the magnitude of welfare provision, and the distribution of taxes or social security contributions to support it, in each country? Tables 11.1 and 11.2 present social expenditures and tax revenue and social security contribution rates, respectively, for several advanced countries. I focus largely on Japan and the United States. The statistics in these tables are shown as percentage shares of gross domestic product (GDP).

The tables highlight a remarkable fact: Japan and the United States have the lowest shares of social expenditure and the lowest burden of taxes and social security contributions among the advanced countries, suggesting that the public sector does not provide a large amount of welfare services. The rates of social expenditure in Japan and the United States in 1993 were

Table 11.1   **Social Expenditures (% GDP)**

	1980	1985	1990	1993	1994
Austria	22.3	24.0	23.6	25.6	n.a.
Belgium	25.4	28.2	26.4	27.2	n.a.
Denmark	27.6	26.5	28.2	31.0	n.a.
Finland	18.9	23.5	25.3	34.8	34.1
France	23.5	27.0	26.0	28.7	n.a.
Germany	25.8	26.5	24.8	29.8	n.a.
Greece	10.8	16.2	17.1	16.9	n.a.
Ireland	19.7	23.3	19.3	21.3	20.7
Italy	18.4	21.7	23.1	25.0	n.a.
Luxembourg	24.8	24.6	23.9	25.3	n.a.
The Netherlands	28.5	28.9	29.2	30.5	n.a.
Portugal	11.6	11.9	14.4	17.5	n.a.
Spain	16.5	18.7	19.8	22.5	n.a.
Sweden	28.9	30.4	31.6	37.5	n.a.
United Kingdom	18.7	21.5	20.2	24.0	n.a.
United States	12.7	12.9	13.8	15.3	n.a.
Japan	10.2	11.3	11.2	12.5	13.0

Source: OECD (1998).

Note: n.a. = not available

Table 11.2   Tax Revenue and Social Security Contribution Rates (% GDP)

	Gross Revenues			Personal Income Tax			Social Security						Other Taxes		
							Employee			Employer					
	1991	1993	1995	1991	1993	1995	1991	1993	1995	1991	1993	1995	1991	1993	1995
Austria	41	43	42	9	9	9	6	6	7	7	7	7	20	21	20
Belgium	45	45	46	14	14	15	5	5	5	10	10	9	16	17	17
Denmark	49	50	51	26	26	28	1	1	1	n.a.	n.a.	n.a.	21	22	22
Finland	45	47	46	17	16	16	0	1	2	11	10	10	19	18	18
France	44	44	45	6	6	6	6	6	6	12	12	12	20	20	21
Germany	38	39	39	10	11	11	6	7	7	8	8	8	14	14	14
Greece	38	40	41	5	4	5	5	6	7	8	8	8	14	14	14
Ireland	35	35	34	11	11	10	2	2	2	3	3	3	19	19	19
Italy	40	44	41	10	12	11	3	3	3	9	9	9	17	20	19
Luxembourg	43	44	44	9	9	9	5	5	5	6	6	5	23	24	24
The Netherlands	47	47	44	12	12	8	11	11	12	3	3	3	20	21	21
Portugal	32	31	34	6	6	6	3	3	3	5	5	5	18	17	19
Spain	35	35	34	8	8	8	2	2	2	9	9	8	16	15	15
Sweden	54	50	50	18	18	18	n.a.	1	2	15	13	12	21	18	18
United Kingdom	36	33	35	10	9	10	2	2	3	4	3	3	19	18	20
United States	27	27	28	10	10	10	3	3	3	4	4	4	10	11	11
Japan	31	29	29	8	7	6	4	4	4	5	5	5	14	13	13

Source: OECD (1997).

Note: n.a. = not available

12.5 percent and 15.3 percent, respectively, much lower than the rate of the average European country. The rates of government revenue for both countries were below 30 percent in 1993, again much lower than the average rate among European countries. The public sector in Japan and the United States does not play an important role in welfare provision.

Very high shares of social expenditure, tax revenues, and social security contributions are observed in Scandinavian countries like Denmark, Finland, and Sweden, which are known as welfare states. The public sector plays a very important welfare provision role in these countries. Tables 11.1 and 11.2 suggest that both Japan and the United States are representative examples of nonwelfare states.

Tachibanaki (2000b) provides an extensive discussion of the reasons why Japan is a nonwelfare state. The paper emphasizes the roles of both family and firms in welfare provision, which diminish the role of the public sector. Rein (1996) stresses that focusing only on the state leads to an underestimate of the level of social protection in society, suggesting that the United States is not the exceptional case of a welfare laggard. Welfare is provided not only by the public sector in the United States, but also by individuals and enterprises, as represented by health insurance programs and enterprise pension systems.

Scandinavian countries are the other extreme because they are welfare states, with welfare levels much higher than that of the United States. Also, the income distribution is much more equal in Scandinavia, for the following two reasons: First, pretransfer income is more equally distributed. Second, a stronger redistributive policy through tax and social security systems is in place. Freeman, Topel, and Swedenborg (1997) have published an interesting book about the difference between the American and Swedish views on the welfare state.

What is the role of firms in welfare provision? Figure 11.1 presents a time series of the contributions of firms to social security. Figure 11.2 presents the shares of social security funding, including those of beneficiaries' contributions and tax revenues, for several countries. These figures were published by Katsumata and Morita (1999) and Katsumata (2000).

They show several interesting results regarding the role of firms in welfare provision. First, both Sweden and France have very high rates of contributions by firms. About two-thirds of total social security costs are borne by firms in Sweden, and about half in France. It is interesting to note that Denmark, which is one of the welfare states, is quite different from Sweden. The role of the firm is very minor in Denmark: Seventy percent of social security financing comes from general tax revenues. Thus, there are differences even within Scandinavia regarding the financial sources of welfare provision.

Second, the firm contribution shares for Germany, Japan, the United Kingdom, and the United States look similar, ranging from 20 to 30 per-

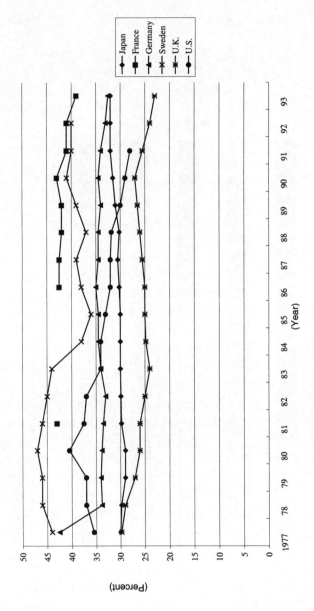

Fig. 11.1 Share of social security costs borne by firms (%)

Source: Katsumata and Morita (1999)

Note: A firm's share of social security costs is the ratio of the firm's contributions to total social security costs.

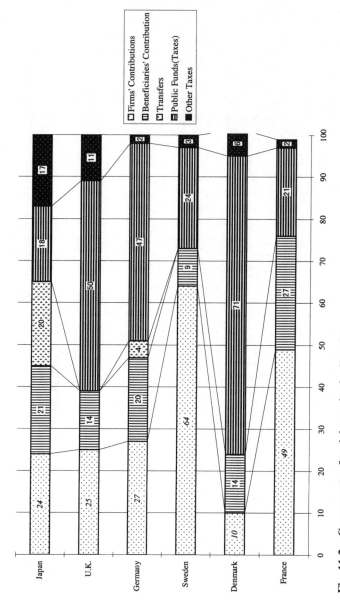

Fig. 11.2 Components of social security funding (%)

Source: Katsumata (2000)

cent. The contributions of firms to welfare provision are modest in these countries. If we rank these countries according to the role of firms, Germany ranks highest, followed by the United Kingdom, Japan, and the United States. It is again striking that both Japan and the United States are at the bottom for this measure.

Despite the fact that firm contributions to welfare provision play a minor role in both Japan and the United States, there are differences between the two countries. Japanese firms, in particular larger firms, make fairly significant contributions in the form of nonstatutory fringe benefits. American firms contribute to enterprise pensions and health insurance systems that are not managed by the public sector. The Japanese nonstatutory fringe benefit system will be discussed below.

Third, it is necessary to understand why several European countries like France, Germany, and Sweden have high rates of firm contributions to social security. For Germany, it is widely known that the Bismarckian social insurance system encouraged firms to contribute to social security along with workers in order to enhance worker productivity. This is sometimes called a carrot-and-stick policy, and it led the Prussian society and economy into the Industrial Revolution. It is the origin of a social policy that was popular both before and after World War II. It is ironic that German social policy was applauded by the Marxist school of economics in this period in Japan. It has, to a certain extent, dominated Japan's labor and social security policy during the postwar period. It is not an exaggeration to say that welfare policy in Japan followed the tradition of social policy in Germany and that this is still reflected in the current system, although there have been modifications.

For France, there are two possible explanations. First, there is a tradition of social insurance systems that are delineated by occupation, firm, or both. Each occupational group or firm has its own separate social insurance system. In such a case, firms are normally willing to contribute more to employees because they can expect high employee motivation in return. Second, the French trade union movement has been fairly strong, and thus it has had a strong voice to use against employers during the postwar period. It is not surprising that firms have to accept a high share of social insurance costs under such circumstances. It is, nevertheless, necessary to take into consideration the incidence of firms' contributions to social insurance in France in order to draw a clear conclusion concerning the above two forces.

For Sweden, a story similar to that of France can be applied to explain the high contributions of firms. Trade unions, in particular blue-collar unions, have been fairly powerful. Additionally, the welfare state has received wide support. Thus, all economic agents, including firms, have been willing to contribute to welfare provision.

11.3 Japan

Having examined international statistics, my next task is to evaluate the contribution of firms to welfare provision in Japan. There are basically four important components of firms' contributions to welfare. The first is statutory contributions to social security, which account for about 50 percent of nonwage labor payments. The second is nonstatutory fringe benefits. The third is retirement allowances (or severance payments). The residual fourth is the sum of payments toward real goods, expenditures on education and training for employees, hiring costs, and so forth.

Table 11.3 shows the share of each component as a fraction of total labor costs. The largest share is that of statutory contributions to social security, about 8 to 10 percent. The second largest share is accounted for by severance payments, and the third is due to nonstatutory fringe benefits. Table 11.3 reveals significant differences in nonwage payments by firm size. This is particularly true in the case of retirement allowances (severance payments) and nonstatutory fringe benefits, whereas there is no difference in statutory contributions to social security. The differences in severance payments and nonstatutory fringe benefits can be explained by the "ability to pay" hypothesis: Larger firms are able to offer higher severance payments and nonstatutory fringe benefits than smaller firms, due to their extra revenues. This is probably the most salient feature about firms' contributions to welfare provision in Japan.

How large are the differences by firm size? Table 11.4 gives the answer. First, the largest difference is for housing payments. Larger firms have their own housing facilities for married households and dormitories for singles. Employees can live in these facilities and pay very low rents because they are heavily subsidized by the firms. The higher payments for housing by larger firms reflect the amounts of the subsidies and the purchase costs of these houses and dormitories. Overall, expenditures on housing account for over 46 percent of nonstatutory fringe benefits. This is by far the highest share of any component of these benefits. However, this share varies substantially by firm size. Firms with over 5,000 employees pay an average of 23,600 yen per month, per employee, whereas firms with thirty to ninety-nine employees pay only 6,900 yen per month per employee. Therefore, the payments per employee by large firms are about 3.4 times those by small firms. Payments are probably near zero for the smallest firms, but there are no data with which to confirm this conjecture.

Second, table 11.4 suggests that firms in Japan pay amazingly varied types of fringe benefits, including payments for cultural and athletic facilities, congratulations and condolences, food, and so on. These payments are sometimes called East Asian types of fringe benefits.

The results in tables 11.3 and 11.4 document extraordinary differences in welfare provision by firm size. This is particularly true for severance pay-

Table 11.3   **Components of Nonwage Labor Costs**

Firm Size	Total[a]		Real Goods %	Severance Payments %	Statutory Costs %	Nonstatutory Costs %	Education & Training %	Hiring Costs %	Other %
	Yen	%							
Total	82,360	17.1	0.5	4.3	8.9	2.8	0.3	0.2	0.2
Over 5,000	116,949	19.0	0.6	5.6	8.4	3.8	0.3	0.1	0.2
1,000–4,999	92,531	17.5	0.4	4.5	8.4	3.3	0.3	0.2	0.3
300–999	76,743	16.5	0.5	3.9	9.0	2.4	0.3	0.2	0.4
100–299	64,627	15.6	0.3	3.5	9.3	2.0	0.2	0.2	0.1
30–99	57,710	15.2	0.3	2.8	9.8	1.8	0.2	0.1	0.1

Source: Ministry of Labor (1997).

[a]Per month, per employee.

Table 11.4 **Components of Nonstatutory Fringe Benefits (%)**

			Firm Size			
	Total	5,000+	1,000–4,999	300–999	100–299	30–99
Total	100.0	100.0	100.0	100.0	100.0	100.0
Housing	46.3	49.6	54.1	51.8	33.8	19.4
Medical insurance	5.6	7.9	4.7	3.5	4.7	3.3
Food	10.6	9.8	9.4	10.4	12.7	14.8
Culture and athletics	8.6	8.1	7.1	7.8	9.9	14.1
Private insurance	8.4	3.2	6.8	9.3	14.6	22.5
Additional casualty payments	1.7	0.4	0.6	2.1	3.9	5.8
Congratulations and condolences	3.4	2.7	3.7	3.2	4.0	4.8
Aid to savings	3.9	6.0	3.3	3.1	2.4	1.3
Other	11.6	12.3	10.3	8.7	13.9	13.9
Amount per month per employee (yen)	13,682	23,601	17,439	11,317	8,069	6,907

Source: Ministry of Labor (1997).

Table 11.5 **Components of Statutory Social Insurance Contributions by Firms**

	Percentage of Contribution
Health insurance	32.1
Public pension	52.7
Labor insurance	14.2
Unemployment	7.0
Labor casualty	7.2
Child allowance	0.7
Other	0.4
Total	100.0

Source: Ministry of Labor (1997).

ments and nonstatutory fringe benefits. Tachibanaki (1996), Tachibanaki and Taki (2000), and Tachibanaki and Noda (2000) discuss the dual structure of the Japanese labor market, which implies a significant difference in wages, productivity, employment stability, union behavior, and the like by firm size. Severance payments and nonstatutory fringe benefits are no exceptions to this dual structure.

Table 11.5 shows how firms' statutory contributions to social security are distributed. The highest share, nearly 53 percent, is paid to public pension programs. An additional 32 percent is contributed to health insurance, and 14 percent goes to unemployment insurance and labor casualty insurance. Historically, the role of unemployment compensation has been minor, due to the low rate of unemployment. This is no longer true in light of the fact that the unemployment rate reached over 5 percent in 2003. Nevertheless, public pensions and health insurance account for the vast majority of firms' contributions to social security.

11.4 Theory

This section presents economic theories to explain the considerably high share of nonwage payments, particularly nonstatutory fringe benefits.

It is crucial to understand that a large part of fringe benefits, such as payments to private retirement systems (including severance payments), life insurance systems, health benefits, and other agreed-upon plans, are *deferred* compensation. The intrinsic nature of deferred compensation is the main reason for both employers' and employees' preferences for fringe benefits, although factors that are not associated with deferred payments must also be examined.

Rice (1966) gives four factors for explaining the growth of fringe benefits in the United States: (a) preferential treatment under federal personal income tax laws; (b) savings that are made possible by group purchase of some benefits, notably insurance; (c) efforts to reduce turnover in the face of rising costs of labor turnover; and (d) unionization. Woodbury (1983) adds three factors: (e) preferential treatment under federal corporate income taxes, since contributions by employers to pension funds and insurance benefits are largely deductible from employers' taxable income; (f) the changing age composition of the labor force; and (g) the effect of rising income. Hart (1984) provides a useful survey of these results for the 1960s to early 1980s and analyzes nonwage labor costs.

These factors have been scrutinized recently in an attempt to interpret the rationales behind the payment of fringe benefits, and new factors have been added. I summarize them under the following five headings: (a) agency theory; (b) tax advantage theory; (c) worker preference; (d) cost savings apart from tax advantages; and (e) better industrial relations. These are mainly factors explaining the *level* of fringe benefits. However, by reinterpreting them, I may also use them to explain the *growth* of fringe benefits. I discuss each in turn.

11.4.1 The Agency Model

This model was developed by Lazear (1979, 1981) as an extension of that of Becker (1964). The fundamental idea of this model is that the optimal age-earnings strategy for a firm is to pay workers less than their marginal value product in their early years with the firm and more in their later years. There are several reasons for this strategy. First, an employee who has received costly training may quit before the firm has recouped the cost of training or may engage in a suboptimal level of shirking. Lazear emphasized the importance of deferred compensation to increase the employee's opportunity cost of quitting or shirking, with its attendant prospects of being discharged. Second, fringe payments may increase workers' productivity directly. Third, and somewhat contrary to the second view, Medoff and Abraham (1980) find that productivity grows far less than is proportionate to earnings with length of service in the firm. If this finding is true, a steeper age-earnings profile would increase a worker's incentive to shirk.

Several reservations may be raised about agency theory. First, the model refers implicitly to total labor compensation rather than to fringe benefits only. Second, the causal mechanism is not entirely clear. Third, some empirical evidence on the difference in working hours between younger workers and older workers contradicts the theory. Fourth, it is not easy to distinguish between human capital theory and agency theory using wage data.

11.4.2   Tax Advantage Theory

Tax advantage theory offers three basic arguments. The first is based on the fact that most forms of nonwage compensation are not taxed as income. Standard microeconomic theory leads us to conjecture that employers could reduce compensation costs without reducing employee utility by offering compensation packages that contain untaxed, nonwage employee benefits. This provides employers with an incentive to raise the amount of nonwage compensation.

Second, and somewhat related to the argument of the agency model, Mumy (1985) has shown that deferred payment has a clear advantage when payroll taxes, social security benefits, and income taxes are taken into account. The reason is as follows: When wage income is deferred, the present value of payroll taxes on the income declines. In addition, this wage income later enters the calculation of average earnings for social security payments in an undiscounted manner. In other words, the social security and payroll tax systems provide incentives to defer compensation early in working life, thus avoiding payroll taxes and allowing pension benefits to accrue. The concentration of compensation later in life raises the average earnings base for social security benefits. Again, the same reservations expressed for agency theory are applicable here.

Third, corporate tax laws favor employer contributions to social security and pension funds because of deductibility from employers' taxable income.

In sum, the tax advantage model is quite promising for interpreting the rapid growth of nonwage labor costs and, in particular, pensions. A nice example of the relevance of this theory is provided by the rapid growth in enterprise pension systems, such as 401(k)s, in the United States (e.g., Poterba, Venti, and Wise 1994).

11.4.3   Worker Preference

A large number of empirical studies such as Freeman (1981), Lester (1967), and Woodbury (1983) find that unionized firms provide a higher proportion of total compensation in the form of fringe benefits than nonunionized firms. One exception is Reynolds (1974). Since the union places a greater weight on the preferences of older workers and permanent workers, who are likely to prefer deferred compensation such as health insurance and pensions over wages, unionized firms tend to have higher proportions of fringe benefits. This argument is an application of the median voter model advocated by Freeman and Medoff (1979). See Tachibanaki and Noda (2000) on Japanese unions that prefer such arrangements. The fact that large Japanese firms have reacted positively to their unions' preferences is interesting.

It must be noted, however, that although the theory of union preference is reasonably persuasive, we have to offer an adequate explanation for why nonunionized firms prefer fringe benefits in some countries and why highly unionized countries, such as Germany and Sweden, have low rates of voluntary, nonwage labor costs.

The case of Germany and Sweden is not complicated. These countries have a higher rate of statutory social welfare programs, and thus the necessity of nonstatutory social programs is greatly reduced. It would be interesting, however, to investigate whether relying more heavily on statutory or nonstatutory social welfare programs is more efficient.

The case of nonunionized firms is not as simple. The tax advantage model may provide an adequate explanation. Both employers and employees may agree to raise the share of deferred payments in order to take advantage of the favorable tax treatment of these payments. It is possible that firms also pay fringe benefits on a purely voluntary basis outside of the system of collective bargaining to secure employees' loyalty.

11.4.4   Cost Savings apart from Tax Advantages

A specialized agent, like an insurance company, can offer insurance for a low charge. Each employee's costs are reduced if a large number of workers can form a group insurance program with the consent of an employer. Management costs of pensions and insurance programs can also be reduced if employers and their employees administer, monitor, and evaluate their programs collectively. These cost-saving features encourage employers and their employees to increase the number of fringe benefit programs and concomitant employer expenditures on these programs.

11.4.5   Better Industrial Relations

In section 11.3, I noted the relatively high share of nonstatutory fringe benefits in large firms in Japan. One reason for this phenomenon is that larger firms want to have better industrial relations and so pay higher fringe benefits to their employees. Generous treatment, through better housing facilities, health insurance, free lunches, cultural and athletic facilities, and so forth, attracts more qualified workers and reduces turnover.

Firms can also expect to reap returns from the high motivation and hard work of their employees. In addition, large firms hesitate to pay relatively high wages because harmony in the industry is believed to be important. These are the main reasons why large firms in Japan pay considerably high proportions of compensation in the form of fringe benefits. Trade unions in these firms have responded positively to these benefits. Thus, both employers and employees have been cooperative, as Tachibanaki and Noda (2000) document.

11.5   Tax Incidence and Policy Issues

There are at least five important criticisms of high employer contributions to social security and nonstatutory fringe benefits. First, high rates of contribution increase labor costs in general, which is detrimental to the financial condition of a firm and thus to employment. Second, the increase in labor costs may encourage firms to employ more capital-intensive techniques. This is again harmful to employment. Third, and related to the second point, labor-intensive industries are hurt more than capital-intensive industries. Fourth, nonmanual workers (or skilled workers) will be preferred to manual workers (or unskilled workers) due to the wage ceiling used in the determination of the contribution rate. Fifth, since benefits of welfare provision are enjoyed almost entirely by individual persons, it is conceivable to relieve firms of their contributions to welfare provision. The reduction in these contributions could be used to increase employment, wages, or both.

The extremely important subject of payroll tax incidence must also be considered here. It is crucial to understand who actually bears the burden of employer contributions. Three cases are possible: (a) backward shifting, in which a firm passes employer contributions (payroll taxes) on to its employees; (b) forward shifting, in which a firm passes the tax on to consumers in the form of price increases; and (c) no shifting at all. The previous five propositions regarding the effect of the firm contribution rate on employment are made under the presumption that firms do not shift the burden at all. When the direction and the degree of tax shifting are known, these stories may have to be substantially modified. Several theoretical and empirical results on payroll tax incidence follow.

11.5.1   Payroll Tax Incidence

In a competitive market, the incidence of a payroll tax depends upon two parameters, the elasticities of labor supply and labor demand. If capital is considered an additional factor input, the substitutability of capital and labor also plays an important role. The common technique for estimating the payroll tax incidence was initiated by Brittain (1972), who estimated a labor demand equation derived from a production function. The effect of a payroll tax is then estimated indirectly. This technique is based on a common understanding that payroll taxes are mostly borne by labor in the long run because long-run labor supply is perfectly inelastic (or very inelastic). Break (1974) found this to be mainly true for the United States. In other words, it was believed that employer contributions were fully shifted backward to workers' real wages.

Feldstein (1974) proposes a model of payroll tax incidence that assumes that labor supply is not necessarily inelastic. He also introduces a growth dynamic into the model through capital accumulation. When estimates of labor supply and labor demand elasticities are applied to this model, a slightly different result is obtained. For example, Beach and Balfour (1983) use U.K. data to estimate that only 45 to 60 percent of payroll taxes are shifted back to labor for prime-age males, and 14 to 19 percent for married women. Since the labor supply elasticity of married women is very high— say, 0.8 to 1.1, as compared to 0.08 to 0.20 for men—only a small portion of their payroll tax is shifted back. Thus, the effect of the payroll tax is equally shared between wage loss and employment reduction for married women, and the major effect is on wages for men. Irish results tell a similar story. Kirwan (1979) adopts a higher value of the elasticity of labor supply, 0.74, while Hughes (1985) uses a lower value, 0.21. The estimated results on shifting turn out to be considerably different. Consequently, a hypothetical reduction in the employer contribution rate produces different estimates of job creation for each elasticity estimate. These two studies clearly show the importance of the labor supply elasticity in estimating the incidence of the payroll tax as well as the number of jobs created or lost due to changes in the rate of employer contributions.

Hamermesh (1979) estimates that 36 percent of the U.S. payroll tax is borne by labor as lower wages (his study is restricted to white males). Although his paper acknowledges the differences in labor supply elasticities among demographic groups, he fails to incorporate such differences. Rather, he emphasizes the adjustment process of labor demand and supply. Extending the idea of the adjustment process, Hamermesh (1980) obtains the result that the impact of a change in the payroll tax rate on wages is delayed for several years because the adjustment of both labor supply and labor demand is not instantaneous. He then applies recently estimated values of the adjustment coefficients to estimate his result.

Another important finding of Hamermesh (1980) is that the response to a decrease in the payroll tax is much slower than the response to an increase. This asymmetry arises from the fact that the adjustment of actual to desired labor supply is slower than that of actual to desired labor demand in the Barro-Grossman (1976) employment model he utilizes. The Barro-Grossman employment model specifies that actual employment must be the minimum of labor supplied and demanded. This asymmetry has an important policy implication: When the tax rate is increased, employment adjusts quickly (i.e., employment is cut quickly because labor demand is the binding constraint); when the tax rate is decreased, employment increases only slowly because labor supply is the constraint. Thus, a policy aimed at lowering the payroll tax rate in order to increase employment has only limited value, whereas increasing the tax rate is quite detrimental to employment.

Two reservations are forthcoming at this point. First, it may still be worthwhile to decrease the payroll tax rate in order to increase employment in economies where the observed rate of unemployment is very high, as is the case in several European nations. Second, it is necessary to keep in mind that the supply elasticities for both men and women are considerably higher in countries where the average tax burden (including both income and payroll taxes) is relatively heavy (e.g., Blomquist 1983 on Sweden). In such countries a downward adjustment in employment may be accomplished more quickly than is suggested by the model.

What is the incidence of the payroll tax in an economy in which both factor and product markets are imperfectly competitive? Unions may resist the lowering of real wages in order to maintain real purchasing power. Firms with monopoly power may raise product prices and pass on the tax increases to consumers, that is, forward shifting. Leuthold (1975), among others, tackles this problem for the United States. She concludes that labor contracts and union actions effectively prevent real wages from falling rapidly, but much work is needed to obtain a more conclusive result in this field.

In addition to the common technique described above, several authors have applied another estimation method, a macroeconomic, or Phillips-curve, approach. Perry (1970) proposes that an increase in employer contributions did not lead to any decrease in wages. Gordon (1971), on the contrary, suggests that employer contributions were shifted back to wages entirely. Vroman (1974) shows a result somewhere in between. All of these studies were conducted for the United States, and the results are quite varied. Holmlund (1983) estimates the payroll tax incidence for Sweden using a similar but more sophisticated method. He concludes that only a fraction (roughly 40 percent) of postwar Swedish payroll tax increases were directly shifted back onto labor as lower wage increases. He also finds that around 30 percent of employer contributions in the United States were shifted back.

In sum, studies of payroll tax incidence suggest that only a small portion of employer contributions is shifted back onto labor. The degree depends on many factors and is very sensitive to the elasticity parameters used. However, it must be emphasized that only one study, Perry (1970), has found no backward shifting at all. Some backward shifting almost certainly occurs.

It is somewhat strange that interest in the study of payroll tax incidence has waned in recent years. I suggest the following two reasons for this.

First, there is a widespread belief that only a small portion of employer contributions is shifted back onto labor. Thus, there is no strong incentive to add a new result. Second, several technical issues have not yet been solved. Thus, unless a new estimation method is invented, a different result cannot be expected.

10.5.2   Incidence in Japan

My estimation method is discussed briefly below. There are basically two approaches to estimating payroll tax (i.e., employers' contributions to social security) incidence. The first is a time series estimation method, as utilized by Hammermesh (1980), Beach and Balfour (1983), and Holmlund (1983). The second is a cross-sectional estimation method (i.e., states and occupations), as utilized by Gruber and Krueger (1991). Cross-sectional analyses cannot be easily performed if a national-level social security system applies uniformly to all firms and workers, unlike the American employer-provided health insurance system analyzed by Gruber and Krueger. Since the Japanese social insurance system for employees is fairly universal for all firms and workers, I use a time series estimation method.

The basic method relies on the estimation of the demand for labor, as shown, for example, by Beach and Balfour (1983). The demand for labor under a generalized constant elasticity of substitution (CES) production function is given by equation (1):

(1) $$Y_i = [\alpha_1(e^{\lambda i}L_i)^{(\sigma-1)/\sigma} + \alpha_2(e^{\mu i}K_i)^{(\sigma-1)/\sigma}]^{\sigma/(\sigma-1)},$$

where Y is real output, L is man-hours of labor input, K is capital input, σ is the elasticity substitution between capital and labor, λ and μ are factor-augmenting technical change parameters, and i specifies the time period.

We can write the demand for labor by equating the marginal product of labor to the real wage, as follows:

(2) $$\ln L_i = \alpha + \beta_1 T + \beta_2 \ln(W/P)_i^* + \beta_3 \ln Y_i^* + u_i,$$

where T is a time-trend variable and $*$ implies the optimal level that is calculated using the marginal productivity condition. Gross labor costs are denoted by $(W/P)(1 + St)$ where W is the net wage, $S(0 \leq S \leq 1)$ is the shift parameter, and t is the payroll tax rate. If S is equal to 1 after estimation, there is full backward shifting, implying that the presence of the payroll tax lowers the net wage by the amount of the tax. If S is 0 there is no shifting, implying that the net wage is not affected by the payroll tax. The former signifies full offsets, and the latter signifies no effect. In other words, the former implies that employees bear the entire burden of the payroll tax, whereas the latter implies that employers bear the whole burden.

The demand for labor can thus be estimated by

(3) $$\ln L_1 = \alpha + \beta_1 T + \beta_2 \ln(W/P)_i^* + \beta_2 S \ln(1 + t_i)^* + \beta_3 \ln Y_i^* + u_i.$$

I have to specify the desired level of each variable, namely $\ln(W/P)_i^*$, $\ln(1 + t_i)^*$, and $\ln Y_i^*$, because they are not observed. I do this by assuming a rational-expectations framework, in which $(W/P)_i^* = \ln(W/P)_{i-j}$, $\ln(1 + t_i)^* = \ln(1 + t_{i-j})$, and $\ln Y_i^* = \ln Y_{i-j}$, where j denotes a lag. These values can be estimated with the data.

The estimated result of Tachibanaki and Yokoyama (2002) suggests that it is impossible to find any significant shifting except for a few cases of samples divided by sex and industry. It implies that nearly all employers' contributions to social security are borne by employers (i.e., firms). This gives us important policy implications.

11.6   Recommendations for Japan

Our empirical result regarding the direction and degree of shifting of employers' contributions to social security in Japan suggests the following policy implications. First, employers bear nearly the entire burden of firms' contributions. Thus, if the society had a consensus such that firms should be free from any contributions to social insurance, the portion paid by firms to social insurance could be used freely for purposes other than firms' contributions to social security.

Second, it is reasonable to expect that nearly all of social security benefits should be financed by employees. This is true in particular when the burden of employers' contributions to social security is too high, damaging the investment and employment activities of firms.

Third, Tachibanaki's (1997b) proposal that firm contributions to social security could be transformed into wage payments must be modified in light of the incidence results. The proposal emphasizes that higher wages enable employees to contribute more to social security, and they also provide greater freedom of consumption. Freedom of consumption implies that the wage increase resulting from decreased employer contributions to social security would be spent freely by employees. Great modifications to this proposal, however, are necessary given the current finding that no major part of firm contributions to social security are shifted to employees in Japan.

There are three choices for such modifications. The first choice is to abandon or reduce firms' contributions to social security if the burden is believed to be too heavy, and thus to expect employees to accept a lower level of social security benefits. Since it is not desirable to lower benefits, someone would have to accept a higher financial burden to compensate for the reduction in social security contributions. I suppose that this group will have to be all citizens. The second choice is that only nonstatutory fringe benefits should be transformed into wage payments. The third is to consider a new financing method for social security if employees are not willing to accept lower social security benefits.

My own preference is for a combination of the above choices, for the following reasons. First, it is desirable to reduce the burden of firms' contributions to social security in order to allow firms to better concentrate on their business activities. I add the fact that firms' contributions to social security are likely to have a distortionary impact on labor allocations, as was proposed previously.

Second, there is no strong justification for believing that firms should be responsible for the social security benefits of workers. I believe that a firm's responsibility is to engage in prosperous economic activity and thus to keep employment high, with possibly higher wages. Incidentally, self-employed workers and farmers have no outside support like employer contributions.

Third, it is desirable to have a social security system whose financing is borne by beneficiaries. One way to have such a system is to shift the basis of the financing method from a social insurance principle to a tax principle. Okamoto and Tachnibanaki (2002) performed a simulation study that proposed that the best financing method is to introduce a nonlinear (i.e., progressive) expenditure tax, replacing current social security contributions paid by both employers and employees. "Best" here implies that the impacts on both efficiency and equity were incorporated into the welfare measure.

11.7   Concluding Remarks

This paper proposes that firms in Japan can withdraw from welfare provision. The concrete method is as follows: (a) a transformation of nonstatutory fringe benefits to wage payments; (b) a withdrawal of firms' statutory social security contributions; and (c) an introduction of a progressive expenditure tax to compensate for such a withdrawal.

I offer several reasons why both employers and employees have preferred nonwage payments in the past. It is technically necessary to discuss why these reasons are no longer applicable in Japan. However, since Tachibanaki (1997a,b) and the previous part of this paper engage in such a discussion, here I only briefly describe several items to supplement the justifications of my proposal.

First, the argument of the agency model is no longer applicable because the basis of wage determination is shifting from the seniority system to the merit system, and thus the age-wage profile is flattening.

Second, tax advantage theory has not been a driving force in Japan, unlike in the United States, where preferential tax treatment encourages American firms and workers to adopt employer-provided health insurance and pension programs (see Tachibanaki 2000a) for the case of Japan).

Third, employers wish to reduce the burden of firm contributions to welfare provision, as shown in appendix A. Also, employees want higher wage payments, rather than nonstatutory fringe benefits (appendix B), since there is currently an increasing trend in labor turnover in Japan. The advantages of nonstatutory fringe benefits are greatest when there are few turnovers.

Fourth, the Japanese industrial relations system is changing, and better industrial relations can be achieved without relying on either nonwage payments or nonstatutory fringe benefits. In other words, fair wage payments and promotion systems are more important than generous fringe benefits for sustaining better industrial relations in Japan (see Tachibanaki 1997a and Tachibanaki and Taki 2000 for details).

Finally, trade unions in Japan may be reluctant to accept my proposal because union members are employed in large firms and are therefore the biggest beneficiaries of the current firm-financed system of welfare provision. Two recent phenomena are likely to mitigate this opposition. First, the trade union participation rate is decreasing: It is currently only 22 percent. Second, a large portion of both union and nonunion members now accept the idea that their ultimate goal is to work and to receive fair wage payments and do not expect the welfare provisions that have been offered by firms (see Tachibanaki and Noda 2000).

Appendix A
Firm Attitudes Toward Welfare Provision

This appendix presents results based on the *Questionnaire on Welfare Provisions* survey, prepared by the Cultural Center for Life Insurance in 1998. About 1,400 firms responded. This appendix references only a very small portion of the questions asked in the survey.

One question asks the following: Does your firm increase (a) the share of wages and bonuses, or (b) the share of welfare provision when revenue is distributed? The distribution of each answer was (a), 14.6 percent; somewhat (a), 28.2 percent; indifferent, 32.4 percent; somewhat (b), 18.7 percent; and (b), 6.0 percent. The responses clearly indicate that firms prefer to increase wages (total 42.8 percent) rather than welfare provision (total 24.7 percent).

Another question asks the following: Does (or will) your firm support (a) or (b) regarding the role of welfare provision? Option (a) signifies that firms, rather than employees, are responsible for welfare provision, and (b) signifies that employees, rather than firms, should be responsible. The questionnaire asks for a judgment on current status and future status separately.

The distribution of each answer is as follows: for current status, (a), 7.5 percent; somewhat (a), 22.4 percent; indifferent, 31.1 percent; somewhat (b), 27.4 percent; and (b), 11.3 percent. For future status, (a), 6.0 percent; somewhat (a), 16.4 percent; indifferent, 38.9 percent; somewhat (b), 27.4 percent; and (b), 11.0 percent. The responses indicate that the share of (b) is considerably higher than the share of (a) for both current and future judgment, suggesting that firms believe that employees, rather than firms, should be responsible for welfare provision. The shift from the current judgment to the future is minor; there is a small decrease in the "somewhat (a)" category and an increase in the "indifferent" group.

The final question noted here concerns enterprise pension plans. The question asks, is your firm interested in defined contribution pension plans? The distribution of answers is yes, 11.8 percent; no, 87.6 percent; and no answer, 0.5 percent. It is surprising that the vast majority of firms in Japan shows no interest in defined contribution plans, unlike in the United States, where they are very popular. The reasons defined contribution plans are unpopular in Japan are explained in detail in Tachibanaki (2000a).

Appendix B
Employee Preferences for Welfare Provision

The 1999 *Survey on Life Plan* (2000; sample size 1,350) found that the ratio of nonstatutory, nonwage payments to nonstatutory fringe benefit payments was 0.30, while the ratio of severance payments to enterprise pensions paid was 0.70. One question asks employees the following: What proportion would be ideal, if you had a chance to choose among (a) nonstatutory fringe benefits, (b) severance payments and enterprise pensions, and (c) wage payment? The answer was (a) 0.16, (b) 0.38, and (c) 0.46, implying that employees would like to receive about 50 percent of nonstatutory, nonwage payments as wages. These figures regarding employee preferences strongly support my proposal that a large portion of nonwage payments should be shifted to wages. Employees are less fond of receiving nonstatutory fringe benefits.

References

Barro, R. J., and H. J. Grossman. 1976. *Money, employment, and inflation.* Cambridge: Cambridge University Press.

Beach, C. M. and F. S. Balfour. 1983. Estimated payroll tax incidence and aggregate demand for labour in the U.K. *Economica* 50:35–48.

Becker, G. S. 1964. *Human capital: A theoretical and empirical analysis with special reference to education.* New York: National Bureau of Economic Research.

Blomquist, N. J. 1983. The effect of income taxation on the labour supply of married men in Sweden. *Journal of Public Economics* 22 (November): 169–97.

Break, G. 1974. The incidence and economic effects of taxation. In *The economics of public finance,* ed. G. Break, Washington, D.C.: Brookings Institution.

Brittain, J. A. 1972. *The payroll tax for Social Security.* Washington, D.C.: Brookings Institution.

Cultural Center for Life Insurance. 1998. *Questionnaire on welfare provisions.* Tokyo: Cultural Center for Life Insurance.

Feldstein, M. S. 1974. Tax incidence with growth and variable factor supply. *Quarterly Journal of Economics* 87 (November): 551–73.

Freeman, R. B. 1981. The effect of unionization on retirement. *Industrial and Labour Relations Review* 34 (July): 489–509.

Freeman, R. B., and J. L. Medoff. 1979. The two faces of unionism. *The Public Interest* 57:69–93.

Freeman, R. B., R. Topel, and B. Swedenborg, eds. 1997. *The welfare state in transition.* New York: NBER.

Gordon, R. J. 1971. Inflation in recession and recovery. *Brookings Papers on Economic Activity,* Issue no. 1:105–66.

Gruber, J., and A. B. Krueger. 1991. The incidence of mandated employer-provided insurance: Lessons from workers' compensation insurance. In *Tax policy and the economy,* ed. D. Bradford, 110–43. Cambridge: MIT Press.

Hamermesh, D. 1979. New estimates of the incidence of the payroll tax. *Southern Economic Journal* 45 (April): 1208–19.

———. 1980. Factor market dynamics and the incidence of taxes and subsidies. *Quarterly Journal of Economics* 95 (December): 751–64.

Hart, R. A. 1984. *The economics of non-wage labour costs.* London: Allen and Unwin.

Holmlund, B. 1983. Payroll taxes and wage inflation: The Swedish experience. *Scandinavian Journal of Economics* 85 (1): 1–15.

Hughes, G. 1985. *Payroll tax incidence, the direct tax burden, and the rate of return of state pension contributions in Ireland.* Dublin: Economic and Social Research Institute.

Katsumata, Y. 2000. International comparison of data construction in international comparison (in Japanese). *Kaigai Shakai-Hosho Kenkyu* 130 (Spring): 25–46.

Katsumata, Y., and Y. Morita. 1999. Fundamental data on social security costs: International comparisons and interpretations (in Japanese). *Kaigai Shakai-Hosho Kenkyu* 128 (Autumn): 104–16.

Kirwan, F. X. 1979. Non-wage costs, employment, and hours of work in Irish manufacturing industry. *Economic and Social Review* 10:231–54.

Lazear, E. P. 1979. Why is there mandatory retirement? *Journal of Political Economy* 87 (December): 1261–68.

———. 1981. Agency, earnings profiles, productivity, and hours restrictions. *American Economic Review* 71 (September): 606–20.

Lester, R. A. 1967. Benefits as a preferred form of compensation. *Southern Economic Journal* 33 (April): 485–95.

Leuthold, J. H. 1975. The incidence of the payroll tax in the United States. *Public Finance Quarterly* 1 (January): 3–13.

Medoff, J. L., and K. G. Abraham. 1980. Experience, performance, and earnings. *Quarterly Journal of Economics* 95:703–36.

Ministry of Labor. 1997. *1996 General survey on wages and working hours system.* Tokyo: Ministry of Labor.

Mumy, G. E. 1985. The role of taxes and social security in determining the structure of wages and pensions. *Journal of Political Economy* 93 (3): 574–85.

Okamoto, A., and T. Tachibanaki. 2002. Integration of tax and social security system: On the financing methods of public pension scheme in pay-as-you-go system. In *Social security reform in advanced countries,* ed. T. Ihori and T. Tachibanaki. London: Routledge.

Organization for Economic Co-operation and Development (OECD). 1997. *The tax/benefit position of employees 1995–1996.* Paris: Organization for Economic Co-operation and Development.

———. 1998. *Public management reform and economic and social development.* Paris: Organization for Economic Co-operation and Development.

Perry, G. 1970. Changing labour market and inflation. *Brookings Papers on Economic Activity,* Issue no. 3:411–41.

Poterba, J. M., S. F. Venti, and D. A. Wise. 1994. 401(k) plans and tax-deferred saving. In *Studies in the economics of aging,* ed. D. Wise, 105–38. Chicago: University of Chicago Press.

Rein, M. 1996. Is America exceptional? The Role of occupational welfare in the United States and the European Community. In *The privatization of social policy? Occupational welfare and the welfare state in America, Scandinavia, and Japan,* ed. M. Shalev, London: Macmillan.

Reynolds, L. G. 1974. *Labor economics and labor relations.* Englewood Cliffs, N.J.: Prentice-Hall.

Rice, R. 1966. Skill, earnings, and growth of wage-supplements. *American Economic Review* 54 (2): 583–93.

Survey on life 1999. 2000. Osaka: Kansai Economic Research Center.

Tachibanaki, T. 1996. *Wage determination and distribution in Japan.* Oxford, U.K.: Clarendon.

———. 1997a. Labor policies and welfare programs. In *Long-run perspective of the Japanese economy for the 21st century* (in Japanese), ed. R. Komiya and M. Okuno, 219–38. Tokyo: Toyokeizai Shimposha.

———. 1997b. Labor policies in firms: Wage payments or non-wage payments? In *Support for life in an aging society* (in Japanese), ed. N. Yashiro, 99–116. Tokyo: University of Tokyo Press.

———. 2000a. *Economics of the safety net* (in Japanese). Tokyo: Nihon Keizai Shibun-sha.

———. 2000b. Japan was not a welfare state, but. In *From austerity to affluence,* ed. R. Griffits and T. Tachibanaki, 188–208. London: Macmillan.

Tachibanaki, T., and T. Noda. 2000. *The economic effects of trade unions in Japan.* London: Macmillan.

Tachibanaki, T., and A. Taki. 2000. *Capital and labour in Japan: The function of two factor markets.* London: Routledge.

Tachibanaki, T., and Y. Yokoyama. 2002. The estimation of the incidence of employer contributions to social security. Kyoto University and Kobe University of Commerce. Mimeograph.

Vroman, W. 1974. Employer payroll taxes and money wage behaviour. *Applied Economics* 6:189–204.

Woodbury, S. A. 1983. Substitution between wage and non-wage benefits. *American Economic Review* 73 (March): 166–82.

12

Fringe Benefit Provision for Female Part-Time Workers in Japan

Yukiko Abe

12.1 Introduction

Japan has universal public pension and health insurance coverage. Universal health care coverage is achieved through a combination of an employer mandate and regional plans for self-employed and nonworking individuals.[1] Since coverage is universal, *whether* one is covered is unrelated to his or her labor supply decision. However, *how* one is covered is closely related to his or her employment status. Workers who do not work full-time may not receive coverage through their employers. In this article, I focus on one such group of workers: women who work part-time.

Part-time work has expanded rapidly in Japan in the 1980s and 1990s. According to the *Employment Status Survey* (Statistical Bureau 1984, 1998), the number of female part-time and arbeit workers increased from 3.9 million in 1982 to 8.3 million in 1997.[2] In light of this expansion, labor

Yukiko Abe is associate professor of economics at Asia University.

This paper is part of a project on part-time work conducted by Fumio Ohtake and the author. They thank the Ministry of Labor of Japan for permission to use microdata from the proprietary *General Survey of Part-Time Workers' Conditions* in 1990 and 1995. The author thanks Akira Wakisaka, David Wise, and participants in the National Bureau of Economic Research–Japan Center for Economic Research conference for helpful comments. The author is responsible for all errors. Financial support from the Japan Foundation Center for Global Partnership is gratefully acknowledged.

1. The universal public pension is administered under a similar scheme. Most salary earners are covered through employer-provided plans, whereas the self-employed and farmers are covered by the national pension program. However, unlike the health insurance system, local governments have no discretion over the structure of the national pension.

2. Arbeit workers are nonregular employees who usually work shorter hours than regular employees. When full-time students work for nonregular basis, they usually work under this title. The distinction between part-time workers and arbeit workers is not necessarily clear,

market policies affecting part-time workers have generated increased interest. One such policy concerns social insurance participation. Social insurance programs (in this case public pension, health insurance, and employment insurance) do not require all part-time workers to enroll. Participation is only necessary for workers with sufficiently high working hours, earnings, or both. It has been pointed out that many married women working part-time do not participate in employer-provided plans, but are covered by their husbands' insurance. In this case, neither income taxes nor social security taxes are collected out of the wife's earnings, but she is still eligible for health insurance and public pension benefits through her husband's coverage. This is problematic in terms of both efficiency and equity.

This policy is distortionary because it creates work disincentives for married women. It is not equitable because a married woman will receive benefits even though she (or her husband) does not pay extra insurance premiums for her benefits. In spite of significant interest in this topic, however, social insurance participation has not been analyzed in a systematic way. In particular, some argue that participation is low because employers do not comply with the policy rules, which results in low coverage of part-timers. Others argue that "free" coverage for low-income wives discourages participation by married women.

In this paper I use microdata on part-time workers to examine enrollment patterns of female part-time workers. I examine enrollment in employment insurance (EI),[3] public pensions (EP),[4] and employer-provided health insurance.[5] The conditions for participating in EP and employer-provided health insurance are the same (for those younger than sixty-five): Part-time workers who work thirty hours or more are required to enroll in public pension and employer-provided health insurance.[6] The coverage for

---

but arbeit workers have less attachment to work than part-time workers in that their tenures are shorter than those of part-time workers.

3. This program provides unemployment insurance benefits.

4. Since the focus here is private-sector employees, the applicable public pension system is the employees' pension.

5. Firms with more than 500 employees often form a health insurance society (HIS). An HIS self-insures for the health care expenditures of the enrolled employees and their dependents aged sixty-nine or younger. There were about 1,800 HISs in Japan in 1999. Health care expenditures by people over seventy years old are financed under a different scheme, but HISs usually pay significant "taxes" (contributions for health services for the elderly) to finance the health care expenditures of the elderly. Each HIS sets its health insurance premium rate individually within a range set by the government. The monthly premium for an insured employee is the premium rate multiplied by his or her regular monthly earnings. Employees in smaller firms enroll in governmentally managed health insurance (GMHI). This is a large insurance group consisting of 19.1 million insured employees and 18.2 million dependents. Like the case of HISs, the GMHI self-insures the enrollees aged sixty-nine or younger.

6. The rule actually states that if a worker works at least three fourths of the working hours of regular employees in the same establishment, he or she has to enroll in pension and employer-provided health insurance. Since working hours for regular employees are forty hours per week, the rule is often stated as such in the text.

EI is wider: Workers who work more than twenty hours per week or earn 0.9 million yen or more have to participate in EI.[7]

Some previous studies argue that social insurance benefits are not provided for part-time workers due to employer noncompliance.[8] However, such generalizations do not apply uniformly across categories of workers; this study finds substantial heterogeneity in participation among part-time workers. The following analysis suggests that 86 percent of married female part-time workers who work sufficiently long hours and earn more than 1.3 million yen per year participate in the three social insurance programs above. On the other hand, 83 percent of married female part-time workers with short working hours and low earnings (less than 0.9 million yen per year) do not participate. Of the 64 percent of married female part-time workers who fall between these two groups—working twenty to thirty hours per week, earning 0.9–1.3 million yen or both—43 percent participated in employer-provided plans in 1995. A more detailed analysis of these enrollment patterns is presented below.

12.2   Overview of the EI, EP, and Health Insurance Systems in Japan

12.2.1   Participation Rules for Social Insurance Programs

The rules for participating in social insurance programs are summarized in table 12.1. The Employer Side and Worker Side columns show the requirements imposed on employers and workers, respectively. A number 1 in either of the Employer Side columns indicates that the employer must offer benefits to the specified class of employee; a 1 in the Worker Side column indicates that a worker belonging to the specified class of employee cannot be considered a dependent of another family member (for the purposes of social insurance plans) and must enroll in the social insurance plan by herself.

A worker with weekly hours more than three-fourths those of regular employees in the same establishment is required to participate in EP and employer-provided health insurance. However, if a husband participates in EP and employer-provided health insurance through his employer, his wife can receive basic pension and health care benefits as a dependent of her husband, as long as her earnings are less than 1.3 million yen per year and

7. This is the enrollment condition for EI for short-hour workers that was introduced in 1989. Those who work more than thirty hours per week enroll in EI for regular workers. The benefits of the two differ, but the premium rate is the same. Effective in April of 2001, the threshold for the EI enrollment (0.9 million yen) was repealed. Therefore, under the system at the point of this writing (2002), the cells stratified by the 0.9 million yen threshold do not exist any more. Table 12.4 shows the rules at the point of the data used in the analysis (1990 and 1995).

8. Takayama (1997) notes that "part-time workers who earn 1.3 million yen have to enroll in *national pension insurance* and pay the premium by themselves" (emphasis added; 135).

Table 12.1   **Conditions for Enrollment in Social Insurance**

| | Cell Number | Weekly Hours | Annual Earnings | Employer Side[a] | | Worker Side[b]: |
				EPH	EI	EPH
1990	1	<22	<90			
	2	<22	90–110			
	3	<22	110+			1
	4	22–33	<90			
	5	22–33	90–110		1	
	6	22–33	110+		1	1
	7	33+	<90	1		
	8	33+	90–110	1	1	
	9	33+	110+	1	1	1
1995	1	<22	<90			
	2	<22	90–110			
	3	<22	110+			1
	4	22–33	<90			
	5	22–33	90–110		1	
	6	22–33	110+		1	1
	7	33+	<90	1		
	8	33+	90–110	1	1	
	9	33+	110+	1	1	1

Notes: An entry of 1 on the firm side means enrollment is required. An entry of 1 on the worker side means that the worker cannot qualify as a dependent of another family member and thus must enroll in social insurance individually.
EI = employment insurance
EPH = employees' pension and Health Insurance
[a]Must enroll.
[b]Cannot qualify as a dependent.

less than half of her husband's earnings. For EI, an employee working more than twenty hours per week *and* earning more than 0.9 million yen per year or more is required to participate.

In principle, employers who meet the employer-side conditions must force workers to participate in the social insurance programs, irrespective of their worker-side conditions. For example, if a married, female part-time worker works thirty-five hours per week and earns 1.2 million yen, the employer must enroll her in EP and employer-provided health insurance, even though she could claim benefits from her husband's coverage. Nonetheless, the worker-side conditions may affect participation, even conditional on hours and earnings. Most importantly, as the following analysis confirms, many female part-time workers satisfy some conditions but not others. Most of them work reasonably long hours, but their earnings remain below the threshold for participation in health and EP insurance.

Based on the rules described in table 12.1, I construct nine cells defined by pairs of ranges in weekly hours and annual earnings. They are numbered from one to nine (the second column of table 12.1). The cells differ by whether they meet the conditions for enrollment. For example, workers in cell 1 (the top row for each year) do not satisfy the enrollment conditions for any of the insurance programs considered here; workers in cell nine satisfy hours and earnings conditions for participating in all of the programs. In the analysis below, I classify the observations in my sample into these cells. It is important to bear in mind that measurement error in both hours and earnings might cause misclassification.

12.2.2   Costs Associated with Social Insurance Programs

Participation in social insurance programs requires contributions by both the employer and the employee. For some employers there are costs associated with paying for the benefits. However, benefits are paid out of collected premiums (and accrued interest), so they are not necessarily at a cost to employers. In 1990–1995 (the period for the data used in this paper), employees' pension funds (EPFs) and health insurance societies (HISs) were required to pay benefits, and the value of contributed premiums are not equal for some workers. Most importantly, it is expected that costs will be higher for older workers, although the insurance premium rate does not depend on age.[9]

Insurance Premium Costs

Social insurance enrollees have to contribute a fixed proportion of their regular monthly earnings as insurance premiums. The premium rate is 17.35 percent for EP (for 1996–2002), approximately 8.5 percent for employer-provided health insurance, and 1.15 percent for EI (for 1993–2000). In nominal terms, firms pay half of the EP insurance premium and also approximately half of the employer-provided health insurance premium. For EI, the premium rate is 0.75 percent for firms and 0.4 percent for workers. Regular monthly earnings are approximately equal to monthly earnings if the latter fall within government-specified lower and upper bounds.[10] For EP, the lower bound is 92,000 yen per month and the upper bound is 590,000 (figures are for 1994–2000). For health insurance, the lower bound is 92,000 yen per month and the upper bound is 980,000 (figures are for 1994–2000). Those who earn less than the lower bound pay an insurance premium and receive EP benefits as if their earnings were equal to the lower bound. Similarly, the premium amount and EP benefits for employees with earnings above the upper limit are based on the value of the upper bound.[11]

9. For pensions, this is the same concept as the low marginal tax rate for old employees, as pointed out by Feldstein and Samwick (1992).
10. Bonus payments are not included in regular monthly earnings.
11. The upper bound is similar to the maximum taxable earnings in the U.S. Social Security program.

Costs Associated with Paying Benefits

Most studies of costs of social insurance to the firm focus exclusively on the firm's insurance premium payments. They treat these as taxes on labor income and argue that firms are reluctant to enroll part-time workers in social insurance programs because of these taxes.[12] However, there are important additional costs to the firm arising from benefit payments to the firm's enrollees and retirees.

Under the current system, firms with EPFs or HISs *directly* pay a part of benefits to their enrollees.[13] The EPFs pay the earnings-related portion of the EP benefits and corporate pensions to retirees. The HISs self-insure health care costs for enrollees less than seventy years old. The required expenditure for these benefits may differ substantially across individuals. On the other hand, premium rates for EP and employer-provided health insurance are not allowed to vary across employees. Under such systems, firms with EPSs or HISs will care about whom they include in their insurance plans. For example, if a firm hires a sick worker on a full-time basis, the health care expenditure of that worker may exceed his or her contributions (insurance premiums). The welfare of other members of the HIS would fall because of his or her enrollment.

Small firms are not allowed to form HISs or EPFs. Benefits for enrollees are paid by government agencies (the Social Insurance Agency [EP] or the Governmentally Managed Health Insurance (GMHI). So once employers pay insurance premiums for their employees to the government, the government will pay all benefits to employees. Firms do not have to worry about the costs of paying benefits.

In principle, if the costs of paying benefits are shifted to insurance premiums (with higher-cost employees paying higher premiums), social insurance participation should not be affected by worker characteristics that are associated with higher benefits. If shifting is possible, firms will be indifferent between hiring high-benefit workers and low-benefit workers (assuming the only difference between the two groups is social insurance costs). However, full shifting means wages depend on health status. As explained above, the premium rate is not allowed to vary across workers. It would probably be difficult to fully shift the costs needed to pay benefits onto wages. In the appendix, the cost structure of benefit payments of large firms is discussed in more detail.

---

12. These arguments ignore the fact that a portion of firms' taxes may be shifted to employees in the form of lower wages.

13. Strictly speaking, the entities that pay benefits to a firm's employees and retirees are the HIS (for health care) and the EPF (for the form of corporate pension relevant here), which are distinct from the firm. However, since these organizations handle all the health care and corporate pension payouts to the employees and retirees of the firm, I treat them as the same entity as the firm.

12.2.3 Predictions of the Enrollment Patterns of Female Part-Time Workers

In light of the cost structure of social insurance benefits, I look for evidence of two effects on participation behavior: the marital status effect and the age effect.

Marital Status Effect

As shown in table 12.1, marital status is *not* included in the criteria for participation in any of the three insurance programs. Nevertheless, the fact that married women could receive benefits through their spouse's coverage may reduce participation if their earnings and hours do not exceed the statutory thresholds. Furthermore, if noncompliance exists, it is most likely to occur in cases where workers lose little from nonenrollment. For these reasons, married women should be less likely to participate in EP and health insurance programs than single women. However, differences across marital status should be small for participation in employment insurance.

Age Effect

Older workers are less likely to participate in EP and health insurance, especially in large firms. This is because large firms are more likely to form EPFs, HISs, or both, so they are more likely to be concerned with the costs of paying benefits, which are higher for older workers. Hence, employers are more reluctant to include old part-time workers in their firm-based plans.

12.2.4 Comparison with the U.S. System

The social security systems in the United States and Japan differ in many ways. This section summarizes the differences that are relevant for women with low earnings—the focus of this paper.

First, under the Japanese system, enrollment in EP (the counterpart of U.S. Social Security) is tied to enrollment in employer-provided health insurance for private-sector wage and salary earners. Enrollment in EP means that the employee is eligible for health care benefits. For 1997–2002, if a married woman has her own coverage, the coinsurance rate is 20 percent;[14] if she is covered by her husband's insurance, the coinsurance rate is 30 percent. This is an important difference from the United States, where paying payroll tax is not directly related to the employee's health insurance coverage.

Second, most private-sector employees are subject to paying payroll

---

14. Before 1997, if the wife had her own coverage through her employer, the coinsurance rate for outpatient expense was 10 percent. It rose to 20 percent in 1997. It is scheduled to be 30 percent (so there is no advantage for having own coverage as opposed to being covered as a dependent) after April 2003.

taxes in the United States, whereas in Japan, low-income employees are exempt from paying social security taxes. In the United States, low-income married women are likely to claim social security benefits as their husbands' dependents, so their labor supply does not directly affect their benefit. Therefore, the net marginal social security tax rate is high for such married women (Feldstein and Samwick 1992). In Japan, low-income married women do not pay social security tax as long as their earnings are below 1.3 million yen per year (this value was effective from 1992 to 2002). Earnings of married women below this amount are untaxed by the social security system. Furthermore, if earnings are below 1 million yen per year, a part-time employee owes no social security tax, no national income tax, and no local income taxes.[15] Thus, married Japanese women with earnings below the threshold face a zero marginal tax rate.[16] If their annual earnings exceed 1.3 million yen, they must pay a lump-sum social security tax (so at this point their marginal tax rate is infinity). They also face a very high marginal tax rate beyond this point (over 37 percent, under certain circumstances).[17] Once earnings exceed 1.619 million yen, the employment income deduction becomes more generous, so the marginal tax rate falls.

In sum, under the Japanese system, married women with sufficiently low earnings face a social security tax rate of zero. If a married woman's earnings are above the threshold but not very high compared with those of her husband, she pays social security tax but gains relatively small benefits. This latter case is similar to that of low-income married women in the United States.

15. National income tax is not imposed on employees whose earnings are 1.03 million yen or less. For earnings below 1 million yen, no local income tax is imposed.

16. Since the benefits such married women receive are the same as those enjoyed by nonworking dependent spouses, their *marginal* tax rate is not negative.

17. The U.S. and Japanese systems differ in the way that benefits for retired couples and surviving spouses are determined. Consider a couple in which both spouses worked in their prime (and, in Japan, the wife contributed social security tax since her earnings exceeded the threshold). Assume the husband's past earnings were much higher than that of the wife. For simplicity, assume that the husband dies earlier than the wife. In the United States, if the wife's past earnings were low, the couple receives a benefit equal to 1.5 times the husband's benefit as long as both spouses are alive. If the husband dies, the wife receives the benefit to which the husband is entitled. In Japan, as long as both spouses are alive, each spouse collects benefits based on each individual's contribution. When the husband dies, the wife can choose from one of three options: (a) three fourths of the benefit to which the husband was entitled; (b) the benefit to which the wife is entitled through her contributions; or (c) the sum of one half of the husband's entitled benefit and one half of the wife's entitled benefit. If the wife's past income was low, option (a) dominates the other two. So in Japan, the wife's contribution leads to higher benefits as long as the husband is alive. For this reason, under the Japanese system, if the wife participates in EP (the counterpart of U.S. Social Security) but her earnings are much lower than those of the husband, the wife's net social security tax rate is generally lower than the statutory rate. Furthermore, having her own coverage has the benefit of a reduced coinsurance rate in health care benefits (see above). However, the figures in the text are based on the statutory rate and do not reflect these considerations.

12.3   Data and Sample

12.3.1   Data and Summary Statistics

The data used in this paper come from the *General Survey of Part-Time Workers' Conditions* (GSPWC; Ministry of Labor 1992, 1997) in 1990 and 1995.[18] The GSPWC surveys those workers who are treated as part-time or arbeit workers in the workplace. Therefore, the sample includes nonregular workers who work long hours. According to the 1997 *Employment Status Survey* (ESS; Statistical Bureau 1998), among female part-time workers who either work less than 200 days per year on regular basis or work more than 200 days per year, 28 percent work less than twenty-two hours per week, whereas 31 percent work more than thirty-five hours per week.[19] There is a large wage gap between full-time and part-time female employees.[20] Therefore, defining part-time workers by number of working hours might mask significant differences between full-time workers and part-time workers with long working hours. This data set is unique in that it contains information on participation in all three insurance programs mentioned above.

The sample is restricted to female part-time workers ages twenty-five to fifty-four who (a) were not enrolled in school at the time of the survey; (b) worked at private-sector establishments in manufacturing, service, wholesale, or retail industries; (c) were classified as nonregular workers; and (d) had nonmissing earnings in the previous year. Weekly hours are calculated by multiplying hours worked per day by days worked per week, and so they are measured with error to the extent that working hours per day vary across days or working days per week vary across weeks.

Before proceeding to the analysis, a discussion on the problems with using these data for our purposes is in order. First, an employee who works for an employer for only a short duration (less than one year) is exempt from enrolling in health insurance, EP, and EI, irrespective of her hours of work. For this reason, a part-time worker may be legally exempt from participating in social insurance programs. In fact, about 8 percent of part-time workers in the sample have worked for their current employer

18. Explanations on this survey are found in the Ministry of Labor data (1992, 1997).
19. The proportion of less than twenty-two hours per week is higher than the figures shown in table 12.3. The possible reasons for this difference are (a) sample selection in this paper is restricted in certain ways; (b) the differences in ways that weekly hours are obtained; and (c) the GSPWC is an establishment survey whereas the ESS is a household survey (the GSPWC surveys establishments of at least five employees).
20. This is observed in the ESS. According to the survey, the median of full-time female workers' earnings is between 2.5 million and 3 million yen, whereas that of part-time and arbeit workers is between 0.5 and 1 million yen (earnings are recorded in intervals in this survey).

for less than one year. Second, there may be measurement error in hours and earnings. In particular, the earnings figures in the survey are those for the previous calendar year, but hours are for the survey year. If labor supply behavior in the survey year differs from that of the previous year, the earnings in the two consecutive years may differ. For our purposes, if the previous year's earnings do not exceed the threshold but earnings in the survey year do, there will be a misclassification in assigning observations into the cells defined in table 12.1. However, in a cross-sectional survey, it is not easy to collect contemporaneous information on annual earnings and social insurance participation status; to get both for the same calendar year, participation status and earnings of the *previous* year must be recorded.

Summary statistics for the sample are presented in table 12.2. The top panel of the table shows the pattern of social insurance participation by marital status for each year. Participation in at least one program increased for both married and single women between 1990 and 1995. For married women, the proportion of those who did not participate in any of the programs declined by 12 percent, while for single women the same proportion declined by 7 percent. However, the proportion of those participating in all three of the programs stayed roughly constant for both married and single women.

There are clear differences in participation patterns between married and single women. Although 49 percent of married women did not participate in any of the programs in 1995, only 27 percent of single women fall into this category. The share of those participating in EP and health insurance is 37 percent for married women and 66 percent for single women (the sum of the EPH Only column and the All Insurance column in table 12.2). So married female part-time workers are less likely to be covered by employer-provided plans. The reasons for this are (a) married women work fewer hours than single women, and (b) among those who work a similar number of hours, married women are less likely to participate than single women. The relative importance of these factors is examined below.

The bottom panel of table 12.2 shows the distribution of social insurance participation by whether the firm requires medical checkups at the time of hiring or on a regular basis.[21] Firms who have more part-time workers participating in employer-provided health insurance plans may be more concerned about the health status of their workers and so may be more likely to require medical checkups. On the other hand, whether a firm provides medical checkups should not be related to participation in EI because workers' health status is not related to the firm's burden of providing EI. The pattern shown in the panel is consistent with this hypothesis. Health

---

21. The provision of a medical checkup is surveyed at the establishment level. Here that information is merged with personal information.

Table 12.2   **Summary Statistics for Female Part-Time Workers Aged 25–54**

	Marital Status	No Insurance	EI Only	EPH Only	All Insurance	Sample Size
	Summary of Social Insurance Participation by Marital Status, 1990 and 1995 (%)					
1990	Married	60.70	6.76	1.46	31.07	13,183
1990	Single	33.98	5.76	3.37	56.89	1,997
1995	Married	48.78	14.00	6.89	30.33	8,420
1995	Single	26.63	7.82	7.55	58.00	1,538
	Health Checkup and Social Insurance Participation, 1995 (%)					
Health checkup at hiring?						
Yes	Married	31.52	16.42	3.52	48.55	3,142
	Single	11.18	4.98	3.04	80.79	588
No	Married	54.88	13.15	8.08	23.89	5,278
	Single	32.57	8.91	9.28	49.24	950
Medical checkup on a regular basis?						
Yes	Married	38.41	17.68	3.88	40.03	6,522
	Single	15.95	7.29	4.79	71.97	1,133
No	Married	67.54	7.34	12.34	12.78	1,898
	Single	44.22	8.68	12.08	35.01	405

Summary Statistics, 1990 and 1995[a]

	1990		1995	
	Married	Single	Married	Single
Income in the previous year	99.130	131.174	107.906	143.466
	(1.14)	(3.195)	(1.663)	(4.085)
Earnings > 1M	0.304	0.609	0.310	0.663
	(0.012)	(0.018)	(0.014)	(0.03)
Log hourly wage	6.501	6.564	6.663	6.737
	(0.008)	(0.014)	(0.008)	(0.014)
Weekly hours	31.299	35.374	28.120	33.193
	(0.322)	(0.497)	(0.269)	(0.572)
Days worked in the previous month	20.750	21.370	19.668	20.492
	(0.166)	(0.225)	(0.118)	(0.253)
Age	42.586	39.273	42.736	37.183
	(0.135)	(0.355)	(0.180)	(0.602)
Tenure	5.230	4.745	5.449	4.567
	(0.104)	(0.195)	(0.118)	(0.221)

Source: Author's calculations from the Ministry of Labor (1992, 1997).

Notes: The sample is restricted to private-sector employees in manufacturing, service, retail, or wholesale industries who were classified as part-time workers, were not enrolled in school, and had nonmissing earnings data. All insurance = enrollment in EP, health insurance, and employment insurance. EI Only = enrollment in employment insurance only. EPH Only = enrollment in EP and health insurance, but not in employment insurance. No insurance = enrollment in none of the three.

[a]Standard errors are in parenthesis.

insurance participation is higher for employers with health checkups: Forty-four percent of married female part-time workers in establishments that provide regular health checkups participated in health insurance, whereas only 25 percent participated in establishments without regular health checkups.

12.3.2   Changes in Wage and Labor Supply from 1990 to 1995

The second panel of table 12.2 contains summary statistics for earnings and hours by marital status. These data reveal that weekly hours decreased by about two to three hours from 1990 to 1995, while hourly wages rose by 16 to 17 percent. The hourly wage increase is close to the growth rates of regional minimum wages during this period, which averaged 17 percent. Importantly, earnings did not grow by as much as hourly wages.

Figures 12.1 and 12.2 present the earnings distribution by marital status. As noted in previous research (Higuchi 1995; Nagase 1997; Abe and Ohtake 1997, among others), a tax-free ceiling of 1 million yen has sig-

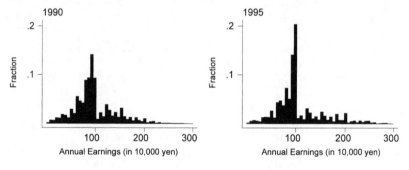

Fig. 12.1   Earnings distribution in 1990 and 1995: Married women
Source: Author's calculations from the GSPWC data.

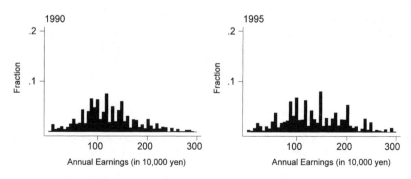

Fig. 12.2   Earnings distribution in 1990 and 1995: Single women
Source: Author's calculations from the GSPWC data.

nificant effects on the labor supply of married women.[22] Married women's earnings are concentrated around 1 million yen, but earnings of single women do not exhibit such a clear concentration at that point. Furthermore, between 1990 and 1995 the earnings of married women below the 1-million-yen ceiling grew. More married women earned between 0.9 and 1 million yen in 1995 than in 1990. However, the fraction earning more than 1 million yen remained unchanged at approximately 30 percent (table 12.2). In response to increases in hourly wages, married women reduced their hours, so their earnings remained constant in nominal terms.

Earnings of single women did not grow much either. In cross section, it is clear that single women's earnings are not as concentrated around 1 million yen as are earnings of married women. However, single women also reduced their hours of work from 1990 to 1995. There are several possible explanations for this reduction. First, during the period analyzed here, working hours of full-time workers were reduced from forty-four hours per week to forty hours per week. Even though there has been no legal initiative to reduce working hours of part-time workers, this regulation may have affected the hours of single female part-time workers, whose hours tend to be relatively long. Second, some single women receive transfer income, which is means tested. In that case, some of these women may have reduced their hours in response to the rise in hourly wages. The change in earnings from 1990 to 1995 can be seen in figures 12.3 and 12.4, where I plot 1990 earnings multiplied by 1.17 and actual 1995 earnings, by marital status. Since wages rose 17 percent on average, had hours remained at their 1990 levels, nominal earnings would have grown by 17 percent. However, as the figures reveal, actual 1995 earnings are concentrated in a lower range for both married and single women.

Table 12.3 shows the share of the sample in each of the nine hours-earnings cells defined by the hours and earnings thresholds for social insurance participation (see table 12.1).[23] The figures in some cells are quite small. For example, the share of workers who work less than the EI minimum hours (twenty-two hours per week in 1990 and twenty hours in 1995) and earn more than the EI minimum earnings (0.9 million yen per year) is less than 3 percent in all four samples. As shown in table 12.3, female part-

22. For earnings up to 1,030,000 yen, a wage earner owes no income tax. For that reason, work disincentives for a part-time worker are often described as the "1.03 million yen ceiling," because such workers try to constrain their earnings to be below 1.03 million yen. The value of the ceiling used to be 1 million yen, so it is sometimes called the "1 million yen ceiling" as well.

23. Higuchi (1995) is one of the earliest studies to calculate social insurance enrollment of part-time workers. He tabulates enrollment rates for health and pension insurance as well as employment insurance for married women of different earnings levels. He finds that participation rises sharply from the 0.9–0.99 million yen range to the 1–1.09 million yen range, and argues that firms may use 1 million yen as the threshold for enrollment in EP and health insurance, even though the threshold in the statute is 1.3 million yen. It seems that he misunderstood the statutory threshold in 1990, believing it to be 1.3 million yen, which is the threshold after 1992, even though it was in fact 1.1 million yen in 1990.

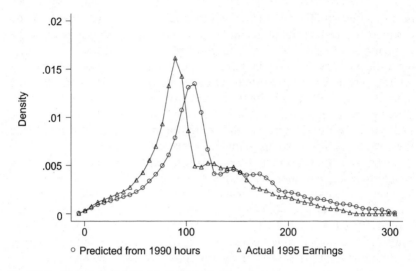

Fig. 12.3   Earnings distribution for married women
Source: Author's calculations from the GSPWC data.

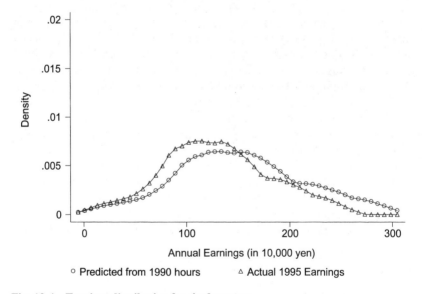

Fig. 12.4   Earnings distribution for single women
Source: Author's calculations from the GSPWC data.

Table 12.3   **Distribution of Hours and Earnings by Marital Status, 1990 and 1995 (%)**

Cell Number	1990				1995			
	Weekly Hours	Annual Earnings	Married	Single	Weekly Hours	Annual Earnings	Married	Single
1	<22	<90	12.84	5.26	<20	<90	9.02	5.58
2	<22	90–110	2.78	1.28	<20	90–130	2.95	0.67
3	<22	110+	0.56	2.44	<20	130+	0.55	1.41
4	22–33	<90	21.47	10.67	20–30	<90	17.26	6.79
5	22–33	90–110	11.75	5.28	20–30	90–130	19.17	6.13
6	22–33	110+	5.70	7.06	20–30	130+	1.97	3.98
7	33+	<90	12.06	9.16	30+	<90	8.95	8.24
8	33+	90–110	10.13	10.45	30+	90–130	19.47	18.74
9	33+	110+	22.72	48.39	30+	130+	20.64	48.46

Source: Author's calculations from the Ministry of Labor (1992, 1997).
Notes: The sample is restricted to female part-time workers aged twenty-five to fifty-four. Annual earnings are measured in 10,000 yen.

time workers work relatively long hours. In 1995, only 13 percent of married female part-time workers worked less than twenty hours per week, whereas 49 percent worked thirty hours or more.

From 1990 to 1995 there were large changes in the distribution of workers over the nine cells, especially for married women. The share earning less than 0.9 million yen per year declined for both married and single women. Due to the increase in hourly wages, it became easier to earn higher income. However, many married part-time workers wanted to constrain their earnings to be less than 1 million yen per year, so the share earning more than 1 million yen remained constant. The changes in the share of workers in each cell in table 12.3 are further complicated by changes in threshold hours. The reduction in the hours threshold acts to increase the share of workers satisfying the conditions for participation. The tendency to constrain labor supply works in the opposite direction, increasing the share of workers who need not enroll.

12.4 Results

12.4.1 The Degree of Noncompliance

Conditional on meeting the participation criteria, noncompliance may be more common among married women than single women.[24]

24. Most of the analysis in this paper is concerned with enrollment in social insurance conditional on labor supply choices. If enrollment behavior were uniform conditional on hours and earnings only, labor supply decisions would basically determine social insurance participation, so there would be no reason to analyze participation conditional on earnings and

Table 12.4 presents 1990 and 1995 participation shares for each of the nine hours-earnings categories. The table lists the results separately by marital status, as labor supply and participation behavior differ between these two groups. Social insurance participation is clearly related to earnings and hours. The share of married women who did not participate in any of the social insurance programs in 1990 is over 97 percent in cell one (weekly hours less than twenty-two and earnings of less than 0.9 million yen), while the same share for cell nine (weekly hours of more than thirty-three and earnings of more than 1.1 million yen) is 10.7 percent. A similar pattern is observed in other groups. So, although noncompliance may exist to some extent, it is not as widespread as some previous research suggests.

In all four samples, almost 80 percent of workers in cell nine participate in all three programs (EP, health insurance, and EI). In this group, married women are no less likely to participate than single women: The option for married women to receive benefits from their husbands' coverage does not seem to affect participation in this range.

For cells seven and eight, nonparticipation is significantly higher for married women than for single women. In 1995, 46 percent of married workers in cell eight did not enroll in any of the insurance programs, compared to 22 percent of single workers. The proportion of workers in cell eight who participated in all of the insurance programs is 31 percent for married women and 52 percent for single women. The larger drop in participation in EP and health insurance from cell nine to cell eight for married women than for single women suggests that "worker-side conditions" significantly affect participation by married women.

Those in cell eight satisfy the conditions for EI participation, yet only 48 percent of married women participated in EI in 1995, whereas 69 percent of single women did. Participation in EI therefore seems to be affected by marital status. Thus, conditional on being in cell eight, EI participation is also correlated with participation in EP and health insurance. In any case, EI participation is not very high among those who satisfy the conditions for EI only (cell five)—for married women, it was 30 percent in 1990 and 43 percent in 1995. Even though EI is mandated for a wider class of part-time workers than are EP and health insurance, EI coverage may not be fully enforced.

---

hours. As the following analysis shows, however, social insurance participation seems to be affected by variables like marital status, age, and firm size, conditional on hours and earnings. The husband's employer may check the income of dependent family members carefully to identify whether they qualify as dependents. If this happens, married women who meet the criteria are not less likely to participate by themselves than are single women, since the benefit for the wife is denied by the husband's employer.

Table 12.4   **Enrollment Behavior Conditional on Weekly Hours and Earnings, 1990 and 1995**

Cell Number	Weekly Hours	Annual Earnings (10,000 yen)	No Insurance (%)	EI Only (%)	EPH Only (%)	All Insurance (%)	Sample Size
			1990, Married				
1	<22	<90	97.52	1.58	0.30	0.60	1,276
2	<22	90–110	92.57	3.39	1.74	2.30	286
3	<22	110+	76.25	0.65	4.43	18.68	77
4	22–33	<90	86.65	7.65	0.91	4.78	2,418
5	22–33	90–110	69.15	15.22	0.90	14.73	1,573
6	22–33	110+	28.33	5.30	1.06	64.81	870
7	33+	<90	71.21	8.83	1.10	18.87	1,270
8	33+	90–110	57.21	9.46	2.34	30.99	1,159
9	33+	110+	10.72	3.12	2.71	83.45	4,254
			1990, Single				
1	<22	<90	93.23	5.09	0.00	1.68	71
2	<22	90–110	98.97	1.03	0.00	0.00	13
3	<22	110+	87.59	0.00	2.61	9.80	37
4	22–33	<90	72.48	8.27	7.13	12.12	145
5	22–33	90–110	54.32	14.83	6.40	24.45	91
6	22–33	110+	41.61	2.63	2.33	53.44	139
7	33+	<90	33.37	4.31	3.29	59.03	174
8	33+	90–110	24.76	9.38	6.10	59.76	179
9	33+	110+	13.40	4.65	2.28	79.67	1,153
			1995, Married				
1	<20	<90	83.41	1.41	13.68	1.50	632
2	<20	90–130	80.69	7.75	9.23	2.33	269
3	<20	130+	17.00	21.16	23.90	37.95	47
4	20–30	<90	78.59	11.57	5.46	4.38	1,065
5	20–30	90–130	51.25	30.31	5.56	12.88	1,533
6	20–30	130+	14.08	8.77	7.53	69.62	204
7	30+	<90	52.74	18.87	11.29	17.10	662
8	30+	90–130	46.05	16.67	6.01	31.26	1,646
9	30+	130+	6.83	2.98	4.42	85.77	2,379
			1995, Single				
1	<20	<90	57.87	0.00	21.43	20.70	56
2	<20	90–130	84.87	6.77	8.36	0.00	17
3	<20	130+	55.15	0.00	40.78	4.06	26
4	20–30	<90	77.28	4.59	11.36	6.76	75
5	20–30	90–130	67.47	5.58	11.59	15.36	66
6	20–30	130+	18.57	3.37	21.68	56.38	44
7	30+	<90	44.34	9.65	3.89	42.12	119
8	30+	90–130	22.10	16.96	8.96	51.97	259
9	30+	130+	8.55	6.21	2.84	82.39	881

Source: Author's calculations from the GSPWC data

Notes: All Insurance = enrollment in EP, health insurance and employment insurance. EI Only = enrollment in employment insurance only. EPH Only = enrollment in EP and health insurance, but not in employment insurance. No Insurance = enrollment in none of the three. For workers under sixty-five, conditions for enrollment are the same for EP and health insurance.

12.4.2   Decomposition of the Enrollment Difference into
Labor Supply Effects and Enrollment Effects

In this section, differences in enrollment patterns of various groups are decomposed into several factors. The first comparison is that of married women and single women. This comparison is important because the low participation rates of part-time workers are partly caused by provisions in the social insurance system that allow married women to receive benefits through their husbands' coverage. Single women do not have such an opportunity, so comparing the two groups reveals the effects of the option to receive benefits from a husband's insurance.[25] I decompose the differences into a labor supply effect and an enrollment behavior effect. The former is the difference in enrollment due to labor supply choices (hours and earnings), and the latter is the difference in likelihood of enrollment conditional on hours and earnings.[26]

The second comparison is that of 1990 and 1995 participation rates. Overall, enrollment in social insurance by part-time workers increased between the two years. As the bottom panel of table 12.2 shows, the proportion who did not participate in any of the three social insurance programs declined 12 percent for married women and 7 percent for single women. These overall changes are decomposed into a labor supply effect, an enrollment behavior effect, and a rule effect. This last one captures the effect of the threshold revisions for hours and earnings that took place between 1990 and 1995.

The decompositions are done in the following manner.[27] Let L be the fraction of workers by labor force status in each of the categories defined by the hours-earnings pairs. The hours-earnings pairs are defined by the thresholds for participation in EP, health insurance, and EI in each year (see table 12.1). Denote L_1 as the distribution of labor force status of the group of interest (for example, married women) and L_0 as the distribution

25. Health insurance (but not pension) coverage can be obtained from another insured and employed family member (for example, from parents). Some single women may have health insurance coverage in this way. However, in 1990, 57 percent of the single women in the sample were divorced or widowed. They are probably less likely to receive health insurance from their parents. The categories of "never married" or "divorced or widowed" were only included in the 1990 survey.
26. Terming the former a labor supply effect may be a bit misleading because it refers here to how the probability distribution over the nine cells changed between the two years. The likelihood of a worker's being included in each of the cells depends on *both* hourly wages and weekly hours.
27. It is possible to perform similar decompositions by using regression coefficients obtained from a model that predicts participation in the two insurance groups (EP and health insurance, and EI). However, such decompositions are quite sensitive to the estimated coefficients. Unless the estimated parameters predict the outcomes well (here, *outcome* refers to the probabilities of the four states that correspond to participation in the two insurance groups), such decompositions may not be reliable. For this reason, the decomposition here is based on simple accounting, which does not use a behavioral model.

of labor force status of the comparison group (for example, single women). Using i to index labor supply categories, L_{i1} in this case represents the fraction of married workers whose labor supply decisions place them in category i. Let p_{jk} be the probability distribution over the four participation states (indexed by j) by workers in the group k ($k = 0,1$). The participation states correspond to (a) not enrolled in employer-provided health insurance nor EP nor EI; (b) enrolled in EI only; (c) enrolled in employer-provided health insurance and EP only; and (d) enrolled in all three. Let β_{ijk} be the probability distribution over the four participation states for those in the kth group and the ith labor supply status category. Then, the difference in the probability of being in participation state j between the two groups can be written as

$$(1) \quad p_{j1} - p_{j0} = \sum_i \beta_{ij1} L_{i1} - \sum_i \beta_{ij0} L_{i0} = \sum_i (\beta_{ij1} - \beta_{ij0}) L_{i1} + \sum_i \beta_{ij0} (L_{i1} - L_{i0})$$

This formula is used to compare the participation patterns of married women to single women.

In comparing participation in 1990 and 1995, it is necessary to control for the changes in the participation conditions that occurred. As explained in section 12.2, the weekly hours thresholds for participation were reduced between 1990 and 1995. For EP and health insurance, the threshold was cut from thirty-three hours per week to thirty hours per week; for EI, it was cut from twenty-two hours per week to twenty hours per week. On the other hand, the earnings threshold for EP and health insurance increased from 1.1 million yen to 1.3 million yen; the threshold for EI remained at 0.9 million yen. These factors will change the likelihood of participation even if hours and earnings are kept constant. To account for this, I decompose the second term of equation (1) into a term that controls for the changes in the rules and a term that captures the changes in labor supply distributions. Specifically, let $\tilde{L}_{i0}$ be the probability distribution over the nine categories of labor supply choices if the 1995 rules were applied to 1990 hours and earnings. Then $\sum_i \beta_{ij0}(\tilde{L}_{i0} - L_{i0})$ corresponds to the changes in participation due to the changes in the rule, evaluated at the participation propensity of group 0 (β_{ij0}). Therefore, in comparing 1990 and 1995 outcomes, the decomposition becomes

$$(2) \quad p_{j1} - p_{j0} = \sum_i \beta_{ij0}(\tilde{L}_{i0} - L_{i0}) + \sum_i \beta_{ij0}(L_{i1} - \tilde{L}_{i0}) + \sum_i (\beta_{ij1} - \beta_{ij0}) L_{i1}.$$

Here, the subscript 1 corresponds to the 1995 outcome, and 0 to the 1990 outcome. The first term is the change in rule term, the second term is the labor supply term, and the final term is the change in participation behavior term.

The results of this decomposition are shown in table 12.5. The changes in rules have mixed effects on participation: The fall in the hours threshold and the rise in the income threshold moved the distribution over the nine

Table 12.5   **Decomposition of Differences in Participation Behavior**

	No Insurance (%)	EI Only (%)	EPH Only (%)	All Insurance (%)
A. Comparison of Married and Single Women, 1995				
Married	48.78	14.00	6.89	30.33
Single	26.63	7.82	7.55	58.00
Difference	22.15	6.18	−0.66	−27.67
Decomposition				
Difference in labor supply	18.11	−0.24	2.15	−20.01
Difference in participation				
behavior	4.03	6.45	−2.80	−7.68
B. Comparison of Married Women, 1990 and 1995				
Actual 1995	48.78	14.00	6.89	30.33
Actual 1990	60.70	6.76	1.46	31.07
Difference	−11.92	7.24	5.43	−0.74
Decomposition				
Difference due to enrollment				
conditions	−0.07	0.59	0.16	−0.67
Difference in labor supply	−0.16	0.52	−0.06	−0.33
Difference in participation				
behavior	−11.70	6.15	5.32	0.23
C. Comparison of Single Women, 1990 and 1995				
Actual 1995	26.63	7.82	7.55	58.00
Actual 1990	33.98	5.76	3.37	56.89
Difference	−7.35	2.06	4.18	1.11
Decomposition				
Difference due to enrollment				
conditions	−3.33	0.60	0.51	2.24
Difference in labor supply	0.24	−0.12	−0.36	0.23
Difference in participation				
behavior	−4.25	1.58	4.02	−1.36

Source: Author's calculations from the GSPWC data

Note: All Insurance = enrollment in EP, health insurance, and employment insurance. EI Only = enrollment in employment insurance only. EPH Only = enrollment in EP and health insurance, but not in employment insurance. No Insurance = enrollment in none of the three. For workers under sixty-five, conditions for enrollment are the same for EP and health insurance.

cells in opposite directions. On the one hand, the reduction in the hours threshold made the fraction of workers who exceeded this threshold go up; on the other hand, the rise in the earnings threshold for EP and health insurance made the fraction of workers in cell nine (who satisfy conditions for participating in all three programs) fall. The upward adjustment of the EP and health insurance threshold is comparable to the rate of general wage increase, so if labor supply decisions had remained the same, the decline in the fraction of workers who meet all the conditions for participation would not have occurred. However, as shown in table 12.3 and figures

12.1 and 12.2, part-time workers generally reduced their work hours during this period, so their earnings growth was limited. Therefore, the fractions in cell five (twenty to thirty hours per week and annual earnings of 0.9–1.3 million yen) and cell eight (over thirty hours per week and annual earnings of 0.9–1.3 million yen) rose. Workers in cell five are not required to participate in EP and health insurance, since hours are less than the threshold. Married women in cell eight are eligible for benefits through their husbands' coverage.

Table 12.5, panel A shows the results of a comparison of married and single women in 1995. Overall, married women are 22 percent more likely to participate in none of the insurance programs, 6 percent more likely to participate in EI only, and 28 percent less likely to participate in all of the programs. A significant portion of each of these differences is explained by the labor supply term. The labor supply factor predicts that married women are 18 percent more likely to participate in none of the programs and 20 percent less likely to participate in all of the programs. Married and single women differ in participation behavior as well. Married women are 4 percent more likely to participate in none of the programs and 8 percent less likely to participate in all of them. Table 12.5, panels B and C, show the 1990 to 1995 comparison separately by marital status. Overall, the fraction participating in none of the programs fell, and the fraction participating in EI only and in EP and health insurance only went up. For single women, the fraction participating in EP and health insurance increased only somewhat. For both groups, the fraction participating in all three programs remained unchanged. The changes in distribution from 1990 to 1995 are largely explained by changes in participation propensity.[28]

12.5   Social Insurance Participation Behavior at the Individual Level

12.5.1   Base Results

In this section, I examine participation behavior at the individual level. Specifically, I look at whether individual participation patterns follow the predictions made in section 12.2.3. I present probit models that predict participation. The dependent variable is either a dummy variable that equals 1 if the worker participates in EP and health insurance and zero otherwise, or a similar dummy for participation in EI. Explanatory variables include dummies for marital status, age category, and firm size, as well as years of tenure and other available controls. If married women are less likely to participate in EP and health insurance, the coefficient of the married dummy will be negative. If older workers are less likely to participate,

---

28. Some of the decomposition results are affected by the order of decomposition, but the general pattern is basically similar.

the coefficients of the older age category dummies will be negative. If large firms are more likely to comply with the rules or if they tend to provide higher benefits, the coefficients of the large firm dummies will be positive.

The four panels of table 12.6 show the regression results from the univariate probit models. Table 12.6, panels A and B, contains results for participation in EP and health insurance, and table 12.6, panels C and D, presents results for EI. Separate regressions are estimated for the sample of workers who meet the conditions for mandatory participation and for the sample of workers who do not.[29] Since participation patterns differ across industries, regressions are also run separately by industry (summary statistics on participation by industry can be found in table 12A.1 in the appendix).

Table 12.6, panel A, lists the estimates from the sample of workers who meet the conditions for mandatory participation in EP and health insurance. Among this sample of workers, neither marital status nor age affects participation. The point estimate of the married dummy is positive, so conditional on satisfying participation conditions, married women are no less likely to participate in EP and health insurance. The coefficients of the age dummies are insignificant, so older workers are no less likely to participate. Participation is higher in larger firms. The coefficients on the 1995 year dummy suggest that the probability of participation increased by 6 percent in the service industry and by 8 percent in wholesale and retail industries. In manufacturing, the coefficient on the 1995 year dummy is small and statistically insignificant. In 1995, the yen appreciated against the dollar significantly, which might have reduced labor demand in manufacturing. Since shorter work hours would reduce the likelihood of participation, participation may not have risen in manufacturing despite the general trend toward increasing participation.

Table 12.6, panel B, shows the estimates from the sample of individuals who do *not* meet all of the conditions for mandatory enrollment in EP and health insurance. As shown in table 12.4, even though participation is not required, some workers do participate. Participation in this group also increased from 1990 to 1995, especially in the service sector. Here, married women are less likely to participate than single women. Older workers are also less likely to participate, suggesting that the higher costs of paying EP and health care benefits to older workers may forestall participation.[30]

Table 12.6, panel C, shows the univariate probit results for EI for work-

29. Regressions presented here are *not* based on a complete model of labor supply and social insurance participation. A complete framework would model the hours, participation in EP and health insurance, and participation in EI decisions simultaneously. Such an analysis is beyond the scope of the paper.

30. I also estimated a similar specification using a subsample of workers in cells seven and eight. Workers in this sample satisfied the employer-side conditions, but not the worker-side conditions. The tendency for older workers to be less likely to participate is stronger in this subsample.

Table 12.6   Probit Estimates of Mandatory and Optional Enrollment

	Manufacturing Sector			Service Sector			Wholesale and Retail Sectors		
	Coefficient	Standard Error	Marginal Effect	Coefficient	Standard Error	Marginal Effect	Coefficient	Standard Error	Marginal Effect
A. Probit Estimates of "Mandatory" Enrollment in EP and Health Insurance									
Year 1995	0.082	(0.137)	0.010	0.255	(0.129)	0.059	0.490	(0.150)	0.081
Married	0.190	(0.156)	0.025	0.161	(0.133)	0.037	0.012	(0.160)	0.002
Age 30–34	-0.119	(0.365)	-0.015	-0.232	(0.206)	-0.057	0.633	(0.325)	0.065
Age 35–39	-0.438	(0.312)	-0.067	-0.132	(0.210)	-0.031	0.594	(0.356)	0.066
Age 40–44	-0.152	(0.310)	-0.019	-0.197	(0.210)	-0.047	0.630	(0.315)	0.076
Age 45–49	-0.144	(0.311)	-0.018	-0.014	(0.195)	-0.003	0.203	(0.314)	0.029
Age 50–54	0.071	(0.319)	0.008	-0.306	(0.236)	-0.076	0.533	(0.368)	0.067
Over 1,000 emp.	1.562	(0.241)	0.143	0.717	(0.258)	0.125	0.924	(0.250)	0.125
500–999 emp.	1.220	(0.248)	0.078	0.447	(0.283)	0.083	0.984	(0.320)	0.086
300–499 emp.	1.173	(0.290)	0.071	0.835	(0.282)	0.125	0.839	(0.325)	0.077
100–299 emp.	0.947	(0.249)	0.069	0.641	(0.237)	0.121	-0.145	(0.285)	-0.023
30–99 emp.	0.631	(0.252)	0.053	0.225	(0.257)	0.047	0.221	(0.269)	0.030
Tenure	0.016	(0.013)	0.002	0.022	(0.022)	0.005	0.043	(0.019)	0.007
Log-likelihood	-1,034.17			-1,004.45			-527.55		
N	4,177			2,465			1,715		

(*continued*)

Table 12.6 (continued)

	Manufacturing Sector			Service Sector			Wholesale and Retail Sectors		
	Coefficient	Standard Error	Marginal Effect	Coefficient	Standard Error	Marginal Effect	Coefficient	Standard Error	Marginal Effect
B. Probit Estimates of Optional Enrollment in EP and Health Insurance									
Year 1995	0.150	(0.082)	0.047	0.543	(0.115)	0.152	0.300	(0.087)	0.080
Married	-0.600	(0.117)	-0.216	-0.421	(0.112)	-0.134	-0.818	(0.142)	-0.280
Age 30–34	-0.295	(0.167)	-0.084	0.108	(0.157)	0.032	-0.146	(0.204)	-0.038
Age 35–39	-0.431	(0.168)	-0.121	-0.199	(0.139)	-0.053	-0.320	(0.208)	-0.080
Age 40–44	-0.473	(0.161)	-0.137	-0.375	(0.149)	-0.098	-0.497	(0.202)	-0.123
Age 45–49	-0.549	(0.166)	-0.154	-0.369	(0.151)	-0.096	-0.455	(0.182)	-0.115
Age 50–54	-0.508	(0.179)	-0.139	-0.241	(0.190)	-0.064	-0.485	(0.210)	-0.113
Over 1,000 emp.	0.991	(0.125)	0.362	0.258	(0.222)	0.078	0.370	(0.161)	0.110
500–999 emp.	0.969	(0.138)	0.357	0.288	(0.147)	0.089	0.504	(0.253)	0.162
300–499 emp.	0.698	(0.162)	0.254	0.298	(0.202)	0.093	0.303	(0.197)	0.093
100–299 emp.	0.468	(0.134)	0.161	0.200	(0.135)	0.060	0.334	(0.191)	0.102
30–99 emp.	0.212	(0.134)	0.069	0.248	(0.158)	0.075	0.187	(0.187)	0.055
Tenure	0.021	(0.010)	0.007	0.037	(0.011)	0.011	0.063	(0.012)	0.018
Log-likelihood	-2,941.04			-2,995.35			-2,371.37		
N	5,655			6,127			4,999		
C. Probit Estimates of "Mandatory" Enrollment in Employment Insurance									
Year 1995	-0.048	(0.091)	-0.016	0.069	(0.117)	0.026	0.127	(0.095)	0.047
Married	-0.507	(0.117)	-0.149	-0.326	(0.129)	-0.120	-0.609	(0.128)	-0.197
Age 30–34	0.029	(0.195)	0.010	-0.085	(0.152)	-0.033	0.249	(0.223)	0.086
Age 35–39	-0.144	(0.177)	-0.050	-0.098	(0.174)	-0.038	-0.299	(0.194)	-0.113
Age 40–44	-0.229	(0.166)	-0.080	-0.239	(0.174)	-0.093	-0.198	(0.197)	-0.073
Age 45–49	-0.198	(0.172)	-0.069	-0.218	(0.160)	-0.084	-0.241	(0.186)	-0.089
Age 50–54	-0.190	(0.179)	-0.066	-0.117	(0.183)	-0.045	-0.180	(0.204)	-0.067
Over 1,000 emp.	1.421	(0.141)	0.355	0.547	(0.235)	0.195	0.824	(0.220)	0.278

	Coef.	(S.E.)	dF/dx	Coef.	(S.E.)	dF/dx	Coef.	(S.E.)	dF/dx
500–999 emp.	1.243	(0.151)	0.289	0.432	(0.174)	0.154	0.658	(0.264)	0.205
300–499 emp.	1.302	(0.196)	0.286	0.751	(0.187)	0.245	0.500	(0.250)	0.162
100–299 emp.	0.666	(0.150)	0.194	0.510	(0.156)	0.183	0.415	(0.233)	0.140
30–99 emp.	0.303	(0.145)	0.097	0.145	(0.167)	0.055	0.299	(0.236)	0.103
Tenure	0.026	(0.008)	0.009	0.047	(0.013)	0.018	0.061	(0.013)	0.022
Log-likelihood	-3,704.55			-2,977.13			-2,176.83		
N	7,099			4,735			3,754		

D. Probit Estimates of Optional Enrollment in Employment Insurance

	Coef.	(S.E.)	dF/dx	Coef.	(S.E.)	dF/dx	Coef.	(S.E.)	dF/dx
Year 1995	0.219	(0.104)	0.071	0.359	(0.101)	0.071	0.242	(0.113)	0.052
Married	-0.452	(0.160)	-0.161	-0.454	(0.119)	-0.107	-0.627	(0.182)	-0.177
Age 30–34	-0.094	(0.197)	-0.029	-0.185	(0.144)	-0.033	-0.508	(0.245)	-0.089
Age 35–39	-0.356	(0.190)	-0.106	-0.126	(0.154)	-0.023	-0.358	(0.289)	-0.068
Age 40–44	-0.401	(0.186)	-0.119	-0.151	(0.158)	-0.028	-0.478	(0.247)	-0.093
Age 45–49	-0.281	(0.194)	-0.085	0.039	(0.175)	0.008	-0.295	(0.239)	-0.060
Age 50–54	-0.090	(0.220)	-0.028	0.159	(0.182)	0.033	-0.153	(0.329)	-0.031
Over 1,000 emp.	1.011	(0.147)	0.374	0.321	(0.175)	0.070	0.780	(0.182)	0.211
500–999 emp.	0.866	(0.161)	0.321	0.309	(0.177)	0.070	0.944	(0.236)	0.292
300–499 emp.	0.842	(0.213)	0.313	0.718	(0.205)	0.194	0.714	(0.286)	0.209
100–299 emp.	0.433	(0.158)	0.151	0.463	(0.150)	0.109	0.892	(0.300)	0.262
30–99 emp.	0.344	(0.153)	0.116	0.439	(0.162)	0.099	0.212	(0.221)	0.050
Tenure	-0.023	(0.014)	-0.007	-0.075	(0.021)	-0.015	-0.024	(0.015)	-0.005
Log-likelihood	-1,448.97			-1,408			-1,179		
N	2,733			3,857			2,960		

Source: Author's calculation from the GSPWC data.

Note: The sample is restricted to workers who either do not satisfy the hours and earnings conditions for EI participation or have worked one year or less for their current employer. The dependent variable is a dummy which takes on a value of 1 if the individual participates in EI, and 0 otherwise. Other explanatory variables are three dummy variables indicating amount of education completed, a dummy indicating location in Tokyo, and four dummies indicating regional minimum wage levels. The excluded age group is twenty-five to twenty-nine year olds. The excluded firm-size group is five to twenty-nine employees. Observations are weighted and standard errors are corrected for correlation across observations in the same establishment. Over 1,000 emp = firms with over 1,000 employees, with similar notation for the other firm-size category dummies.

ers who meet the participation criteria. Unlike the case of EP and health insurance, married women are less likely to participate than single women. As noted in the discussion of summary statistics in section 12.3.1, some married part-time workers who meet the conditions for EI but not those for EP and health insurance do not participate in EI, which may affect the results. This possibility is investigated further below. Most of the age dummy coefficients are insignificant. This is consistent with the hypothesis that, since EI costs are not higher for older workers, older workers are no less likely to participate in EI than younger workers. Again, participation is higher in larger firms.

Table 12.6, panel D, lists results for EI for workers who do not meet the participation conditions. In this specification, married women are less likely to participate and age is not significantly related to lower participation. These patterns are similar to those in table 12.6, panel C.

12.5.2 Correlation between EI Participation and EP and Health Insurance Participation

The results from the EI univariate probit model suggest that participation in EI is influenced by participation in EP and health insurance. To incorporate this effect into the regression models, I estimate a univariate probit model that uses the sample of workers who meet the conditions for EI but do not belong to cell nine. These workers are much less likely to participate in EP and health insurance. The results are shown in table 12.7. For this group, the characteristics that discourage participation in health insurance and EP (marital status or age) generally seem to discourage participation in EI.[31] For example, although participation in EI is considered to be unrelated to marital status, the coefficient of the married dummy in the wholesale and retail sample in table 12.7 is significantly negative. Furthermore, although EI participation is unlikely to be related to age, the marginal effect of older age dummies in manufacturing is significantly negative. So, even though EI has provisions for short-hour workers that allow more part-time workers to participate, participation in EI is affected by factors that are related to participation in EP and health insurance.

12.5.3 Additional Evidence on Participation in Employment Insurance

In section 12.4.2, I showed that the rise in social insurance participation from 1990 to 1995 is largely due to an increase in participation propensity. There are two possible reasons for the increase in participation. One is stricter enforcement of the participation rules. In particular, the short-hour provision of EI that mandates enrollment by workers with twenty-

31. I also estimated an unweighted bivariate probit model for the sample of workers in cell eight. These workers satisfy the conditions for EI participation, but not the worker-side conditions for EP and health insurance enrollment. The model suggests that the error terms in the two equations are highly correlated.

Table 12.7   Probit Estimates of "Mandatory" Enrollment in Employment Insurance by Workers Not in Cell Nine

	Manufacturing Sector			Service Sector			Wholesale and Retail Sectors		
	Coefficient	Standard Error	Marginal Effect	Coefficient	Standard Error	Marginal Effect	Coefficient	Standard Error	Marginal Effect
Year 1995	0.251	(0.105)	0.099	0.142	(0.161)	0.055	0.217	(0.110)	0.086
Married	−0.280	(0.175)	−0.111	−0.208	(0.196)	−0.082	−0.460	(0.175)	−0.180
Age 30–34	−0.202	(0.243)	−0.079	−0.276	(0.236)	−0.104	0.411	(0.300)	0.161
Age 35–39	−0.382	(0.236)	−0.148	−0.185	(0.250)	−0.071	−0.238	(0.267)	−0.094
Age 40–44	−0.526	(0.223)	−0.204	−0.177	(0.264)	−0.068	−0.249	(0.275)	−0.099
Age 45–49	−0.588	(0.230)	−0.227	−0.257	(0.238)	−0.098	−0.119	(0.263)	−0.048
Age 50–54	−0.621	(0.239)	−0.235	−0.010	(0.276)	−0.004	−0.253	(0.280)	−0.100
Over 1,000 emp.	1.173	(0.173)	0.418	0.646	(0.290)	0.253	0.864	(0.256)	0.332
500–999 emp.	1.246	(0.184)	0.431	0.386	(0.216)	0.153	0.736	(0.318)	0.277
300–499 emp.	1.035	(0.196)	0.371	0.670	(0.231)	0.261	0.412	(0.300)	0.161
100–299 emp.	0.428	(0.166)	0.169	0.340	(0.189)	0.135	0.313	(0.281)	0.124
30–99 emp.	0.217	(0.161)	0.086	0.123	(0.202)	0.048	0.471	(0.298)	0.184
Tenure	−0.003	(0.012)	−0.001	0.046	(0.013)	0.018	0.027	(0.017)	0.011
Log-likelihood	−1,723.32			−1,433.43			−1,287.00		
N	2,922			2,270			2,039		

Source: Author's calculations from the GSPWC data.

Note: The sample is restricted to workers who are not in cell nine who satisfy the hours and earnings conditions for EI participation and who have worked more than one year for their current employer. The dependent variable is a dummy which takes on a value of 1 if the individual participates in EI, and 0 otherwise. Other explanatory variables include three dummy variables indicating amount of education completed, a dummy indicating location in Tokyo, and four dummies indicating regional minimum wage levels. The excluded age group is twenty-five to twenty-nine year olds. The excluded firm-size group is five to twenty-nine employees. Observations are weighted and standard errors are corrected for correlation across observations in the same establishment. Over 1,000 emp = firms with over 1,000 employees, with similar notation for the other firm-size category dummies.

two to thirty-two hours or more than 0.9 million yen in earnings was introduced in April of 1989 (the criterion was later changed to twenty to twenty-nine hours per week). As the following data show, enrollment in this category of EI grew rapidly in the 1990s. As the new system became better known among firms and workers, participation in EI may have increased. The second reason is an increased desire to enroll in EP (and health insurance) by single part-time employees. Starting in 1991, those aged twenty and above were required to participate in the public pension program regardless of their earnings. Therefore, a single person without an employer-provided public pension has to enroll in the national pension program and pay a premium of about 13,300 yen per month (1999 premium amount). Before that, participation was voluntary for nonworking or low-income individuals. This change might have made enrollment in EP and health insurance at the employer level a more attractive option for single part-time workers, which might have increased enrollment, leading to higher enrollment in the EP and Health Insurance Only category. Married persons whose spouses enroll in an EP program can be covered without an additional premium (see section 12.2.1).

Here, I present additional evidence on the increase in participation in EI. I use aggregate enrollment data from EI administrative records. Table 12.8 shows the number of women who participated in EI by type of worker (short-hour or regular) and age group. EI for short-hour workers was applied to those who worked twenty-two to thirty-two hours per week in 1992 and twenty to twenty-nine hours per week in 1997. Employment insurance for regular workers was applied to those who worked over thirty-three hours per week in 1992 and over thirty hours per week in 1997. The first two columns show that, from 1992 to 1997, the enrollment of short-hour workers more than doubled for those aged forty-five or over. The next two columns show the ratio of enrollment to the number of workers who work twenty-two to thirty-four hours per week, to control for the possibility that the raw increase in enrollment was caused by an increase in the number of workers.[32] Even controlling for the overall increase in part-time work, enrollment of short-hour workers rose significantly, especially among older workers. This is consistent with the rise in participation in EI only shown in table 12.5. For comparison, changes in the enrollment of regular workers are shown as well (note that part-time workers who work more than thirty hours enroll as regular workers). Since the data do not have infor-

32. For our purposes, it is desirable to use the number of workers whose weekly hours are between the thresholds (twenty to twenty-nine hours per week in 1997). However, such numbers are not published in the nationally representative data set. Not many Japanese governmental surveys ask employment status and weekly working hours in the same survey questionnaire. One such survey is the *Special Survey of the Labor Force Survey,* but the published data do not contain figures for the number of workers who work twenty to twenty-nine hours per week.

Table 12.8   **Employment Insurance Participation, 1992 and 1997**

Age	Raw Enrollment (thousands)		Ratio of Enrollment to the Number of workers	
	1992	1997	1992	1997
Employment Insurance Participation by Short-hour Workers, 1992 and 1997				
<20	1.77	3.17	0.032	0.053
20–24	11.97	20.64	0.082	0.092
25–29	21.73	33.61	0.112	0.143
30–34	24.21	41.64	0.105	0.150
35–39	39.42	66.58	0.107	0.175
40–44	73.08	101.71	0.126	0.208
45–49	59.95	143.17	0.128	0.227
50–54	42.00	94.47	0.124	0.232
55–59	23.41	59.49	0.112	0.197
60–64	13.29	31.29	0.113	0.184
Employment Insurance Participation by Regular-hour Workers, 1992 and 1997				
<20	450.04	223.64	0.872	0.793
20–24	2515.78	2191.34	0.862	0.836
25–29	1566.04	1955.48	0.804	0.840
30–34	834.05	1061.05	0.707	0.798
35–39	817.02	861.52	0.648	0.736
40–44	1256.42	984.72	0.698	0.721
45–49	1111.16	1399.15	0.718	0.749
50–54	1047.28	1098.75	0.764	0.778
55–59	768.00	908.48	0.778	0.810
60–64	320.29	387.67	0.725	0.814

Source: Enrollment data are from the Annual Report on Employment Insurance (various years). Number of workers working twenty-two to thirty-four hours per week are based on the published data from the Statistical Bureau (1984 and 1998).

Notes: Short-hour workers are defined as working twenty-two to thirty-two hours per week in 1992 and twenty to twenty-nine hours per week in 1997. Regular-hour workers are defined as working at least thirty-three hours per week in 1992 and at least thirty hours per week in 1997. Number of workers (in the denominator) is defined as those working at least thirty-five hours per week. Many public-sector employees who are not covered by EI are counted in the denominator. Therefore, the ratio is not the enrollment rate.

mation on EP and health insurance participation or marital status, it is impossible to assess the effect of the system on participation in detail. Nonetheless, the figures suggest that one of the reasons for higher participation in later years is stricter enforcement of the new rules.

12.6 Conclusion

In this paper, I examine the social insurance participation of a group of Japanese female part-time workers using microdata. There are four main conclusions. First, there has been an increase in social insurance participation by female part-time workers from 1990 to 1995. This increase is a result not of changing labor supply behavior, but of increased policy compliance and higher participation by those for whom enrollment is not mandatory. Second, conditional on satisfying the participation conditions for EP and health insurance, married women are no less likely to participate in social insurance than single women. However, among those who do not meet the conditions for mandatory EP and health insurance, married women are significantly less likely to participate. The provision that married women can claim benefits from their husbands' coverage discourages participation by this group.

Third, participation in EI is not very high among those who work twenty to thirty hours per week and earn 0.9 million to 1.3 million yen. Even though EI has provisions for short-hour workers that mandate participation, these provisions may not be very well enforced. Fourth, participation by part-time workers who meet the conditions for mandatory EP and health insurance is unrelated to age. Older part-time workers are no less likely to participate than younger part-time workers. However, among workers who only partially meet these conditions, older workers are less likely to participate than younger workers. This latter finding is consistent with the hypothesis that paying benefits to older workers is more costly than paying benefits to younger workers.

Appendix

The Cost of Paying EP Benefits for Firms with EPFs

If a firm has an EPF, the EPF pays the earnings-related portion of public pension benefits (except for adjustments for inflation and wage increases).

The EPFs are firm pension plans that pay supplemental pensions for retired employees. The EPFs are closely linked to EP programs through a system called "substituting the payment of employees' pension (*daikoseido*)."[33] The EP benefit has an earnings-related portion that is proportional to one's contributions at young ages. If a firm has an EPF, the earnings-related portion of the benefit (excluding the part for indexation to wage growth and inflation) is paid by the EPF of the firm. The present discounted value of the future benefits of an older employee is higher than

33. This had been mandated for the EPFs until March 2002. However, starting April 2002, the EPFs were allowed to transfer the obligation to substitute the payment of EP to the government. If the firm transfers, the argument here may not apply. But in 1990 and 1995 (the years for the data used in this paper), the EPFs were required to substitute the payment, so the argument here is applicable.

that of a younger employee because the benefits for an old employee will be paid in the near future, whereas those for a young employee will be paid in the remote future. Therefore, for firms with EPFs, pension benefit costs of older employees are higher than those of younger employees. Other things being equal, firms may be cautious in hiring older workers because the burden of their pension benefits is greater.

The Cost of Paying Health Care Benefits

If a firm forms an HIS, the firm self-insures its employees and dependents younger than sixty-nine (inclusive). However, the insurance premium rate is not allowed to vary across insured workers within an HIS. Therefore, healthy workers pay more in premiums than they spend on health care, while less-healthy workers spend more than they pay. Given this structure, attracting enrollees with large health expenditures would weaken the financial condition of an HIS. Health expenditures are likely to vary considerably across individuals. Since old workers are less healthy than young workers, firms may be cautious about including old workers in the HIS. Firms may keep the working hours of old part-time workers low so that they do not have to include them in the firm's health insurance plan.

Considerations for Part-Time Workers

Conditional on enrollment, there is no difference in health care benefits and health insurance premium rates between full-time and part-time workers. In other words, full-time and part-time workers who participate in health insurance are treated the same.

There is an important difference between full-time and part-time workers in the firm portion of the EPFs. Part-timers are usually ineligible for corporate pension benefits (due to the way firms typically set up their corporate pension plan). However, part-time workers who work in a firm with an EPF must participate in the firm's EPF for the purposes of receiving the earnings-related portion of their pension. If a worker enrolls in the EPF for more than ten years, the earnings-related portion of her EP benefits are paid by the EPF (rather than the Social Insurance Agency). On the other hand, if an employee works for a firm for less than ten years, the earnings-related portion is not paid by the firm's EPF, but by the Association of Employees' Pension Funds (AEPF). However, when the worker leaves the firm, the firm pays the present discounted value of the earnings-related portion of the worker's future benefits to the AEPF. Since the present discounted value of future benefits are higher for older employees (because they will start receiving benefits in the near future), the pension cost for the firm in this case is higher for older employees.

Table 12A.1   Social Insurance Participation by Industry

Year	Marital status	Industry	No Insurance (%)	EI Only (%)	EPH Only (%)	All Insurance (%)
1990	Married	Manufacturing	47.35	7.47	1.33	43.85
		Service	72.45	3.81	1.02	22.72
		Wholesale and retail	65.36	7.77	1.80	25.07
1990	Single	Manufacturing	18.27	4.23	1.59	75.91
		Service	48.86	6.29	3.31	41.55
		Wholesale and retail	33.54	6.25	4.34	55.87
1995	Married	Manufacturing	41.92	15.24	5.27	37.57
		Service	50.74	10.14	10.23	28.89
		Wholesale and retail	51.65	14.76	6.53	27.07
1995	Single	Manufacturing	24.11	7.21	4.83	63.85
		Service	32.59	5.68	10.50	51.23
		Wholesale and retail	23.98	9.27	6.72	60.03

Source: Author's calculations from the Ministry of Labor (1992, 1997) data.
Notes: EI = employment insurance; EPH = employees' pension fund.

References

Abe, Y., and F. Ohtake. 1997. The effects of income tax and social security on the part-time labor supply in Japan. *Review of Social Policy*, no. 6:45–64.

Feldstein, M., and A. Samwick. 1992. Social security rules and marginal tax rates. *National Tax Journal* 45 (1): 1–22.

Higuchi, Y. 1995. The economic consequences of protection policies for nonworking married women. In *Economic analysis of protection policies for the "disadvantaged"* (in Japanese), ed. T. Hatta and N. Yashiro, 105–219. Tokyo: Nihon Keizai Shimbun sha.

Ministry of Labor, Government of Japan. Various years. *Annual report on employment insurance.* Tokyo: Ministry of Labor.

———. 1992. *Report on the general survey of part-time workers' conditions, 1990* (in Japanese). Tokyo: Ministry of Labor.

———. 1997. *Report on the general survey of part-time workers' conditions, 1995* (in Japanese). Tokyo: Ministry of Labor.

Nagase, N. 1997. Part no chingin ha naze hikui ka? Shoseido no ashikase (Why are part-time wages so low? Obstacles by institutions). Ochanomizu University, Graduate School of Humanities and Sciences. Mimeograph.

Statistical Bureau, Prime Minister's Office. 1984. *Employment status survey, results for Japan 1982.* Tokyo: Statistical Bureau.

Statistical Bureau, Management and Coordination Agency. 1993. *Employment status survey, results for Japan 1992.* Tokyo: Statistical Bureau.

Statistical Bureau, Management and Coordination Agency. 1998. *Employment status survey, results for Japan 1997.* Tokyo: Statistical Bureau.

Takayama, N. 1997. Public pension reform. In *Income maintenance policies in an aged society* (in Japanese), ed. Naohiro Yashiro, 119–36. Tokyo: University of Tokyo Press.

13

Unions, the Costs of Job Loss, and Vacation

Fumio Ohtake

13.1 Introduction

Many researchers have pointed out that Japanese workers' effort level is high. They often cite the low nonattendance rate in Japan as evidence of high worker effort since it is difficult to measure actual effort levels (Koshiro 1978, 1980; Ishida 1985).[1] This paper investigates the effects of human resource management systems, such as steep tenure-wage profiles, nonvested retirement allowance systems, and labor market conditions, on the amount of vacation time taken by workers in Japan.

The fact that wages are cut proportionally in response to nonattendance in Japan would seem to imply that nonattendance does not affect productivity. However, nonattendance has potential productivity effects, as pointed out by Koike (1981) and Weiss (1985). First, nonattendance reduces working hours. Second, nonattendance increases costs because firms are forced to reallocate workers in order to cover for absent workers. The characteristics of both the jobs and skills of workers can alter the productivity effects of nonattendance. For example, in auto assembly plants, where the complementarity of workers on a line is very high, nonattendance should have negative productivity effects. If nonattendance has negative productivity effects, firms should have employment systems with in-

Fumio Ohtake is professor at the Institute of Social and Economic Research at Osaka University.

The author thanks Richard Freeman, Hideshi Itoh, Takenori Inoki, Hisako Ishii, Megumi Nakamura, Hajime Miyazaki, Atsushi Seike, participants in the National Bureau of Economic Research–Japan Center for Economic Research Hawaii conference, and participants in the Seventh Labor Economics Conference for helpful comments on an earlier draft.

1. For example, Koike (1981) points out that worker morale affects absenteeism.

centives designed to reduce nonattendance, such as counting it in merit ratings and making it a factor in dismissal decisions.

We should distinguish between good and bad vacation time. Good vacations are paid holidays, sick leaves, or legal or contracted vacations. Bad vacations consist of nonattendance due to absenteeism, shirking, and absence without leave. Bad vacations have larger negative productivity effects than good vacations. However, the distinction between these two types of vacation is relatively weak in Japan, as will be explained presently.

This paper compares the effect of the costs of job loss (to workers) on the amount of vacation time taken in firms with and without unions. The cost of job loss is high when the tenure-wage profile is steep, retirement allowances are nonvested, or finding an alternative job is difficult. According to the bonding hypothesis of Lazear (1979), steep tenure-wage profiles and nonvested retirement allowances increase worker effort by increasing the opportunity cost of shirking because workers are fired if their shirking is detected. The efficiency wage hypothesis can also explain the amount of vacation time taken. Both higher unemployment rates and higher wage rates increase the costs of job loss; therefore, workers will increase their effort correspondingly.

Although no worker shirks (and thus is dismissed) in equilibrium in these theoretical models, it is an important assumption that firms can dismiss workers if they do shirk. However, it is very difficult to dismiss full-time workers in unionized firms in Japan. Although Japanese firms have long-term employment practices with high employment security, widely known as lifetime employment, Japan does not have legislation generally prohibiting dismissals without just cause. Restrictions on dismissals are provided by case law.[2] Since employment security is provided by case law, workers must file suit in court in order to challenge dismissals (Araki 2002). Although workers in unionized firms are protected by case law because unions can support workers undergoing legal proceedings, workers in nonunionized firms may be dismissed more easily. This is because it is difficult for a worker to file suit in court without union support due to high legal costs.[3]

Under this legal system, the effectiveness of internal and external threats in reducing vacation time is affected by the presence or absence of a union. Internal threats include the costs of job loss due to a wage system with a steep tenure-wage profile and a nonvested retirement allowance system. External threats include the difficulty of finding alternative jobs due to high wages at the current job and high unemployment. Because unions reduce

2. The costs of illegal dismissals for firms are very high. If the employer's exercise of the right to dismiss is judged to be abusive and invalid, the employer is obligated not only to give the employee back pay covering the period of dismissal, but also to reinstate him or her.
3. There is no low-cost individual dispute settlement system specifically provided for workers, as is available in European countries.

the potency of internal and external threats of job loss (by making it more difficult for employers to dismiss workers), vacation time taken by employees should be less responsive to such threats in unionized firms than in nonunionized firms.

We should take into account Japanese employment practices when we analyze the determinants of vacation time. First, the Labor Standards Law in Japan stipulates a minimum length of paid vacation apart from any union contract. Second, Japanese workers often use granted annual paid leave retroactively. As Dore (1973, 187–88) writes:

> It is almost universally the practice to ask that days taken off for sickness should be counted as part of one's annual holiday. (That way one gets a perfect attendance record which automatically gets one some way towards a good merit rating.) The next, more or less legitimate, claim on holidays is for attending weddings and funerals. Those who do not use up their ten, fifteen or twenty day's holiday in these ways, may take other days off with the foreman's agreement, though it may be a rather unwilling ex post facto agreement.

Moreover, until recently, many Japanese firms accorded disadvantageous treatment to workers who had taken paid annual leave. As Sugeno (1992, 269) writes: "There are still a significant number of enterprises in which the taking of annual leave would have a negative effect on various allowances (e.g., a perfect-attendance allowance), bonuses and wage raises."[4] These employment practices may partly explain the low level of vacation taken in Japan. Thus, in this paper, I examine both pure vacation time and a broader definition of vacation time, including used annual paid leave.

This paper is organized as follows: Section 13.2 briefly surveys the literature on the economic analysis of vacation; section 13.3 discusses the data; section 13.4 presents the models; section 13.5 discusses the estimation results; and section 13.6 concludes.

13.2 Vacation Determinants: Theory and Evidence

13.2.1 The Contracted Working Hours Model and the Worker Discipline Model

There are two main economic explanations for vacation. First, workers use vacation to minimize discrepancies between contracted working hours and optimal working hours, which maximizes utility at a given wage rate. Second, workers use vacation time to shirk under imperfect monitoring (Brown and Sessions 1996; Barmby, Sessions, and Treble 1994).

---

4. The 1988 law revising the Labor Standards Law provided that "an employer must not reduce the wages or otherwise accord disadvantageous treatment to a worker for having taken paid annual leave" (Supp. Provns, Art. 134).

In order to reduce vacation time taken due to shirking under imperfect monitoring, firms can increase the costs of job loss by paying an efficiency wage (Shapiro and Stiglitz 1984) and providing a bonding system, such as a nonvested retirement allowance or a steep tenure-wage trajectory (Lazear 1979). An important assumption in the models of Shapiro and Stiglitz (1984) and Lazear (1979) is that shirking workers who are detected by a firm will be dismissed. Thus, I call these two models worker discipline models.

Efficiency wages or bonding mechanisms will not work unless the dismissal probability is higher for workers who take more vacation. Ferguson and Filer (1986) find empirical evidence consistent with these theories in U.S. data. In Japan, the retirement allowance system may work to reduce vacation time. According to the *Survey on Honor and Disciplinary Action* by the Institute for Labor Administration (Romu Gyosei Kenkyusho 1997), workers who are absent more than two weeks without leave are dismissed in disgrace in most Japanese firms; 91 percent of firms do not pay any allowance on principle in disciplinary dismissals.

The efficiency wage model also suggests that the business cycle should affect vacation. According to the efficiency wage model, vacation should change procyclically (Leigh 1985; Kaivanto 1997) since the cost of job loss is lower in periods of low unemployment.[5]

Thus, the basic hypothesis of vacation determination models based on the worker discipline theory is represented by the following vacation time function:

(1) $\text{Vac} = f(cjl, X), f_{cjl} < 0,$

where Vac is vacation time, *cjl* is cost of job loss that is affected by the steepness of the tenure-wage profile and the size of the retirement allowance in the bonding model and the active ratio of job openings to applicants in the efficiency wage model,[6] and X represents other factors affecting vacation time.

13.2.2   Unions and Vacation

The effect of unions on vacation time is theoretically ambiguous. Both union voice and union wage effects should decrease vacation time. If unions can improve working conditions, they may reduce vacation time by

---

5. This model is often called the worker discipline model. Another explanation for procyclical changes in vacation time is given by the selection bias model. This model posits that, in recessions, workers with high vacation levels are dismissed so that average vacation time decreases.

6. Since unemployment rate by prefecture is not available for the survey years, I use the active ratio of job openings to applicants, which is often used as a measure of the tightness of the labor market in Japan.

increasing workers' satisfaction. If unions can increase wages, the discrepancy between contracted working hours and optimal working hours will be reduced.[7]

On the other hand, since unions may reduce the potency of internal and external threats of job loss (by making it more difficult for employers to dismiss workers) as Green and MacIntosh (1998) showed, vacation time should be less responsive to such threats in unionized firms than in nonunionized firms. Since employment security is provided by case law, workers need to file suit in court in order to be protected against dismissal. Although workers in unionized firms are protected by case law, workers in nonunionized firms may be dismissed easily because of high legal costs in Japan. I express this hypothesis as

$$(2) \qquad \frac{\partial f}{\partial cjl}\bigg|_{\text{nonunion firms}} < \frac{\partial f}{\partial cjl}\bigg|_{\text{union firms}} \leq 0.$$

Moreover, because of high firing costs, managers in unionized firms may increase monitoring costs instead of paying efficiency wages or creating a bonding system. Workers in unionized firms may accept high levels of monitoring through performance evaluation in exchange for high job security.[8] Another possibility is that unionized firms try to screen for workers with a low tendency toward taking vacation since it is more difficult to dismiss union workers.

13.3   Data

I use firm-level microdata from the 1985 and 1993 *General Survey on Working Hours and Conditions* (GSWHC) conducted by the Ministry of Labor in Japan. Firms with more than thirty employees are surveyed about various issues concerning working conditions every year. I selected the 1985 and 1993 surveys because these two surveys asked firms about both retirement allowance systems and vacation.

There were 4,910 firms included in the 1985 survey, and 4,951 firms in the 1993 survey. When I restrict the sample to records without missing values for the retirement allowance question, 3,117 records remain. I use this smaller sample to estimate my models.

To measure vacation, I use average days of vacation for full-time workers in each firm. I use two definitions of vacation: bad vacation only and total vacation. Bad vacation only is defined as worker absence except for annual holidays, paid vacation, and special vacation, such as sick leave. Total

---

7. Here, I assume that the substitution effect is larger than the income effect.
8. The merit pay system is applied to blue-collar workers as well as to white-collar workers in Japan (Fujimura 1989).

Table 13.1   **Bad Vacation Rate and Days, by Firm Size**

Firm Size	1985 ($N = 4,910$)	1993 ($N = 4,951$)	Total ($N = 9,861$)	Union ($N = 4,614$)	Nonunion ($N = 5,247$)	Total ($N = 9,861$)
			Bad Vacation Rate (%)			
5000+	0.472	0.426	0.447	0.452	0.365	0.447
1,000–4,999	0.509	0.518	0.514	0.482	0.651	0.514
300–999	0.806	0.499	0.635	0.646	0.620	0.635
100–299	1.240	0.862	1.034	0.907	1.110	1.034
30–99	1.694	1.055	1.354	1.039	1.406	1.354
Total	1.518	0.963	1.220	0.888	1.322	1.220
			Bad Vacation Days			
5000+	1.234	1.069	1.145	1.158	0.937	1.145
1,000–4,999	1.366	1.351	1.357	1.250	1.806	1.357
300–999	2.240	1.289	1.710	1.721	1.695	1.710
100–299	3.547	2.317	2.878	2.496	3.105	2.878
30–99	4.942	2.884	3.848	2.914	4.002	3.848
Total	4.406	2.618	3.446	2.453	3.751	3.446

Source: Author's calculation from the 1985 and 1993 GSWHC.

vacation is the sum of bad vacation only and days of used annual paid leave (good vacation). Annual paid leave is defined as the amount legally stipulated by article 39 of Japan's Labor Standards Law.

The supplementary provision of article 134 in the 1987 revision of Japan's Labor Standards Law states that the "employer must not reduce the wages or otherwise accord disadvantageous treatment to a worker for having taken paid annual leave." However, "there is a case which holds that the treatment of consumed annual-leave days as absences for bonus purposes does not violate public policy and good morals because of the extent of disadvantageous treatment" (Sugeno 1992, 281).

Most Japanese workers do not use all of their annual paid leave. The average utilization ratio of annual paid leave is about 50 percent according to the 1993 GSWHC. According to the 1997 Japan Institute of Labor survey on sick leave (JIL 1998), 77.5 percent of workers reported that they did not use all of their annual paid leave because they had made provisions for sickness and injury. The 1997 JIL survey also shows that Japanese workers tend to use annual paid leave rather than sick leave for short-term illness.

Tables 13.1 and 13.2 show mean bad vacation and total vacation time by firm size, calculated from the full sample of 9,989 firms. The bad vacation rate was 1.5 percent in 1985 and 0.96 percent in 1993.[9] The bad vacation

---

9. A possible institutional reason for the fact that the bad vacation rate was lower in 1993 than in 1985 is the revision of the Japanese Labor Standards Law. The 1987 revision increased the starting number of annual paid leave days from six to ten. It supplemented this increase with a provision that confirmed that disadvantageous treatment of workers who take annual leave violates the principle guaranteeing such leaves.

Table 13.2   **Total Vacation Rate and Days, by Firm Size**

Firm Size	1985 ($N = 4{,}910$)	1993 ($N = 4{,}924$)	Total ($N = 9{,}834$)	Union ($N = 4{,}608$)	Nonunion ($N = 5{,}226$)	Total ($N = 9{,}834$)
		Total Vacation Rate (%)				
5000+	4.072	5.059	4.598	4.632	4.013	4.598
1,000–4,999	3.721	3.950	3.852	3.990	3.268	3.852
300–999	3.298	3.612	3.472	3.834	2.967	3.472
100–299	3.442	3.618	3.537	3.924	3.308	3.537
30–99	3.592	3.464	3.524	3.965	3.451	3.524
Total	3.545	3.523	3.533	3.941	3.408	3.533
		Total Vacation Days				
5000+	10.563	12.519	11.606	11.689	10.173	11.606
1,000–4,999	9.839	9.906	9.877	10.192	8.542	9.877
300–999	8.965	9.158	9.072	9.992	7.794	9.072
100–299	9.648	9.444	9.535	10.468	8.980	9.535
30–99	10.355	9.297	9.794	10.847	9.619	9.794
Total	10.109	9.342	9.699	10.552	9.436	9.699

Source: Author's calculation from the 1985 and 1993 GSWHC.
Note: Total vacation is the sum of bad vacation and the used annual paid leave.

rate is lower in larger firms than in smaller firms. Average days of bad vacation are 3.4 days for the full sample and about 1 day for a sample of large firms only. This may be explained by evidence that the sick leave system is more prevalent in larger firms in Japan, as found in the 1997 JIL survey and the 1997 GSWHC. In the United States and the United Kingdom, on the other hand, absence rates are higher in larger firms (Winkler 1980; Allen 1981; Allen 1982; and Wilson and Peel 1991).

On average, the bad vacation rate is lower in union firms than in nonunion firms. However, for firms with more than 300 employees, both bad and total vacation rates are higher in union firms than in nonunion firms.

13.4   Estimation Model and Descriptive Statistics

13.4.1   Estimation Model

I test the worker discipline hypotheses by specifying linear functions for vacation taken in firm i, Vac_i, by union status:

$$(3) \qquad \text{Vac}_{Ui} = \alpha_U \text{Ret}_{Ui} + \beta_U \text{Fwage}_{Ui} + \gamma_U \text{JOA}_{Ui} + \delta_U \mathbf{X}_{Ui}$$

$$(4) \qquad \text{Vac}_{Ni} = \alpha_N \text{Ret}_{Ni} + \beta_N \text{Fwage}_{Ni} + \gamma_N \text{JOA}_{Ni} + \delta_N \mathbf{X}_{Ni},$$

where U and N represent unionized and nonunionized firms, respectively. Ret, Fwage, and JOA are proxies for the costs of job loss to workers. Ret_{Xi}

is the ratio of retirement allowance to wage at the mandatory retirement age. Fwage is the wage at the mandatory retirement age. JOA is the ratio of active job openings to applicants in the prefecture where the firm is located. X is a vector of other firm characteristics. The predictions in equation (2) are then represented by the following hypotheses:·

HYPOTHESIS 1. $\alpha_N < \alpha_U \leq 0$

HYPOTHESIS 2. $\beta_N < \beta_U \leq 0$

HYPOTHESIS 3. $\gamma_N > \gamma_U \geq 0$

Hypotheses 1, 2, and 3 state that internal and external costs of job loss motivate greater effort and reduce vacation and that the effects are greater in nonunionized firms than in unionized firms because of reduced threat credibility in the latter. A stronger version of these hypotheses is that costs of job loss have *no* impact in the unionized sector because it is too difficult to dismiss workers in unionized firms in Japan.

13.4.2   Explanatory Variables

Table 13.3 lists the explanatory variables used in the estimation. The average number of days of bad vacation is defined as total days of bad vacation divided by the number of full-time workers. As explained above, I also use a total vacation measure, which is defined as the sum of bad vacation days and used days of granted annual paid leave, since workers often use granted annual paid leave retroactively when they are absent due to sickness.[10]

Average wage at the mandatory retirement age is a proxy for the steepness of the tenure-wage profile if we assume that starting wages for new graduates are the same for all workers in Japan.[11] In the survey, firms are asked about the average monthly wages of workers who separate from the firm in the survey year due to mandatory retirement.

I use the sum of lump-sum retirement allowance payments and the present value of the company pension plan at the mandatory retirement age as a measure of the size of the retirement allowance. This retirement allowance is the average retirement allowance for workers who are dismissed during the survey year due to mandatory retirement.[12]

---

10. Of course, a high average vacation rate may mean good working conditions and may boost worker morale and productivity.

11. This assumption is reasonable because wage differences among young workers are small in Japan. The dispersion of earnings in 1993 was only 1.58 for workers aged twenty to twenty-four, as compared to 3.16 for workers aged sixty to sixty-four, where dispersion is measured as the ratio of the upper earnings limit of the 9th decile of male workers to the upper earnings limit of the 1st decile (D9/D1). The dispersion of starting wages in 1993 was only 1.16 for university graduates and 1.23 for high school graduates, according to the *Basic Survey on Wage Structure* (Policy and Research Division, Ministry of Labor 1993).

12. There are potential problems with using information about retirement allowances in cases of mandatory retirement. First, the retirement allowance system for retired workers may not be the same as for current workers. In this paper, I assume workers have static expecta-

Table 13.3   **Sample Means**

Variable	Description/Units	Full Sample	Union	Nonunion
Bad vacation rate	Percent	0.972	0.821	1.177
		(1.351)	(0.950)	(1.731)
Bad vacation days	Average days absent per worker	2.658	2.233	2.826
		(3.833)	(2.664)	(3.949)
Total vacation rate	Percent	4.034	4.281	3.701
		(1.945)	(1.848)	(2.025)
Total vacation days	Number of days	10.777	11.268	10.097
		(5.324)	(4.961)	(5.714)
Firm size	Number of workers	545.670	804.403	196.936
		(2416.282)	(3130.041)	(540.607)
Annual paid leave	Number of days of entitled	14.888	16.212	13.103
	annual paid leave	(4.124)	(3.965)	(3.634)
JOA	Active ratio of job openings to	0.789	0.764	0.820
	applicants in firm's prefecture	(0.292)	(0.283)	(0.301)
Retirement	Amount of retirement allowance	1280.014	1375.786	946.874
allowance	(in 1995 yen)	(775.77)	(772.246)	(691.834)
Wage	Monthly wage at retirement (in	32.224	33.819	30.075
	1995 yen)	(10.432)	(10.592)	(9.816)
Point system	Dummy for point-based retire-	0.055	0.063	0.027
	ment allowance system	(0.228)	(0.243)	(0.163)
University ratio	Share of university graduates	0.110	0.129	0.085
	among workers subject to	(0.266)	(0.273)	(0.253)
	mandatory retirement			
High school white-	Share of high school graduates	0.288	0.297	0.277
collar ratio	among white-collar workers	(0.392)	(0.371)	(0.419)
	subject to mandatory retirement			
High school blue-	Share of high school graduates	0.180	0.191	0.165
collar ratio	among blue-collar workers	(0.344)	(0.335)	(0.356)
	subject to mandatory retirement			
Six-day workweek	Six-day workweek dummy (Six-	0.130	0.0988	0.146
	day workweek = 1, five-day	(0.336)	(0.298)	(0.353)
	workweek = 0)			
Union	Union firm dummy (union = 1,	0.574	1.000	0.000
	nonunion = 0)	(0.495)	(0.000)	(0.000)
Log bad vacation	Log of bad vacation days	0.238	0.114	0.405
		(1.328)	(1.319)	(1.322)
Log total vacation	Log of total vacation days	2.243	2.306	2.157
		(0.552)	(0.522)	(0.580)
Log retirement	Log of retirement allowance	6.961	7.062	6.609
allowance		(0.661)	(0.606)	(0.722)
Log wage	Log of monthly wage at retire-	3.423	3.475	3.353
	ment	(0.316)	(0.305)	(0.318)
Log annual holidays	Log of number of annual paid	2.654	2.752	2.522
	leave days	(0.333)	(0.281)	(0.352)
Log firm size	Log of firm size	5.212	5.660	4.609
		(1.245)	(1.260)	(0.932)
Log JOA	Log of active ratio of job open-	−0.310	−0.340	−0.269
	ings to applicants	(0.386)	(0.384)	(0.385)
N		3,117	2,421	696

Source: Authors' calculations from the 1985 and 1993 GSWHC.

Notes: Observations with missing values, extreme values, or both are dropped. Extreme values are defined as those that are at least 4 standard deviations away from the mean. Wages and retirement allowances are standardized to 1995 yen using the Consumer Price Index (CPI).

The JOA is the active ratio of job openings to applicants in the prefecture where the firm is located. To capture information about contracted working hours, I incorporate a dummy variable for the length of the workweek. This dummy variable takes on a value of 1 if the firm has a six-day workweek and a value of zero if the firm has a five-day workweek. Firm size is defined using the sum of full- and part-time workers. The average number of legally stipulated annual paid-leave days is calculated for full-time workers in each firm.

If firms use a performance-evaluation system to determine wages and retirement allowances, they can rely on threats of changes in these compensation factors in addition to worker dismissal in order to reduce vacation. Although the survey does not include information on performance-evaluation systems, firms were asked about the introduction of a point-based retirement allowance system. In such systems, the amount of the retirement allowance is determined as a multiple of the monthly wage at the time of the worker's separation from the firm. The multiplier is a function of the length of tenure and the reason for separation. In some firms, only the length of tenure determines the amount of the retirement allowance. Under the point-based system, however, the amount of the retirement allowance is determined by the past performance of the worker. In this system, a worker with a high propensity for vacation will receive a smaller retirement allowance even if he or she is not dismissed in disgrace.

A worker's education level also affects his or her incentives. The steeper tenure-wage profile for more educated workers, as well as their preferences for time off, may affect vacation time taken. Since information about the education level of current workers is not available in the data, I use the distribution of education levels for retired workers in the survey year.

In the estimation of total vacation, I include the number of legally stipulated annual paid-leave vacation days as an explanatory variable, since a worker's tenure determines the number of legally stipulated holidays.

The expected signs of the coefficients on wage at retirement and retirement allowance are negative. According to the worker discipline hypothesis, the expected sign of the coefficient on JOA is positive. However, there is also a possibility of a negative coefficient for JOA. If firms can control the utilization rate of annual paid leave by workers in accordance with the business cycle, vacation time may increase in recessions when firms can more easily adjust to it.[13] In this case, vacation may be regarded as a

---

tions about their future retirement allowance system. Second, the selected sample is limited to firms with workers who quit the firm due to mandatory retirement. As a result, there is a sample selection bias in favor of larger firms. Although the mean firm size in the full sample, used in tables 13.1 and 13.2, is 201, that of the sample used in the estimation is 546.

13. Dore (1973) reports the actual practices of vacation in the Japanese company Hitachi: "Foremen are reluctant to have people take leave because they have a stake in a high attendance record and high production figures, and when order books are long, they are likely to be under considerable pressure from enthusiastic managers" (188).

method of labor adjustment.[14] Finally, the six-day workweek dummy variable is expected to have a positive effect on vacation time because the number of workers needing to be absent on workdays due to sickness or errands would be higher.

13.4.3   Descriptive Statistics

Table 13.3 reports descriptive statistics of the sample used in the estimation. The sample consists of 2,421 unionized firms and 696 nonunionized firms. The average firm size is 804 in unionized firms and 197 in nonunionized firms. The average bad vacation rate is about 1 percent, which is smaller than the average for the full sample in table 13.1. This reflects the bias toward large firms in the estimation sample. The average number of bad vacation days is 2.7. On average, bad vacation time is lower in union firms. On the other hand, unionized firms have a higher incidence of total vacation. The mean retirement allowance and monthly wage at retirement for the entire estimation sample are 12,800,000 yen and 320,000 yen, respectively.

13.5   Estimation Results

Table 13.4 reports regression results for a pooled estimation of unionized and nonunionized firms. Tables 13.5, 13.6, and 13.7 report results from specifications distinguishing between unionized and nonunionized firms. Table 13.5 employs bad vacation time as the left-hand-side variable, table 13.6 uses good vacation time, and table 13.7 utilizes total vacation time.[15]

Table 13.4 supports the worker discipline model because the wage at retirement and the retirement allowance have negative effects on bad and total vacation time taken. Table 13.5 reveals, however, that these effects do not differ between unionized and nonunionized firms.

The introduction of a point system for retirement allowances is predicted to have a negative effect on vacation time as long as it entails more precise monitoring: Table 13.5 shows that this theoretical prediction is borne out empirically and the reduction is greater in unionized firms than in nonunionized firms.

White-collar workers and workers with high levels of education take fewer bad vacation days. The steeper tenure-wage profile for highly educated workers and their preferences for vacation time may affect this result.

The JOA has a significant negative effect on bad vacation time in union-

14. Hildreth and Ohtake (1998) analyze an automobile assembly company that uses worker utilization rates as a method of labor adjustment in addition to changes in working hours.

15. I conduct an F-test for the equality of all estimated coefficients between the union and nonunion samples. The null hypothesis of equality of the coefficients is rejected. I estimated equations for the rate of absence as well as for days absent. The results are qualitatively the same. I also estimated equations using only firms with fewer than 1,000 employees and, again, did not find significantly different results.

Table 13.4   Estimation Result for All Firms and All Vacation Types

Dependent Variables	Bad Vacation	Good Vacation	Total Vacation
Log wage	−0.534***	−0.039	−0.092**
	(0.100)	(0.056)	(0.041)
Log retirement allowance	−0.253***	−0.046**	−0.075***
	(0.042)	(0.024)	(0.017)
Log JOA	0.074	0.071**	−0.006
	(0.059)	(0.033)	(0.024)
Log firm size	−0.091***	0.020*	−0.052***
	(0.021)	(0.012)	(0.008)
Log annual paid leave	−0.379***	0.235***	0.555***
	(0.071)	(0.039)	(0.029)
Point system	−0.374***	−0.029	−0.097*
	(0.125)	(0.070)	(0.051)
University ratio	−0.278***	−0.073	−0.234***
	(0.102)	(0.058)	(0.042)
High school white-collar ratio	−0.306***	0.068*	−0.174***
	(0.067)	(0.038)	(0.027)
High school blue-collar ratio	−0.174**	0.084**	−0.031
	(0.070)	(0.039)	(0.028)
Six-day workweek	0.212***	−0.014	0.096***
	(0.073)	(0.041)	(0.030)
1993 year dummy	−0.045	0.165***	0.083***
	(0.049)	(0.028)	(0.020)
Union	0.128***	0.166***	0.154***
	(0.052)	(0.029)	(0.021)
Constant	5.359***	1.357***	1.795***
	(0.342)	(0.192)	(0.139)
N	3,117	3,083	3,117
R^2	0.157	0.053	0.190

Source: GSWHC (1985, 1993).

Note: Standard errors are in parentheses. Sampling ratios are used as weight.

*Statistically significant at the 10 percent level.

**Statistically significant at the 5 percent level.

***Statistically significant at the 1 percent level.

ized firms and a significant positive effect on bad vacation time in non-unionized firms. The positive effect of JOA on bad vacation time in nonunionized firms is consistent with the worker discipline hypothesis. The negative effect of JOA on bad vacation time in unionized firms can be explained as follows. Since labor adjustment costs are high in unionized firms, such firms use bad vacation time as an additional control variable for labor adjustment. Unions may agree to this employment practice in exchange for employment security.

Lastly, the five-day workweek reduces days absent in unionized firms but has no significant effect on vacation in nonunionized firms.

Table 13.5   **Estimation Results for Bad Vacation**

Union/Nonunion Firms	Model 1		Model 2	
	Main Effect (Nonunion)	Interaction with Union Dummy	Main Effect (Nonunion)	Interaction with Union Dummy
Log wage	-0.592***	0.236	-0.486***	
	(0.149)	(0.202)	(0.100)	
Log retirement allowance	-0.211***	-0.074	-0.242***	
	(0.061)	(0.085)	(0.042)	
Log JOA	0.382***	-0.538***	0.381***	-0.539***
	(0.091)	(0.119)	(0.090)	(0.116)
Log firm size	-0.127***	0.046	-0.096***	
	(0.039)	(0.046)	(0.021)	
Log annual paid leave	-0.538***	0.431***	-0.554***	0.431***
	(0.097)	(0.144)	(0.095)	(0.142)
Point system	0.058	-0.518*	0.047	-0.489*
	(0.248)	(0.287)	(0.246)	(0.284)
University ratio	-0.119	-0.269	-0.278***	
	(0.163)	(0.209)	(0.101)	
High school white-collar ratio	-0.347***	0.082	-0.309***	
	(0.100)	(0.135)	(0.066)	
High school blue-collar ratio	-0.332***	0.347**	-0.325***	0.333***
	(0.102)	(0.139)	(0.099)	(0.129)
Six-day workweek	0.038	0.570***	0.0192	0.583***
	(0.111)	(0.153)	(0.109)	(0.146)
1993 year dummy	0.052	-0.213**	0.052	-0.169*
	(0.086)	(0.106)	(0.083)	(0.102)
Constant	5.900***	-1.728**	5.632***	-1.209***
	(0.506)	(0.708)	(0.378)	(0.386)
N		3,117		3,117
R^2		0.177		0.168

Source: GSWHC (1985, 1993).
Note: Standard errors are in parentheses. Sampling ratios are used as weight.
*Statistically significant at the 10 percent level.
**Statistically significant at the 5 percent level.
***Statistically significant at the 1 percent level.

Table 13.6 shows the differences in workers' behavior regarding good vacation time between unionized and nonunionized firms. In nonunionized firms, steepness of wage profile (wage at retirement) has negative effects on good vacation time. In nonunionized firms, this negative effect of steep wage profile on good vacation time disappears. There is no difference between union and nonunion firms for the effects of the amount of the retirement allowance on good vacation time. The estimation results for nonunion firms are consistent with the worker discipline hypothesis. The results for unionized firms are also consistent with the hypothesis shown in

Table 13.6   Estimation Results for Good Vacation

Union/Nonunion Firms	Model 1		Model 2		Model 3	
	Main Effect (Nonunion)	Interaction with Union Dummy	Main Effect (Nonunion)	Interaction with Union Dummy	Main Effect (Nonunion)	Interaction with Union Dummy
Log wage	-0.225***	0.314***	-0.252***	-0.277***	-0.063*	0.013
	(0.083)	(0.113)	(0.079)	(0.105)	(0.032)	(0.044)
Log retirement allowance	-0.032	-0.034				
	(0.034)	(0.048)				
Log JOA	0.192***	-0.196***	0.201***	-0.201***	0.192***	-0.198***
	(0.051)	(0.067)	(0.050)	(0.066)	(0.051)	(0.066)
Log firm size	0.144***	-0.173***	0.141***	-0.178***	0.136***	-0.165***
	(0.022)	(0.026)	(0.021)	(0.025)	(0.021)	(0.026)
Log annual paid leave	0.192***	0.132*	0.191***	0.110	0.169***	0.152**
	(0.054)	(0.080)	(0.054)	(0.079)	(0.053)	(0.080)
Point system	-0.104	0.055	-0.118	0.078	-0.105	0.058
	(0.138)	(0.160)	(0.138)	(0.159)	(0.138)	(0.160)
University ratio	-0.242***	0.195*	-0.261***	0.211**	-0.326***	0.315***
	(0.091)	(0.117)	(0.089)	(0.116)	(0.086)	(0.109)
High school white-collar ratio	0.012	0.130*	-0.007	0.127*	-0.054	0.213***
	(0.056)	(0.075)	(0.056)	(0.075)	(0.050)	(0.070)
High school blue-collar ratio	0.164***	-0.135*	0.157***	-0.132**	0.150***	-0.120
	(0.057)	(0.078)	(0.057)	(0.078)	(0.057)	(0.078)
Six-day workweek	-0.052	0.010	-0.041	0.023	0.050	0.001
	(0.062)	(0.086)	(0.061)	(0.084)	(0.062)	(0.086)
1993 year dummy	-0.021	0.273***	-0.018	0.271***	-0.046	0.308***
	(0.048)	(0.059)	(0.047)	(0.059)	(0.047)	(0.058)
Constant	1.599***	-0.4340	1.503***	-0.465	1.175***	-0.173
	(0.283)	(0.396)	(0.264)	(0.378)	(0.236)	(0.326)
N	3,083		3,083		3,083	
R^2	0.0859		0.0845		0.083	

Source: GSWHC (1985, 1993).

Note: Standard errors are in parentheses. Sampling ratios are used as weight.

*Statistically significant at the 10 percent level.

**Statistically significant at the 5 percent level.

***Statistically significant at the 1 percent level.

Table 13.7   Estimation Results for Total Vacation

	Model 1		Model 2		Model 3	
Union/Nonunion Firms	Main Effect (Nonunion)	Interaction with Union Dummy	Main Effect (Nonunion)	Interaction with Union Dummy	Main Effect (Nonunion)	Interaction with Union Dummy
Log wage	-.0137** (0.060)	0.129 (0.081)	-0.226*** (0.057)	0.169** (0.076)	-0.128*** (0.023)	0.076** (0.032)
Log retirement allowance	-0.109*** (0.024)	0.058* (0.034)				
Log JOA	0.187*** (0.037)	-0.337*** (0.048)	0.217*** (0.036)	-0.364*** (0.048)	0.187*** (0.037)	-0.337*** (0.048)
Log firm size	-0.075** (0.015)*	0.025 (0.019)	-0.086*** (0.015)	0.030 (0.018)	-0.080*** (0.015)	0.030 (0.018)
Log annual paid leave	0.386*** (0.039)	0.371*** (0.058)	0.382*** (0.039)	0.356*** (0.057)	0.372*** (0.038)	0.385*** (0.058)
Point system	0.212** (0.100)	-0.386*** (0.116)	0.166* (0.100)	-0.334*** (0.116)	0.212** (0.100)	-0.386*** (0.116)
University ratio	-0.179*** (0.066)	-0.105 (0.084)	-0.244*** (0.064)	-0.045 (0.083)	-0.230*** (0.062)	-0.058 (0.078)
High school white-collar ratio	-0.138*** (0.040)	-0.028 (0.054)	-0.156*** (0.040)	-0.015 (0.054)	-0.178*** (0.036)	0.011 (0.050)
High school blue-collar ratio	-0.091** (0.041)	0.151*** (0.056)	-0.115*** (0.041)	0.172*** (0.056)	-0.099** (0.041)	0.159*** (0.056)
Six-day workweek	0.074* (0.045)	0.124** (0.061)	0.112** (0.044)	0.104* (0.061)	0.076* (0.045)	0.123* (0.061)
1993 year dummy	0.080** (0.035)	-0.017 (0.043)	0.091*** (0.034)	-0.027 (0.043)	0.065* (0.034)	-0.003 (0.042)
Constant	2.736*** (0.204)	-1.875*** (0.286)	2.410*** (0.191)	-1.642*** (0.273)	2.480*** (0.170)	-1.635*** (0.235)
N	3,117		3,117		3,117	
R^2	0.225		0.219		0.224	

Source: GSWHC (1985, 1993).

Note: Standard errors are in parentheses. Sampling ratios are used as weight.

*Statistically significant at the 10 percent level.

**Statistically significant at the 5 percent level.

***Statistically significant at the 1 percent level.

equation (2). The effects of firm size on good vacation time are different between unionized and nonunionized firms. In nonunionized firms, good vacation time increases as firm size increases. In unionized firms, firm size is independent of good vacation time. The 1993 year dummy has a positive effect on good vacation time in unionized firms.

The estimation results for total vacation time show clear differences in worker behavior in unionized versus nonunionized firms (table 13.7). The absolute value of the coefficient on wage at retirement in unionized firms is about one-tenth that of nonunionized firms. The absolute value of the coefficient on retirement allowance in unionized firms is about half that of nonunionized firms. Thus, when I use total vacation in the estimation, hypotheses 1 and 2 are supported. Hypothesis 3 is also supported by table 13.5, although γ_U is negative.

An additional difference between unionized and nonunionized firms is the coefficient on entitled annual paid leave. In unionized firms, the elasticity of total vacation time with respect to entitled annual paid leave is about 0.76, whereas in nonunionized firms it is approximately 0.35 to 0.55. Unionized workers use more legally stipulated annual paid leave than nonunionized workers.[16]

I decompose the effects of unions on vacation time using the Oaxaca decomposition. The difference in mean log vacation days is decomposed into two parts: the difference due to union and nonunion differences in the characteristics of both firms and employees, and the difference due to differences in coefficients.

$$(5) \qquad \overline{\text{Vac}}_U - \overline{\text{Vac}}_N = \sum (\overline{X}_{Uk} - \overline{X}_{Nk})\beta_{Nk} + \sum \overline{X}_{Uk}(\beta_{Uk} - \beta_{Nk}),$$

where $\overline{\text{Vac}}_i$ is the mean of log vacation days, $\overline{X}_{ik}$ is the mean of the kth explanatory variable, and β_{ik} is the estimated coefficient in unionized firms (U) or nonunionized firms (N).

Table 13.8 shows the decomposition for bad vacations. The overall difference in bad vacation time between unionized and nonunionized firms is –28 percent. This is mainly caused by the difference in characteristics between unionized and nonunionized firms. The total mean difference effect is –43.9 percent. On average, unionized firms enjoy 43.9 percent less bad vacation time because of higher retirement allowances, steeper tenure-wage profiles, larger numbers of employees, and more days of entitled annual paid leave than nonunionized firms. However, the total difference due to coefficients is positive. This is mainly caused by the difference in the coefficients on days of entitled annual paid leave. In nonunionized firms, bad vacation time decreases in days of entitled annual paid leave. This negative relation is very weak in unionized firms.

---

16. A possible reason for this is that de facto vacation is more likely to be counted a part of annual holidays in union firms than in nonunion firms.

Table 13.8   **Decomposition of Union and Nonunion Difference in Bad Vacation**

	Mean Difference Effects	Coefficient Difference Effects	Total Effect
Log wage	-0.059	0.000	-0.059
Log retirement allowance	-0.109	0.000	-0.109
Log JOA	-0.027	0.183	0.156
Log firm size	-0.101	0.000	-0.101
Log annual paid leave	-0.128	1.186	1.058
Point system	0.017	-0.031	-0.014
University ratio	-0.012	0.000	-0.012
High school white-collar ratio	-0.006	0.000	-0.006
High school blue-collar ratio	-0.008	0.064	0.055
Six-day workweek	-0.001	0.058	0.057
1993 year dummy	-0.004	-0.092	-0.096
Constant	0.000	-1.209	-1.209
Total	-0.439	0.158	-0.281

Note: Decomposition is based on the estimation results for model 2 in table 13.5.

Table 13.9   **Decomposition of Union and Nonunion Difference in Good Vacation**

	Mean Difference Effects	Coefficient Difference Effects	Total Effect
Log wage	-0.027	1.091	1.064
Log retirement allowance	-0.014	-0.240	-0.255
Log JOA	-0.014	0.067	0.053
Log firm size	0.151	-0.979	-0.828
Log annual paid leave	0.044	0.363	0.407
Point system	-0.004	0.003	0.000
University ratio	-0.011	0.025	0.015
High school white-collar ratio	0.000	0.039	0.039
High school blue-collar ratio	0.004	-0.026	-0.022
Six-day workweek	0.002	0.001	0.003
1993 year dummy	0.001	0.149	0.150
Constant	0.000	-0.434	-0.434
Total	0.134	0.059	0.193

Note: Decomposition is based on the estimation results for model 1 in table 13.6.

Table 13.9 shows the decomposition of union and nonunion difference in good vacation. On average, unionized firms have higher level of good vacation by 19.3 percent. Most of the differences between union and nonunion firms come from differences in coefficients. The largest difference comes from the differences of coefficient of wage at the retirement. In unionized firms, steep wage profile does not reduce good vacation time. Workers in unionized firms enjoy taking good vacation without fear of dismissals.

Table 13.10   **Decomposition of Union and Nonunion Difference in Total Vacation**

	Mean Difference Effects	Coefficient Difference Effects	Total Effect
Log wage	−0.017	0.448	0.432
Log retirement allowance	−0.049	0.410	0.360
Log JOA	−0.013	0.115	0.101
Log firm size	−0.079	0.142	0.063
Log annual paid leave	0.089	1.021	1.110
Point system	0.008	−0.024	−0.017
University ratio	−0.008	−0.014	−0.021
High school white-collar ratio	−0.003	−0.008	−0.011
High school blue-collar ratio	−0.002	0.029	0.026
Six-day workweek	−0.003	0.012	0.009
1993 year dummy	−0.005	−0.009	−0.015
Constant	0.000	−1.875	−1.875
Total	−0.084	0.246	0.162

Note: Decomposition is based on the estimation results for model 1 in table 13.7.

Table 13.10 shows the decomposition for total vacations. On average, total vacation time in unionized firms is 16.2 percent greater than in nonunionized firms. This is mainly due to the differences in coefficients. In unionized firms, an increase in entitled annual paid leave does not decrease bad vacation time. The job security effects of unions increase total vacation time in unionized firms, and the vacation-reducing effects of steep tenure-wage profiles and retirement allowances are weaker in unionized firms.

13.6   Conclusion

I hypothesize that the presence or absence of a union mediates the effectiveness of internal and external threats in reducing vacation time taken. Internal threats include costs of job loss due to a nonvested retirement allowance system and a steep wage-tenure profile. External threats are characterized by the unemployment rate and potentially lower wages in jobs outside the firm. In particular, I argue that because unions reduce the potency of the internal and external threat of job loss (by making it more difficult for employers to dismiss workers), vacation time is less responsive to such threats in unionized firms than in nonunionized firms. The results of analysis of data from the 1985 and 1993 GSWHC in Japan support this hypothesis.

Since case law in Japan severely restricts unionized firms from dismissing workers, the simple worker discipline model based on dismissal does not apply. Unionized firms use more costly monitoring and merit pay systems than nonunionized firms. Therefore, the efficiency wage explanation of the dual market model by Bulow and Summers (1986) is not applicable to the Japanese labor market. However, the efficiency wage implication is supported in the nonunionized sector in Japan. Thus, it may be more appropriate to characterize the Japanese labor market as a three-sector market, with a unionized sector of full-time workers, a nonunionized sector of full-time workers, and part-time workers.

References

Allen, P. T. 1982. Size of workforce, morale, and absenteeism: A re-examination. *British Journal of Industrial Relations* 20 (1): 83–100.

Allen, Steven G. 1981. Compensation, safety, and absenteeism: Evidence from the paper industry. *Industrial and Labor Relations Review* 34 (2): 207–18.

Araki, Takashi. 2002. *Labor and employment law in Japan.* Tokyo: Japan Institute of Labor.

Barmby, Tim, John G. Sessions, and John G. Treble. 1994. Absenteeism, efficiency wages and shirking. *Scandinavian Journal of Economics* 96 (4): 561–66.

Brown, Sarah, and John G. Sessions. 1996. The economics of absence: Theory and evidence. *Journal of Economic Surveys.* 10 (1): 23–53.

Bulow, Jeremy I., and Lawrence H. Summers. 1986. A theory of dual labor markets with application to industrial policy, discrimination, and Keynesian unemployment. *Journal of Labor Economics* 4 (3): 376–414.

Dore, Ronald. 1973. *British factory-Japanese factory: The origins of national diversity in industrial relations.* London: George Allen & Unwin.

Ferguson, Ronald, and Randall Filer. 1986. Do better jobs make better workers? Absenteeism from work among inner-city black youths. In *The black youth employment crisis,* ed. Richard B. Freeman and Harry J. Holzer, 261–95. Chicago: University of Chicago Press.

Fujimura, Hiroyuki. 1989. International comparison of merit rating. *Journal of Japan Institute of Labour* no. 362:26–37.

Green, Francis, and Steven McIntosh. 1998. Union power, cost of job loss, and workers' effort. *Industrial and Labor Relations Review* 51 (3): 363–83.

Hildreth, Andrew K. G., and Fumio Ohtake. 1998. Labor demand and the structure of adjustment costs in Japan. *Journal of the Japanese and International Economies* 12 (2):131–50.

Ishida, Hideo. 1985. *International personnel management of Japanese firms* (in Japanese). Tokyo: Japan Institute of Labor.

Japan Institute of Labor. 1998. Research on the sick leave system in Japan. Research report no. 105. Tokyo: Japan Institute of Labor.

Kaivanto, Kim. 1997. An alternative model of pro-cyclical absenteeism. *Economic Letters* 54 (1):29–34.

Koike, Kazuo. 1981. *Skill-formation in small and medium firms* (in Japanese). Tokyo: Dobunkan.

———. 1991. *Economics of jobs* (in Japanese). Tokyo: Toyokeizai Shinposha.

Koshiro, Kazutoshi. 1978. Work incentive and labor relations in workers in large Japanese factories: Basic indexes for international comparison (in Japanese). In

International comparison of labor relations, ed. Mikio Sumiya, 91–116. Tokyo: University Press of Tokyo.

———. 1980. Quality of life of Japanese workers (in Japanese). *Journal of Japan Institute of Labor* no. 255 (June): 15–23.

Lazear, Edward P. 1979. Why is there mandatory retirement? *Journal of Political Economy* 87 (6): 1261–84.

Leigh, J. P. 1985. The effects of unemployment and the business cycle on absenteeism. *Journal of Economics and Business* 37 (2):159–70.

Ministry of Labor. 1985. *General survey on working hours and conditions.* Tokyo: Ministry of Labor.

———. 1993. *General survey on working hours and conditions.* Tokyo: Ministry of Labor.

Policy and Research Division, Ministry of Labor. 1993. *Basic survey on wage structure 1993* (in Japanese). Tokyo: Rodo Horei Kyokai.

Romu Gyosei Kenkyusho (Institute for Labor Administration). 1997. Chokai seido no jishhi jyokyo to unyo no jittai (Survey on disciplinary systems). *Rosei Jiho* no. 3322:2–27.

Shapiro, Carl, and Joseph E. Stiglitz. 1984. Equilibrium unemployment as a worker discipline device. *American Economic Review* 74 (3):433–44.

Sugeno, Kazuo. 1992. *Japanese labor law,* trans. Leo Kanowitz. Tokyo: University of Tokyo Press.

Weiss, Andrew. 1985. Absenteeism and wages. *Economics Letters* 19 (3): 277–79.

Wilson, Nicholas, and Michael J. Peel. 1991. The impact on absenteeism and quits of profit-sharing and other forms of employee participation. *Industrial and Labor Relations Review* 44 (3): 454–68.

Winkler, Donald R. 1980. The effects of sick-leave policy on teacher absenteeism. *Industrial and Labor Relations Review* 33 (2): 232–40.

Contributors

Yukiko Abe
Faculty of Economics
Asia University
5-24-10, Sakai, Musashino-shi
Tokyo 180-8629 Japan

Hiroyuki Chuma
Institute of Innovation Research and
    Faculty of Economics
Hitotsubashi University
Naka 2-1, Kunitachi
Tokyo 186-8603 Japan

David M. Cutler
Department of Economics
Harvard University
Cambridge, MA 02138

Matthew J. Eichner
U.S. Securities and Exchange
    Commission
450 Fifth Street NW
Mail Stop 10-01
Washington, DC 20549

Richard B. Freeman
Department of Economics
Harvard University
Cambridge, MA 02138

Yuji Genda
Institute of Social Science
University of Tokyo
7-3-1 Hongo, Bunkyo-ku
Tokyo, Japan 113-0033

Takehiko Hagino
Japanese Center for Economic
    Research
Nikkei Kayabacho Building
Nihombashi Kayabacho
2-6-1 Chuo-ku
Tokyo 103 Japan

Takao Kato
Department of Economics
Colgate University
13 Oak Drive
Hamilton, NY 13346

Mark B. McClellan
Department of Economics
Stanford University
Economics Building, 224
Stanford, CA 94305-6072

Yoshifumi Nakata
Doshisha Management School
Doshisha University
Karasuma-Higashi-iru, Imadegawa-dori
Kamigyo-ku, Kyoto 602-8580 Japan

Seiritsu Ogura
Department of Economics
Hosei University
4342, Aihara-machi, Machid-shi
Tokyo 194-0211 Japan

Fumio Ohtake
Institute of Social and Economic
    Research
Osaka University
6-1 Mihogaoka, Ibaraki
Osaka 567-0047 Japan

Andrew Samwick
Department of Economics
Dartmouth College
6106 Rockefeller Hall
Hanover, NH 03755-3514

Toshiaki Tachibanaki
Institute of Economic Research
Kyoto University
Yoshida Honmachi
Sakyo-ku
Kyoto 606-8501 Japan

Ryoji Takehiro
Department of Economics
Doshisha University
Karasuma-Higashi-iru, Imadegawa-dori
Kamigyo-ku, Kyoto 602-8580 Japan

David A. Wise
John F. Kennedy School of
    Government
Harvard University
79 John F. Kennedy Street
Cambridge, MA 02138

Tadashi Yamada
Institute of Policy and Planning
    Studies
University of Tsukuba
Tsukuba City, Ibaraki Prefecture 305-
    8573 Japan

Tetsuji Yamada
Department of Economics
Rutgers University
The State University of New Jersey
Camden, NJ 08102

Author Index

Subject Index